Buying sequence and

# The New Economic Mind

What are the influences of
economies on people's objectives?

tap into
This.

⊕ - wealth.

— unemployment

pressures          Fears
Social.            worries.
debt.
Conditioning
branding.  —————      desire ⊕ of
                     goods.

# The New Economic Mind
## The Social Psychology of Economic Behaviour

**Alan Lewis**
*Reader in Economic Psychology, University of Bath*
**Paul Webley**
*Senior Lecturer in Psychology, University of Exeter*
**Adrian Furnham**
*Professor of Psychology, University College London*

HARVESTER
WHEATSHEAF

New York   London   Toronto   Sydney   Tokyo   Singapore

First published 1995 by
Harvester Wheatsheaf
Campus 400, Maylands Avenue
Hemel Hempstead
Hertfordshire, HP2 7EZ
A division of
Simon & Schuster International Group

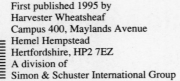

Typeset in 10/12pt Times
by Columns

Printed and bound in Great Britain by
Hartnolls Ltd, Bodmln, Cornwall

Library of Congress Cataloging in Publication Data

Lewis, Alan, 1952–
    The new economic mind: the social psychology of economic
behaviour / by Alan Lewis, Paul Webley and Adrian Furnham.
        p.     cm.
    Includes bibliographical references and index.
    ISBN 0–7450–1325–2
        1. Economics—Psychological aspects.   2. Social psychology. e.
I. Webley, Paul.   II. Furnham, Adrian.   III. Title.
HB74.P8L48 1995
330'.01'9—dc20                                      94–31583
                                                    CIP

British Library Cataloguing in Publication Data

A catalogue record for this book is available from
the British Library

ISBN 0–7450–1325–2

    2   3   4   5   99   98   97

To all our friends

# Contents

# Figures

# Tables

# Acknowledgements

Thanks to Colin Lawson for his advice on developments in central Europe and to John Cullis for his elliptical comments on health economics and other matters. John and Colin are both members of the Bath University Centre for Economic Psychology (BUCEP) but nevertheless all responsibility for errors remains with the authors. Thanks also to Debbie Lewis (no relation) for secretarial help.

# PART I

# Apéritif

# Chapter 1

# The social psychology of economic behaviour

Today I (Alan) went to the bank, drew some money out from an automatic teller machine using my credit card and made an appointment for next week to talk about my mortgage. My wife (Sandie) is to have a company car; I am working at home (writing this), so when I left the bank I picked up some brochures for cars for her to look at when she comes home. On the way home Sandie has promised to purchase some groceries, particularly for my elderly father, about to make one of his infrequent visits for lunch tomorrow. Tonight will find my wife at the theatre with friends, the car will need some fuel; I am hoping to go to the pub for an hour before cooking supper.

All these events are economic events, but they are also social and psychological events – all of them involve the economic mind. In everyday life each of us is faced with a series of economic decisions, some trivial, others of great significance. The thesis of this book is that we do not deal with economic matters like a logistic machine would, we do not dispassionately weigh up alternatives, considering which option is most likely to result in, to use the jargon of economics, utility maximisation. Economic life forms part of our psychological life and vice versa.

Sandie's car: we plan to share it, for pleasurable purposes outside business hours; we have not, we will not, sit down and assess the relative merits and costs of public transport compared to private transport, or for that matter the depreciation, fuel economy, acceleration of a wide range of cars. As most people do, we have made a decision about the decision and we know already what we like. Of course, economic factors matter but they are only part of the equation; we are driven by cultural values, attitudes, beliefs, perceptions, idiosyncratic preferences even: I dislike the colour red.

Automobiles are important purchases, second only in importance to house purchases for most of us. Consumer demand is strong; there are plenty of models to choose from, marketing personnel are keen to differentiate their products. For the top and most successful models the 'objective' differences between them are very

3

small, what is marketed instead is 'style', 'sex' or what ownership of such a car says about you as a person – 'subjective' features unrecognisable to a hard-nosed analyst. Sandie and I, I suspect, will buy a fuel-injected model. Neither of us drives quickly, although the extra acceleration is helpful overtaking at lower speeds, but it is not this and this alone, if we were to be honest. It is that a car without fuel injection is too pedestrian, too ordinary, too average; we have a little more verve than that, it is how we see ourselves – somewhere between a vicar and a boy racer in his turbo-charged cabriolet.

At the bank today it was all right. I know what a bank is for, what is expected of me, I put a credit card in the cash dispenser and not a banana; I pressed the correct buttons in the correct order. I spoke to the enquiry clerk about making an appointment to discuss my mortgage. She was polite, she understood I was the customer and she the bank employee, we knew our respective positions. I had come to the right place.

What do children think banks are for? Economic socialisation is an essential part of our enculturation and learning processes, the domain of anthropology, sociology and especially psychology. There is now a growing literature produced by developmental and other psychologists addressing this question: how and when do we become competent members of society, how and when do we learn the economic and social rules? And what of Eastern Europe – some economies in transition want capitalism but have no real experience of what a bank does and its purposes.

Sandie and I have an account at the bank. That is why they let us take cash. The bank, my wife and I, we have an understanding, though sometimes there is a misunderstanding. Our salary cheques are paid straight to the bank; we draw on this account, the bank charges us for its services, cheque books, credit cards and so forth; sometimes we even earn a little interest. Everything is running smoothly. Earlier this summer it was not so friendly. We returned from holiday having spent too much and had the embarrassment of having our credit card rejected at the Chinese 'take-away'. How could we let this happen? We are not stupid. The economic calculations are quite straightforward. All we had to do was plan a little more, deliberate. It is a common experience that the deliberative aspect of rational decision making is far from omnipresent; planning too carefully is not really fun, while impetuosity sometimes is; we are risk seeking as well a risk averse.

Talking with friends uncovers 'anomalies', which we (the authors) prefer to see as psychological generalisations rather then exceptions to rationality assumptions. For instance, people with household incomes comparable to ours have several accounts running at once, being in debt on one account at a bank while saving on another, even, would you believe, at the same bank. Arrangements such as these have been dubbed 'mental accounts' (Thaler, 1990). Economists assume that money is 'fungible', that it will be moved around in a 'rational' way. Given that interest paid on sums borrowed will exceed that gained on sums saved, robbing Peter to pay Paul, especially when Peter and Paul are one of the same, makes little sense at all. Or does it? Certainly from a psychological point of view it makes sense and people who are not economists see little strange in their behaviour, as it is for them obvious that money used in different ways or for different purposes should be compartmentalised. The reason, they say, why we are overdrawn on our current bank account is that we are spending too much on groceries and there have been unanticipated expenditures on replacement kitchen machinery and automobile parts; our savings account is for our holiday and 'we don't want to touch it'.

Thinking of groceries and my domestic vignette, you will recall that Sandie buys them. Perhaps you think I should? My wife and I negotiate, to an extent, who does what. An economist might like to describe this as the 'domestic division of labour'. Reasoning runs that, as domestic tasks have to be done and money earned, it makes sense for the person who can earn the most 'in the market' to do so while the other completes 'unpaid' domestic tasks which, if completed by the individual with the highest potential income, with the time taken up in such tasks would constitute inefficiency in terms of household income maximisation (Becker, 1976).

Economics likes to see itself as a 'value-free' science, yet for non-economists when economists turn their attention to love, relationships and marriage in their analysis, they are at their most value-laden, most offensive (McKenzie and Tullock, 1978).

We need to keep a collective cool head. It is not our brief to show how economists have got it wrong where psychologists could get it right. The domestic division of labour, as an analytic, is logical; psychologists should not put themselves in the position of appearing illogical. What is missing from the analysis is any consideration of the family, of marriage as an institution, as dependant upon gender and social identity, on preferences, on changing values. The domestic division of labour is not settled; it is constantly shifting, not just as a consequence of changing market conditions but because of the values of the participants, what they think an intimate partnership should be, what the appropriate roles of women and men should be and what the legal and cultural influences are.

Psychologists are concerned mainly with synthetic science rather than analytic science; it is a natural step for psychologists to want to hear what people have to say, to listen to their explanations of their own behaviour rather than to impose such explanations, however elegant in their simplicity and consistency. Certainly qualitative studies of household values, perceptions, are in their infancy and little account has been taken of the domestic economy from women's point of view, but there are encouraging signs (Kirchler 1988; Burgoyne, 1990; Burgoyne and Lewis 1994).

## A student's life

Youthful readers will be reading this introduction at a time of flux, at a time of developing personal and economic independence, distinct from parents and guardians. How have you fared? How are you faring? How will you fare? It is a busy and troublesome initiation into the economic world. My economic world may seem alien to you but your economic mind is hard at work as well. How are your tuition fees to be paid for, your living and accommodation costs? Countries differ in the amount of financial support given to students at universities, nevertheless student loan schemes are now familiar with many undergraduates working in part-time paid employment. You must think it is worth it; or are you just doing it to please your parents, because of the culture you live in, are you just doing what is expected of you, what is 'normal'?

Let us guess that at least in part you are doing a university course because you want something from it, something to improve you; but in what way? You will have learnt that economists prefer to deal with tangibles rather than intangibles, and of the tangibles in your case life-time income would be top of the list. On average, graduates have greater life-time incomes than non-graduates. So you may not know it, but it is as if you have made a rational decision about your life-time income, if the positive correlation between years in education (at least to this point) and life-time income approached zero you simply would not be where you are today. You may not like to see yourself this way, that you are searching instead for intellectual and artistic growth, a deeper understanding, or a thirst for knowledge for its own sake.

It is most likely that the economic mind is driven by a mixture of motives, *homo economics* and *homo psychologicus* entwined: we are selfish *and* generous, base *and* aspiring, calculating *and* impetuous, ignorant *and* insightful.

You have subjective expectations too. You do not know exactly how your life is going to pan out (no one does). You may aspire to the medical profession, the law, business, even psychology, but you are expecting better things, higher income, possessions – a car, a house. Best of luck to you; but things *do* go wrong. What happens when your loan, your credit becomes a debt? What happens when you buy your first house, you lose your job and the real price of your property falls? What are interest rates? What are the best forms of credit? Where can you get the best advice?

As psychologists, we believe choices are determined not just by economic antecedents but by attitudes, values, beliefs. Furthermore people bring their own baggage with them, their socialisation; they may choose what they want to see and what they do not. It is wise to think of people with neither perfect nor imperfect information but with perceptions and knowledge that can be understood by studying the psychological processes that underlie them.

## A brief history

### The past

Only a few years ago a faculty at Bath had lengthy and heated debates about what it should call itself: the School of Humanities and Social Sciences; the School of Social Sciences; the School of Economics and Social Sciences? These kinds of discussion reflect the history of economics, with its beginnings in philosophy and ethics, its brief early flirtation with the social sciences in the first parts of the twentieth century (Tarde, 1902) and its present mainstream position stripped of its psychological and sociological content, with more in common, if not in content but in method, with mathematics. Bath eventually settled for the simplest title of School of Social Sciences, but the economists took some persuading.

Within the discipline of economics theoretical economists have the highest status and those agricultural economists who actually get their feet dirty collecting data have the least. Theoretical economics generates analytical, mathematical formulae and models of various aspects of the economy, even the economy as a whole. A number of assumptions are made about people, the economic actors in the model: for instance, they have transitive choice orderings, they are utility maximisers, etc. Most economists are not bothered about whether these assumptions are empirical 'facts'. Psychological, sociological, even political influences on individual action is outside the economic models, they are 'exogenous' factors.

Psychology, on the other hand, is a synthetic science. Although not entirely devoid of theoretical underpinning, it is largely driven by observations, by the testing of hypotheses against data. Economists test hypotheses against data too but their emphasis is on deduction rather than induction. One of the consequences of these differences is that economists really only have one theory and psychologists have quite a large number of 'guiding ideas', none of which has the status of a fully fledged theory. The one theory of economics is that of Rational Economic Man. In social psychology alone sixteen 'guiding ideas' have been identified including 'Attribution', 'Consistency', 'Categorisation', 'Role-playing' (McGuire, 1980). It is tempting to suggest that economics should open its well-guarded perimeter to some fresh ideas while psychology could do well to produce a more co-ordinated and disciplined research programme.

As to the status of Rational Economic Man (and presumably Rational Economic Woman), it is unclear whether it constitutes a theory or a hypothesis (Hollis and Nell, 1975; Marr and Raj, 1983). Whatever the case may be, the concept has changed very little this century, which suggests either that all the 'facts' fit or that the concept is unfalsifiable (Sen, 1977). One group of economists treat Rational Economic Man as a fact; a second group, a fiction; a third, one or the other depending on what suits the situation.

But we do not want to get bogged down in trying to demonstrate to economists that the assumption of human rationality is misguided. Lea, Tarpy and Webley (1987) have argued that psychologists' preoccupation with rationality is sterile, since Rachlin (1980) has shown that any behaviour that is consistent can be described as maximising something. Even if people do behave in ways that very obviously maximise their utility, we still need to understand the psychological mechanisms which underly their behaviour.

Things have changed, though, on the 'boundaries' of economics: some economists with more imagination have taken the trouble to learn some psychology (Earl, 1983). Historically the two most important psychologists to have made a contribution to economics have been Herbert Simon, a Nobel prize winner in economics, and George Katona.

The 'Rationality' part of Rational Economic Man can mean different things to different people; the concept itself may even be tautological. Simon makes a useful distinction between 'substantive' and 'procedural' rationality. Substantive rationality is the concept most commonly held among economists and refers to the achievement of given goals within the limits imposed by given conditions and constraints, search costs and time constraints, but within these limits the consumer 'rationally' pursues self-interest and maximises utility. 'Procedural' rationality is more understandable to psychologists as it refers to the internal environment, an individual's ability to deliberate and reason within the constraint of circumstance and cognitive capacity (Simon, 1976). Some considerable advances have been made in cognitive science, decision making and experimental economics making it plausible and desirable to include aspects of procedural rationality in the more formal models. (The most frequently quoted of contemporary research is by Kahneman and Tversky (1979), but more of this later.)

George Katona's main claim to fame is his measurement of 'subjective expectations' (Katona, 1975). Most economists are wary of delving into the internal environment of the economic mind and prefer to predict economic outcomes from economic antecedents. Sticking with automobiles for a moment, predicting the aggregate consumer demand for automobiles in the United States next year (the dependent variable) would necessitate assessing such economic independent variables as inflation rates, family income and expenditure rates – figures available from social surveys and other statistics: there are no 'people' in this equation at all. Katona's simple and persuasive idea was that people buy cars, and other commodities, when they think it is a good time to do so, when their consumer 'sentiments' are favourable.

Economists too have used expectations in research on changes in employment, inflation, exchange and interest rates (Shackle, 1949; Carlson and Parkin, 1975; Hudson, 1982).

Using questionnaires, Katona was able in 1946 to predict that the US economy was about to enter a consumer-led boom when conventional economic indicators were predicting a recession (Katona, 1975) and these subjective measures have been shown over the years to be predictive of the behaviour of the economy. Whether these attitude measures give us information that cannot be obtained from conventional economic indicators is arguable. Surveys of consumer sentiment have been regularly conducted now for forty-five years in the United States and for twenty years in the European Community, and analyses of this enormous block of data suggest that consumer attitudes often add nothing to the usual predictors of economic trends (see van Raaij, van Veldhoven and Wärneryd, 1988). But to dismiss this work on these grounds would be a mistake; there is an important distinction between being able to predict a behaviour and understanding the behaviour. The work of Katona and others goes some way to exploring the mechanisms that underly the connections between conventional economic indicators, the economic mind and actual economic behaviour: though we are not sure how seriously to take this, recent research has suggested that the coverage of the economy in newspapers and the pessimism found in pop-song lyrics have been found to predict, with a time-lag, consumer sentiments and movements in the economy (Zullow, 1991).

Among economists the boundaries have been expanded particularly by Duesenberry (1949), Leibenstein (1976) and Scitovsky (1976). Duesenberry (1949), like the so-called 'Austrian' School of Economists (von Mises, 1978), has given more attention to the internal environment: people are viewed as active participants in the economy rather than the passive pawns of economic forces. In studies of consumer behaviour Duesenberry drew attention to the role of habit: purchases are often not deliberated about; the purchasing decision is in some senses already solved. Likewise Duesenberry treats income constraints not as objective facts but dependant upon perception of them by consumers and their relative position to other people's incomes and expenditure. In this way Duesenberry's work bears some resemblance to the work in social psychology and sociology on perceptions of equity, reference groups, social comparisons and relative deprivation (Stouffer, *et al.* 1949).

Leibenstein (1976) also agreed that interpersonal relationships are important, but in particular emphasised the concepts of 'inertia' and 'x-efficiency'. Both are concerned with 'non-optimal' behaviour. People within the traditional economic units of the firm and the household often do not react to domestic changes until the need for change becomes paramount. There is an inertia and sluggishness in decision making. Economic decisions, say within the firm, are dependant upon negotiation and are constrained by the nature of the environment of jobs and occupations, and the structure of the firms themselves. Not everyone is equal within an organisation and firm; it depends where you are in the hierarchy. Leibenstein recognises the cognitive element in decision making, and recommends further research to examine the degree of 'x-efficiency', by which is meant the difference between maximal effectiveness and actual effectiveness.

Scitovsky (1976) takes issue with the static nature of aspiration and motivation implied in economic theory. Motivation is variable. Borrowing from animal and experimental psychology (Hebb, 1955; Berlyne, 1960), economic motivation is examined in terms of the need of individuals for optimal arousal (a plateau between sluggishness and catastrophic overarousal) stimulation and the spur of curiosity.

## The present

The developments of the last fifteen years have been remarkable. Textbooks dealing with economic psychology abound, such as Maital (1982), Furnham and Lewis (1986), MacFadyen and MacFadyen (1986), Lea, Tarpy and Webley (1987), van Raaij, van Veldhoven and Wärneryd (1988); and there are some excellent edited collections (Grunert and Olander 1989; Lea, Webley and Young, 1992; Maital and Maital, 1993).

There are specialist journals too: *The Journal of Economic Psychology, The Journal of Socio-Economics*; even 'mainstream' psychology journals and mainstream economics journals have given the topic the royal nod of approval, such as

*Journal of Social Psychology, Journal of Personality and Social Psychology, Journal of Economic Perspectives, American Economic Review.*

Economics is too important to be left to economists it seems and interdisciplinary research is on the increase (Himmelstrand, 1992). There are a number of disciplines besides economic psychology and it is well to talk about these before talking mainly about economic psychology. Not that we want to draw any strict boundaries, but the emphases and aims of these groups are different.

*Experimental economics* uses the experimental method to investigate behaviour, such as auctions and a whole host of economic actions open to empirical test (Smith, 1991; Hey, 1992; Güth, Wärneryd and Lea, 1992). Most of the participants in this group are economists; it matters to them whether the 'assumptions' of economics are factual, a very different position from that of Milton Friedman, who has argued that unrealistic assumptions can lead to better economic predictions and are consequently acceptable.

The work of experimental economists is accessible particularly to experimental psychologists and is to be welcomed as a step in the right, behavioural, direction. Nevertheless the contemporary critique of the experimental method when applied to human behaviour still holds: for example, the disagreeable need to manipulate people, to treat them as subjects; the use of isolated, restricted and unrealistic environments; the use of subterfuge; the use of detailed instructions often associated with a lack of interest in what participants in experiments think they are doing and how they explain their own behaviour, all add up to indictment of the artificial nature of experiments and to comments about their external validity. People are right to worry about external validity but not because of artificiality. What matters is whether important variables have been operationalised so that they engage the same psychological processes as their real-world counterparts. Setting up the situation so that it involves a real monetary loss or gain is seen as crucial by experimental economists (e.g. Güth and Tietz, 1990), though in our view monetary payment is secondary to involvement. If people are involved or psychologically engaged in the situation, their decisions will be meaningful – they do not need to be taking decisions about real money.

The findings generated from experimental economics is not solely of interest to economists and some economic psychologists but also to cognitive psychologists and those interested in decision making and competitive behaviour.

## Behavioural economics and psychological economics

Experimental economics and behavioural economics (psychological economics) are closely allied, the latter employing social survey techniques, even interviews as well as experiments as research tools. Again like experimental economics, the group is comprised mostly of economists but there have been contributions from sociologists, political scientists and psychologists as well. The cement to this group is that not only are the methods of the behavioural and social sciences deemed

worthwhile but some of the concepts as well; social comparisons, dissona
ry, equity considerations, subjective expectations are examples. And this g....
claim a number of 'historical' figures among its friends, such as Simon, Scitovsky,
Katona, Shackle and – among the more contemporary researchers – Earl.

The aim is to take the best and most reliable of the findings from psychology and
the other social sciences and add them to existing economic models, rather like
notions of uncertainty and risk aversion have been employed in the past. Such addi-
tions are hoped to improve the realism, comprehensiveness and particularly the predictive qualities of a more eclectic economics.

## Socio-economics

Socio-economics is something different. It is no longer the case of psychologists
and sociologists helping the economic discipline out; instead socio-economics is
driven by the intent of re-inventing economics, of creating a new economics.
Whatever the rhetoric of the movement itself, this feels more like competition than
co-operation between disciplines.

The leading light of the movement is the sociologist Amitai Etzioni (Etzioni,
1988). The rationality and self-interest provisions of economics are criticised
because of their lack of realism, for their lack of humanity and their reductionism.
Etzioni argues that choices are rarely made dispassionately and that people are
motivated by their value systems and beliefs, systems which have no proxy in utility maximisation. In his persuasive writing style Etzioni leads the reader on to the
wholly plausible view that people have mixed motives; yes, we can be selfish but
we have moral obligations too: an economic system, or indeed a social system,
where all participants were merely self-interested in the narrow sense would soon
disintegrate. A central theme is that the economic system, that economics itself, is
inextricably linked to a wider social culture. It makes no sense to think of individuals as mindless calculating machines, it is better to think of them as members of
social groups, classes, cultures with their concomitant social identities and social
values. Many of the points Etzioni makes are ones that strike a chord for social psychologists, there are many shared interests in this approach.

Most controversially, at least as far as economics is concerned, is the socio-
economic attack on the 'value-free' claims of positive neo-classical economics. To
summarise a complex debate, economists generally argue that they are neutral
about the preferences and values of individual economic actors and do not want to
make recommendations about how people ought to behave (Caldwell, 1984).
Critics point out that the assumptions of rationality and self-interest are hardly neutral; rather, they are ideological and have ideological consequences as they legit-
imise selfishness, that this is somehow the 'natural' state of affairs. Socio-economics favours communitarianism over utilitarianism.

The atmosphere of socio-economics is not one, understandably, that many economists want to breath. Socio-economics is strong on rhetoric and weak on empirical

studies but there can be little doubt that the organisation is international in its scope, its reputation and intellectual influence are blossoming.

## Economic psychology

Economic psychology is mostly, but not exclusively, for psychologists. The main branches of psychology represented are developmental, cognitive, social and experimental. Developmental – what do children know about money, exchange, the bank; when and how do they learn these things? Cognitive – how do people make economic decisions; what do they take into account; what do they ignore? Social – how much are my economic decisions influenced by my values; would I be prepared to buy a product that was environmentally safe but cost 10 per cent more than its competitor? Experimental – would I be more likely to evade tax in a computer simulation 'game' if my chances of detection were 1 in 10 and the size of fine 5 times the amount evaded or where the chances of detection were 1 in 20 and the size of fine 20 times the amount evaded?

These examples are in a sense ordinary and familiar psychology applied to economics. Once it is decided that economics is part of mental life, that economic behaviour is everyday behaviour, economics simply becomes another, important, aspect of psychological study.

For some people this is quite enough to be going on with but for us we also see other intellectual challenges that motivate our endeavours. It is a bizarre but intriguing notion for psychologists that economists should believe in a single motive for human behaviour. It is equally bizarre to economists that psychologists should build models of behaviour without recourse to economics. It is fashionable to talk of the incommensurability of ideas (Kuhn, 1970) as of psychology and economics having different rhetorics, languages without shared meanings (McCloskey, 1987; Klamer, 1988), making effective communication impossible. The arguments of course are not to be dismissed out of hand but we nevertheless find such a position rather negative. We are nagged instead by such questions as the following:

> If economics can do so well without psychology, could it not be that some at least of the economic assumptions about behaviour have psychological validity?
>
> What 'facts' are there in psychology? What trends can we predict as psychologists that we feel confident will be reliable in aggregate, that cannot be reduced to the economic and are statements not open to tautological criticism?

But first let us get on with looking at economic behaviour through a psychological lens, not with a view solely to see what this can tell us about social, cognitive, developmental and experimental psychology but with an eye too on what this can tell us about economics and social problems.

## Plan and content

Part II of the book is dedicated to economic socialisation and the psychology of money. How do children learn about economics? At what ages do children grasp notions of buying and selling, of savings and spending? How do parents and schools socialise children? How does the distribution of pocket-money influence childrens' attitudes? Do children from different socio-economic backgrounds have varying beliefs about the ownership of property, entrepreneurship and income inequalities?

For economists money is a medium of exchange, a unit of account, a standard of deferred payment and a store of value. From a psychological point of view money is much more than this. People treat money differently depending on where it comes from, whether it is a windfall or whether it is 'earned'. Meaning is added to this 'neutral medium of exchange', even the size, colour and in the case of coins, weight, count.

Part III is dedicated to social issues and social problems. The first chapter deals with the problems of addictive spending and gambling. As a partial antidote, studies on savings behaviour are also reviewed: not only do people spend when they ought to be saving but many individuals save when the economically rational thing to do is to spend. The rest of the chapter relies heavily on 'lay' explanations research. 'Lay' beliefs are what 'ordinary' people think, they are frequently different from elite opinion or the views of those highly informed. Why are some people poor and others not? Are the wealthy different from the rest of us? What causes unemployment and how can it be cured? Lay explanations have been sought for all of these questions.

Why do 'lay' economic beliefs matter? First of all a good deal of social psychology is concerned with the structure and content of attitudes and beliefs, how they change, how they are sustained, how they are shared by particular social groups. Findings on 'lay' economic beliefs clearly fit with this but there is more to it than that. The politico-economic structure of a society is in part determined and maintained by its citizens; within democratic systems a political party is more likely to stay in power if its rhetoric and policies are similar to those popularly held by the electorate; government policy can be legitimised by lay beliefs. If people generally believe that high income is a just reward for effort, qualifications and risk taking, that poverty is brought about by laziness, a lack of drive and imagination, it is much easier for a government to reduce its intervention, to cut back on any 'social engineering', to let 'nature' take its course, to let the cream rise to the top, to reduce taxation and social benefits provided by the state.

'Morals and the market' is the title for Part IV. Moral questions influence many economic decisions at both the collective and the individual level. How should scarce resources for health and education be distributed? Should it be left solely to the market? Would it matter if this meant children of wealthier parents received a better education and were likely to live longer, healthier lives? If the market mechanism is inappropriate, should decisions about health and education be left to politicians, bureaucrats, doctors, teachers? How should the state 'interfere' with the market in order to protect fairness and equity?

The part starts with a brief review of research on fairness in economic transactions, business ethics, medical ethics, green and ethical investing. In a competitive market is it in the interests of one company purposely to mislead another? When is a price a fair price – is it simply the one people are prepared to pay? Is the production of 'green' products in the shops just a gimmick? Can a change in consumer preferences save the planet? Is it possible to be good and amass investment income as well or is it camel and needle time?

The later sections present a brief review of voters' (and others) attitudes' towards public expenditure and taxation and the perceived appropriate roles of state and the market in distribution and production of goods. Tax evasion is considered in some depth. What makes people evade tax? Is it just a function of opportunity and the rational calculation of getting caught or are we motivated too by notions of fairness, obligation, a willingness to stay within the law for its own sake?

Part V discusses the work ethic and economies in transition: the new market economies of Central and Eastern Europe. It has long been recognised that work is not for pay alone. People in work, if they are fortunate, will build up social relationships with colleagues, benefit from some level of job satisfaction and raised self-esteem, all of which can be lost if redundancy strikes. The first chapter concentrates on the experimental and social survey data on the Protestant work ethic (PWE) and examines its value as an explanatory variable in individual motivation. The traditional Weberian studies of PWE were conducted at a different level of analysis more familiar to sociologists, namely cultures and societies. Some combination of these levels of analysis becomes necessary when trying to interpret the impact of economic and social change in Central and Eastern Europe. While the introduction of democracy and the liberation of markets are indeed revolutionary changes, the communist economic mind cannot be changed into the capitalist economic mind overnight; old ways will persist mixed with the new perhaps in a novel configuration influencing work practices, the mobility of labour, the growth of industry and entrepreneurial activity. It is here that the power of the economic mind is at its most apparent.

Speculations about the future of economic psychology, the related interdisciplinary groups and the social psychology of economic behaviour are offered in the last chapter which comprises Part VI. Economists have even begun to look at themselves, to discuss how they generate economic knowledge, although it has mainly been left to sociologists to investigate the 'social construction' of economics. Contemporary research, especially in Europe, has more in common with radical philosophy, linguistics, rhetoric and the sociology of science than 'traditional' psychology. So where should we go from here?

All the authors, like so many of the applicants to psychology courses I see, want to find out 'what makes people tick'. The choice of words could be improved but the sentiment is apt: if we can tell you something valuable about the minds of men and women it will be worthwhile.

# PART II

# Socialisation and the psychology of money

# Chapter 2

# Socialisation and economics: children's understanding of and behaviour in the economic world

## Introduction

Although there have been a very large number of studies concerned with children's and adolescents' cognitive development relating to the physical world, comparatively few studies have been done on their understanding of the social and economic world. A major exception is Berti and Bombi (1988). The former studies have nearly all been in the Piagetian tradition and have been concerned primarily with the stages that children pass through in the understanding of physical concepts (Shultz and Coddington, 1981). Related research on social development in children and adolescents has been concerned with such things as political socialisation (Furnham and Gunter, 1984) and moral development (Haste and Torney-Purta, 1992).

Socialisation is generally defined as a process through which individuals learn to interact in society. It concerns learning social roles and acquiring the knowledge and skills related to them. So far less research has been carried out on economic socialisation than on other parts of social development (e.g. political socialisation or moral development) although interest in the area has accelerated over the past few years.

A detailed examination of the economic and political socialisation of children and adolescents is of both academic and applied interest. In Great Britain in 1990 14–16-year-olds had nearly £10 per week each in disposable cash. West German 7–15-year-olds received 7.5 billion DM of pocket-money and monetary gifts in 1988 and the spending-power of 12–21-year-olds amounted to 33 billion DM annually. And of course in most western democratic countries teenagers of 18 years are allowed to vote in local, municipal and national elections.

Many different aspects of young people's understanding and perception of the economic and political world, their attitudes towards money and possessions, their spending and consumption habits are relevant to the teaching of economic principles in schools as well as to the research of psychologists, educationalists, marketing people and even to economists.

It is only comparatively recently that there has been much research on young people's understanding of the economic world and their economic behaviour (Lea, Tarpy and Webley, 1987; McNeal, 1987). There are two good reasons why the topic of economic socialisation and education is an important one. Firstly, it is likely that adult habits of spending, saving, investing, gambling and purchasing are established in childhood or adolescence (Furnham and Lewis, 1986). Though Maital (1982) described economic man as an obstetric marvel, who leapt fully formed from the womb, we know that real humans are not capable of such athletic feats. So if we wish to understand any economic behaviour we have to know something about its origin and development. Secondly, it is clearly desirable to teach economic concepts and behaviour to children and adolescents on the grounds that their knowledge is not extensive (Leiser, 1983; Ingels and O'Brien, 1985), their buying power is considerable (Davis and Taylor, 1979; Furnham and Thomas, 1984b) and there is accumulating evidence that training at a young age is both possible and effective. Such education will benefit not just the individual but also the society of which s/he is a member.

There appears to be a relative paucity of research on adolescent economic beliefs, values and behaviour. This is perhaps surprising as there are both practical and theoretical reasons for wanting to know how adolescents participate in the economy and what they think about its workings. Two 'practical' reasons seem obvious. Firstly, adolescents have considerable buying power – for instance, in America, even in the 1980s, children spent over $4 billion annually and teenagers spent over $40 billion; while British 5–16-year-olds had an estimated £780 million to spend in the early 1980s on preferred goods and services – and it is of considerable interest to people in trade how, where and why that money is spent. Secondly, teachers of economics are clearly interested in the way economic concepts and behaviours are acquired so that they may teach them more effectively at the appropriate age (Kourilsky, 1977; O'Brien and Ingels, 1985, 1987). There are also many interesting theoretical questions concerning adolescent understanding and beliefs about the economy (trade, work, consumption, advertising), such as at what age various sophisticated economic concepts are grasped and what socialisation experiences determine the extent and structure of economic beliefs and the nature of economic behaviour. McNeal (1987) in fact listed twenty of these that could guide studies on children as consumers. He also noted the number of agents in the socialisation process whereby children learn to become consumers: parents, peers, teachers and businesses. Visits to shops, advertising, features, functions and packaging for young people's products are all considered.

Concept growth is very difficult to investigate clinically, let alone empirically. One has to be particularly sensitive to which variables, experiences and situations precipitate concept stage growth. Specific examples only hint at the multitude of problems arising from the interaction of the numerous factors which simultaneously influence the development of the conceptual processes. The effect of sex differences, variations in parental and wider societal attitudes, disparate schooling and all the rest, must be taken into consideration. It is not surprising that, in designing research work, the emphasis tends to be a simplification and elimination of variables. Attempts to isolate factors, however, can be no substitute for the study of the complex interactions themselves.

Hurlock (1972) maintains that money concepts, unlike time and number concepts, tend to lag behind those of many other concepts. Many of the things Hurlock says have not been substantiated by recent research, possibly due to her selection of articles. However, more recently there has been a great deal of research in this area. One theme of the earlier work which is still apparent in current research are studies on the developmental stages that children pass through in the acquisition of various economic concepts. The stage-wise approach to development is very much out of fashion though retained for heuristic reasons. Frequently rather different stage-wise models compete in the description of phenomena. Yet there are a number of characteristics common to all stage-wise theories:

A stage is a structured whole in a stage of equilibrium.
Each stage derives from the previous stage, incorporates but transforms the previous one and prepares for the next.
Stages follow in an invariant sequence.
Stages are universal to all humans at all times in all countries.
Each stage has a stage from coming-into-being, to being.

All stage-wise theories appear to have a number of implicit assumptions: that the sequence of development is fixed, that there is an ideal end-of-state towards which the child and adolescent inevitably progresses and that some behaviours are sufficiently different from previous abilities that we can identify a child or adolescent as being in or out of a stage. Non-stage theories do not see people progressing inevitably to a single final stage since environmental forces are given more power to create a diversity of development responses. At the one end of the stage/non-stage continuum is the view that most of a young person's time is spent in one of several specific stages with short, relatively abrupt transitions between stages. As the length of time spent in a stage is perceived to be shortened and the time in transition is lengthened, one moves along the continuum until all the time is seen as spent in transition, and development is seen as continuous and non-stage. Since a non-stage theory does not necessarily dictate a specific end stage or single development sequence, the study of individual differences assumes more importance.

## Developmental stages

In a very thorough early study Strauss (1952) studied five boys and five girls at each age between $4\frac{1}{2}$ and $11\frac{1}{2}$ years interviewing them using 71 predetermined questions. Strauss believed that even before 4 years children have experience of money though they may not realise that it is connected with buying. From his study

Strauss drew up nine different stages or transformations through which a child passes as s/he becomes acquainted with money. He argues that as new stages are reached the meanings of old relationships change, become revised and qualified, so that little remains of the initial or early meanings of the concepts. For him insightful learning, conditioning and rewards cannot fully account for cognitive development.

Danziger (1958), in a later article on children's early conceptions of economic relations, maintains that the development of social concepts may follow paths of their own that may not fall into line with the theoretical model elaborated in connection with physical concepts. Using interviews with children 5–8 years old, he asked them about the meaning of rich and poor, the uses of money and the position of the boss at work. He found a variety of replies from the fantastic to the fairly accurate, and attempted to codify these into four clear developmental stages:

1. An initial precategorical stage occurs when the child lacks economic categories of thought altogether. There appears to be no special subsection of economic concepts differentiated from social concepts in general.
2. At a second categorical stage the child's concepts appear to represent a reality in terms of isolated acts which are explained by a moral or voluntaristic imperative.
3. At the third stage the child becomes able to conceptualise relationships by virtue of the fact that a reciprocity is established between previously isolated acts. However, these relationships are isolated.
4. At the fourth stage these various isolated relationships become linked together to form a system of relations.

Danziger noted that most children were at the lowest of his four levels since most had had the experience of purchasing but not of work. He believed like Strauss that the development in the stages of economic understanding are not simply a consequence of internal maturation, but depend on experience with money and economic exchange. This, it is argued, accounts for class, regional and national differences in the development of economic understanding, a point demonstrated twenty-five years later (1983).

Later Sutton (1962) maintained that theory and research on the attainment of economic concepts have attempted to answer five questions:

1. How do children achieve information necessary for isolating and learning a concept?
2. How do children retain the information from encounters so that it may be useful later?
3. How is the retained information transformed so that it may be rendered useful for testing a hypothesis still unformed at the moment of first encountering new information?
4. What are the general features in the growth of economic concepts?
5. To what extent are the concepts of children a cultural product of the environment?

In her study Sutton asked 85 children randomly chosen from the first to the sixth grade, twelve questions such as 'How do people get money?', 'What is a bank?', 'Why do people save?', etc. The 1,020 replies were arranged into six (developmental) categories:

1. No replies (1 per cent).
2. Pre-categorical stage where objects are named but with little understanding of economic meaning (63 per cent).
3. A category of moral value-judgements (good/bad, right/wrong) irrespective of economic function (18 per cent).
4. Two isolated acts/factors that are economically significant (people save just to be saving) (12 per cent).
5. Two acts involving a reciprocity which cannot be explained by other economic relationships (if you put money in a bank you get more back) (5 per cent).
6. The subjective explanation gives rise to the objective: the single act derives its significance from its position in a system of relationships that is no longer conceived in an isolated way.

Sutton found that age, intelligence or socio-economic background variables did not make any difference in the children's understanding, yet argued that external stimuli were important in understanding the development of economic concepts. Precisely what experiences facilitate or hinder a child's economic growth were, however, beyond the scope of this study.

Essentially all these early (and later) studies of monetary and economic understanding have isolated three major phases. In the first the child does not understand the role of money in everyday transactions, though realises that money is required in transactions. In the second phase the child may understand the nature of the immediate exchange but not the network of exchanges within the monetary and economic system, the divisibility of money and its origin. The third stage is characterised by the understanding of most but not all (e.g. profit, investment) types of exchange.

More recently studies into the development of economic concepts have become more conceptually and methodologically sophisticated. Burris (1983) interviewed 30 4–5-, 7–8- and 10–12-year-old children who were chosen as representative of the distinct Piagetian developmental stages (pre-operational, concrete operations and formal operations). The children were interviewed with regard to six basic economic concepts: the commodity (products exchanged in the marketplace), value (that which governs the production and circulation of a commodity), exchange (economic transaction in the market economy), property (the nature and ownership of property), work (social relations at work) and income (payment from work). Within each area the author found qualitatively different types of responses and significant levels of association between types of response and age levels of the children. For instance, when asked why some people get more money than others for the work that they do, the youngest group argued that it was because some people work more, harder or longer; the next group said it was because some people's work is more important, functional or helpful to others; while the oldest group argued that people get paid more because their work requires more skill, training or education. The results suggest that the younger children tended to represent social phenomena in terms of natural or physical categories (value is identified with physical size; income with the physical quantity of labour). Furthermore the younger children exhibit extreme 'realism' in that they do not understand the conventionality or normativeness associated with social phenomena or institutions; they are accorded the same ontological status as physical laws or objects.

In a similar study using 89 Israeli children aged 7–17, Leiser (1983) asked (by interview and questionnaire) questions about prices, salaries, strikes, savings and investments, factories and banks and the Mint. He found that younger children (8–9) interpret economic transactions from the perspective of individual participants having no awareness of the system of economic forces. Older children integrate their economic knowledge, become aware of conflicts and try to resolve them; for instance, children believe simultaneously that 'government sets all the prices' and yet 'shopkeepers are free to change them'. Similarly once children realise the concept of profit on a fair transaction they are able to resolve the apparent contradiction between 'buying as an exchange of money for something of equivalent value' and 'selling goods as a way of earning a living'. Thus when asked how a shopkeeper would feel about a drop in the prices of their goods all the children realised that there would be a diminished profit, yet only 25 per cent of the youngest but 75 per cent of the oldest realised that this would probably also be accompanied by an increase in sales. Also when asked what would happen if the economy was suddenly injected with a massive distribution of money, 21 per cent of the youngest (8–9), 31 per cent of the intermediate (11–12), yet 89 per cent of the oldest group (14–15) successfully predicted negative economic consequences (rising prices, shortage of goods, people's unwillingness to work). The more abstract and complex the phenomena (e.g. inflation, market forces) and particularly the more difficult it is to personify, the less children (even up to the age of 15) can understand it. Children, it seems, can understand the motives of individual actors, but not the cumulative or aggregated effect of people's economic actions. It is only when children have some conception of the structure and function of society at large that they can begin to comprehend macro-economic changes.

More recently Leiser (1983), Schug and Birkey (1985) and Sevon and Weckstrom (1989) supported these findings. Schug and Birkey (1985), like Danziger, also stressed that children's economic understanding varies somewhat depending upon their own economic experiences, though the quality of the evidence they acquired is debatable. Sevon and Weckstrom characterised younger children's perception of the economy as from the viewpoint of *homo sociologicus* (driven by moral and social norms) and the one of older children more as of *homo economicus* (striving for personal hedonic satisfaction). Of the three age groups (8, 11 and 14) the youngest group, when asked about the thinking and acting of economic agents first felt the need to decide whether these agents, would become happy or unhappy before thinking about why this was the case (e.g. 'The shoe retailer would be happy about the reduction in shoe prices because people can save their money . . .'). The answers of the younger children thus described moral or 'Christian' (concern for other people, other people's approval or disapproval of own behaviour important) rather than economic thinking (other people as means, constraints or obstacles to personal satisfaction). Some of the older children, however, saw the economy more as an instrument and the action of the individual as led by the search for opportunity to increase his/her own wealth. This is partly due to their increased ability to think more abstractly but as adults also sometimes argue from a moral viewpoint, intellectual sophistication cannot be the only explanation, but family values and secondary socialisation clearly play a part.

Although most researchers largely seem to agree on a Piagetian view about the development of economic concepts in the child they apparently have identified different numbers of stages. This might be due to several reasons: the differing age ranges of the subjects; the differing number of subjects in each study (sometime perhaps too small to be representative); each researcher's precision in the definition of where one stage ends and the next starts, thus the assignments of the subjects to the respective stages vary; the methodologies used are different in precision, etc. These are possible explanations although they do not all necessarily have to be true for every single study.

Table 2.1 shows that there is disagreement about the number of stages, points of transition and content of understanding at each respective stage. The trend among the more recent studies, though, seems to be that the number of (sub-)stages are summarised and three broad main phases are defined: (1) no understanding, (2) understanding of some isolated concepts and (3) linking of isolated concepts to full understanding. By no means do these stages suggest, though, that the child's understanding of different economic concepts always advances simultaneously. As Danziger (1958) stressed, a child's understanding of, for example, buying and selling may be more advanced than his/her understanding of work, as the child might have had experience of the former but not of the latter. It would therefore be of great interest to further investigate if, and what, other factors (e.g. parental practices, social class) actually tend to speed up or perhaps slow down the transition from one stage to the next. Nearly all the relevant research consists of self-report studies using interviews. Most Piagetian work is task-based (role-play, games, etc.) and it may well be that experimental studies on economic concepts would yield clearer, more interesting results. Also, most of these studies have been conducted in

**Table 2.1** Number of stages in the development of economic concepts

|  | Year | Subjects | Age range | Stages |
|---|---|---|---|---|
| Strauss | 1952 | 66 | 4.8–11.6 | 9 |
| Danziger | 1958 | 41 | 5–8 | 4 |
| Sutton | 1962 | 85 | Grade 1–6 | 6 |
| Jahoda | 1979 | 120 | 6–12 | 3 |
| Burris | 1983 | 96 | 4–12 | 3 |
| Leiser | 1983 | 89 | 7–17 | 3 |
| Berti and Bombi | 1988 | 100 | 3–8 | 4 |

western, industrialised, capitalist countries and, if economic education and experiences are relevant to the development of economic concepts, studies need to be done in third-world or socialist countries.

Webley (1983) and others have criticised the application of the standard Piagetian approach and argued in favour of looking for what is distinct about economic concepts instead of treating economic cognition as just another area where general principles of cognitive development apply. He reproached researchers for their use of a static standard approach towards the investigation into children's development of economic thinking and regretted that no attempts have been made to 'produce a characterisation of the environment which might allow variations in the development of economic thought apart from social class distinction'. What is special about economic factors (e.g. property) is that they form the basis of power in society and interpersonal relations and the concepts/ideology a child develops are therefore of vital concern to the possessing. The need to relate to the economic structure of the society – an idea more radically expressed by Cummings and Taebel (1978) – and the importance of characterising a child's environment (e.g. exposure to own economic experience) are therefore aspects that might distinguish the development of economic concepts from others. In this sense the understanding of economics, history and politics is different from that of physics, chemistry and, say, meteorology. Social values and ideology are more obviously bound up with the latter and can influence understanding profoundly.

Without exception all studies agreed that there are changes in economic reasoning with age. But not all agree how much the following factors influence economic understanding: (1) accumulation of knowledge and experience from primary and secondary socialisation and education; (2) general ability to complex reasoning increases; (3) diminishing egocentrism ; (4) change in role behaviour – with increasing age children assume more of the adult behaviour in the economy etc. It is impossible to calculate how much cognitive development can be attributed to each process (and others) as they are interdependent and vary with each individual.

## The development of economic concepts and behaviour

Although numerous studies of children's understanding of different aspects of the economic world have been carried out, it appears they have concentrated on some topics rather than others. There have been even fewer studies of economic behaviour, a fact bemoaned by Webley and Lea (1993b). Relatively few studies exist on young people's knowledge of betting, taxes, interest rates, the ups and downs of the economy (boom, recession, depression, recovery, etc.) or inflation. This might be because these concepts are considered to be too difficult for children to understand, although in a study in the former Yugoslavia by Zabukovec and Polic (1990) the children's answers clearly reflected aspects (e.g. inflation) of the then current economic situation, which shows that the 'difficulty' always depends on the circumstances (exposure to the economic world). There is, however, fairly detailed and replicated research on topics like possession and ownership, wealth and poverty, entrepreneurship, prices, wages, money, buying and selling, profit and the bank. However, the common denominator of all economic interactions in the western world obviously is money and therefore its understanding is a prerequisite for all other concepts.

A number of studies have made attempts to trace the development of certain specific economic concepts. Not only have the areas researched been very diverse but also experimental and investigative methods have differed widely. Despite these differences there are coherent patterns of results in the literature. Here we consider a selection of topics, concentrating on economic understanding (as that reflects the state of the literature) but devoting two subsections to forms of economic behaviour (saving and swapping) that have been the subject of sustained investigation.

## Buying and selling

Central to any economic activity is buying and selling. Yet for the child these transactions are by no means easy to grasp. Furth (1980) has noted how difficult it is for the child to understand the transaction particularly those of 5 or 6 years who have not even mastered the number system. On the scheme outlined in Figure 2.1 he attempts to explain the various concepts that the child must master. It can be seen that the child has to master a number of observed and non-observed transactions. The child must understand the origin of money, the function of change, the ownership of goods. Children must also integrate the payment of wages, shop expenses and the shop owner's money into the system in order to understand the pricing of goods.

For Furth (1980) there appear to be four major stages concerned with the understanding of buying and selling: no understanding; understanding of payment of customer but not of the shopkeeper; understanding and relating of both the customer's and the shopkeeper's payment, but not of profit; understanding of all these things. A very similar picture emerges from the extensive cross-cultural work reported by Leiser, Sevón and Lévy (1990). They describe 8-year-olds as understanding the exchanges involved in trade (that is money – goods), and industry (money – work) but not having an integrated picture of the two, which only emerges at around age 11.

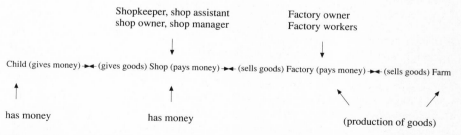

**Figure 2.1**   Schematic outline of the shop's business. Reprinted by permission of the publisher from Furth, *The World of Grown-ups*. Copyright 1980 by Elsevier Science Publishing Co., Inc.,

## Profit

G. Jahoda (1979) conducted two studies, one involving role-playing and the other semi-structured interviews, in order to investigate 6–12-year-olds' conceptions of profit. In the role-playing study children played the role of shopkeeper and the experimenter those of customers and suppliers. The critical test involved the difference in the price that the child expected to buy the goods from the supplier and sell them to the customer. Where the buying price was consistently lower than the selling price, the child was credited with an understanding of profit; when the two prices were consistently identical, lack of such understanding was recorded; and a mixture of responses was regarded as transitional. It seemed that it was not until the age of about 11 that most children began to understand the concept. The interview study showed in more detail the child's development from no grasp of any transaction system to the development of two unconnected systems to an integrated system. Younger children simply accept givers and make up nonsensical answers on being questioned, whereas older children try to make sense of economic relationships but fail to arrive at the correct solution. Children at earlier stages are aware that some people are engaged in the buying and selling of goods, and that people give their work in return for wages. When an adult points out that buying and selling is also a job for which people are paid s/he draws attention to the relationship between the two systems (mentioned above) and poses the problem for children. Younger children tend to deny that buying and selling can be a job but older children are able to think through the problem and emerge with the answer. Jahoda (1983) replicated this study with young African children in Zimbabwe. His hypothesis was that, owing to their greater exposure to relevant experiences (notably in trading), African children will acquire the concept of profit more rapidly than European children, that is, the traditional 'culture lag' between European and non-European children will be reversed. The results confirmed the hypothesis; being active in trading makes for an earlier grasp of the concept of profit. Indeed the Zimbabwean children were shown to be significantly in advance of British children within the same age range.

Tan and Stacey (1981) in a study of the understanding of socio-economic concepts of Malaysian Chinese school children found, however, that developmental trends were:

> highly similar to that found among previous Western samples of children studied . . . but there was also a suggestion that there may be (a) less of a tendency for young Chinese children to refer to an imaginary source of money and to refer to parents or work as a source of money, than Western children.   (p. 44)

More recently Nakhaie (1993) looked at the effects of age, mother's education, education at home and various other demographic variables on knowledge of shop profit and bank interest in 8–11-year-old Canadian children. The most powerful predictors were mother's level of education and the extent to which children are educated at home.

These findings point to the influence of mothers who are entrusted with child care and education in the domestic division of labour. It may be that it is not being a mother or father as such which is an important determinant of the child's economic knowledge, but it is the time availability of either parent as a role model which enhances children's economic knowledge. Of course, the overall contribution of the mother need not to be a result of direct parental teaching about the appropriate economic principles and the consequent development of economic cognition among children; it may instead be explained by cultural capitals (values, traits and characteristics) of mothers transmitted to their children. It is possible that highly educated mothers are involved in more positive interaction with their children. Importantly, however, the present findings support the argument that the type of learning environment that the child encounters in the home accentuates the positive element of social cognition and that children's economic cognition may be a product of a genuine intellectual construction. They also note in their study that children with mothers who have a high level of education seem to benefit from the transmission of cognitive skills and attitudes, which enabled these children to understand remote and abstract concepts such as interest. There was no significant father effect. These two findings together support the instrumental role of the mother, as against the father, in the economic socialisation of children and question the importance of inherited intelligence.

## Banking

G. Jahoda (1981) followed up the study on profit with a study on children's conceptions of banking, a complex and often remote economic concept for children. Eleven-, 13- and 18-year-old children were first put through the shop transaction study in order to ascertain whether the subject understood the notion of profit. They were then asked a number of questions about the functions of a bank such as: 'Supposing I put £100 into a bank, and after one year I take my money out again, would I get back more, less or the same?' And 'Supposing I borrow £100 from a bank to pay back after one year. Would I have to pay back more or less or the same?' The responses of the children were categorised thus:

1. No knowledge of interest (get or pay back the same amount).
2. Interest on deposits only (get back more but pay the same).
3. Interest on both, but more on deposit.
4. Interest same on deposits and loans.
5. Interest higher on loans (not fully understood).
6. Interest on loans (fully understood).

Although there was some evidence of class differences (the middle-class children functioning at a slightly more advanced level), the difference was not significant. However, the developmental trends were striking and highly significant. Only a quarter of the 14-year-olds fully understood the function of the bank and this number showed no increase for the 16-year-olds.

This study was, in fact, replicated by Jahoda and Woerdenbagch (1982) in Holland. They found that while primary pupils in both locations overwhelmingly saw the bank as simply a place that keeps money, twice as many as the older Dutch subjects realised that one borrowed money from a bank compared with the older Scottish subjects.

Ng (1983) replicated and extended G. Jahoda's (1981) study with 96 6–13-year-old children from Hong Kong. Although he found much the same developmental trend, a full understanding of the bank emerged at 10 while the idea of profit emerged at 6 years old. Thus for both concepts the Chinese children were more precocious than the Scottish (and Dutch) sample. As in previous studies Ng examined the dynamics of conflict between schemes in the child: for instance, to induce cognitive conflict the interviewer deliberately asked the child to explain how the bank obtained money to pay its employees, electricity charges, etc., while yet having the same interest charges on money lent and borrowed. Although the impact of this conflict instruction was not significant it seemed to be useful in examining economic development. Ng (1983) concludes:

> The exceptional maturity of the Hong Kong children probably reflected their high level of economic socialisation and consumer activity, and the business ethos of the society at large. Socially, life would be difficult for them if they did not grasp socio-economic concepts at an early age. Their maturity represents, in short, a case of socio-economic reality shaping (partly at least) socio-economic understanding.   (pp. 220–1)

Ng's results are not unique. Using a similar approach, Wong (1989) also found that children in Hong Kong had a more sophisticated understanding of banking than those in the United States and Leiser, Sevón and Lévy (1990) report that children in Denmark and Finland have a more sophisticated understanding than those in Algeria, Yugoslavia, Norway and Austria. These comparisons demonstrate that developmental trends are not necessarily always similar throughout different countries, although they may prove to be so in many cases. A decisive factor seems to be the extent to which children are sheltered from, exposed to, or in some cases, take part in economic activity. This is borne out by the initially surprising findings of Takahashi (in press), who found that Japanese children lagged behind those of Hong Kong and western children in their understanding of banks. Though members of an economically sophisticated and prosperous society, Japanese children may well be sheltered from economic activity.

This all raises question of exactly what kind of experiences influence the understanding of which economic concepts at what age. This means that there sometimes may even be greater differences within the same country than between different countries, depending on the way parents raise their children, and explain and show to them how banks operate.

## Ownership and possessions

Berti *et al.* (1982) have been particularly interested in children's conceptions of the means of production and ownership. They argued that children pass from an initial stage of complete ignorance about the productive function of means to recognising that various means have to do with work and money and the production of goods. Finally when a coherent and comprehensive view of the network of economic exchanges has been formed the child will understand that the sale of the produced goods permits the owner to realise a profit and pay his/her employees.

Over 120 Italian children were interviewed in order to determine whether the child recognised (a) the existence of an owner for various objects, who s/he was, and how s/he became owner; (b) the existence of agricultural and industrial products, and whose they were; and (c) what advantage the child thought the owner derived from each means of production. From their interviews of who owns such things as factories, five levels were distinguished:

1. The owner is the person found in spatial/temporal contact with the production means (passengers own the bus).
2. The owner is the person who exercises an appropriate use of or direct control over the producing means in question (drivers own the bus).
3. The owner is the one who not only directly uses the producing means in question but also controls its use by others (the boss owns the bus).
4. The owner is clearly differentiated from the employee, in that s/he has the function of giving orders.
5. The owner is at the top of the hierarchy of command, and the boss at an intermediate position between the owner and worker.

The authors also identified five different levels for the perceived ownership of products. These include a stage where the children believe products are owned by anybody, followed by a stage where they are seen to be owned by those closest to them or using them, and then a stage where product ownership is seen through ownership of the means of production. Only at the final level do children realise that products belong to the owner of the means of production and that the employees are compensated for their work by a salary.

Various statistical analyses showed that children's ideas about different production means develop with different speeds but through the same sequences. Furthermore the parents also had a 'developmental' view of their children in that parents of the youngest children said that they had not been told or asked about jobs and ownership, while the opposite was true for older children.

The authors argue that understandings about the value of money and its use in the act of buying and selling occur at the same time as the development of logical–arithmetic operations. They argue that for children to have a grasp of ownership and other economic relationships they need to be in Piaget's formal operation period.

Cram and Ng (1989) in New Zealand examined (172 subjects of three different age groups: 5/6, 8/9, 11/12 years) children's understanding of private ownership by noting the attributes the subjects used to endorse ownership. Greater age was associated with an increase in the endorsement of higher-level (i.e. contractual) attributes and in the rejection of lower-level (i.e. physical) attributes, but there was only a tendency in this direction. Already 89 per cent of the youngest group rejected 'liking' as a reason for possessing, which increased to 98 per cent in the middle and oldest group, whereas the differences on the other two levels were more distinct. This indicates that surprisingly 5–6-year-olds are mainly aware of the distinction between personal desires and ownership. This does not necessarily contradict earlier work but makes it necessary to interview children younger than the ones in this study to find out whether and at what age egocentric ownership attributes are endorsed during earlier stages of development.

Furby's comprehensive work on property and possessions (summarised in Furby, 1991) takes a rather different view. She emphasises that possessions are extensions to the self which help the child to control the environment. Those objects that a child is allowed to explore come to be regarded as theirs and somehow part of them: those objects towards which their behaviour is restricted are defined as part of the other. So the most important characteristic of possession is the very high degree of control involved: one has essentially as much control over one's possessions as over one's body. Given this, it is no surprise that possessions are included in one's concept of self.

Furnham and Jones (1987) studied children's views regarding possessions and their theft. One hundred and two subjects aged 7–8, 9–10, 12–13 and 16–17 filled out a questionnaire based on work by Furby (1980a, 1980b, 1991) and Irving and Siegal (1983). Results indicated that, as hypothesised, views about possessions become more sophisticated and 'realistic' with age. The type of favourite possessions proved to be age-dependent, varying from toys to sound and sports equipment, computers and clothes. The younger groups showed no preference for the means of acquisition of an object whereas the older groups attached great importance to self-bought and individually owned objects motivated by a desire to effect and control their environment.

As with increasing age the child's self-concept gradually depends more and more on possessions, reactions towards theft become harsher and empathy with the victim increases, even under mitigating circumstances. Most of the younger subjects simply demanded a return of the stolen object, creating mitigating circumstances (i.e. poverty or unhappiness) even where there were none, whereas older subjects demanded conditional discharge or prison sentences of different durations as a punishment. Although the oldest group was relatively stringent in their actual demands for punishment, in moral terms they were rather lenient. This is understood as a pragmatic acceptance of the need for law and order to provide general safety.

For children of all ages the element of control over their environment seems to be the most important characteristic of possessions. For older children who are more active consumers themselves, possessions often imply power and status and an enhancement of personal freedom and security. This suggests that in societies or groups (like a kibbutz) where ownership is shared, young people acquire the understanding about possessing in a quite different way.

Concepts relating to means of production seem to develop similarly to those of buying and selling. They also advance through phases of no grasp of any system, to unconnected systems (knowledge that the owner of means of production sells products but no understanding of how s/he gets the money to pay the worker) and to integrated systems (linking the worker's payment and sales proceeds), depending on the respective logical–arithmetical ability of the child. Although these concepts seem to follow the same developmental sequence, it cannot be said whether, to what extent and how the same factors (experimental, maturation, educational) contribute equally to the development of each concept.

## Labour and management

Haire and Morrison (1957) set out to measure American school children's perceptions of labour and management to get some idea of the origin and development of these attitudes. They gave 755 12–16-year-olds five short tests including cards with stereotyped pictures; sentence completion tests 'A union is . . .'; ten statements about union management and labour which they could agree on; a word form test where they were asked to underline two words which best described union, job, etc.; and finally a socio-economic questionnaire. They found that even by the age of 12 there was a clear distinction between the attitudes of children from high and low socio-economic backgrounds. The latter were predictably much more strongly pro-labour, showed more undifferentiated approval of the workers involved, agreed with them on most issues, and tended to identify with them. As the children got older they tended to move in a pro-labour direction; however the basic difference between the class groups remains stable. They also found that where they could differentiate the effect of schools and homes on children's perceptions and attitudes the evidence suggests the school is the major determinant.

Finally they found that lower socio-economic status (SES) groups showed less differentiation in their perceptions of labour–management relations, although this did not prevent their taking sides. Further, low-SES children tended to describe the union in terms of an economic function, while high-SES income groups tended to describe it in terms of a simple aggregate of people. High-SES groups tended to see the boss in terms of power, money and intelligence, with unilaterality of action, while low-SES children saw him/her simply in terms of telling people what to do.

In a more recent British study, Patterson and Locksley (1981) tried to determine how a large group of London fifth-formers (15–16-year-olds) see the unions. Although most students knew who a shop steward was, less than a quarter knew who the 'father of a chapel' was. Just under half the children thought the media treated the unions fairly but generally they were negative towards the unions: nearly a half thought them too greedy, and a fifth too extreme. The majority believed that unions have benefited their members fairly well but were against the closed shop. However, the children did not feel that they had been taught enough on the subject of trade unions.

## Inequality and poverty

In 1975 Zinser, Perry and Edgar conducted a study to determine the importance of the affluence of the recipient to preschool children's sharing behaviour. Most of the children favoured sharing with poor recipients over rich recipients. They were also more generous with low-value items than with high-value items and these findings were consistent over all three (4–6) ages. There are two possible explanations for this behaviour: (a) societal values, for instance, society already has communicated to these young children that poor people are more deserving as recipients of sharing than rich people; or (b) empathy, for instance, perceived need arouses affective reactions in the children that motivate sharing, which in turn reduces affective reactions.

Siegal (1981) set out to determine children's perceptions and evaluations of adult economic needs. Children aged 6–13 were asked to distribute token money to dolls dressed as a doctor, shopkeeper, bus driver or waiter by the question: 'Show me how much money each needs to take care of his children.' They were also asked whether their (unequal) distributions were fair and about the amount of effort required in the various professions. The results showed that the youngest children did not realise that unmet needs exist, while older children were divided on the issue of equality: some believed that needs should be met regardless of the bread-winner's occupational efforts while others believed that inequality is fair and that effort and ability should be rewarded irrespective of need. These findings are explained in terms of the work ethic in that 'those children for whom work efforts are equated with rewards might be more likely to maintain that inequality is fair than those for whom the relationship between effort and reward is loose and non-existent' (p. 301).

Winocur and Siegal (1982) predicted that older adolescents would be more likely to base judgements on equal pay for equal work, while younger children would be more likely to advocate that pay should correspond with family needs. Further they hypothesised that though girls may be more likely to treat male and female workers equally, they would be more conservative in their achievement judgements than boys. Although they found support for the former hypothesis, they did not find it for the latter. Thus concern for family needs appears to decline with age, and objective work outcomes take precedence over need in adolescents' allocations of economic rewards.

In a later study Irving and Siegal (1983) investigated the effect of various mitigating circumstances (including economic need) on children's perceptions of criminal justice. They found that younger children were harsher in their judgements than older ones, but that their leniency and acceptance of mitigating circumstances were highly dependent on the situation. Older children did not consider economic need to be a valid defence.

Leahy (1981) was specifically interested in the development of class concepts (specifically comparisons between rich and poor people) in cognitive developmental terms. Over 700 children in four age groups (mean 6, 10, 14, 17 years) were interviewed and asked to describe rich and poor people and distinguish between them. These responses were classified into categories of person description, including peripheral (possessions, appearances and behaviours), central (traits and thoughts) and sociocentric (life-chances and class-consciousness) categories. The

ANOVAs on the content analyses categories revealed numerous significant age effect findings. Lower- and working-class subjects were more likely than upper-middle-class subjects to mention life-chances and thoughts in describing the rich and the poor, while upper-middle-class subjects were more likely than subjects from the other classes to mention the traits of the poor. As the subjects got older there was an increasing tendency to view classes of rich and poor people as not only differing in their external, observable qualities, but as being different kinds of people. As children got older they placed more emphasis on individual differences in effort, ability and other salient personality traits.

The author offers two explanatory models to account for his findings: a cognitive developmental model and a general functionalist model. As regards the former model, the results are similar to other findings on the descriptions of peers, social roles and sex roles and suggests that later adolescence is characterised by an increased awareness of the nature of complex social and economic systems. Hence, class differences and economic inequality are seen not only in terms of an individual's characteristics but also in terms of his/her relationship to other classes. According to the second model, socialisation results in considerable uniformity among classes and races as to the nature of the social world. This uniformity retains stability in social institutions while also providing a rationale for the unequal distribution of assets.

Although most of the research to date does suggest that there is a consensus about the justice of inequality, this may be because it has focused on the explanations for inequality that are given by children of different ages. Emler and Dickinson (1985) took an alternative approach and explored class differences in children's beliefs about the nature of social and economic inequalities. They asked children aged 7–12 from middle- and working-class backgrounds to estimate the incomes of people in a range of occupations (doctor, teacher, bus driver, road sweeper) and make judgements about the fairness of the income differences. The middle-class children made higher estimates of income, but also believed that inequalities of income were greater than did the working-class children. Most children from both classes believed that the inequalities were justified, but the middle-class children were more committed to the justice of the inequalities. A similar pattern was found in adolescents (Dickinson, 1990). Most adolescents think income inequalities are legitimate, with the middle-class providing most support, though it is striking that few class-differences were found in the explanations and justifications offered.

Emler and Dickinson explain these findings using Moscovici's (1981) ideas about social representations. Children will assimilate those social representations that are dominant in their community. This suggests that social representations of economic inequalities are more detailed and important for the middle classes. Children of this group therefore pick up these representations quickly. For the working class the same ideas are less significant and so children of this group have a more tenuous grasp of them.

Class differences in explanations were also found by Furnham (1982d) in his study of adolescent school children's (15-year-olds) explanations for poverty. Public-school boys (primarily middle-class) tended to offer more individualistic explanations for poverty than comprehensive (primarily working-class) school boys who in turn tended to rate societal or structural factors as more important. On the whole public-school boys tended to blame the poor for their condition. The two most important explanations for poverty among public-school boys were 'Lack of thrift and proper money management', and 'No attempts at self-improvement'. On the other hand, for the comprehensive-school boys the two most important explanations for poverty were 'Failure of industry to provide enough jobs for poor people' and 'Low wages in some business and industries'. Curiously one of two items that might have been expected to reveal significant difference did not, namely 'Failure of society to provide good schools' – clearly a salient variable for school children. There were no differences between the groups regarding fatalistic explanations which were by and large considered unimportant. These results have been found with adult samples (Feagin, 1972; Feather, 1974; Furnham, 1982b). Yet it should be pointed out that comprehensive-school boys saw both individualistic and fatalistic explanations as relatively unimportant in explaining poverty. That is, the major differences between the groups lay in the importance that they attached to societal explanation. Roker (1990) also reports that adolescents from private schools are more likely to blame the poor themselves for poverty, whereas those attending state schools see government policy as the main causal factor.

The estimates of the annual incomes of the poor given by Furnham's (1982d) sample also showed interesting results. With one exception all of the ANOVAs showed significant differences in the predicted direction; namely that public-school boys gave higher estimates than comprehensive-school boys. They are interesting for a number of reasons. The first is that by and large the estimates are rather low, in that many people on social security or supplementary benefits earn more money than those estimates. Secondly there appears to be an element of sexism in their estimates; women need less money to be poor than men, and a man supporting a wife and child needs no more money than a man just supporting a child. But both these results probably reflect the adolescents' understanding of the economic world rather than bias or prejudice. It is known, for instance, that children underestimate both poverty and wealth because of their own experience of money (Danziger, 1958). Presumably adolescents also tend to underestimate, but not to the same extent. Interestingly more comprehensive-school boys estimated the amount in weekly wages than public-school boys, who in turn preferred to make estimates in terms of annual amounts. This may reflect what they have learnt from their parents, some of whom are probably paid monthly (middle-class) and some weekly (working-class).

Stacey and Singer (1985) had 325 teenagers of $14\frac{1}{2}$ and 17 years from a working-class background complete a questionnaire, probing their perceptions of the attributes and consequences of poverty and wealth following Furnham (1981). Regardless of age and sex, all respondent groups rated familial circumstances as most important and luck as least important in explaining poverty and wealth. With

internal and external attributions for poverty and wealth rating moderately important, these findings differ slightly compared to Leahy's (1981) results, as here adolescents clearly thought sociocentric categories to be more important than the
other two. A reason for this might be that here all subjects were from a working-
class background and, as Furnham (1982b) found out, subjects from a lower socio-
economic background tend to attach more importance to societal explanations than
subjects from a higher socio-economic background, who tend to offer more individualistic (e.g. lack of thrift and proper money management) explanations for
poverty.

Most of the studies in this field have tried to describe the levels which children
go through in their understanding of certain economic notions. The occasional disagreement as to the number of levels and points of transition is probably mostly a
matter of methodology; and results have generally been interpreted within the
Piagetian developmental framework though more socio-economic interpretations
have been suggested (e.g. by Emler and Dickinson, 1985). Most of the researchers
already agree that external stimuli (socio-economic environment, personal experience with money, formal teaching, parental practices) have great influence on the
child's development of economic thinking and may contribute to pre-mature
knowledge. For instance, Wosinski and Pietras (1990) discovered in a study with
87 Polish subjects of ages 8, 11 and 14 that the youngest had in some aspects (e.g.
the definition of salary, the possibility of getting the same salary for everybody, the
possibility of starting a factory) better economic knowledge than the other groups.
They attributed this to the fact that these children were born and had been living
under conditions of an economic crisis in Poland. They had experienced conditions
of shortage, increases in prices, inflation and heard their family and television programmes discuss these matters. This, too, represents 'a case of socio-economic
reality shaping (partly at least) socio-economic understanding' (Ng, 1983: 220–1).

It therefore seems to be that up to a certain extent the development of economic
notions can be accelerated through experimental and educational factors, which still
merit further study.

## Economic relations and justice

A few studies have been carried out which attempt to understand how children perceive and understand political and economic relationships. For instance, Miller and
Horn (1955) were interested in children's perceptions of debt. They chose twenty
actual court cases involving debt that would be interesting and easy for children to
interpret as well as being representative of a broad area of debt, credit, promises
and related contracts. These were given to a panel of adults closely associated with
debt or ethics to obtain their opinions concerning the 'best' ethical responses to
these cases. They were also shown to 1,297 children, ranging in age from 10 to 18
years. One of the major findings was the lack of agreement between the consultants
and the children on 47 of the 129 items. The children of varying ages, sexes and
socio-economic backgrounds tended to disagree with the ethical consultants on the

following points which they and the courts had accepted:

1. Debtors ought not to be jailed or forced to labour because of their debt.
2. All acts of the courts should be upheld and respected, despite personal or contingent circumstances.
3. Gambling losses do not constitute legally enforceable obligations.
4. Using credit in making purchases is not morally wrong.
5. Warranties of quality are implied in sales on the open market.
6. Banks and depositors have well-established responsibilities towards one another.

Predictably they found evidence of age differences. Older (14 and above years) children showed greater tolerance and ability to differentiate among various kinds of promises as to their cruciality and seriousness. On the other hand the younger children (10- and 12-year-olds) strongly believed that performance of promises should be compelled, and debt-evasion should be punished. Involuntary bankruptcy was also viewed as a legitimate means of collecting debts. The authors concluded that children should be explicitly taught in school elements of debt, credit, promises and simple contract.

Irving and Siegal (1983) were interested in children's perception of justice in relation to crimes concerning assault, arson and treason, each with the respective mitigating circumstances of brain damage, passion and economic need. Seven- to 17-year-old children were asked to judge the appropriate punishment given to these various cases. Although younger children were harsher in their judgement than older children, their leniency and acceptance of mitigating circumstances were highly dependent on the situation.

## Saving

A topic that has only recently received empirical attention is that of children's saving (Webley, Levine and Lewis, 1991; Sonuga-Barke and Webley, 1993). Sonuga-Barke and Webley (1993) chose an experimental approach and a degree of abstraction in the use of a 'play economy' in their study of economic socialisation. The play economy of Sonuga-Barke and Webley (1993) had a common format through a series of experiments. In the play economy, children took part in a board game using tokens which they had previously earned. The board game was structured to operationalise aspects of temptation to spend and the threat of losing savings. The details of the board game varied from study to study, but all had a toy shop (containing the long-term goal the children were saving for), a sweet shop (a temptation) and a bank.

The major improvements in economic performance occurred between the ages of 6 and 9. At age 4, the use of the bank was essentially random. To the 6-year-old, it appeared that money saved was money lost. Yet they did save, as they believed it was something they ought to do. In contrast, the 9-year-olds viewed saving strategically and were aware that savings could be used for expenditure in the future and that saving and expenditure were related, not distinct activities.

Webley, Levine and Lewis (1991) had thirty children, ten each aged 6, 9 and 12, take part in a 'play economy' which consisted of four adjoining rooms, representing opportunities to save (one room contained a 'bank') or temptation to spend, such as another room containing a sweet shop with real sweets. Children were given 90 tokens during the period of the game and had to save 70 in order to purchase a desired toy which had been chosen at the outset. While the results showed a predictable pattern of increased understanding of savings (especially institutional saving) and improved savings 'success' rates with increasing age, the information gathered from the accounts showed that younger children developed 'rational' strategies which were not necessarily inferior when viewed in a wider social context. They concluded:

> studies such as the present one are of some interest to economists who are concerned with the development of economic preferences and, at a practical level, to marketing personnel searching for the best ways of increasing institutional saving. More fundamentally perhaps, the current paper is a small contribution to the re-psychologizing of the study of saving. The early economists made extensive use of psychological concepts in devising an 'impatience' model of saving but since Keynes such ideas have played little part. In the dominant economic model of saving of today, the life-cycle hypothesis, there is no psychology; every concept is economic or demographic or is translated into such terms. We believe that stripping out psychology in this way is a mistake and that an improved model of saving should utilise insights from psychology and sociology.   (p. 145)

## Entrepreneurship

For economists, sociologists and informed lay people the entrepreneur is a risk-taking individual, who seeks new markets, promotes new methods of production, has a future time orientation and is able to fill gaps in services or demands. Though nice distinctions may be made between 'real' craftsmen and 'quasi'-opportunistic entrepreneurs, there is no doubt both that adults recognise the qualities of an entrepreneur and that entrepreneurship is one prerequisite for economic growth. Kourilsky and Campbell (1984) set out to determine children's (938 8–12-year-olds) beliefs about entrepreneurship before participation in an instruction system designed to encourage economic success, risk-taking and entrepreneurial persistence. They were also very interested in sex differences. Results indicated that the stereotypic entrepreneur was male, yet the effect of the instruction and role-playing exercises was to encourage girls to be more interested. Perhaps the most important aspect of this study was however the demonstration that various entrepreneurial behaviours could be taught and measured. Economic success was measured by profit made in a mini-business; risk-taking was measured by exposure to loss and disadvantages; and persistence as the tendency to stick to a task till completed.

## The playground economy

So far we have only considered children's economic understanding and behaviour in so far as it impinges on the adult economic world. But in addition to coming to understand the adult world of banks, shops and work and learning to budget and save money, children also construct an economic world of their own. Webley and Lea (1993b) describe a number of studies of this 'playground economy' which reveal that it is economically quite sophisticated. For example, a child (the worker) who is skilled but has no marbles may 'work' for a child (the capitalist) who owns lots. If the worker wins some marbles they share the proceeds; though they claim that these should be split equally, in fact the marble capitalist always takes a bigger share than the marble worker. In this marble economy the value of the different kinds of marbles ('oilies', 'grandmas', etc.) is crucial but, interestingly, is determined by local supply and demand and not the price of marbles in the shops. The children seem to understand supply and demand in the playground; they can easily explain why one would need to give three 'ordinaries' for a 'grandma'; they seem to understand this much better than they do if they are asked questions about the 'real' (but for them probably less important and more abstract) world of the adult economy. Studies of swapping shed a rather different kind of light on the playground economy. Swapping appears to be an act with an economic content but a social function and seems to correspond to the kind of world of part-time trading described by Henry (1978). Children will make unequal swaps but only for good reasons (usually as an overture to friendship); they have a good grasp of the relative value of things.

This research is still in its early stages, and is methodologically rather weak. But it does suggest that researchers should perhaps be less concerned with answering the question of how children come to understand the economic world of grown-ups and focus instead on how children understand and solve the economic problems they are faced with. The economic world of the playground matters to children; and it is important that we investigate behaviour that matters to the children concerned.

## Money

As money is the basis of almost all economical actions today, its full understanding clearly is a prerequisite for other, more abstract concepts (e.g. credit or profit). Children's first contact with money happens at a quite early age (watching parents buying or selling things, receiving pocket-money etc.) but research has shown that this does not necessarily mean that although children use money themselves they fully understand its meaning and significance. For very young children, giving money to a salesperson constitutes a mere ritual. They are not aware of the different values of coins and the purpose of change, let alone the origin of money. Children thus need to understand the nature and role of money before being able to master more abstract concepts.

Pollio and Gray (1973) investigated different 'change-making' strategies in children and adults. Five groups of subjects ranging in age from 7 to 20 years were asked to do mental arithmetic on the giving of change. Whereas the younger children tended to make mistakes, by the age of 13 the children were accurate nearly all the time. Although children of all levels knew the various coin equivalencies, younger children used smaller coins by preference when making change while older children used all the coins available. This was interpreted to mean that coin equivalencies are probably learned as specific response pairs and that in making change younger children use untransformed base units such as pennies and dimes, largely because the computational demands placed by change-making operations force them to minimise the number of non-computational transformations used (p. 173).

Hitchcock, Munroe and Munroe (1976) hypothesised that as people in poor countries have greater material need than persons in wealthy countries a country's coinage allows institutional expression of a level of need. They therefore compared 84 countries' gross national product with their mean coin size and found, as predicted, a negative correlation. This indicates, in their view, the potential usefulness of viewing institutional-level data from a psychological perspective.

In a longitudinal study conducted in Italy, Berti and Bombi (1981) attempted to ascertain 3–8-year-olds' conceptions of money and its value. They showed children a variety of coins and notes which they were asked to identify; asked what (from a chocolate bar to a motor car) they could buy with this money; and took part in a shopkeeper game sequence to determine whether the child would pay for the purchase (as a customer) and give change (as a shopkeeper). From the work of Strauss (1952) and others they hypothesised six stages:

1. No awareness of payment.
2. Obligatory payment: recognition of the need for exchange but does not discriminate between various amounts of money.
3. Realisation that not all types of money can buy everything: not all money is equivalent.
4. Realisation that money is insufficient for certain goods.
5. Strict correspondence between money and object.
6. Correct use of change: the realisation that the excessive value of money may be compensated for by the shopkeeper's giving the difference in money to the customer.

As predicted, they found a clear developmental sequence in which

> the acquisition of understanding about money can be interpreted as a process of differentiation and articulation which allows the child to construct usage rules that are increasingly more precise and complex . . . the progression through the first four stages is developed around pre-operational thinking and precisely during that chronological period in which such thinking is dominant. In contrast, the fifth and sixth stages imply the use of logical and arithmetic operations.   (p. 1182)

In an earlier study Berti and Bombi (1979) concluded that the idea of payment for work emerges from a hinterland of spontaneous (and erroneous) beliefs developed by children to explain the origin of money. In effect the idea of this topic is only acquired in a verbal way: if a child occasionally notices that his/her parents (and other adults) take part in extra domestic activities, this is not defined as work and the child cannot have any direct knowledge of payment. Verbal information about this constitutes initially a strange body in childish thought, in which predominate the spontaneous ideas of the origin of money. Only when the understanding of work is substantially developed does it support the spontaneous beliefs about the origin of money.

It was also established that the links between money and work is initially understood asymmetrically. Children affirm that parents work for earnings but do not understand that there is a need for money which can be obtained through working. This indicates the existence of systems of ideas that are relatively independent, although they possess certain facts in common. In fact, the ideas that we found can be divided into two heterogeneous categories, the one containing spontaneous and fantastic ideas about the origin of money, the other containing information about the work of parents.

More recently in an investigation of incentive effects Witryol and Wentworth (1983) found that 7-year-old children confused the two American coins (a dime and a nickel), yet by 9–12 years none chose the nickel over the dime.

Supporting the idea of gradually integrating subsystems, Berti, Bombi and de Beni (1986) pointed out that the concepts about shop and factory profit in 8-year-olds were not compatible. Despite improving their understanding of shop profit after receiving training, the children were not able to transfer their knowledge onto factory's profit, thinking that prices were set arbitrarily. Berti, Bombi and de Beni (1986) showed that, by training, children's understanding of profit could be enhanced. Both critical training sessions stimulating the child to puzzle out solutions to contradictions between their own forecasts and the actual outcomes and ordinary tutorial training sessions (information given to children) that consisted in similar games of buying and selling proved to be effective. However, the results of the post-tests also showed that neither kind of experience was sufficient in itself to lead children to a correct notion of profit, partly due to lack of arithmetical abilities. Nevertheless the authors suggested that although arithmetical abilities are essential: 'making children talk about economic topics they have not yet mastered, far from being an obstacle to learning may contribute to their progress, constituting in itself a kind of training, as G. Jahoda (1981) also found in different circumstances' (p. 28).

In a study with 11–16-year-olds, Furnham and Cleare (1988) also found differences in understanding shop and factory profit. 'Of 11–12-year olds, 7% understood profit in shops, yet 69% mentioned profit as a motive for starting a factory today, and 20% mentioned profit as an explanation for why factories had been started' (p. 475). The understanding of the abstract concept of profit, which depends on the previous understanding of the basic concept of buying and selling, grows through different phases. Young children (6–8 years) seem to have no grasp of any system and conceive of transactions as 'simply an observed ritual without further purpose' (Furth, Baur and Smith, 1976, p. 365). Older children (8–10 years) realise that the shop owner previously had to buy (pay for) the goods before he can sell them. Nevertheless, they do not always understand that the money for this comes from the customers and that buying prices have to be lower than selling prices. They thus perceive of buying and selling as two unconnected systems. Not until the age of 10/11 are children able to integrate these two systems and understand the difference between buying and selling prices. Of course, these age bands may vary slightly among children (or cultures) as experimental factors play a part in the understanding of economic concepts.

## Economic socialisation: pocket-money

In reviewing the literature on economic socialisation Stacey (1982) concluded that:

> In the first decade of life, the economic socialisation of children does not appear to be strongly influenced by their own social backgrounds, with the exception of the children of the very rich and possibly of the very poor. In the second decade of life, social differences in the development appear to be more pronounced.   (p. 172)

One important way in which parents socialise their children in monetary and economic matters is through their pocket-money, a weekly or monthly allowance given either unconditionally or for some work. Until recently there has been little academic research in this area and most of the information comes from marketing studies. In Britain, for example, a regular survey of pocket-money has been carried out by Bird's Eye Walls. This reveals that the average pocket-money in 1989 was £1.40, that it increases with age, that boys get on average slightly more than girls and that the highest rates of payment are in Scotland, where average payments are almost half as much again as in the south-west of England. Though in some years pocket-money has gone up by less than the rate of inflation and in other years by more, overall it was 25 per cent higher in 1989 than it would be if it had simply kept pace with inflation since 1975 (Walls, 1989). French surveys paint a similar picture but also reveal that parents report giving much lower amounts than children report receiving, essentially because parents focus only on pocket-money whereas children count all the money they receive (Micromegas, 1993). This gives an idea of when pocket-money may be an important socialising agent since it constitutes 100 per cent of the income of French 4–7-year-olds but only 14.5 per cent of the income of 13–14-year-olds (half of French 14-year-olds work regularly).

The comparative lack of a firm basis of academic research has not inhibited the publication of handbooks and articles that guide parents in the economic socialisation of their children, though ideas about what is appropriate have changed drastically during the last hundred years. At the beginning of the century parents were encouraged to link pay with children's work, whereas current rhetoric favours a regular allowance that is not tied to work (Zelizer, 1985). The following is typical:

> The allowance should be paid weekly on the same day each week to younger children, and monthly to kids as they approach their teens. The shift to a monthly payment is not for your convenience but is for the purpose of encouraging more careful attention to

budgeting and planning ahead on the part of your teenager. The important thing is that the payment should represent a predictable source of income that the child can count on. (Davis and Taylor, 1979: 46)

What evidence is there that such parental practices have the desired effect? Marshall and Magruder's (1960) study appears to be the first that specifically investigated the relationship between parents' money education practices and children's knowledge and use of money. Amongst the many hypotheses examined were: 'Children will have more knowledge of money use if their parents give them an allowance' and 'Children will have more knowledge of the use of money if they save money'. They found, as predicted, that children's knowledge of money is directly related to the extensiveness of their experience of money – whether they are given money to spend; if they are given opportunities to earn and save money; and their parents' attitudes to, and habits of money spending. Thus it seems that socialisation and education would have important consequences on a child's or adolescent's understanding of economic affairs. However, they did not find any evidence for a number of their hypotheses. These were: children will have more knowledge of money use if their parents give them an allowance; if children are given allowances, less of the family's money, rather than more, will be taken for children's spending money; if children are given opportunities to earn money, they will have more knowledge of money use than children lacking this experience; children will have less knowledge of money use if money is used to reward or punish their behaviour; and children will have the attitudes about the importance of money and material things that are expressed by their parents.

More recently, Abramovitch, Freedman and Pliner (1991) have investigated how spending in an experimental store was affected by children's' experience of money. Their participants (aged 6, 8 and 10) were given $4 either in the form of a credit card or in cash to spend in an experimental toy store which offered a variety of items priced from 50 cents to $5. They were allowed to take home any unspent money. Children who received an allowance spent roughly the same amount in the cash and credit card condition ($2.32 vs $2.42) but those who did not receive an allowance spent much more with a credit card ($2.82) than when they only had cash ($1.76). After they had finished in the store the children were given a pricing test in which they had to say how much familiar items (e.g. running shoes, television) cost; children who received an allowance scored higher on this test, as did the older children. These results suggest that receiving an allowance may facilitate the development of monetary competence. Since there was no difference in the incomes of the allowance and non-allowance groups, we can exclude the possibility that this is simply the result of amount of experience with money.

Though the limited evidence does suggest that allowances are effective, it seems as if parents make only limited use of their potential as a vehicle for economic socialisation. Sonuga-Barke and Webley (1993) focused specifically on whether parent's used pocket-money to teach children about saving. They found that for most parents, pocket-money was seen as money to be spent, not money to be saved.

Though there were some half-hearted attempts to foster saving (e.g. by parents offering to match any money saved by the child) this opportunity was rarely taken up.

Parents are concerned with more than merely turning children into effective economic agents, however, and two studies cast some light on other aspects of parental views about pocket-money, those of Furnham and Thomas (1984b) and Feather (1991).

Furnham and Thomas (1984b) investigated adults' perceptions of the economic socialisation of children through pocket-money. Over 200 British adults completed a questionnaire on their beliefs concerning, for instance, how much and how often children should be given pocket-money, as well as such things as whether they should be encouraged to work for it, save it, etc. There were a number of differences based on sex, age, social class and whether the subjects did or did not have children. Females turned out to be more in favour of agreeing with children in advance on the kinds of items pocket-money should cover, more in favour of giving older children pocket-money monthly, and also more in favour of an annual review of a child's pocket-money, than males. Thus, all of these differences show females more willing to treat children as responsible individuals. It is possible that this is due to the tendency for women, both at work and in the home, to have greater contact with children and therefore a better understanding of their capabilities.

The age differences showed, as expected, that older adults were more likely to expect children to spend less on entertainment and more on reading materials, than younger adults. Further, as expected, older adults disagreed less than younger adults that boys should be given a little more pocket-money than girls. Younger adults were also more in favour of pocket-money being linked to the performance of household chores. Younger adults tend to view pocket-money more as a contractual arrangement between adult and child than older adults. Middle-class adults were more in favour of giving children pocket-money and of starting to give pocket-money at an earlier age than working-class adults. Over 90 per cent of the middle-class adults believed that by the age of 8 years children should receive pocket-money, while just over 70 per cent of working-class adults believed that children of 8 should receive pocket-money. All middle-class adults believed that by the age of 10 the pocket-money system should be introduced, yet only 84 per cent of working-class adults agreed. Indeed some working-class respondents did not believe in the system of pocket-money at all. A similar class difference was revealed in the question concerning when children should receive their pocket-money. Whereas 91 per cent of the middle-class believed children should receive it weekly (and 4 per cent when they need it) only 79 per cent of working-class adults believed children should receive their pocket-money weekly (and 16 per cent when they need it). Furthermore significantly more working-class adults believed that boys should receive more pocket-money than girls.

These class-difference findings are in line with previous studies on childhood socialisation (Newson and Newson, 1976) and with figures on class differences in

general. That is, working-class adults introduce pocket-money later and more errat-
ically than middle-class parents. However, the study of Furnham and Thomas
(1984a) revealed far fewer class differences which may be the result of the fact that
a greater range of ages were considered in this study.

Feather's (1991) concerns were more psychological. He focused on the relationships between parental beliefs, values and pocket-money practices. The amount of
money that children received was related to the age of the child and the importance
that parents placed on the need to foster a strong and harmonious family unit. In
other words, parents who rated reasons for giving pocket-money like 'it helps to
reduce conflict in the family' and 'because it improves one's relationship with the
child' as important tended to give more of it. Mothers placed more emphasis on
children's needs than fathers.

Probably the most detailed analysis of parent–child money transfer is that of
Newson and Newson (1976). They carried out an extensive study of over 700
7-year-olds. They found that most of their sample could count on a basic sum of
pocket-money, sometimes calculated on a complicated incentive system. Some
children appear to be given money which is instituted for the express purpose of
allowing the possibility of fining (confiscating); others are given money as a substitute for wages; while some have to 'work' for it. Over 50 per cent of the sample
earned money from their parents beyond their regular income but there were no sex
or social-class differences in this practice. This means that it is difficult to determine how much money children get per week as it varies. They did, however, find
social-class differences in children's unearned income and savings. Middle-class
children received less (18 vs 30p) than working-class children, and saved more (90
vs 48 per cent). That is, 52 per cent of class V children always spend their money
within the week, whereas only 10 per cent of class I or II children do so. The
authors conclude: 'Having cash in hand is equated with enjoying the good life: the
relationship between money and enjoyment is specific and direct . . . the working-
class child already begins to fall into this traditional pattern of life in his use of
pocket money' (p. 244).

Furnham and Thomas (1984a) set out to determine age, sex and class differences
in the distribution and use of pocket-money. They tested over 400 7–12-year-old
British children. They predicted, and found, that older children would receive more
money and take part in more 'economic activities' such as saving, borrowing and
lending. Class differences were also apparent: working-class children received
more money but saved less than middle-class children. Middle-class children also
reported more than working-class children that they had to work around the house
for their pocket-money and tended to let their parents look after the pocket-money
that they had saved. Overall, however, there were surprisingly few class differences.

All this research on pocket-money suggests that although its role in childhood
economic socialisation may be important, it should not be considered in isolation.
Parents also provide other resources ('holiday money', 'comics', etc.) and the
'parental package' should be considered as a whole. In particular we need to con-

sider what use children make of money they obtain from other sources and how the experience of adolescents with money they have earned affects later personal financial management. One also wonders about the extent to which different mental accounts (discussed in Chapter 4) may have their origin in the different sources of income that children have.

## Children's consumer socialisation

### Children as customers

Government researchers and consumer advocate groups are concerned about the extent to which children should be participating in the consumer role. Many believe that the young person lacks the skill and knowledge to be a fully fledged consumer or they simply assume s/he is not a qualified consumer.

The results of studies of children's consumer behaviour remain relatively few. Results are fragmented and do not allow for substantial conclusions. There are probably two main reasons for the paucity of investigations of children's consumer behaviour. First, children are difficult to study: the difficulties in formulating questions, organising the children for research and obtaining and holding their attention. The methodological quality of the studies in this area are noticeable.

A second reason for the scarcity of studies of children's consumer behaviour is the question of ethics. Is it proper to study the consumer behaviour of children if the results benefit the businessman more than the child? Socio-political beliefs on the part of many researchers have presented good research on this important topic. For some, studies of children's consumer behaviour are always assumed to contribute to the profit motive by either intent or default. Consequently, neither government nor business, parent nor teacher, seems very willing to engage in research activities related to the child consumer unless such efforts are clearly labelled as public policy studies.

In spite of the paucity of information about the consumer behaviour of children, the few studies conducted have produced remarkable similarities in findings. They show the child at age 4 and 5 to be entering the consumer role with enthusiasm, but limited knowledge. But by ages 9 and 10 young people are performing as consumers with as least as much confidence and expertise as they display in any other societal roles. A child sees consuming as a logical role to assume, and recognises that basic needs such as affiliation and self-esteem can be fulfilled in the marketplace with ease. How does the young person (say 10–18 years old) differ from the average adult consumer? Mainly, s/he is younger!

### Socialisation agents

Consumer socialisation is the process 'by which young people acquire skills, knowledge, and attitudes relevant to their functioning in the market-place'. This s is influenced by several socialisation agents: parents, peers, teachers and ___ ≥dia. A very important part clearly is played by parents as they are the ones with whom children have their first consumption and purchasing experiences. Already at a very young age children are taken to supermarkets where they watch their parents compare brands, products, prices and expiry dates. At home children ask their parents about products and advertisements they might have seen on television and their parents' answers help shape the child's ideas about consumption. Children are thus implicitly taught consumer behaviour before even going to school. As early as 1945 a study was undertaken by Prevey enquiring into family practices in training children in the use of money. She found that 'parent practices in training children in the use of money tended to be positively related to later ability to utilise financial resources in early adulthood'. The kind of parental economic education children are exposed to thus has an impact throughout their whole later life.

Peers also exert considerable influence on children. From elementary school, being accepted by the group starts to depend on the right clothing, food and toys and therefore a lot of attention is paid to peers' recommendation of certain products. The impact peers' approval may have on a child's self-esteem and self-confidence thus is quite considerable.

Teacher's influence on the child's consumerism may also be exerted in many ways. When talking about the environment and the threats that it faces, discussions about and testing of 'green products' during chemistry lessons are just one example.

Industry influences children's consumer socialisation through advertising, shops and the products themselves. Advertisements specifically targeted at children (forbidden in Britain and Canada) suggest fun and easiness ('. . . get it . . .' instead of '. . . buy it . . .'). Shop owners' display of certain products at children's eye level is another way of targeting children.

In their study, Schug and Birkey (1985) suggested that ideas related to television advertising, similar to those of exchange, develop more quickly than rather fundamental concepts such as opportunity costs and monetary value, for example, as again children possess substantial personal experiences with television advertisements. The youngest subjects (4–5 years) either had difficulties in distinguishing commercials from other types of programme or thought the purpose of commercials was to give the viewer a break. Most of the older subjects (6–9 years), though, regarded the reason for advertising as providing consumers with information about available goods and services and some even suggested that commercials manipulate consumers by making them want to buy things. When asked about the truthfulness of television commercials the youngest group again turned out to give the most unreflected answers and stated that as they had seen the products in the shop, the commercial was accurate, ('In the toy commercials they really tell us the truth because I believe them because I've seen the He Man figures before', p. 15). The older subjects started to realise that advertised products did not always measure up to claims ('They said that Fiesta, the new soap called Fiesta, that it will make you sing, and I tried it and it never made me sing', p. 15) when using the product at home. Television commercials seem to be present in children's minds from a cer-

Strength of
Brand

tain age (6–7 onwards). In order to persuade children to purchase, advertising thus must induce favourable attitudes towards the advertised goods and make children want them. Therefore advertising targeted at children promotes different products (more desirable for children, e.g. sweets instead of margarine) than the ones targeted at adults and also uses different means of persuasion (fun instead of facts). In an experiment by Resnik and Stern (1977) children were given the choice of two different potato crisps after a commercial for a new brand and it turned out that 57 per cent chose the advertised brand. The authors thus concluded that 'a child is more likely to choose a brand that he has seen advertised on television over another previously unknown brand that he has not seen advertised' (p. 16).

Carlson and Grossbart (1988) administered a study on parental style and consumer socialisation of children: 451 questionnaires were filled in by mothers of elementary school children (kindergarten up to sixth grade). According to the answers, they were grouped into Authoritarian, Permissive, Rigid Controlling, Authoritative and Neglecting. The hypotheses were that parental styles differ in fostering consumption autonomy (i.e. Authoritarians grant less autonomy), that they differ in parent–child communication about consumption (with Authoritarians communicating more than the others), that Authoritarians have more consumer socialisation goals, that they differ in restriction and monitoring of consumption and media exposure (with Authoritarians restricting consumption and media exposure more). The difference assumed in the first hypothesis was found to be non-significant but all other hypotheses were more or less supported. It thus seems that the pronounced differences between parental styles in fostering general autonomy are not transferred to consumption autonomy. Consistently throughout all styles more consumption autonomy (pocket-money) was granted to older children and boys.

Authoritarian parents on the whole were found to be the most active in consumer socialisation and although all parental style groups were rather negative about advertisements, this was most pronounced for Authoritarian parents.

When trying to explain the differences in parents' consumer socialisation tendencies, parental style clearly seems to be one explanation. However, it would be fruitful to extend this research on fathers' styles to see whether the same results would be obtained. Furthermore it would be interesting to examine whether there is a link between parents' income and style. Since parental style determines the extent of contact children have with the other socialisation agents, parents must definitely be the most important factor in the child's consumer socialisation until the child detaches him/herself from home (adolescence) where parents lose influence and peers gain importance.

## Economic education

Formal instruction is one means by which young people acquire an understanding of the economic and political world. Much more research has gone into economic than political education, however.

## The effect of economic instruction

Whitehead (1986) investigated the eventual change in students' attitudes to economic issues as a result of exposure to a two-year 'A' level economics course. The 16–18-year-old subjects were divided into a test group of 523 and a control group of 483. The questionnaires did not test economic knowledge but economic attitudes (dis/agreement on, for example, private enterprise as the most efficient economic system; capitalism is immoral because it exploits the worker by failing to give him full value for his productive labour). In absolute terms, considerable correspondence existed between the responses of experimental and control groups with respect to those items where a large majority expressed either conservative or radical attitudes. On the whole, experimental and control groups held completely differing views only on three items. For six out of the eighteen items on the scale, students who had studied for 'A' level economics, though, showed a significant shift in their economic attitudes.

In a similar study O'Brien and Ingels (1987), who developed the economics values inventory (EVI), an instrument aimed at measuring young people's values and attitudes regarding economic matter, also had their hypothesis confirmed that formal education in economics influences students' economic attitudes. The teaching of economics therefore not only increases children's understanding of certain economic contexts but also may help them review their values and attitudes, which are mostly influenced by or even taken over from their parents. Understanding societal independencies better may help learning to question prejudices and therefore contribute to increased maturation.

## Economics instruction in primary grades

Economics as a subject is mostly not taught before university and in almost all cases not before secondary school. The majority of adolescents who drop out of school after nine or ten years of education, therefore never receive economics instructions. As macro-economic knowledge obviously cannot be learned by observation (purchasing something or filling in a cheque might be, but certainly not other fields of economic exchange such as the working of banks or even government borrowing and spending), there obviously is a need for the teaching of economics.

Kourilsky (1977) proved, however, that even kindergarten is not too soon to start educating economically literate citizens. In the 'Kinder Economy', an education programme, children became acquainted with the concepts of scarcity, decision making, production, specialisation, consumption, distribution, demand/supply, business, money and barter. Her study examining 96 subjects aged 5 or 6 was supposed to answer four questions:

1. Is the child's success in economic decision making and analysis related to instructional intervention or to increased maturity inherent in the passage of time?
2. To what extent and degree, through intervention, are children able to master concepts that, psychologically, they are considered too young to learn?

3. What type of school, home and personality variables are predictors of success in economic decision making and analysis?
4. What are the parents' attitudes towards the teaching of economic decision making and analytical principles as a part of early childhood education?

The examination of the first question showed a significant difference between the scores of the subjects in the Kinder Economy and in the control group which proved that significant progress was induced by instruction. Four out of the nine topics covered yielded mastery levels of more than 70 per cent, the total average being 72.5 per cent. The mastery level was set at 70 per cent, as a previous testing of 40 elementary-school teachers yielded an average of 68.5 per cent on the same test. This shows that children are in fact able to learn concepts which developmentally they are considered to be too young to learn. To answer the third question, six predictor variables were examined: parent report, verbal ability, maturation level, general ability, social ability and initiative. The first three proved to be the best predictors of success in economic decision making, the strongest, parent report, accounting for 62 per cent of the total variance.

Parents' attitudes towards the teaching of economics in kindergarten turned out to be rather positive: 96.7 per cent of the parents were in favour and 91.3 per cent thought that an economics programme should be continued throughout the rest of the grades. Some even mentioned that they were embarrassed to find out that their children knew more about economics than they did, encouraging them to increase their own knowledge. These findings and the general ignorance of children and adults concerning economic interdependencies and contexts seem to give clear evidence for the importance of economic education as early as possible.

Fox (1978), however, challenged the view that 'any topic can be taught effectively in some intellectually honest form at any stage of development'. She cited three things that children already possess (in their mental knapsack) when going to school: economic attitudes ('parent tapes' and proverbs), unprocessed direct experience (e.g. shopping trips) and cognitive capacities (level of cognitive development). Considering that children on the pre-operational level are not able to think very abstractly (centred, static and irreversible). Fox saw difficulties in formal teaching of economic concepts to children who are, for instance, unable to understand the transaction of economic exchange in a shop. She warned that 'The fact that kinder-garten children can learn economic terms is not compelling evidence that the concepts underlying those terms are in fact understood.' (1978: 481) Instead she pleaded for using direct experience as a basis for economic education in primary school and suggested that teachers use everyday situations of economic behaviour in the classroom to help children make sense of what they already know, always considering the level of the child's cognitive abilities. This contradicts Kourilsky's findings that children are to some extent able to master concepts that psychologically they are considered too young to learn. This contradiction might be an indication that Piaget's stages of general cognitive development, originally 'trying to explain the way that the individual represents physical reality' can simply be transferred into economics without any alteration.

Lea, Tarpy and Webley (1987: 376) pointed out that 'Since we learn about some aspects of the economic world mainly by actually engaging in the behaviour and not, as with the physical world, in two ways – both directly and didactically via the mediation of other – the nature of the construction may be different.'

In the *Journal of Economic Education*, solely dedicated to research into the teaching of economics, Davidson and Kilgore (1971) presented a model for evaluating the effectiveness of economic education in primary grades. Five hundred and four second-grade pupils in 24 classes from different socio-economic backgrounds were subjects in one control and two different experimental groups. Pupils in the control group were taught their regular social studies curriculum, the first experimental group was taught with 'The child's world of choices' materials and the teachers in the second experimental group additionally received in-service training. Analysis showed that both experimental groups scored significantly higher results on the post Primary Test of Economic Understanding (PTEU) than the control group, but no experimental method proved to be superior to the other. Pupils from lower socio-economic backgrounds (target schools) scored significantly lower on both PTEU pre- and post-tests than pupils from non-target schools. It could thus be concluded that elementary-grade children can be taught basic economic concepts and growth in understanding them can be measured. Specially designed material prompted the pupils' growth in understanding but an additional full-scale programme in economic education for teachers did not have any significant effects on pupils' advancement. As to the 'how' of teaching of economics concepts to children, Waite (1988) suggested that the child must be the centre of activity, as case studies have shown that the acceleration of children's conceptual understanding, can be achieved using a number of different strategies. Since the child's economic awareness is acquired through information channels outside the classroom, case studies seem to be a good way of teaching children about the economy. Ramsett (1972) also suggested to shy away from the traditional lecture approach and use daily life classroom events which are either directly or indirectly relevant to economics as a basis for further discussion and explanation (e.g. if a pupil's family has to move away because his/her mother or father has accepted a new job, the teacher could take this opportunity to discuss employment, incomes, dependencies, etc.).

Chizmar and Halinski (1983) described the impact of 'Trade-offs', a special series of television/film programmes designed to teach economics in elementary school, on the performance in the Basic Economic Test (BET). The results indicated that (1) as the number of weeks of instruction increased, the rate of increase in student score was significantly greater for students using 'Trade-offs'; (2) there were no sex differences in scores for students using 'Trade-offs' whereas for those being instructed traditionally gender was a statistically significant predictor of student scores (girls outperforming boys). Furthermore the grade-level and teacher training (see also McKenzie, 1971; Walstad, 1979; Walstad and Watts, 1985) in economics were significant positive determinants of BET performance. These findings may indicate that gender differences here could possibly be attributed to the way instruction was given, as boys performed better under "Trade-offs" than under traditional instruction. Under this premise it would be interesting to examine how sex differences found in other studies possibly could have been caused.

Hansen (1985), acknowledging that the teaching of economics to elementary-school children has proved effective, demanded a firm installation of this subject into the curriculum of the primary grades. He briefly summarised the basic knowledge about children and economic education, which is as follows:

What happens in a child's early years – before the end of the primary years – has lasting effects into adulthood.

Children enter kindergarten possessing an experience-based economic literacy.

Children can acquire economic concepts and can do so earlier than previously thought.

A variety of economic materials and teaching approaches are both available and effective.

Evaluation procedures are available, and new ones are being established even though they need continued refinement.

Economic education programmes show greater student gains where teachers are well versed in economics.

As long as economics are not part of the curriculum and thus goals, materials and schedules, they will not reach the classroom. At present the apparent opportunity cost of economics (teaching and testing of reading and mathematics, which still have top priority before any other subjects in today's primary schools) still are deemed too high to introduce economics into primary schools. If economics was not considered as a subject to be studied on its own, competing with other subjects in the curriculum, but rather being experienced in connection with already existing subjects such as mathematics (case studies), this problem could be avoided.

## Reasons for goals and economic education

In order to decide what should be taught in economics courses and how such economics instruction should take place, an explicit goal needs to be defined. Horton and Weidenaar (1975) tried to do just this and interviewed more than 200 economics educators, economists, other social scientists, trainers of social studies teachers, businessmen and others. Three goals were singled out:

1. To help us to be more capable as direct participants in the economy – that is, as consumers, workers, businessmen or investors.
2. To 'improve' decisions when we act in our society as citizens.
3. To improve our understanding of the world in which we live.

All three goals appear to be of equal importance and probably cannot be separated completely from one another anyway. Still, depending on the emphasis that is put on each goal, an economics course would probably touch slightly different topics. The authors suggest that for the third goal an economics course might cover such concrete questions as 'why automobile mechanics often earn more than English teachers; why teenagers, females and nonwhites are disproportionately unemployed; and why more money for each of us would do so little to meet our fundamental economic problem of relative scarcity' (p. 43).

Possessing a better knowledge of the economic aspects of our environment makes us better prepared to analyse and interpret the situations and problems we face. As with any knowledge this gives us a vaster and better choice of possible solutions and considering the widespread ignorance about economic topics in both children and adults, economics instruction seems necessary.

## Conclusion

The literature on children's and adolescents' understanding of the economic world is highly diffuse and of varying quality. Most of the research has attempted to describe the stages through which children pass in their understanding of a specific concept. There is, however, a good deal of disagreement about the number of stages, the points of transition and the exact understanding in each stage. Considerably less work has gone into describing those factors which speed up or slow down the transition from one stage to another or individual differences within the various stages. Social class, exposure to the economic world and parental practices seem most important determinants of children's knowledge and use of money, though there may well be other important determinants.

The importance of this area cannot be underestimated, as it seems that habits of using money (spending, saving, gambling, etc.) are established in childhood. Studies on children's pocket-money, for instance, suggest that class attitudes towards money may be established even before adolescence. This is in accordance with the literature on the Protestant work ethic (see Chapter 10), which suggests that early socialisation in gratification postponement, internal locus of control and need for achievement lead directly to later success in the adult world.

One of the more interesting applications of research on children's acquisition of economic concepts is the teaching of these concepts in schools. Certainly, the widespread ignorance about economics in children, adolescents and adults suggests the importance and relevance of the teaching of the subject even in kindergarten.

# Chapter 3

# The psychology of money

## Introduction

Despite its importance as the primary medium through which goods are exchanged, until recently there has been little serious academic research into the psychology of money, though there are numerous popular books on the topic. A surprisingly diverse and very unrelated series of studies have been carried out on such things as the perceptions of coins and notes, and a few on people's attitudes towards money (Lea, Tarpy and Webley, 1987). There are also various theories as to the origins of beliefs and behaviour concerning money and a few studies of its symbolism. There is, however, no coherent theory or body of research on the psychology of money; this chapter will attempt to review the work which has been done so far.

Economists, anthropologists and historians have pointed out that as people went from barter societies to more advanced economies money had to be invented. Galbraith (1977) has noted that money has been an everyday fact of life for at least 2,500 years. There were tremendous abuses of coined money (in terms of weight, metal content, etc.) until the nineteenth century. Given its functions, almost anything will serve as money, though of course it is preferable for money to be durable, portable, consistent and inherently valuable. Coins, now largely redundant, were for centuries the main source of money. Many characteristics, and terms still associated with them, served interesting functions: coins have milled edges to prevent people shaving away a little of the valuable metal from which the coin is made; the term 'debasing the currency' came about because of the practice of adding base metals (lead, iron) to gold and silver to increase the number of coins made. In Europe coins were the major form of transaction until the creation of banks, which, because they could lend money, could 'create it'. Coins were invented by the Greeks (or perhaps the Lydians – see Grierson, 1978) but it was the Italians, Dutch, French and British who developed banks. Paper money (notes, bills), which were promises of real money (gold or silver), originated in China in the ninth century (Grierson, 1978), although their use in the Western world came from America and was popularised by Benjamin Franklin.

Of course, other disciplines – particularly economics and to a lesser extent anthropology and sociology – have taken a great deal of interest in the origins, functions and use of money. Economists argue that money in any form fulfils a number of functions:

1. *A medium of exchange:* to avoid the necessity of finding the double coincidence of wants.
2. *A unit of account:* a way of simplifying and summarising the worth of goods that are exchanged.
3. *A standard of deferred payment:* to be used to separate in time the exchange of a good or service and the payment for goods or services.
4. *Store of value:* to be able to receive payment at one moment and postpone purchase until a later date.

Apart from its obvious and above-stated virtues, economists have also attempted to define the reasons why money is desired. These include the following:

1. *Transactions:* to be able to make planned transactions.
2. *Precautionary:* to be able to cope with unplanned expenditures and circumstances.
3. *Speculative:* to be used as an asset to accrue more money.

Furthermore, there are a number of different economic definitions of money. These include currency (fiat money); demand deposits, which are the amounts people and organisations have in their various accounts; narrow money, which is a combination of hard currency and demand deposits; and near money, which are moneys which pay interest to the owner.

There are many theories concerning the value and importance of money. For instance, Fisher (1911) provided a simple formula which determines the value of money:

$$P = MV/T$$

Where $P$ = prices, $M$ = the quantity of money in circulation, $V$ is the velocity or speed at which money is spent, and $T$ is the number of transactions.

Monetarism and related monetarist policies are currently popular theories based on the quantity of money in circulation or the cost of credit. Ways of controlling the money supply include central banks' lending rate as well as government control over lending. It is, however, debated by monetarists whether priority should be attached to the quantity of money or the cost of credit, though the two are obviously related. As well as macro-economic theories of money, there are micro-economic theories concerned with such things as what economic factors (bank rates, inflation) affect individual saving, investment, etc.

It is, of course, impossible to do justice to the range and complexity of economic theories of money in a single chapter. Economists differ from psychologists on two major grounds, though they share the similar goal of trying to understand and predict the way in which money is used. Economists are interested in aggregated data at the macro level: how classes, groups and countries use, spend and save their money under certain conditions. To this extent economists have more in common with sociologists than with psychologists, who are interested in individual and small-group differences. Thus, whereas economists might have the goal of modelling or understanding the money supply, demand and movement for a country or continent, psychologists would be more interested in understanding how and why different groups of individuals with different beliefs (e.g. in the Protestant work ethic) or different backgrounds (e.g. middle vs working class) use money differently. Whereas individual differences are 'error variance' for the economists, they are the 'stuff' of social psychology. Secondly, whereas economists attempt to understand monetary usage in terms of rational decisions of people with considerable economic knowledge and understanding, psychologists have not taken for granted the fact that people are logical or rational in any formal or objective sense, though they may be subjectively rational or self-consistent. Indeed it has been the psychological, rather than the logical, factors that induce people to use money the way they do that has, not unnaturally, fascinated psychologists.

There are no psychological 'theories' of money as such, although various psychological paradigms or traditions have been applied to the psychology of money. These include psychoanalytic theories, which are discussed later in this chapter, Piagetian developmental theories, which are covered in Chapter 2 on socialisation, and behaviourist learning theory. As well as the bigger theoretical traditions in psychology, money as a variable plays a part in 'smaller', more specific theories such as exchange or equity theory. In this approach there is a wage–work bargain (Behrend, 1988) where the input of effort, experience, training and performance at work is measured against the output of money and other reward variables. Equity theory often considers the role of money at work.

Behaviourist research has been concerned with how money becomes a conditioned reinforcement and hence a valued and meaningful object. Research in this tradition has been limited to studies on animals in which animals of various sorts (rats, chimpanzees, cats) perform a task in order to get tokens (poker chips, iron balls, cards) which, like money, can be exchanged for desirable objects such as food. Hence money is valued because it represents or is associated with various desirable objects. However, it should be pointed out that in most experiments of this sort money is not strictly a generalised conditioned reinforcer but a specific reinforcer or a symbol of a specific reward. Hence animal studies do not fully test or prove behaviourist theories.

As well as animal studies there is a vast literature on 'token economies' which is effectively the application of behaviourist 'monetary' theories to clinical populations such as mental patients (particularly schizophrenics), disturbed adolescents and recidivists. The idea is based on the well-established principles of operant conditioning, that is that behaviour followed by positive consequences tends to occur more often than if followed by negative consequences. A token economy is a self-contained economic system where clients/patients are paid (reinforced) for behaving appropriately (socialising, working), and in which many desirable commodities (food, entertainment, cigarettes) must be purchased. Thus luxuries (indeed necessities) must be earned. Token economies are based on various principles (Ayllon and Azrin, 1968) which include the following:

1. Specifying the target behaviours that are rewarded so that reinforcement is consistent.
2. Specifying the 'token', which is a medium of exchange and a representation of more primary reinforcers.
3. Specifying the back-up reinforcers, which are the goods and services for which tokens are exchanged and which must be desirable over time.
4. Specifying the exchange rate, which is the number of tokens necessary for each good or service and which are realistically priced to maximise performance.

Numerous studies have shown the benefits of token economies (Ayllon and Roberts, 1974) but have also received various criticisms on clinical grounds. These include the fact that as there is little comparative research (only a no-treatment control condition); it is difficult to establish whether token economies are better or worse than other conditions; that token economies are often aimed at institutional rather than individual needs; that token economies violate many individual rights in total institutions; but perhaps most importantly, that conditioned behaviour does not generalise to new environments where the token economy does not operate (Bellack and Hersen, 1980).

Finally, it should be pointed out that there is a fairly large literature, in the behaviourist tradition, on the effects of monetary incentives on various cognitive tasks (Eysenck and Eysenck, 1982). Most of this work has demonstrated that motivation (through monetary reward) controls attention and hence learning, which in turn affects memory.

A popular topic that excites attention from working managers is the role of money as a motivation at work. Some argue that there are both intrinsic and extrinsic rewards and that money is only one of many extrinsic rewards like working conditions, status and job security. Hence it may be perfectly acceptable, more efficient and ultimately more effective to use other rewards. However, it has been argued that money can serve as a highly efficient 'motivator' under three conditions: when the employee has a high net preference for money; when employees see that greater performance is directly related to more money; and when effort at work is seen to lead to improved performance. Suffice to say that the role of money as a work-related performance motivator remains a highly debated topic.

## The psychology of money usage

There have been a number of empirical studies on the psychology of money. Wernimont and Fitzpatrick (1972) used a semantic differential approach to attempt to understand the meaning that different people attach to money. In their sample of over 500 subjects they had such diverse people as secretaries and engineers, nursing sisters and technical supervisors. Factor analysis revealed a number of interpretable factors, which were labelled shameful failure (lack of money is an indication of failure, embarrassment and degradation), social acceptability, pooh-pooh attitude (money is not very important, satisfying or attractive), moral evil, comfortable security, social unacceptability, and conservative business values. The subjects' work experiences, sex and socio-economic level appeared to influence their perceptions of money: for instance, employment status showed that employed groups view money much more positively and as desirable, important and useful, whereas the unemployed seemed to take a tense, worrisome, unhappy view of money. They conclude that money does have a good deal of symbolic value and means quite different things to different people, which may go in developmental stages. Important individual attitudes to money include sex, associates, economic status and personality.

Some researchers have looked at personality and money. Luft (1957) found, for instance, that a person's weekly income determines how s/he is perceived. Hypothetically rich people were seen as relatively healthy, happy and well adjusted, while the poor person was seen as maladjusted and unhappy. Rim (1982) looked at the relationship between personality and attitudes towards money. He administered the Eysenck Personality Inventory and a number of questions concerning money, and found that over half showed significant differences on the extraversion factor, and a third on a neuroticism factor. Predictably, stable extraverts seemed more open, comfortable and carefree about their money than unstable introverts. Rim's pilot study appears to be the only one concerned with individual differences but is completely atheoretical. It was, in fact, based on another large-scale survey which attempted to measure Americans' attitudes towards money.

Rubinstein (1980) devised a money survey for *Psychology Today* to investigate readers' attitudes and feelings about money, to get an idea of its importance in their lives, what associations it evokes and how it affects their closest relationships. Although over 20,000 responses were received from a moderately well-distributed population, the results were only analysed in terms of simple percentages and few individual difference variables were considered. Some of these questions were later combined into a 'Midas' scale but no statistics were presented. They found that spenders, as opposed to self-deniers, were healthier and happier. The Midas respondents (self-deniers) were more unhappy about their finances, personal growth, friends and jobs. They are more pessimistic about their own and the country's economic future, and appear to have more psychosomatic symptoms than spenders. Rubinstein found that people were still secretive about money: 57 per cent of the sample believed it prudent to conceal one's income from family and friends. As regards disclosing one's income, 97 per cent of men were prepared to disclose the amount to their spouse, 52 per cent to their parents, 44 per cent to their friends, 29 per cent to their co-workers and 18 per cent to their siblings. The proportion of respondents who concealed their financial worth increased with income. Also, with two-income families, money appears to be a frequent source of friction, and over 40 per cent agreed that money made them envious, aspiring to material goods beyond their means.

On the basis of a number of questions (e.g. how rich or poor they feel; how often they think about money; how unhappy they are with their financial situation) respondents were divided into the money contented and the money troubled. The troubled want things they cannot afford, are in debt and have saved little. They believe their friends to have more money than them; that they deserve more; that they lack financial control over their lives. They also lacked a secure sense of self and were more dissatisfied than others with friendships. Unhappiness at work and at home was also associated with money discontent. Over half of the sample associated the following negative emotions with money: anxiety, depression, anger and helplessness. Finally half of the sample were pessimistic about the future of the economy which was independent of their income.

A study such as this has, of course, major problems: the representativeness of the sample, the analyses performed, the applicability of the questions, and so on. Perhaps the most important criticism of this work is that there is a confounding of correlation and cause: that is, it is not certain whether one's attitude to inflation, material possessions, happiness, etc. is a cause or a consequence of one's income.

Goldberg and Lewis (1978) considered the numerous paradoxes, hypocrisies, inconsistencies and lies surrounding money. They suggest that the main symbolic factors associated with money are security, power, love and freedom. They claim that people who turn to money for security inevitably become alienated from others and their fear about being hurt or rejected by others is manifested in a paranoid fear that they will deprive them of their money. Among the security collectors that Goldberg and Lewis describe are the compulsive saver, the self-denier, the compulsive bargain hunter, the fanatic collector, all concerned with the safety-first syndrome. That is, the security collectors are primarily concerned with safety rather than happiness, success or productivity. Power-oriented people are greedy for money, which is power they never had during infantile omnipotence. The power-grabbers fit into various categories: the manipulator, the empire-builder, the godfather are all aggressive attempts to build barriers between them and a threatening world. Others give and withhold money and gifts as tokens of love. People attempt both to buy and sell love. Finally, there are those who perceive money as bringing freedom for themselves but as a possible enemy of freedom for others because of its power over them.

Each of these 'clinical' types is illustrated by a number of case histories which are interesting and convincing. However rich these case histories might be, the empiricist is no doubt frustrated by the lack of coherent evidence for the typology outlined. Furthermore, important questions are neglected, such as how easy it is for each of these money types to change in their beliefs and behaviour; the incidence of these types over different groups, cultures and societies, etc.

Some studies have, however, attempted to do more systematic research in this field. Yamauchi and Templer (1982) attempted to develop a fully psychometrised money attitude scale. A factor analysis of an original selection of 62 items revealed five factors labelled power-prestige, retention-time, distrust, quality and anxiety. From this a 29-item scale was selected which was demonstrated to be reliable. A partial validation – correlations with other established measures such as Machiavellianism, status concern, time-competence, obsessionality, paranoia and anxiety – showed that this questionnaire was related to measures of other similar theoretical constructs: 'The correlations are in agreement with ostensibly suggested motives such as power and prestige. And the evidence is viewed as congruent with less surface psychodynamic formulations such as the relationship of money retention to the obsessive-anal character structure' (p. 528). Most interestingly the authors found that money attitudes were essentially independent of a person's income.

While Yamauchi and Templer's (1982) study is to be welcomed, it did appear to have a number of shortcomings. Although the authors obtained a large and fairly heterogeneous sample, they failed to investigate any demographic differences (age, sex) save income. Secondly their partial validation seemed too concerned with psychopathological correlates of money attitudes rather than on normal social beliefs and attitudes. Finally the study makes no attempt to trace the aetiology of these beliefs.

Furnham (1984a) attempted to overcome these shortcomings in an empirical study in Britain. The study had three aims: (1) to develop a useful, multifaceted instrument to measure money beliefs and behaviour in Britain; (2) to look at the relationship between various demographic and social/work beliefs and people's monetary beliefs and behaviour; and (3) to look at the determinants of people's money beliefs and behaviour in the past and the future.

The importance of the demographic and belief determinants of money beliefs and attitudes lies mainly in the clues it gives to the aetiology of these beliefs. Primary and secondary socialisation and later experience have important effects on people's monetary habits and beliefs. Parental factors such as income and education, as well as social and political conservative beliefs and Protestant work ethic values no doubt determine certain child-rearing practices of independence, saving, achievement, motivation, etc. (Furnham and Bland, 1983). Studies of children's pocket-money and allowances suggest that factors such as class and age have very important effects on children's spending and saving habits, even before they reach the age of 10 (Furnham and Thomas, 1984a).

First, the study aimed to investigate subjects' perceptions of the way in which they had experienced money in the past and anticipated using it in the future. Although there may be various memorial and attribution errors involved in such a procedure, which casts some doubt on the usefulness of this approach to collect valid information about the past, a number of very interesting findings emerged. Predictably, older less well-educated people believed their early childhood to be poorer than younger better-educated people, reflecting both the average increased standard of living and the class structure of society. Overall there were few differences in the subjects' perception of money in the past, but a large number regarding money in the future. Older people were more worried about the future than younger people, and richer people were more concerned about the future than poorer people. Conservative voters believed that the country's economic future was bright, while Labour voters and those with high alienation and those with conservative social attitudes believed that it would get worse. Although these questions may seem vague, they are not trivial because presumably people act on their beliefs about future trends (Rubinstein, 1980). That is, if one believes that future economic trends mean that one might be substantially worse off one might take steps to avoid this.

The results were not dissimilar from related American studies (Rubinstein, 1980; Yamauchi and Templer, 1982). Attitudes towards money are by no means unidimensional: factor-analytic results yielded six clearly interpretable factors that bore many similarities to the factors found in Yamauchi and Templer (1982) such as power, retention and inadequacy, as well as the hypothetical factors derived from psychoanalytic theory (Fenichel, 1947). Whereas some of the factors were clearly linked to clinical traits of anxiety and obsessionality, others are more closely related to power and the way in which one obtains money. Also some factors more than others proved to be related to the demographic and belief variables: obsession with money showed significant differences on sex, education and income and all the belief variables (alienation, Protestant work ethic, conservatism), whereas the inadequacy factor revealed no significant differences on either set of variables.

Other results showed an interesting and predictable pattern of results with age, education and the Protestant work ethic values discriminating most strongly. These differences would not have been predicted by psychoanalytic theory. It should also be noted that feelings of alienation did not discriminate very clearly, so casting doubt on a narrowly clinical approach to money beliefs and attitudes. From a social psychological perspective these results are quite sensible – as one gets older and one's needs change so money takes on new meanings. Furthermore, as one might predict, education makes a difference to one's beliefs about money (see Chapter 2).

The canonical correlation yielded three significant varieties which described the relationship between the independent (attitudes to money) and dependent (demographic belief) variables. The first two significant varieties both showed a relationship between specific independent variables and two of the dependent factors, namely obsession with money and beliefs about whether one gets money through ability or effort. Females more than males, high Protestant work ethic scorers rather than low, low- rather than high-income earners and less rather than more alienated people tend to be obsessed by money and to believe that the accumulation of money is due to effort and ability. The third significant variate showed that age, education and sex were related to conservative monetary beliefs as well as feelings of inadequacy about money. Case studies on people with money obsessions indeed point to the importance of the above factors (Goldberg and Lewis, 1978).

Hanley and Wilhelm (1992) in fact used the Furnham measure to investigate the relationship between self-esteem and money attitudes. They found, as predicted that compulsive spenders have relatively lower self-esteem than 'normal' consumers and that compulsive spenders have beliefs about money which reflect its symbolic ability to enhance self-esteem.

Lynn (1991) used some of the items from Furnham's (1984a) scale to look at national differences in attitudes to money over forty-three countries. He argued that various studies have shown that people respond with greater work effort when they are offered financial incentives. It is probable, however, that people differ in the importance they attach to money and therefore in the degree to which they will work hard in order to obtain it and it may be that there are national differences in the strength of the value attached to money.

The results of the study for the valuation of money scale are given in Table 3.1, which shows the means for the nations weighting the sexes equally. The correlation between the mean for males and females across countries is 0.87. This is highly statistically significant and indicates a high level of consistency between scores of the two sexes across the nations.

The correlations between the valuation of money scale and economic growth and per capita incomes are shown in Table 3.2. The correlations are given for the whole sample of nations, the whole sample omitting the United Arab Emirates, and for the economically developed and developing nations as separate groups. It will be seen that there are positive correlations between the Valuation of Money Scale and economic growth rates in all four samples, although the correlation of 0.26 among the economically developing nations does not reach statistical significance. The pattern of correlations suggests that the degree to which people value money may be a determinant of economic growth rates at all levels of economic development. This is essentially the thesis proposed for the low economic growth of Britain during the present century and the findings lend some support to this theory.

There are also statistically significant negative associations between the valuation of money and per capita income among all four samples of nations. The result suggests that as people become more affluent they attach less value to money, as might be expected. There are also high correlations between the valuation of money and competitiveness across nations, where the correlation is 0.72, and among individuals within nations.

The sex differences show a general trend for males to attach more value to money than females. The male scores are higher than females in forty of the nations, and only in India, Norway and Transkei is this tendency reversed. A possible explanation for this sex difference is that males generally tend to be more competitive than females and money is valued partly as a symbol of competitive success. Striking sex differences are also reported by Prince (1993a, 1993b), who devised his own 'money style' questionnaire. He found that although both young men and young women see money as linked with esteem and power, men feel more competent in dealing with money and take more risks to accumulate it whereas women express more frustration at not having enough money and are more envious of others.

**Table 3.1**    Means and standard deviations for the valuation of money scale

| Country | Total | |
|---|---|---|
| Argentina | 7.85 | (4.97) |
| Australia | 7.12 | (5.91) |
| Bangladesh | 14.60 | (6.30) |
| Belgium | 7.11 | (6.07) |
| Brazil | 13.16 | (5.99) |
| Bulgaria | 11.09 | (7.38) |
| Canada | 9.07 | (6.67) |
| Chile | 11.78 | (5.98) |
| China | 11.76 | (6.27) |
| Colombia | 12.64 | (5.79) |
| Egypt | 11.18 | (6.57) |
| France | 9.12 | (6.34) |
| Germany | 5.70 | (5.17) |
| Greece | 13.75 | (5.62) |
| Hong Kong | 13.45 | (5.66) |
| Iceland | 7.53 | (6.27) |
| India | 12.52 | (7.30) |
| Iraq | 13.77 | (5.88) |
| Ireland | 7.84 | (6.05) |
| Israel | 10.37 | (6.45) |
| Japan | 11.01 | (5.22) |
| Jordan | 12.81 | (6.98) |
| Korea | 10.89 | (6.56) |
| Mexico | 10.86 | (6.27) |
| New Zealand | 8.55 | (6.21) |
| Norway | 4.25 | (4.66) |
| Poland | 7.04 | (6.05) |
| Portugal | 10.32 | (5.24) |
| Romania | 9.95 | (5.88) |
| Singapore | 8.51 | (6.32) |
| South Africa | 12.90 | (5.62) |
| Spain | 9.24 | (5.65) |
| Sweden | 4.14 | (4.19) |
| Switzerland | — | |
| Syria | 13.01 | (5.98) |
| Taiwan | 14.50 | (6.07) |
| Transkei | 15.32 | (7.34) |
| Turkey | 11.20 | (6.35) |
| United Arab Emirates | 10.66 | (6.72) |
| United Kingdom | 6.11 | (5.77) |
| United States | 10.69 | (6.55) |
| Venezuela | 10.39 | (6.06) |
| Yugoslavia | 10.70 | (6.85) |
| Mean | 10.34 | (6.06) |

*Source*: reprinted with permission from *The Secret of the Miracle Economy*, published by the Social Affairs Unit (SAU).

More recently Tang (1992) developed what he called the Money Ethic Scale. He found, using this scale that one's ability to budget money was correlated with age and sex (female). Higher-income respondents tended to think that money revealed much about one's achievements and was not evil, though young people were more

**Table 3.2** Correlations between national means for the valuation of money and economic growth and per capita incomes (decimal points omitted)

|  | All countries | 41 countries | Developed countries | Developing countries |
|---|---|---|---|---|
| Economic growth | 26* | 46** | 56** | 26 |
| Per capita income | −52*** | −61*** | −45* | −40* |

*Source*: reprinted with permission from *The Secret of the Miracle Economy*, published by the Social Affairs Unit (SAU).
* $p < 0.05$
** $p < 0.01$
*** $p < 0.001$

oriented to see it as evil. Those who endorsed the Protestant work ethic reported that they budgeted properly and associated money with freedom and power. Social values were clearly related to money issues. Further, the desire to have more freedom and power from money were associated with lower satisfaction with work, pay, co-workers and overall life satisfaction.

In another study, this time in Taiwan, Tang (1993b) showed how his Money Ethic Scale was systematically related to other measures like the work ethic and locus of control.

Money style, money attitudes and money ethics are associated in the popular mind with the concept of materialism. Materialists are seen as being concerned to acquire money and wealth for its own sake and in order to display their wealth to others (Fournier and Richins, 1991). According to Belk (personal communication), status-seeking ostentation was a consistent theme of interviews on the meaning of materialism carried out in a variety of countries. But we can probably identify at least three different themes which underlie everyday discussions of materialism. The first is the tendency to use money as the measure of all things (in other words, a concern with the things money can buy). The second is a concern for possessions *per se*. The last is the idea of goods being used for ostentation rather than for a specific function.

The two main scales that have been devised to measure materialism (Belk, 1984; Richins and Scott, 1992) place different emphases on these themes. Belk's scale consists of three components: envy, possessiveness and non-generosity which tie in with the last two themes but not the first. Belk (personal communication) argues that money is a medium of materialism rather than the focus of materialism and that it is not the attitude towards using money in particular ways (e.g. to acquire possessions or to facilitate ostentatious display). Richins and Scott conceptualise materialism as a consumer value and their scale has three components: possession-defined success, acquisition as the pursuit of happiness and acquisition centrality. High scorers on the scale were more concerned with financial security than interpersonal relationships and spent more on themselves (and less on others). Reassuringly, both in this study and in Belk (1985) materialists were less satisfied with their lives.

More recently researchers have concentrated on such things as the use of money in marriage. Burgoyne (1990), for example, looked at how patterns of money allocation in a marriage both reflect and conceal power. A couple's report that they pool their income (perhaps in a joint bank account) can give the erroneous impression that resources are shared equally. What seems to be particularly important are the 'rights' of ownership that are associated with having earned the income. This can lead to a pattern of control which is to the detriment of a non-earning partner (often, though not always, the wife). There also continues to be a great deal of speculation as to the meaning of money to ordinary people. Thus Belk and Wallendorf (1990) argue that in order to better understand people's use of money it is necessary to consider the non-economic sacred function that money may have originally served, and still serves in modern economic communities.

## Experimental studies on coins and notes

One experiment published in 1947 has meant that considerable research has been done on the psychology of coins from various countries. Bruner and Goodman (1947) argued that values and needs play a very important part in psychophysical perception. They entertained various general hypotheses: the greater the social value of an object, the more it will be susceptible to organisation by behavioural determinants (i.e. perceptually accentuated) and the greater the individual need for a socially valued object, the more marked will be the operation of behavioural determinants. Rich and poor 10-year-olds were asked to estimate which of an ascending and descending range of circles of light corresponded to a range of coins. Another control group compared the circle of light to cardboard discs of identical size to the coins. They found, as predicted, that coins (socially valued objects) were judged larger in size than grey discs, and that the greater the value of the coin, the greater is the deviation of apparent size from actual size. Secondly, they found that poor children overestimate the size of coins considerably more than did the rich children. Furthermore this was true with coins present and from memory.

   Because this experiment demonstrated that subjective value and objective needs actually affected perception of physical objects, this study provoked considerable interest and many replications have been carried out. Studies have been done in different countries (McCurdy, 1956; Dawson, 1975) with different coins (Smith and Razzell, 1975) and with poker chips as well as coins (Lambert, Soloman and Watson, 1949) and found that although there have been some differences in the findings, the effects have been generalisable. Tajfel (1981) noted that about twenty experiments have been done on the 'overestimation effect' and only two have yielded unambiguously negative results. Nearly all the researchers have found that motivational or valuable stimuli had effects on subjects' perceptual judgements of magnitude as well as size, weight, number and brightness.

   Tajfel (1981) has made some important observations and criticisms of this work. He notes that two aspects of this experiment need to be considered: the interserial effect (the perceived relationship between any stimulus of the value series and the neutral stimuli) and the intraserial effect (the relationship between the stimuli of a value series as compared with the corresponding relationships in an objectively identical neutral series). He thus stresses the accentuation of differences as an explanatory device which suggests that polarisation effects should operate systematically at either extreme of the response continuum.

Two other, methodologically different studies have looked at the value size hypothesis. Hitchcock, Munroe and Munroe (1976) compared eighty-four countries' per capita income and the average size of the currency to determine whether 'persons in poor countries have greater subjective need than persons in wealthy countries, and that a country's coinage allows institutional expression of the level of need' (p. 307). They found a correlation of –0.19 ($p < 0.05$) between GNP per capita and the mean size of all coins minted for a country, and a correlation of –0.25 ($p < 0.025$) between GNP per capita and the size of the least-valued coin. They conclude that these data indicate the potential usefulness of viewing institutional-level data from a psychological perspective.

Furnham (1985a) did an unobtrusive study on the perceived value of small coins. It was assumed that the finder's behaviour (either picking up the coin or not) is an index of the perceived worth of the coin at the time. Specifically it was hypothesised that the value of the coin would be linearly related to the number of times that it was picked up. The four smallest coins of the country (Britain) were dropped in the street and observers recorded how people who saw the coins reacted. In the study 56 people who saw the smallest (half-pence) coin ignored it, 44 ignored the one-pence coin, 16 the two-pence coin and 10 the five-pence piece. It was concluded that because of the fact that money is both a taboo and emotionally charged topic unobtrusive measures such as these are particularly useful, especially in times of high inflation, unemployment, or where there were changes in the coinage. Boustead *et al.* (1992) replicated Furnham's study five years later and found that the probabilities of people picking up coins had decreased (presumably as inflation in the intervening years had lessened their real value) and, more interestingly, that the probability of the smaller new five-pence coin being picked up was less than the old five-pence coin, despite it having the same nominal value. This suggests that size does indeed affect the perceived value of a coin.

The psychological factors associated with actual coins and notes have received some attention. Bruce and her colleagues (Bruce *et al.*, 1983a; Bruce, 1989) were interested in the introduction of two new coins into British currency which were small relative to their value compared with other coins present in the system. This was done because small coins are cheaper to produce, easier to handle, and bring British coinage into line with the coins of other nations. A number of studies were done on members of the public. In a preliminary series of studies they found that it was not the colour of a coin (gold vs copper vs silver) that made it appear more valuable, but rather its thickness and elaborate edge. Further in Britain, 'seven-sidedness', rather than a purely circular coin is seen as more valuable. In the main study they found that their adult subjects appeared to apply specific 'rules' about the value-conferring features of coins. These rules refer to the shape, colour, edge and sidedness of the coins.

In a second series of studies Bruce *et al*. (1983b) looked at the extent to which the new British one-pound coin might be confused with existing coins. In a series of studies they found that the new coin could easily be confused with a coin one-twentieth of its value and a different colour, but a similar circumference. Where coins have the same shape and circumference it is most important that the thickness of the more valuable is sufficiently great to make the weight difference between the two coins very easily detectable. They concluded that more ergonomic work is needed before coins are introduced into circulation in order to minimise the possibilities of confusion in the public.

Both of the Bruce *et al*. (1983a and 1983b) studies were concerned with how natives recognise their own currency: however, some work has also been done on how people identify coins they are not familiar with. Furnham and Weissman (1985) showed all the British coins to over sixty Americans (in the United States) who had never been to Britain, nor previously seen British currency. Only one subject was able to rank order the coins correctly according to worth. Whereas over half of the sample could identify the relative worthlessness of the two smallest coins (one-pence, half-pence) less than a third correctly identified the rank of the top five coins. In a second study the authors asked 4–5- and 9–10-year-old children various questions about British coins when showing them all the coins of the realm: for instance, 'Which coin can you buy most with?'; 'Point at the ten-pence piece'. They found that whereas the 9–10-year-olds were accurate in their answers (90 per cent or more) in each case the 4–5-year-olds were often wrong. The 4-5-year-olds seemed to be operating on much the same principles as the American adults had done: that is, given the choice, the children (and foreign adults) assumed that size was positively correlated with worth (circumference, not volume) and that silver coins were more valuable than copper or gold-coloured coins.

Two studies have looked at the effects of inflation on the perception of money, one using coins, the other notes. Lea (1981) showed that subjects tended to overestimate the sizes of identical coins as a function of inflation. That is, subjects made bigger estimates of coins given their old predecimalisation names (two shillings) than their new name (ten pence). Although there are some alternative hypotheses that may be entertained, the most satisfactory explanation appears to be that because inflation has reduced the actual worth of the same sized coin, they are perceived as smaller. Furnham (1983c) found evidence of the same phenomena when considering notes. Subjects were asked to identify rectangles corresponding in shape to a one-pound note withdrawn from circulation in 1979, and a one-pound note currently being used. The notes differed slightly in colour, shape and design but were broadly similar. As predicted, subjects tended to overemphasise the size of the old note (10.714 cm vs 9.692 cm) and underemphasise the size of the new note (8.243 cm vs 9.045 cm).

Together these studies provide evidence for the value/need money perception hypothesis and the effects of inflation on the perceived size of money.

# The psychoanalysis of money

In an essay entitled 'Character and anal eroticism' Freud (1908) argued that character traits originate in the warding-off of certain primitive biological impulses. In this essay he first drew attention to the relationship of adult attitudes to money as a product of anal eroticism. Many psychoanalytic thinkers have developed these notions: for instance, Ferenczi (1926) described the ontogenic stages through which the original pleasure in dirt and excreta develops into a love of money. Freud (1908) identified three main traits associated with people who had fixated at the anal stage: orderliness, parsimony and obstinacy with associated qualities of cleanliness, conscientiousness, trustworthiness, defiance and revengefulness.

The child's interest in its faeces turns first to such things as mud, sand, stones, thence to all manufactured objects that can be collected, and then to money. Essentially the Freudian thesis may be spelt out thus: children all experience pleasure in the elimination of faeces. At an early age (around 2 years) parents toilet-train their children some showing enthusiasm and praise (positive reinforcement) for defecation, others threatening and punishing a child when it refuses to do so (negative reinforcement). Potty- or toilet-training occurs at the same stage that the child is striving to achieve autonomy and a sense of worth. Often toilet-training becomes a source of conflict between parents and children over whether the child is in control of its sphincter or whether the parental rewards and coercion compel submission to their will. Furthermore the child is fascinated by and fantasises over its faeces, which are, after all, a creation of its own body. The child's confusion is made all the worse by the ambiguous reactions of parents who on the one hand treat the faeces as gifts and highly valued, and then behave as if they are dirty, untouchable and in need of immediate disposal.

If the child is traumatised by the experience of toilet-training, it tends to retain ways of coping and behaving during this phase. The way in which a miser hoards money is seen as symbolic of the child's refusal to eliminate faeces in the face of parental demands. The spendthrift, on the other hand, recalls the approval and affection that resulted from submission to parental authority to defecate. Thus some people equate elimination/spending with receiving affection and hence felt more inclined to spend when feeling insecure, unloved or in need of affection. Attitudes to money are then bimodal; they are either extremely positive or extremely negative.

Evidence for the psychoanalytic position comes from the usual sources, patients' free associations and dreams. However, Freudians have attempted to find evidence for their theory in idioms, myths, folklore and legends. There is also quite a lot of evidence from language, particularly from idiomatic expressions. Money is often called 'filthy lucre', and the wealthy are often called 'stinking rich'. Gambling for money is also associated with dirt and toilet-training: a poker player puts money in a 'pot'; dice players shoot 'craps'; card players play 'dirty-Girty'; a gambler who loses everything is 'cleaned out'.

Families, groups and societies which demand early and rigid toilet-training tend to produce 'anal characteristics' in people, which include orderliness, punctuality, compulsive cleanliness and obstinacy. Hence one can be miserly about knowledge, time and emotions as much as money. These effects may be increased or reduced depending on whether the child grows up in a socialist or capitalist country, in times of comparative expansion or depression, or whether one is part of a middle- or working-class family. Parents' belief in the Puritan or Protestant ethic may also alter money beliefs and habits.

The extent to which money is imbued with psychological meaning is clearly apparent from the following quote by Wiseman (1974):

> One thinks of kleptomaniacs, or of the women who drain men of their resources, to whom money, which they are always striving to take away, symbolizes a whole series of introjected objects that have been withheld from them; or of depressive characters who from fear of starvation regard money as potential food. There are too those men to whom money signifies their potency, who experience any loss of money as a castration, or who are inclined, when in danger, to sacrifice money in a sort of 'prophylactic self-castration'. There are, in addition, people who – according to their attitudes of the moment towards taking, giving or withholding – accumulate or spend money, or alternate between accumulation and spending, quite impulsively, without regard for the real significance of money, and often to their own detriment every man has, and the pricelessness of objects, and the price on the outlaw's head; there are forty pieces of silver and also the double indemnity on one's own life.
>
>   Behind its apparent sameness lie the many meanings of money. Blood-money does not buy the same thing as bride-money and a king's ransom is not the kind of fortune as a lottery prize. The great exchangeability of money is deceptive; it enables us to buy the appearance of things, their physical form, as in the case of a 'bought woman', while what we thought we had bought eludes us.   (pp. 13–14)

There have been both speculation and empirical attempts to categorise or taxonomise different attitudes to money. For instance, Goldberg and Lewis (1978), who were particularly interested in the paradoxes, hypocrisies, inconsistencies and lies associated with money, identified four forms of 'money madness':

1. Security collectors such as compulsive saver, self-denier and fanatic collectors who distrust others and find having money reduces anxiety because one is less dependent on others.
2. Power grabbers, who might be business empire builders or 'godfathers', tend to see money as a form of strength and power and its loss as being rendered helpless, weak, scorned and humiliated.
3. Love dealers, who buy, sell and steal love see either love as money or money as symbolic of love or as a commodity that can be bought or sold.
4. Autonomy worshippers, who hope to buy or fight for the freedom that they see money providing.

They stress the many emotions such as greed, fear, envy, anger, contentment and that money neither be worshipped nor denounced. Money behaviour frequently involves unconscious motivation, but people have the ability to control rather than be controlled by it.

A rather different, but overlapping, taxonomy has been proposed by Forman (1987), who listed five money complexes! He too points out that money is frequently equated with love, self-worth, freedom, power and security. His five types are as follows:

1. The miser, who hoards money that is itself completely fascinating. They tend not to admit being niggardly, have a terrible fear of losing funds and tend to be distrustful, yet have trouble enjoying the benefits of money.
2. The spendthrift, who tends to be compulsive and uncontrolled in their spending and do so particularly when depressed, feeling worthless and rejected. Spending is an instant but short-lived gratification that frequently leads to guilt.
3. The tycoon, who is totally absorbed with money making, which is seen as the best way to gain power status and approval. They argue that the more money they have, the better control they have over their worlds and the happier they are likely to be.
4. The bargain hunter, who compulsively hunts bargains even if they are not wanted because getting things for less makes people feel superior. They feel angry and depressed if they have to pay the asking price or cannot bring the price down significantly.
5. The gambler feels exhilarated and optimistic by taking charge. They tend to find it difficult to stop even when losing because of the sense of power they achieve when winning.

Forman considers in some detail some of the more fascinating neuroses associated with everyday financial and economic affairs like saving, paying insurance and taxes, making a will, using credit cards. For instance, he looks at the issue of borrowing and the occasional obsessive, persistent, unrealistic and intense phobia surrounding this. He gives examples of the fear and avoidance of lending institutions, partly from fear of dependence or punishment if loans are not repaid. The essence of this work, as with so many other books on this topic, is that because money is imbued with so much meaning there are a large number of neuroses and compulsions associated with it. Furthermore, as with all self-help approaches, the author attempts to help people recognise and change the nature of their behaviour. Forman (1987) concludes with such a table (p. 235), set out in the following list:

*The money sanity transition from neurotic to well*

From 'Money as Inner Tormentor' (neurotic)
To 'Money as Inner Mentor' (non-neurotic)

You use money to impress and influence other people.
To feel powerful and to gain status, you flaunt your wealth.

You are comfortable and at ease in the world.
You know that power and status come from within.

You amass money as an end in itself.
You like to have money for its own sake.

You value money for what it can do.
You can distinguish between worldly desires and emotional needs.

You feel anxious, tense, worried, when you think about money. You are relaxed about money and can think about it in a logical way.
You distrust other people around your money and you suspect that they are trying to take advantage of you.

You are self-confident and have a good self-image. You know your friends like you, not your money.
You hoard money in an attempt to protect yourself. Your desire to save is healthy.

You have trouble controlling your spending and you tend to buy things impulsively.
You like to gamble.
You are a good money manager.

Psychoanalytic ideas have inspired a good deal of empirical work (Beloff, 1957; Grygier, 1961; Kline, 1967). Although there are a number of measures that have been constructed to measure dynamic features Kline (1971) developed his own test of the anal character. Examples of this scale include the following:

1. Do you keep careful accounts of the money you spend? (Yes/No)
2. When eating out, do you wonder what the kitchens are like? (Yes/No)
3. Do you insist on paying back even small trivial debts? (Yes/No)
4. Do you like to think out your own methods rather than use other people's? (Yes/No)
5. Do you find more pleasure in doing things than in planning them? (Yes/No)
6. Do you think there should be strong laws against speeding? (Yes/No)
7. There is nothing more infuriating than people who do not keep appointments. (Yes/No)
8. Do you often feel you want to stop people and do the job yourself? (Yes/No)
9. Most people do not have high enough standards in what they do? (Yes/No)
10. Do you make up your mind quickly rather than turn things over for a long time? (Yes/No)
11. Do you think envy is at the root of most egalitarian ideals? (Yes/No)
12. Do you like to see something solid and substantial for your money? (Yes/No)
13. Do you easily change your mind once you have made a decision? (Yes/No)
14. Do you disagree with corporal punishment? (Yes/No)
15. Do you regard smoking as a dirty habit? (Yes/No)

This scale has been used in Ghana as well as Britain.

The empirical research into the anal character has been reviewed by Hill (1976) and Kline (1972). Both reviewers were critical of the methodology of studies done in this area, but came to the conclusion that the evidence for the existence of the anal character as described by the psychoanalytic thinkers is poor.

# The symbolism of money

The fact that money is emotionally charged and highly symbolic has already been mentioned. There is a great deal of speculation about this but comparatively little empirical work in this field. For instance the introduction and/or removal of a coin from circulation causes a great public outcry. The use of credit cards as opposed to cash has also altered the way in which people use and perceive money. For Lea and Webley (1981):

> The essence of money is that it carries meanings. It involves multiple symbolisation. It is not simply a symbol of ordure (Freud), nor only a symbol of what it has bought in the past (Skinner); neither only a symbol of what it could buy in the future (as indicated by some anthropologists), nor only a symbol of the most valuable objects in a society (as other anthropological data suggest); nor is it only a symbol of the world of dehumanised salaries and payments (as Deci says, or some Marxists). Money symbolises all these things, and furthermore many others.   (p. 12)

Consider, for example, two areas in which some research has been done: the use of tips and, more importantly, the exchange of gifts. It has been suggested that the word 'tip' stands for 'to insure prompt service' and is given for services in such places as hotels and restaurants, barbers and hairdressers. A tip is often a symbolic gesture of satisfaction with service, though it may be a requirement in some organisations. Tipping is related to bill size and ratings of service, but not with ratings of food or alcohol consumption, which is consistent with the view that people tip in order to buy social approval and maintain equitable relationships with waiting staff (Lynn and Grassman, 1990). Shamir (1983) has pointed out two interesting features of the tip. First, in that a tip is a tangible form of feedback from clients, workers who receive tips may be thought of as more highly satisfied and motivated compared with workers who do not. Second, people who receive tips are often put in conflicting roles between the management/superiors and the customer but they are more likely to side with the latter as opposed to the former which would be more true of those who do not receive tips. In a study it was demonstrated that tip recipients experience more conflict yet were more favourable to their customers, but were less satisfied than those not receiving tips. The author suggests that his results provide more support for the boundary role perspective (conflict between roles) than for the motivation theory perspective. The dependence on the customer is probably more a source of stress for occupants of subordinate service roles than a source of reward or satisfaction.

The exchange of money as a gift reveals most clearly the symbolic nature and psychological quality of money. Webley, Lea and Portalska (1983) set out in a series of four studies to investigate the unacceptability of money as a gift. They found that money or a cheque was less acceptable than a gift token or a selected present as a gift to the respondents' mother. A third study considered why the gift of money was inappropriate. The top three reasons were: that a gift ought to be something one would not usually buy for oneself and hence chosen by the giver, whereas with a cheque this cannot be the case; a cheque involves no thought devoted to choosing the present; money given as a gift would be used for general expenses. In the fourth study of students' mothers' reactions to gifts the researchers found that the mothers indicated that a cheque would be less acceptable than a selected present or gift token, but that they did not expect more to be spent on a cheque than on other gifts. Hussein (1985b) partially replicated these results in Cyprus, though there was little consensus there about the reasons why money gifts were inappropriate. Webley and Wilson (1989) followed these studies up by exploring the unacceptability of money as a gift in relationships varying in relative status and intimacy. They found that intimacy dictated the amount spent on a present whereas relative status had more effect on the unacceptability of money as a gift. Burgoyne and Routh (1991) took this further by carrying out a more ecologically valid investigation, an extended-diary study of Christmas gift-giving. Their results indicated that a gift needs to have characteristics that can communicate love and respect. Where certain kinds of intimacy can be assumed, money may be acceptable (e.g. from an older to a younger member of a family), but since it may also communicate inappropriate messages relating to status it is not a suitable gift for a higher status individual. Extending this work in another direction, Webley and Lea (1993a) found that money was also unacceptable as a way of repaying neighbourly help. Only in the case of repaying a 'loan' of food was money felt to be acceptable. All of these results suggest that 'modern, Western money is like primitive moneys in that there are taboos on its use. Whatever the institutional position, therefore, in psychological terms money does not meet the economist's definition of being a universal medium of exchange' (Webley, Lea and Portalska, 1983: 237).

# Economic anthropology and primitive money

Unlike psychology, anthropology has long been interested in economics and consumption (Douglas and Isherwood, 1980). Economic anthropology is concerned with the economic aspects of the social relations of persons. Indeed there are a number of standard textbooks on economic anthropology (Thurnwald, 1932; Herskovitz, 1952; Dalton, 1971). Although there have been a number of well-established authorities in this field, Polanyi's work is perhaps the best known. Anthropologists have long been aware that nearly all economic concepts, ideas and theories are based on only one type of economy – industrial capitalism. Some have argued that these modern economic concepts (maximising, supply, demand) are equally applicable to primitive societies, while others are not convinced.

One of the major tasks of economic anthropology is to detect economic universals in human society by sampling the many forms in which they are manifest across cultures: for instance, whereas the deferment of wants, through saving and investing, may be considered good for some cultures, most primitive cultures dictate that resources be expended.

First, it should be pointed out what all economies have in common. Dalton (1971) has noted three features: a structured arrangement with enforced rules for the acquisition or production of material items and services; rules whereby natural resources, human co-operation and technology are combined to provide materials and services in a sustained, repetitive fashion; and the existence of superficially similar institutional practices in the form of marketplaces, monetary objects, accounting devices and external trade. However, he is much more impressed by the differences in economies in terms of their organisation, performance, change, growth and development.

Anthropologists have been concerned with all aspects of economic activity, including barter, the market, distribution of goods and wealth, ownership and property, etc. There are certain similarities between primitive societies' economic behaviour: for instance, Thurnwald (1932) noted that a characteristic failure of most primitive economies is the absence of any desire to make profits from either production or exchange. Many studies have looked at the symbols of value and money stages of evolution of money, and the diverse number and type of object used as units of barter, including shells, dogs' teeth, salt and copper bracelets. Various distinctions have been made such as objects which are treated as treasure and hoarded as such or an article of daily use; whether the object is regarded as capital capable of yielding profit; and also whether the object is the potential source of others of its own kind. Certainly what is interesting about anthropological studies of money is not only the range of objects used as money but the fact that primitive money does not fulfil many of the functions that current money does.

Whereas economists seem concerned with only non-social aspects of money, such as its worth, divisibility, etc., anthropologists look at money which is used in reciprocal and redistributive transactions, in terms of the personal roles and social context of what occurs. The exchange of whatever serves as money – be it armbands, pigs' tusks, shells or stones – as well as its acquisition and disposition is a structured and important event that often has strong moral and legal obligations and implications and which might change various status rights and social roles. Because money is a means of reciprocal and redistributive payment used fairly infrequently to discharge social obligations in primitive societies its portability and divisibility are not very important. The introduction of western-style money does more than just displace indigenous money; it has inevitable repercussions on the social organisation of a people. This is because western-style money allows both commercial and non-commercial (traditional) payments to be earned with general-purpose money earned in everyday market transactions. Hence patrons, elders and heads of families and clans lose some control over their clients and juniors who can earn their own cash and dispose of it as they wish.

The essence of the anthropological message is this: money has no essence apart from its uses which depend on the traditional transactional modes of each culture's economy. Money is what it does and no more.

# A new psychological theory of money

Dissatisfied with the fact that no psychological theory of money can account for the interesting but diffuse data available on money usage and belief, Lea, Tarpy and Webley (1987) have attempted to devise a 'new' psychological theory of money. They note that money is multiply symbolic and, building on Codere's (1968) analysis, point out that it can operate at various levels of measurement, namely nominal, ordinal, interval and ratio. At a nominal level, the only relationship involved is that of equivalence. So money of this kind could only be exchanged for a particular good or category of goods. An anthropological example that comes close to this is the Trobriand kula exchange where the two types of valuables are exchanged solely for other instances of the same type. Money operating at the ordinal level would have various forms which could be placed in rank order. Although one form would be more valuable than another, the difference in value between any two forms would not be the same. With money operating at the interval and ratio level scale we know the size of the differences between numbers. This is the kind of money that exists in most money-using societies.

From this perspective hypothecation (the allocation of money from a specific source to a specific expenditure) can be seen as the intrusion of a nominal heuristic in an interval system. Developmentally children appear to go through a nominal stage when they believe that a twenty-pence piece can only be used to buy a twenty-pence tube of sweets.

Money is then, according to Lea *et al.*, a multiple symbol that can operate at various levels of measurement. This idea is taken further using Lancaster's (1966) characteristics approach to consumer demand. Lancaster assumed that people do not demand goods as such but rather the characteristics that goods possess and by a simple extension it can be argued that people similarly demand the characteristics of money rather than money *in toto*. These characteristics may be economic (rate of interest, liquidity, predictability) or psychological (physical form, whether it has a limited sphere of exchange, its 'cleanliness' in a Freudian sense). It is clear that the most crucial characteristic that differentiates money is value (Snelders *et al.*, 1992 found that this was the main dimension that respondents used in comparing differing money items) but in certain contexts, such as gift-giving, other features will be highly salient. A change in physical form (from one-pound note to one-pound coin), for example, was shown to change the way money was spent. Hussein (1985b) paid subjects for their participation in an unrelated experiment with either a one-pound coin or a one-pound note and asked them to return the following day. This revealed that the one-pound coins were much less likely to still be in people's purses (indicating that they were spent quicker), a result which confirms the findings of Webley, Lea and Hussein (1983).

# Conclusion

Psychological research on money is diffuse and varied. Yet there appears to be a consistent theme running through all the literature from studies on perception through to psychoanalytic observations: money is not simply a convenient medium of exchange, it is a complex and richly imbued symbol.

To understand how and why people spend, save and perceive money as they do requires some understanding of the sociological, economic and historical nature of the society in which they live (i.e. post-industrial, liberal capitalism, pre-industrial, peasant economy) as well as a knowledge of the personal development of the individual, for whereas there are culturally shared beliefs, taboos and symbols surrounding money there are also individual patterns of beliefs and behaviours.

Each of the different branches of psychology has something to contribute to the study of money: developmental psychology (how and when money concepts and behaviours are learnt), experimental psychology (distortions in the perception of familiar and unfamiliar money), occupational psychology (the use of money as a reward and incentive for labour), personality psychology (individual differences in the use of money), and social psychology (individual, group and societal attitudes to money).

Perhaps the psychological significance of money is seen most clearly when it changes: that is, when coins and notes appear, disappear or are interchanged; at times of inflation; when the use of money is being replaced by other tokens such as cheques and cash cards. Governments can radically alter the way in which people use and perceive money by changing its form: changing the name of the currency (and little else), by decimalisation, but perhaps most commonly and effectively by changing notes into coins. Another innovation is the payment of wages and salaries directly into bank and building society accounts, which has an influence on and hopefully leads to less immediate expenditure and saving. Inflation is another important factor in the understanding of money. Epstein and Babad (1982) found that variation in income was not as relevant as people's subjective appraisal of the threat of inflation in predicting their expenditure.

The future of money in many advanced western countries, however, appears to be in doubt: that is, with the introduction of more and more 'plastic' money in the form of credit cards, cash in the form of notes and coins appears to be being used less and less. However, as the work on token economies has shown, there is no reason to suspect that the psychological significance and symbolism of present-day coins and notes might not be equally appropriate to the understanding of money substitutes.

As has been stressed before, this is a rich and neglected area of research made all the more interesting by rapid changes in the use of money and its substitutes. For the economic psychologist it would be very interesting to see whether the use of credit cards increases expenditure; whether credit cards are used for some interactions rather than others, and why; whether the credit card reduces guilt and/or changes attitudes about being in debt, etc. It is already apparent that credit cards have assumed a disclosive/display role in that the colour of the card (e.g. gold vs green) indicates one's credit limit which is itself an indication of annual income. Thus a credit card enables one to disclose more about one's income than was allowed by simple cash or cheques, and hence, they may take on a more important psychological role. Individual preferences for cards, cash or cheque books may also be a useful indicator of socialisation experience (class).

# PART III

# Social issues and social problems

# Chapter 4

# Debt, gambling, addictive spending (and saving)

## Introduction

There is a coherence to the topics dealt with in this chapter that might not be apparent at first sight. Debtors and savers are often seen as opposites, both in everyday conversation and in economics and psychology. In everyday speech, savers are characterised as patient, controlled and sensible; in contrast, debtors and gamblers are seen as impatient, reckless and indulgent. Similarly, from an economic perspective, borrowing (and thereby incurring a debt) is the mirror image of saving. Saving is putting consumption – spending – off into the future and generally receiving some reward for doing so (in the form of interest). Borrowing is bringing future consumption forward into the present, and generally paying some price (in the form of rather higher interest). The same range of academic questions are posed by debt and borrowing as by saving, but with a somewhat sharper edge. Addictive spending and gambling can also be seen as the opposite of saving, since the latter involves restraint. It has also been argued that some gambling and some forms of saving are compulsive (hoarding and miserliness) and so understanding addictive economic behaviour may aid our understanding of both saving and gambling. Another link is that addictive spending and gambling can lead to debt problems (Faber and O'Guinn, 1988).

Treating these topics in one chapter also highlights some important issues in economic psychology, most notably the different assumptions that are made about the nature of the self in theorising in this area. We will see from our concluding discussion that we have a long way to go to get to a theory of the self that is acceptable to social psychologists whilst being usable by economists.

### Some definitions

Definitions may be as dry as dust, but it is best to start dry and quench one's thirst later. We all think we know what debt, gambling and saving are: gambling is betting on the Derby, buying lottery tickets and playing cards for money; saving is making regular contributions to a pension plan, putting money aside to buy a new washing machine or, for children, saving up to buy Christmas presents. The meaning of borrowing, debt and even addictive spending seem similarly self-evident. But things are not that simple.

Gambling, in everyday speech, has come to mean little more than taking a risk, so we talk about gambling that a friend will be in when we call round. But in a formal sense, gambling involves three things. First, there is an exchange, where the winner (e.g. the betting shop) gains at the expense of the loser (the punter). Second, this exchange is determined by the as yet unknown outcome of a future event (e.g. the horse race) which is at least partly a matter of chance. Finally, and most importantly, the gamble is unnecessary: we cannot avoid the risks involved in crossing the road but we can avoid the potential loss of our stake simply by not gambling.

Defining saving is rather more complicated. At an abstract level, since income must be spent or saved, saving can be defined as unspent income. To put it formally:

income earned + amount borrowed = spending + saving.

But there are a number of problems with this. First, we must specify a time period. If one of us saves $400 a month for six months and then spends it all on a holiday (we can but dream), then he would have done a lot of saving per month but none over the year. Once we have specified a time period, a decision to save can be seen as a decision to defer consumption to a future time period. Similarly, a decision to borrow can be seen as a decision to bring forward consumption to the current time period. But the amount of consumption brought forward or deferred need not be same as the amount of consumption forgone or made possible in the future; savings (and borrowings) can shrink and they can grow.

Katona (1975) has made some useful distinctions. First, there is a distinction between voluntary and involuntary saving, which can be extended to borrowing. Involuntary saving occurs when there is no intention or decision to save. Households which pay their gas bills through a regular payment scheme may well discover at the end of the year, when they get a rebate, that they have been saving involuntarily. Conversely, if they then get a bill from the gas company, they have been borrowing involuntarily. Voluntary saving and borrowing are, of course, the opposite, but may take some unusual forms. Cordes, Galper and Kirby (1990) point out that overpayment of federal income tax is found in three-quarters of all individual tax returns in the United States and that the average overpayment is $1,000. The evidence suggests that people are using the tax system to engage in forced saving, so that they will get a refund later. Katona has made a further distinction between two other forms of saving: contractual saving such as pension plans, which are fixed, regular obligations which require no new decisions but are not always regarded by the individual as saving *per se*; and discretionary savings, which are deposits of income in various places and seen as a means of accumulating reserve funds.

There are some further fine distinctions that need to be made in the area of borrowing. Lea, Webley and Levine (1993) have argued that credit implies a willing lender (in fact the loan is often made on the lender's initiative) while debt implies an unwilling lender. So 'debt' refers to an obligation that the borrower either cannot discharge or does not want to discharge, whereas by 'credit' is implied a planned arrangement to borrow money over a period, with an assumption that repayment over that period will be within the borrower's means. The problem with this definition is that it 'privileges' the lender's viewpoint – there is no real justification (other than an operational one) for regarding the view of the lender as more important than that of the borrower. Borrowers do not seem to have a simple or consistent view of debt at all. Lea, Walker and Rooijmans (1992) report that twelve items (out of a list of twenty) were judged to be a kind of debt and that these fell into three categories: formal and agreed in advance (e.g. mortgage, bank loan), formal but unplanned (being behind with the bills, not paying your monthly credit card bills) and informal (IOUs, owing your friends money), whereas Lunt and Livingstone (1992) report that unplanned and informal debt are more consensually judged a debt than negotiated borrowing such as bank loans, and that mortgages were seen by half of their sample as not a debt at all.

The distinction between debt, borrowing and credit and between different kinds of saving is not merely a definitional issue; it has important implications for the way we ask people about their financial behaviour and for the kind of theories we construct. The reader needs to bear this in mind in subsequent pages – one study of peoples' savings may well have used a different definition from another.

Finally, there is a potentially important distinction between addictive and compulsive consumption. Compulsive buying or consumption is the more common term but we have preferred that of addictive consumption here. Scherhorn (1990) makes the difference clear: 'Addictive behaviour runs out of control because of an overpowering but initially welcome desire: compulsive behaviour, on the other hand, is controlled by an unwelcome pressure which the person experiences as alien to himself' (p. 34). In other words, addiction is a pathological habit and is something to which we are all prone. With an addiction we feel driven by an urge, perhaps an irresistible one, but we experience it as our urge whereas with a compulsion we feel pressed to do something, like repeatedly washing our hands, against our will.

## Why do people save, spend addictively, gamble and get into debt?

With the definitional groundwork out of the way, we can turn our attention to the crucial questions. Why do people save, spend addictively, gamble and get into debt? Most theories are based on individualistic notions of rational action and see saving and gambling as functional; we will begin with these and then turn our attention to those approaches that see these behaviours as expressive, social or in some way deriving from childhood experiences.

## Functional theories

We will start with the relationship between income and saving, as this has been the launch pad for many later theories of saving and, by extension, of borrowing and debt. The early theories claimed that the amount of saving was essentially determined by income. Thus Keynes (1936) asserted that the proportion of income that an individual saves is constant; a person with a marginal propensity to save of 0.1 will save £1,000 if s/he earns £10,000 and £2,000 if s/he earns £20,000. In a famous passage, Keynes noted,

> These considerations will lead, as a rule, to a greater proportion of income being saved as real income rises. . . . We take it as a fundamental psychological rule of any modern community that when its real income is increased it will not increase its consumption by an absolute equal amount, so that a greater amount must be saved.　(Keynes, 1936: 96)

This has sometimes been called the absolute income hypothesis of saving and it has been challenged by economists as well as by sociologists. Only in the United Kingdom and the United States do time series data show the propensity to save staying constant; in most other countries the savings ratio has increased over time with income (Kuznets, 1966). More importantly cross-sectional studies show that the savings ratio is higher with higher incomes (e.g. Bean, 1946).

These problems led to the relative income hypothesis of Duesenberry (1949). This theory related the propensity to save to an individual's income relative to other members of the community. This idea can be neatly illustrated by Duesenberry's comparison of black and white Americans. At each income level, American whites save less than American blacks. Duesenberry's explanation for this is that the white group is richer than the black group and so for a given income, the position of a white relative to the white group is worse than for a black relative to the black group. The white, who is relatively worse off, should therefore save less.

Duesenberry also showed how it was possible for there to be a constant average propensity to save as average income changes over time (Keynes' 'fundamental psychological rule') whilst at any particular time those with a higher income save more than those with a lower income.

However, although Duesenberry's approach is attractive to a social psychologist (because he proposed a theory that saw economic behaviour as interdependent and used notions such as social comparison), it actually gives us no insight at all into why people save. Saving (and borrowing) is just a residual, what is left over after people have made their consumption decisions. It also implies that people will not save and borrow during the same time period.

The most influential economic theories assume that the prime motive for saving today is so that one can consume tomorrow; in other words that people are making choices between spending now and spending later. Most theoretical effort has been concentrated on the issue of how individuals deal with variations in income across their life-span. The best known of these theories is the life-cycle hypothesis, developed by Modigliani and Brumberg (1954). Thaler (1990) provides a succinct summary:

> The essence of the life-cycle theory is this: in any year compute the present value of your wealth, including current income, net assets, and future income; figure out the level of annuity you could purchase with that money; then consume the amount you would receive if you in fact owned such an annuity.   (Thaler, 1990: 193–4)

This suggests that people are rationally determining how much they can consume over the remainder of their life so as to maximise utility and that in any given year the difference between this level of consumption and income will be the amount saved (or the amount borrowed). Young people will borrow to pay for consumption, the middle-aged save for retirement and the old spend those savings (this is the so-called 'hump'-shaped age–saving profile).

A rather similar theory is Friedman's (1957) permanent income hypothesis. Friedman claims that people have a notion of what their mean permanent income will be across a time period and aim to consume a fixed proportion of it during that time. Their actual income and consumption may well vary from the permanent income and saving (and borrowing) will take up the slack. One important difference between this and the life-cycle hypothesis is that the permanent income is not the same as expected life-time earnings; Friedman recognised that individuals make calculations based on a time-horizon that does not necessarily extend to their deaths!

Though these theories are elegant, they do not really correspond with the data; consumption (and therefore savings) seems to be very sensitive to income (Thurow, 1969). So the young and the old consume less (save more) than they should according to the life-cycle hypothesis and the middle-aged save too little. A further problem is that those in retirement often add to their savings.

A most recent version of the life-cycle model (the behavioural life-cycle hypothesis of Shefrin and Thaler, 1988) goes some way to overcoming these problems by incorporating concepts from psychology such as self-control and framing and using Thaler's (1990) notion of mental accounts. The traditional life-cycle model assumes that people work out an optimum consumption plan and then stick to it. However, a large body of evidence shows that people have great difficulty in delaying gratification and if offered a choice between a small reward now or a larger one later are likely to take the small immediate reward. A simple demonstration of this effect is reported in Lea, Tarpy and Webley (1987). Participants were shown two envelopes and asked to imagine that one contained a cheque for £5 dated on the day of the experiment and the other contained an undated cheque for £10. The question for the participants was how far in the future the second cheque would have to be dated in order for them to prefer the £5 now to £10 later. The median answer was approximately two months, which would be rational only if there was a contract out on a participant's life or if the rates of interest were around 5,000 per cent. Even when real money is involved (Kurz, Spiegelman and West, 1973 offered people actual cheques), subjective interest rates range from 22 to 60 per cent. Systematic experiments, for example by Abdul-Muhmin, Nyhus and Rønqvist (1993), also reveal high subjective interest rates, although it should be pointed out that the rate depends on a number of factors, notably the amount of money involved (Benzion,

Rapoport and Yagil, 1989) and whether one is choosing between losses and gains (Lowenstein, 1988).

All this suggests that, as the early economists like Böhm-Bewark (1891) recognised, people are impatient and that to save requires self-control (Wärneryd, 1989). Thaler and Shefrin have dealt with this by treating the individual as an organisation containing a far-sighted planner and a myopic doer, both of whom operate rationally but with different preference functions. The planner is concerned with maximising lifetime utility whilst the doer wants immediate gratification. So the planner invents self-imposed rules and makes use of external rules (such as commitments to save regularly through a pension plan) to control the doer's behaviour.

Shefrin and Thaler also propose that people have a number of mental accounts at their disposal which operate fairly independently of each other. In a simple stylised version, these accounts are hierarchically organised according to the source of income: current disposable income, assets and future income. Individuals are predisposed to spend money from these different accounts (a psychological equivalent of the jamjar on the mantelpiece) differently; they will spend most of their current income and almost none of their future income with the propensity to spend assets falling somewhere between these two. Notice that this means that people may borrow whilst they have savings; they may borrow to buy a car knowing that the bank will ensure that they repay the loan whilst keeping their savings intact because of a fear that they, unassisted, would be unable to build them up again.

The final feature of the Shefrin and Thaler model is the idea of framing, which essentially asserts that income will be spent differently depending on how it is perceived by the recipient. This very closely resembles the idea of mental accounts, however, and it is not clear what it adds to the overall theory.

The behavioural life-cycle hypothesis is quite striking. It does a good job of accounting for the data (although few of its predictions have so far been directly tested) but, more interestingly, it is explicitly (if extremely simplistically) psychological. The two-self model may seem very naive, but it is one step on a road to the fusion of economic and psychological models. Despite the modifications to the initial life-cycle model, this approach is still firmly based on the idea of individual rational action: both the doer and the planner 'act' rationally according to their preferences.

This core idea also underlies those theories which treat saving as a goal in itself. Katona (1975), for example, claimed that savings (an adequate reserve of money) is a consumer good which people want to acquire, an idea expressed even more boldly by Clower and Johnson (1968), who proposed that accumulated savings were an autonomous source of utility. This idea is then developed along standard utility-maximising lines.

It is perhaps not surprising that explanations for saving and borrowing have been predominantly functional. That addictive spending and gambling have also been treated in this way is more unexpected. Becker and his associates (Stigler and Becker, 1977; Becker and Murphy, 1988; Becker, 1992) have done just that for addiction. According to Stigler and Becker, the real change that occurs when someone becomes addicted is an increase in the price of achieving satisfaction. They claim that an addiction, for example to alcohol, occurs when two conditions obtain: first of all, the substance, whatever it is, must satisfy a basic need – in economic terms, the demand for the good must be inelastic; second, consumption of the good must involve rapid habituation so that the more it is consumed, the less satisfaction it gives (a regular drinker requires much more alcohol to attain a certain level of intoxication than at least one of your clean-living authors). This means that the real price, for example of intoxication, goes up over time as an individual habituates to the effects of alcohol. If both of these conditions are met, the individual will end up spending more and more on the substance as more and more of it is consumed. It is not that the addict lacks self-control; simply that s/he is satisfying a basic need through a substance that becomes more costly over time.

Other economic models of the addictive process make the link with saving and borrowing more obvious. Winston (1980), for example, describes the addict's behaviour as involving a switching between two states of consciousness, the myopic or addicted state and a state in which one is aware of the long-term consequences and of one's long-term preferences. Though the terminology is slightly different (states of consciousness rather than selves) the similarity between this model and that of Shefrin and Thaler is clear.

As Lea, Tarpy and Webley (1987: 270) point out:

> gambling seems to differ from many other economic phenomena in that we are unusually aware of its excessive forms. However, saving is done by misers, food-buying by compulsive eaters and work by workaholics and yet these pathological cases have not dominated our discussion of work, buying and saving.

It is this awareness of gambling's excessive forms that makes functional accounts of gambling seem inappropriate. Though pathological gambling does have many features in common with other addictions (arousal as the major reinforcing factor, withdrawal symptoms, dependence and tolerance – see Dickerson, 1984), normal gambling (which is what the vast majority of people engage in; Cornish, 1978) does not lead to financial ruin and family break-up. Functional accounts of gambling are straightforward and assume simply that gamblers are trying to maximise their subjective expected utility. Though the objective expected value of commercially available bets is always negative (on average you lose), a gambler may overestimate the chances of winning (so the subjective probabilities of winning are greater than the objective probability) or value the outcome more highly. These approaches have been much criticised but if it is recognised that excitement of gambling itself contributes to the utility, they become much more plausible (Kanto, Rosenqvist and Suvas, 1992). This is very clear in Griffiths' (1990) interview study of young male fruit machine users, who openly confess to playing with money rather than for it. Their aim was to stay on the machine for as long as possible – exactly the same aim as a video game player.

All of these models give essentially the same answer to why people save, spend addictively, gamble or get into debt: they do these things because they are trying to maximise their utility. A short time horizon may mean that individuals may find themselves addicted or in debt but such individuals should be regarded as unfortunate rather than irrational. This is a bold approach (and Becker, in particular, has made strong claims for it) but is to some extent unconvincing. We have two main objections: first, the approach is individualistic and does not take into account the importance of the social groups to which people belong and how this relates to their selves; second, the distinction made by Scherhorn (1990) between choice and decision casts doubt on the adequacy of this approach to certain classes of economic behaviour. Scherhorn points out that choice means more than just preferring an option – it implies that selection of an option is guided by the self. The addict has no choice; s/he feels driven by an irresistible urge. So although an alcoholic decides to have yet another drink, or the compulsive gambler decides to lay another bet, s/he is not choosing to do this because s/he wants to obtain a particular level of intoxication or excitement – in some sense the addict has no say in the matter.

## Expressive, social and developmental models

We get rather different kinds of explanations from sociologists, psychologists and anthropologists. Some of these theories look for the roots of behaviour in childhood experiences, others consider the social context of economic behaviour. Probably the oldest of the developmental theories is Freud's psychodynamic theory. In his essay on Dostoevsky, Freud (1928/1961) identified 'self-destruction' as the common theme running through his life and work. Freud's interpretation of this was that this stemmed from guilt caused by Dostoevsky's Oedipal desire to destroy his father; gambling was just one way of punishing himself for this guilt. An alternative psychoanalytic explanation for gambling was put forward by Bergler (1958): for him, gambling was a neurotic aggression against logic, intelligence and morality (qualities instilled by parents) and a denial of the reality principle. Bergler also claimed that the gambler had an unconscious wish to lose money to punish him/herself for this neurotic aggression, so although the cause of the guilt is different in the two psychoanalytic approaches, both see gambling as expressing an unconscious desire for self-punishment. Psychoanalytic approaches have also been applied to other economic behaviour, for example Freud's theory of money (1908). According to Freud, faeces are the first property of the young child, and they are a property that gives it some power over its parents, since appropriate defecation will please them and inappropriate defecation will anger them. Children also enjoy playing with these 'toys'. This anal behaviour is transformed during development into economic behaviour, so that an anally retentive child (who derived pleasure from not defecating) will be a thrifty adult and an anally expulsive child (who got their fun from releasing faeces) will be a profligate spender.

Though this is quite an entertaining theory, the evidence for it is thin on the ground. Kline's (1967) paper-and-pencil test of the anal personality does include some items on saving and these do correlate with the rest of the scale but there is nothing that links anality directly with saving behaviour. Webley, Lea and Walker (1993) report a negative correlation between general planfulness (which is associated with the kind of obsessionality at the core of the anal personality) and not being in debt, but the association is a weak one and it may be that being in debt reduces your ability to plan rather than that planfulness keeps you out of debt.

A different kind of theory has been proposed to account for addictive spending. Faber and O'Guinn (1988), using Jacobs' (1986) theory, suggest that individuals prone to become compulsive spenders have had experiences in childhood that have made them feel unwanted, inferior and rejected by significant others and have an arousal state that is either chronically depressed or excited which some substances or activities can alter to make it more optimal. Such individuals can, through their compulsive spending, escape from painful reality and experience, albeit temporarily, by being important and admired. A simpler explanation could be that children model their behaviour on that of their parents, which suggests that compulsive spenders will tend to have children who spend compulsively. Faber and O'Guinn (1988) studied a group of self-identified compulsive consumers using a mail questionnaire and intensive interviews. They found some support for Jacobs' ideas, in that compulsive buyers seemed to believe that their siblings were loved more by their parents and that although they had tried hard to please their parents, they had failed. For example, one interviewee commented:

> I was always trying to win their (parents) approval but couldn't. You know you could have stood on your head and turned blue and it wouldn't matter. . . . That's probably why I went out and bought all of that stuff for my kids because I was reliving in my own mind, this is what I should have had.   (p. 10)

The quantitative data showed that compulsive consumers got less verbal approval from parents than a control group of consumers, which also supports Jacobs' interpretation. But the parental behaviour which most differentiated compulsive consumers from others was the use of money or gifts to reward behaviour. Money or gifts then become a substitute for other signs of caring – and buying becomes a means of obtaining feelings of affection. Other studies of addictive buyers give a similar picture: Scherhorn, Reisch and Raab (1990) showed that addictive buyers have lower self-esteem than buyers in general and that their data are consistent with the idea that such people are 'filling-up' the empty self with external gratifications; and Hanley and Wilhelm (1992) also showed that these people have a lower self-esteem than the average consumer and have a need to spend money in a way that reflects status and power.

The problem with this work is that, in most cases, it is hard to know whether the differences between compulsive and non-compulsive buyers are a cause or a consequence of compulsive buying and whether compulsive buying is qualitatively different from normal buying. We suspect that buying to compensate for disappointment or alleviate boredom is very common but that only some people, with specific experiences, become dependent on this compensatory buying.

Focusing on the social context of saving, borrowing and debt gives us an alternative perspective. Most influential has been the approach of Mary Douglas (Douglas and Isherwood, 1980; Douglas, 1982), who treats the goods that people buy as a system of communication. Thus:

> [People] need goods to involve others as fellow-consumers in . . . consumption rituals. Goods are for mobilizing other people. The fact that in the course of these rituals food gets consumed, flags waved and clothes worn is incidental. Subsistence is a fortunate by-product.   (Douglas, 1982: 23)

This does not imply that saving is simply what is left after people have finished communicating via consumption. On the contrary, saving and borrowing are themselves communicative acts; just as people may bandy around the names of cars and holiday destinations so too can they talk about types of pension funds and investment trusts. Getting into financial difficulties can also be seen as communicative; just as attempted suicide is sometimes a cry for help, so too (sometimes) is getting into debt.

Saving has also been conceived as a form of coping (Lunt and Livingstone, 1991), which follows from Keynes' (1936) identification of precaution and foresight as two of the important motivations to save. Lunt and Livingstone suggest that savings will be linked to people's general coping strategies and the way that they use social support. The evidence they present provides some support for this view: when they explored what factors discriminated savers from non-savers they found that non-savers could be characterised as people who give up control over their finances, who prefer flexible financial strategies and keep their finances private. Savers, on the other hand, talked to friends and relatives about financial matters and so would get information about how to cope as well as social support for their approach to money.

## Individual and group differences

Most of the work described above makes the assumption that we can find a single simple explanation for saving, borrowing and debt, whether this is economic or social psychological. But it is clear that people differ considerably in a variety of ways that can be related to their individual financial behaviour, and it is to these differences that we now turn. There may be relevant differences at a variety of levels: we might consider dispositions (like risk aversion), abilities (such as the abilities to plan and to defer gratification), preferences (e.g. time preference) or motivational differences, though there may well be others.

Risk aversion is an excellent place to start. Many kinds of economic behaviour involve risk taking in one form or another: so, for example, choosing to put one's savings in BCCI or a rock-solid institution like Citibank or the Abbey National may reflect not only an assessment of the likely rate of return and the financial security of the two options but a more general disposition to take risks. Dahlbäck (1991) investigated the relationship between the propensity to take risks and saving and being in debt, using data from 178 single-person Swedish households. He used mail questionnaires that covered socio-demographic details, measures of risk taking and a variety of measures of saving. The results suggested that risky individuals had a higher burden of debt and less money in bank accounts than the more cautious respondents, though there was no relationship between riskiness and the measures of total savings. Attempts to find a link between measures of risk taking and gambling have not been very successful, but one consistent finding is that horses with low odds (favourites) are underbet and outsiders are overbet (Thaler and Ziemba, 1987; Kanto, Rosenqvist and Suvas, 1992). This means that in the long run favourites give higher rates of return than outsiders: since the expected utility of each type of bet should be equal, this implies that there must be some non-pecuniary advantage of betting on outsiders, which is most probably that it is more exciting. According to Rachlin's (1989) analysis, veteran gamblers will tend to bet on outsiders and naive gamblers on favourites and he does present some related evidence which supports this idea, so it is quite possible that gamblers (unlike Dahlbäck's savers) like risk.

The idea that risk aversion or preference is relevant to saving and gambling is plausible, but there are problems with the notion of a general propensity to take risks. Many have been sceptical of this, although Dahlbäck (1990) claims there is good evidence for it. The fact that all of Dahlbäck's measures of savings were based on self-report is worrying and it is possible that part of his results can be explained by people's desire to present a consistent image of themselves.

Risk aversion has only recently been linked to saving. By contrast, the concepts of time preference (in economic terms) and ability to delay gratification (in psychological terms) have long been associated with saving (Wärneryd, 1989), although they have only recently been linked with gambling (Rachlin, 1989). The terms used may have been different (Fisher (1930) talked about 'impatience' and Thaler and Shefrin (1981) about 'self-control') but the basic idea, that there are consistent individual differences in people's preference for present consumption over future consumption, remains the same. But although saving and time preference have often been linked and delay-of-gratification experiments used as an (imperfect) analogy for saving (see Lea, Tarpy and Webley, 1987), there have been comparatively few empirical studies of the relationship between the two. One recent example is the work of Abdul-Muhmin, Nyhus and Rønqvist (1993). They explored two hypotheses: that for those who are impatient saving is more likely to be a residual and that patient individuals will be more likely to save a fixed amount every time period. They distributed questionnaires to employees of the Norwegian School of Economics which included four different measures of time preferences and some simple self-report measures of saving behaviour. They found some weak evidence for their hypotheses but, more significantly, found very low inter-item correlations between the measures of time preferences, which suggests either that the idea of general impatience is unsound or that much more work needs to be done on devising a reliable form of measurement for time preference. We incline to the latter view, as the evidence that time preference does play a part in explaining other behaviour is growing: Hornik (1989), for example, has shown that heavy smokers have a greater preference for immediate satisfaction and Fuchs (1982) showed that time preferences help explain health behaviour. Ritzema (Ritzema and Homan, 1991; Ritzema, 1992) made use of the NIPO panel, a representative sample of the Dutch population who, in return for a micro-computer with a modem, answer questions via the computer on a wide variety of topics. In this instance, questions covered saving, borrowing and assets. Ritzema showed that time preference was significantly related to the likelihood of financial problems and total debt and improved the ability of a behavioral life-cycle model to predict borrowing.

It is possible to take a more holistic view of individual differences. Brandstätter, for example, has in recent years stressed the importance of personality structure in explaining economic behaviour (Brandstätter, 1992, 1993a, 1993b) and has claimed that Cattell's sixteen personality factors do a good job of accounting for variations in economic behaviour. He has shown that how leisure time is spent, the number of hours worked per day and the success of entrepreneurs all depend heavily on personality structure. In his most recent work, Brandstätter (1993b) has demonstrated that a simple personality adjective list (the 16 PF) helps explain aspects of saving behaviour.

A rather different approach is to look for different types of savers, borrowers or gamblers. For example, Moran (1970) distinguished four different categories of compulsive gamblers: psychopathic (where the gambling was only part of a global disturbance of behaviour), impulsive (gambling associated with lack of control), neurotic (gambling used to relieve problems) and subculture (where people gambled excessively because their friends did so). This may be useful descriptively but leaves the question of causation open. Others have argued (including us in our earlier *Economic Mind*) that it is important to consider different categories of non-compulsive gamblers: those who bet on horse races are clearly different from those who play on fruit machines, although here one suspects that aspects of the underlying psychology are common to both (e.g. the importance of arousal and excitement – see Griffiths, 1991).

Based on Maslow's notion of a hierarchy of needs, Lindqvist (1981) suggested that there was a corresponding hierarchy of saving needs. These needs, or reasons for saving, are of four kinds. At the bottom of the hierarchy is the need for cash management; here savings are simply deposits of money that have not yet been spent. Next is the need to have a reserve of money for emergencies, a buffer against the unexpected. Third is the need to have a large sum of money to pay for something costly, like a house (goal-directed saving); and finally there is the need to manage accumulated wealth. This idea was elaborated by Wärneryd (1983), who proposed that these needs could form the basis for a typology of savers. Wahlund and Wärneryd (1988) carried out a cluster analysis of a series of surveys on household economic behaviour to see if there was an empirical support for this idea. They found that there were indeed four types of savers. Two of the groups (the cash managers and the wealth managers) were much as expected: the cash managers had low incomes and low savings which were used mostly to pay bills; the wealth managers were middle-aged with high incomes, having lots of savings that they expected to increase over the next year. The other two groups, although fitting the bill as far as their saving behaviour was concerned, did not have the expected demographic characteristics. The buffer savers had the lowest incomes and were the youngest group (contrary to expectations). They had more savings than the cash managers, were planning to increase these savings over the coming year and rated 'having a buffer' as more important than the other groups. The goal-directed savers considered saving to get interest and to buy something as more important than the other groups, had reasonable incomes and were surprisingly the oldest group.

Gunnarsson and Wahlund (1993) have followed up this work and report an initial analysis of 189 households who have been asked about their savings, borrowing and a range of related variables. They too found four groups: the cash managers had the lowest incomes and few assets; the buffer savers slightly higher incomes and held their savings in traditional and safe places (banks, savings bonds); and the wealth managers were again middle-aged with high incomes and had a widely spread portfolio of savings. The fourth group were better characterised as 'gamblers' than goal-directed savers. Their incomes were comparable to the wealth managers and their average regular monthly savings were also similar to this group but they had much bigger debts, half the overall wealth and had concentrated their resources into riskier assets. The groups also differed in their time preferences and risk aversion: the cash managers were significantly more 'impatient' but also less risky than the other groups.

This kind of typological approach is helpful but, as it stands, far too static and descriptive. We need to know where these individuals are in their life-cycle and whether the differences between them are a cause or a consequence of the differences in their saving and borrowing behaviour. To answer questions like these a different kind of approach is needed – an issue to which we will return later.

An alternative typology has been proposed by Lunt and Livingstone (1992), which depends upon people's saving behaviour and whether or not they have debts. Table 4.1 gives a breakdown of their sample (of 279 respondents) according to this classification.

**Table 4.1.** Mean income and savings of six groups classified according to their savings and debts (figures in pounds sterling, amount of savings in square brackets, £1 = $1.5)

| Savings | | | |
|---|---|---|---|
| | none | don't save regularly but have savings | save regularly and have savings |
| Have debt | 5,484 | 6,588 [2,016] | 8,509 [2,587] |
| Debt | | | |
| No debt | 6,607 | 6,759 [12,740] | 7,975 [11,083] |

*Source:* reprinted with permission, Lunt and Livingstone (1992: Table 3.3)

Interestingly, the income differences between the groups are not significant so these different strategies of personal financial managment are not simply the result of obvious economic factors. The groups did not, in fact, differ in voting patterns, educational qualifications, disposable income or outgoings on accommodation and food. None the less, using their family circumstances, attitudes and other variables, it is possible to classify correctly 95 per cent of the respondents. We can summarise the most important differences. Let us start with debtors. Why would people keep their debts when they have some savings? Compared with debtors without savings, debtors with savings are more likely to buy themselves something as a reward, are less well educated, more often blame their problems on losing a job and think they manage their finances better than their friends. They have probably had a previous period of higher earnings and are hoping that things will get better. Some debtors save regularly. Compared with debtors who do not save, debtors who save are more satisfied with the state of the economy, think getting a good job depends on luck, blame demands from children for their financial problems and possess more consumer durables. They maintain repayments and saving concurrently, which suggests that 'being in debt may be a particular financial management decision, not simply an unpleasant situation to escape if at all possible' (Lunt and Livingstone, 1992: 56). Another group of interest is those who neither save nor borrow. They think less often about decisions before taking action, think that success depends on luck, operate fixed styles of budgeting and are less willing to use credit cards. They are somehow detached from the consumer society.

Though Lunt and Livingstone do refer to life-cycle effects (and provide an analysis of credit, borrowing and debt according to stage in the life course), they do not refer to Shefrin and Thaler (1988) and in general make little use of economic theory. But we would argue that their account can easily be integrated with the behavioral life-cycle hypothesis. Remember that Shefrin and Thaler propose that people have a number of mental accounts at their disposal which operate fairly independently of each other. These accounts are hierarchically organised according to source of income, current disposable income, assets and future income. That there are debtors with savings, for example, would result from the fact that the marginal propensity to consume assets is different from the marginal propensity to consume disposable income. Whatever the merits of this particular suggestion, we would argue that Lunt and Livingstone's findings make it clear that we cannot consider saving or borrowing or debt in isolation. We can understand all of these behaviours better if we look at them within the context of general financial management.

## Multi-factor approaches

Most economic psychologists working in this area favour neither the elegance of utility-maximising models nor the complexity (and lack of clarity?) of social and developmental approaches, but espouse an eclectic multi-factor approach. An early example of this was Lindqvist's (1981) study of the saving behaviour in a sample of over 400 Swedish households. Lindqvist investigated the best predictors of four separate measures of saving behaviour (e.g. changes in bank savings over three months, repayment of debts). The independent measures included socio-economic characteristics (income, level of education) as well as attitudinal measures. The picture Lindqvist paints is somewhat surprising: none of the variables, not even income, predicted changes in bank savings; income did predict repayment of debts but psychological measures had no explanatory value; and attitudes and income both predicted changes in total savings. Since the explanatory power of the set of predictors was overall rather low, it is possible that the measures of savings used were not really adequate, though Lindqvist does report some kind of check on his self-reported savings measures.

Furnham (1985) did a rather similar job for gambling, setting out to examine the determinants of people's attitudes to gambling as well as their gambling habits. He found that attitudes towards gambling were far from unidimensional or even bipolar: in fact, his attitude scale turned out to have a five-factor structure, with two factors concerned with the clinical aspects (pathology and addictiveness), one with gambling as innocent fun, another with moral issues and another with economic issues (losses). Older, alienated and conservative people tended to be more against all forms of gambling than younger, less alienated, liberal respondents. The less well educated indulge in bingo, dog-racing and slot machines whereas the better educated bet on horse races. As one might expect, gambling attitudes are not independent of gambling habits. Those who gamble frequently and in a variety of ways find the activity harmless and exciting and resist legal or financial restraints, whereas the opposite is true of those who rarely, if ever, gamble. Furnham argues that the types of, motivation for, satisfaction derived from, attitudes to and habits of gambling are interrelated and multi-dimensional. The motivations for gambling – ranging from social contact through physiological arousal to the desire for self-punishment – are as varied as are satisfactions derived from gambling. Like Lindqvist's study, this investigation also suffers from relying on self-report.

Lunt and Livingstone's recent studies of saving and debt (Lunt and Livingstone 1991, 1992; Livingstone and Lunt, 1992) have been of the same genre but much more successful. They studied a pseudo-random sample of 279 members of the general population. This group completed a twenty-page questionnaire which covered a wide range of areas including socio-demographic measures, financial arrangements, attitudes towards debt and credit use, patterns of shopping, spending and credit use and many other relevant domains. For different measures of both saving and debt they report a series of hierarchical regression analyses, which have the great advantage of assessing the influence of each group of variables (e.g. demographic, economic, psychological) after the effect of previous groups of variables have been taken into account. This kind of analysis enables one to say whether or not 'softer' psychological and sociological measures actually add any predictive power to the 'harder' economic and demographic ones. It is important to realise that a psychological variable may on its own predict a relevant dependent variable (say credit card debt) without adding to our ability to predict credit card debt given that we know, for example, income, education and so on.

To predict both recurrent and total saving, Lunt and Livingstone entered groups of variables into the analysis in the following order: demographic, economic, attitudes and values, economic attributions, economic talk, economic behaviour. For both kinds of savings, economic variables accounted for approximately 45 per cent of the variance; so, for example, disposable income was, as expected, a significant predictor of how much people regularly save. What is more intriguing is that for recurrent saving demographic variables were irrelevant and psychological variables important whilst for total savings the pattern was reversed, with demographic variables accounting for twice as much variance as psychological ones. This makes good sense. People's total savings are likely to increase with age as they accumulate savings, receive lump-sum payments of one kind or another and inherit money from their parents and other relatives. Having children is also clearly likely to reduce total savings, as, in addition to the obvious costs when children are young, parents tend to help their adult children in a variety of ways. Recurrent savings are more under individual control and so we might expect psychological variables to be more important. The surprising result here is that the amount of money that people spend on clothes is a good predictor of the amount they save regularly. One possibility is that those who save more are more concerned with their social image – another option is that purchasing clothing may be seen as a way of investing in long-lasting objects which one can use in the future.

Livingstone and Lunt (1992) approached the analysis of the debt data in a similar way, with demographic variables being entered first and psychological factors last into a hierarchical discriminant function analysis. This revealed that debtors were younger, had less savings, had a positive attitude towards credit, felt less in control of their finances and made more impulse purchases. Surprisingly, neither disposable income nor the number of children was associated with debt – a result which we are inclined to attribute either to the methodology (a postal questionnaire eliciting measures of self-reported debt) or the nature of the sample. Berthoud and Kempson (1990), who carried out intensive personal interviews with almost 2,000 British households, are quite clear that debt is a consequence of financial difficulties; debtors in their sample were distinguished by having a low income and having more demands on that income (i.e. children).

Lea, Webley and Levine (1993) followed the same multi-factor strategy as Lunt and Livingstone, but with an important difference. Instead of relying on people's self-reports of indebtedness, they were able to use creditor records. A large utility company (Welsh Water p.l.c.) identified the names and addresses of people in three credit status groups: non-debtors (those with no outstanding debt to the company), mild debtors (those to whom a 'final' demand had been sent) and serious debtors (those who had been taken to court to recover the money owed). Appropriate steps were taken to ensure anonymity. Questionnaires were sent to over 2,500 households. The questionnaire covered social, demographic, occupational and economic status, attitudes to debt, spending and saving, current financial status, urgency of repaying various debts and the perceived social support for being in debt. The response rate was rather poor (23 per cent in the non-debtor and 11 per cent in the debtor category) but there was a reasonable correspondence between self-report debt and credit groups; 72 per cent of the serious debtors admitted that they were in debt to the water company, which given that a number of those in the serious debtor group would have paid off their debts to Welsh Water in the period between the lists of addresses being prepared and the questionnaires being sent out, indicates that respondents were generally being very truthful.

The picture that emerges from this research is that debt is primarily a problem of family poverty. The serious debt group had lower incomes, were less likely to own their homes, were younger and had more children. This is quite consistent with those cross-sectional studies of saving that show that as income decreases, a steadily reducing proportion of it is saved; running up debt is simply taking this a stage further. A hierarchical analysis on this data (with groups of variables being entered in the following order: economic resources, economic need, social support for debt, attitude-forming variables, attitudes) revealed that adding each group significantly improved the prediction of debt, but that the increase in predictive power with extra groups is small. This runs counter to the results of Lunt and Livingstone but is in accord with those of Berthoud and Kempson.

Later studies by Lea and his team, also carried out in collaboration with Welsh Water, confirm this picture. A second large survey (Webley, Lea and Walker, 1993) made fuller use of Welsh Water's records and so sharper distinctions could be drawn between the credit groups – thus over the past three years the non-debtors had incurred no debt to the company and the mild debtors had been sent at least two 'final demands'. The questionnaire used in this survey included a psychometrically more adequate debt attitude scale and focused on money management both now and in the distant past. But despite being a 'better' scale, attitudes towards debt did not predict indebtedness; again it was the 'harder' variables (income, housing and age) that were the best predictors. There were marked differences in relation to the number of children in the household: the mode for both debtor groups was two, but for the non-debtors none.

The results of these large survey studies were fleshed out with some qualitative research (Lea, Walker and Webley, 1992). Intensive interviews were carried out in a depressed area of Cardiff with individuals classified by Welsh Water as debtors or non-debtors. The debtors fitted the profile described above; they were council tenants, young, had more than one dependent child and were often single parents. Some of the 'non-debtors' fitted the same profile – but they also had large amounts of debt. This suggests that at a certain point economic resources and needs will almost guarantee debt problems. What was surprising was how easy it was for these individuals to get credit; as one interviewee put it 'you see loans are easy for, what, like parties, when you need what you want for the kids'. Given that the interviews were carried out in the summer, it was also striking how often Christmas was mentioned by the debtors. So we hear that 'the loan always seems to help me out at the time, Christmas time . . . and it's just gone on from there really'; 'I finish up these loans before Christmas now, and then I've got to renew them, to get ready for

Christmas again for my kids' and, in answer to the question, 'Why did you go into loans?', 'Because I just could not buy anything for my children at Christmas.'

These interviews give us some insight into how poverty leads households into debt. Part of the answer seems to be that credit, particularly informal credit, is readily available and it is easy to use credit when family, friends and neighbours do so. Another part is that the interviewees were determined that their children should enjoy the same things as their peers.

A multi-factor approach has also been taken to addictive buying, and Tokunaga (1993) has neatly combined the investigation of addictive buying and debt. Tokunaga compared a sample of people who had experienced financial problems as a result of using consumer credit (particularly credit cards) excessively with a control group who had not. The credit problem group were recruited through the Northern California Credit Counselling Services, which limits the generalisability of the study somewhat, as all these people had sought out assistance for their problems. Despite this and the poor response rate (13 per cent), the study does shed some further light on debt and addictive buying, since the participants completed very long questionnaires covering a variety of areas. Measures were taken of locus of control, self-efficacy, self-esteem, attitudes towards money, decision making under risk, sensation seeking, life events and a range of demographic and economic indicators. A hierarchical discriminant analysis was used with groups of variables being entered in the order: background characteristics (including financial situation), adverse life events, psychological variables. Only the addition of the psychological variables significantly improved ability to identify correctly people with credit problems, though given that the control group was contructed to be similar to the credit-problem group in terms of age and socio-economic representation, this is not surprising. More interesting was the similarity between the profile of the typical person with a credit problem and an addicted buyer. Those with credit problems had low self-esteem, low self-efficacy and an external locus of control, which mirrors the picture of addicted buyers presented above.

## The future?

Since the publication of the old *Economic Mind* back in 1986, there has been a vast number of investigations into personal financial management and gambling. At that time there had been almost no research into compulsive consumption, only fragmented work on debt and, other than the extensive econometric literature, only exploratory work into saving (e.g. Furnham, 1985). We have tried to give an overview of just some of these studies in this chapter; now it is time to look to the future.

Our view is that, in this area, psychologically minded economists and economically minded psychologists and sociologists have been moving closer in their understanding, but that there remains an important gap. This was dramatised for two of us, who participated in a workshop on saving held at Tilburg University in

December 1992. Peter Lunt gave a very interesting talk based loosely on the ideas of Mary Douglas and others, which stressed the importance of culture, communication and social groups in explaining economic behaviour. At the end of this, one of the economists present put a long and complicated maximisation equation on the blackboard and said 'I think what Peter is saying is this' (or words to that effect). But this was not what Peter had been saying; on the contrary, he had been highly critical of the individualistic maximisation model. Economists have been happy to incorporate ideas from psychology that they can use in their models (such as time preference) and other social sciences have acknowledged that economic factors play a crucial part in explaining saving and debt – but so far we lack an integrated model that draws on insights from all sides.

So the first need is for further integrated theoretical development. Our feeling is that this will need to focus on the nature of the self in economic psychology. It has been taken for granted in the past in economics that this is unitary; hence the idea of self-interest (in other words, utility maximisation). All the evidence from the other social sciences suggests that it is not. Crucially it is also not divorced from the social context: selves are related to social group membership and so individualistic theories will always miss something.

The second need is for developments in methodology. There is an over-reliance by current researchers on the questionnaire; there is an assumption that self-report is reliable, that people are able and willing to tell researchers about their financial behaviour and that scales that measure time preference, risk aversion, attitudes to debt, attitudes to gambling, etc. reflect fairly consistent and persistent individual differences and do not depend on the situation and the desire to present a coherent self-image. The evidence from other areas is that this assumption is not justified; many people are ill-informed about their own financial state and may wish to present an idealised picture of their position. Investigators have also, with some honourable exceptions, tended to use methods which provide a snap-shot of the situation, which means that we are unable to make clear statements about causality and have to rely upon recollections to derive a picture of, for example, a debtor's or gambler's 'career'. Groenland (1992) has suggested that one possibility would be to use a 'Dynamic Process Tracing Approach' since there is not one decision to save or not save, or bet or not, or take out a loan or not, but a string of serially ordered decisions and acts. This would involve selecting a homogeneous group and first carrying out in-depth interviews to find out the major dynamic patterns for this group. A questionnaire would be developed based on these interviews which could be personalised and would be administered by a computer – this means that questions referring to individual acts and decisions would depend upon the answers to previous questions. Alternative methods (e.g. diary studies) may also be appropriate. Whatever the merits of Groenland's proposal, we have probably gone as far as we can with the mail questionnaire; it has given us the bare bones but can do little more. To put flesh on the bones (or better still, to animate the result) will need a Steven Spielberg of an economic psychologist.

# Chapter 5

# Poverty: aspects of the psychological literature

## Introduction

In contrast to many of the other social sciences – anthropology, economics, political science, sociology – psychology has not paid particular attention to poverty. It is even true that if one examines the few existing texts in economic psychology it is rare to find 'poverty' in the index. Why is poverty as a topic neglected? Surely its cause and alleviation are worthy of study? Is it merely a result of uneven distribution of wealth? Why does poverty exist in a rich country? Can it be prevented? All these questions (which clearly have major social policy implications) have not caught the imagination of psychologists. Paradoxically, in times of economic expansion (the 1960s) and in rich countries (the United States) psychologists appear to have taken most interest in poverty (Allen, 1970). Another paradox explored by some psychologists is that many poor people appear to express considerable life satisfaction (Olson and Schober, 1993).

However the economic downturn of the late 1980s throughout almost all of the western world has caused mass unemployment, homelessness and of course concomitant poverty which has in fact been addressed by psychologists. Thus Shinn and Weitzman (1990) argue that research on homelessness has focused on the problems of homeless individuals, sometimes diverting attention from underlying causes and reinforcing stereotypes about the population. They believe it is necessary to integrate studies that focus on individual-level, social *and* socio-economic context factors associated with homelessness. They are also sensitive to the issue of causality:

> Many factors listed as potential precursors of homelessness are also potential consequences of it. For example, although studies of people who are already homeless typically find that they have few social supports, a study of families at the point of requesting shelter found that they had slightly more relatives and friends than a comparison sample of poor housed families, and they had been in contact with them more recently, presum-

ably in a failed effort to avoid entering shelter. Thus the state of being homeless may disrupt social ties. There is also evidence that people may wear out their welcomes in the homes of relatives and friends before becoming more literally homeless. Many other variables, especially at the individual and social level, share this causal ambiguity. As already noted, homelessness might precipitate depression or a psychotic episode, lead to poor health or job loss, induce substance use, or deplete coping resources.   (p. 6)

Nearly all researchers in this field are concerned that psychological, sociological and economic research inform social policy. Blasi (1990) noted that:

If research is to inform efforts to end mass homelessness, the focus of current research must be broadened and research questions redefined. Epidemiological studies can indicate only who is likely to lose in the competition to find housing. But the causes of homelessness may ultimately have much more to do with social facts that account for the distribution of housing and other resources than with specific characteristics of individual homeless people. Much useful research remains to be done on such things as how images of homelessness are communicated through the mass media, the determinants of attitudes of both ordinary citizens and policy-making elites toward the poor and homeless, how and why organized advocacy on these issues has succeeded, and how and why it has failed.

Suffice to say that some of the most important topics in poverty research have been almost totally neglected by psychologists. These include the definition, measurement, incidence and characteristics of poverty; the life of the poor; the causes of and remedies for poverty; and politics, social policy and poverty. Poverty for the psychologist is a sort of Pandora's box – the obvious problems are immediately apparent. Poverty is a comparative, economic concept that can rarely be isolated from more general questions of inequality. Because the definition of poverty is problematic and many of the questions concerning poverty are structural, involving macro-economic or political factors, psychologists have been hesitant to apply psychological concepts to poverty. Furthermore, others have been convinced that any psychological analysis would be a fundamental attribution error in that one would erroneously focus on individuals and their behaviour rather than economic and industrial organisations and institutions.

However more recently psychologists have attempted to consider their role in the analysis of poverty. Harper (1991) believes much previous research has been laden with pathologising victim-blaming and ethnocentric assumptions. Others have also argued that attempts to 'psychologise' political and economic problems are both unproductive and unmoral. Thus Connolly (1985) has wondered whether we need to develop theories and methodologies in psychology specifically for third-world countries.

Harper (1991) believes that one of the major contributions of psychology to both alleviating and understanding poverty is research on the images of the poor, perhaps promoting ideas that the poor are actively working to resolve their problems. He believes:

the psychologist has much to offer in describing perceptions of poverty and in designing interventions for attempting to change such perceptions. Psychologists can also offer useful analysis of the organisational processes responsible for the creation of poverty. Although there is little psychological research on such institutional influences there is a vast body of organisational psychology literature.   (p. 99)

Poverty can be defined both relatively and absolutely. In absolute 'objective' terms it can be defined in terms of total (weekly or monthly) earnings which are insufficient for a maintenance of basic physical and mental health. A minimal amount may be specified by government agencies and all falling below this amount can then be said to be poor by definition. Alternatively, an 'objective' definition could be the 10 (or so) per cent of the population who earn the least. That is, one can have a relative objective definition. It is also possible to make some 'subjective' (non-economic) definition of poverty in terms of people's experience. Townsend (1979) has, however, argued:

> definitions which are based on some conception of 'absolute' deprivation disintegrate upon close and sustained examination and deserve to be abandoned. Poverty has often been defined, in the words of an OECD review, 'in terms of some absolute level of minimum needs, below which people are regarded as being poor, for purpose of social and government concern, and which does not change through time'. In fact, people's needs, even for food, are conditioned by the society in which they live and to which they belong, and just as needs differ in different societies so they differ in different periods of the evolution of single societies. Any conception of poverty as 'absolute' is therefore inappropriate and misleading.
>
> The second conclusion which might be drawn is that, though the principal definitions put forward historically have invoked some 'absolute' level of minimum needs, they have in practice represented rather narrow conceptions of relative deprivation and deserve to be clarified as such. Thus Seebohm Rowntree's definition mounted in effect to a conception of nutritional deprivation relative to the level believed to be required for members of the manual working class at the turn of the century to function efficiently. That definition corresponded with contemporary Liberal interpretations of the rights and needs of labour in industrial society and was class standard. The US Social Security Administration Poverty Index is similar in basic respects. It is a stringent view of nutritional deprivation relative to the minimally adequate diets achieved by low-income families in 1959 who were managing their budgets economically.   (p. 39)

Townsend (1979) insists on the distinction between subjective, collective and objective definitions of poverty and suggests that to understand poverty properly it is important to document all public and private resources which contribute to actual standards of living but which are inequally distributed. Nevertheless he admits that a definition of poverty must involve value-judgements but feels it is important to make the criteria for the definition as objective as possible.

Notwithstanding serious problems in the definition and measurement of poverty there exist a number of theories for the causes of poverty. These theories – because they come from different disciplines – focus on different factors, operate at different levels of abstraction and are made explicit by people with different values and axioms. Sullivan *et al.* (1980) have attempted to classify how three classic perspectives on social problems view poverty:

From the *functionalist* perspective, poverty becomes a social problem when it no longer performs this function of motivating people to make productive contributions to society. This might occur if there were large numbers of poor because the system was unable to reward all those who performed important tasks; or it might occur if, because of some inequalities in the system, the performance of important tasks only carried a small likelihood of moving up in the stratification system ... Poverty becomes a social problem, from this perspective when the poor are no longer able to adapt to their plight and thus pose a threat to the functioning of society. ...

For the *conflict* theorist, it is not the breakdown of the culture of poverty that constitutes a problem: rather the culture of poverty itself is a social problem because it inhibits the ability of the poor to struggle with other groups over scarce resources. ...

From the conflict perspective, poverty becomes a social problem when some group feels that the existing distribution of resources is unfair and unjust and that something can and should be done about it. ... For the conflict theorist, the emphasis is on more relative criteria. One is poor relative to what other groups have. Rather than establishing absolute cut-off points, one must think in terms of relative inequality. ...

For *interactionists*, poverty is a matter of shared expectations – and the poor often share the negative definition of themselves that is held by others in society. Those who are the objects of such labelling are stigmatised and may begin to behave in accordance with those expectations. The interactionist emphasises that poverty is not just a matter of economic deprivation, but involves the person's self-concept. (pp. 376–8)

Of course there are both orthodox and radical economic theories. Orthodox theories have not tended to look much at the distribution of personal incomes, preferring instead to look at aggregate data (Townsend, 1979). However, where they have, it is assumed that there is a strong positive relationship between income and productivity, the latter of which is determined by such factors as ability, education, skills and expertise. Thus the focus of these theories is on the individual differences in school achievement, education, etc. rather than on institutional or government factors. Alternative more radical economic theories have stressed various other forces which determine wage levels and the demand for labour, such as the influence of trade unions and government. These radical theorists see the labour market divided by class into primary (stable, well-paid) and secondary (unstable, badly paid) sectors which determine both a worker's productivity and his/her income. These radical theories are proposed by both economists (Gordon, 1972) and sociologists (Coates and Silburn, 1970; Townsend, 1979) and are heavily influenced by Marxist ideas. However, there are other sociological and anthropological theories which are much more socio-psychological in nature. Three will be considered, the last of which has probably attracted most attention.

## Minority group theory

This represented an early attempt by Rowntree (1901) not so much to discuss the ultimate causes of poverty, but to describe the characteristics of the poor. His 'theory' has three interesting facets. First, there was a distinction between primary and secondary poverty, which had different causes:

| *Primary poverty* | *Secondary poverty* |
|---|---|
| Death of wage-earner | Drink |
| Incapacity of wage-earner (accident, illness) | Betting and gambling |
| Chief wage-earner unemployed | Ignorant/careless housekeeping |
| Chronic irregularity of work | Irregularity of income |
| Largeness of family | |
| Lowness of wage | |

In a sense this represented an attempt to distinguish the deserving from the non-deserving poor. Secondly, Rowntree hinted at, but never fully explored, the concept of a cycle of poverty with certain categories of people descending into and unable to escape from poverty. Thirdly, and related to the above, this early theory began to typologise the poor into various groups: the old, the unemployed, the sick, etc. The idea of a minority group was to have an important influence on how others saw the behaviour of the poor.

It is perhaps incorrect to describe the minority-group approach as a theory but it clearly had important ideas in it. Indeed running through a good deal of the social psychological studies on poverty is the idea of *labelling* which has been applied to all minority groups.

## Functional analysis of poverty

Functional analysis – the sociological idea that persistent social patterns and structures fulfil important basic functions – has also been applied to poverty. Gans (1972) has argued that poverty fulfils a number of important functions for special interest or socio-economic groups, though of course it is dysfunctional for others. He lists fifteen functions which include the economic, social, cultural and political:

1. The existence of poverty makes sure that 'dirty work' (dangerous, temporary, undignified, menial) is done.
2. The poor, either directly or indirectly, subsidise many activities that benefit the affluent such as consumption and investment in the private economy (by virtue of the low wages that they receive), and through paving regressive taxes.
3. Poverty creates jobs and markets to serve the poor such as social workers, prostitutes and peacetime armies.
4. The poor buy products (second-hand clothes, stale food) not wanted by others and consult professionals too old or poorly trained to attract more affluent clients.
5. The poor may be labelled and punished as deviants in order to uphold the legitimacy of dominant social norms regarding, for instance, work and health care.
6. The disabled or unlucky poor provide the better-off with opportunities for emotional satisfaction in the form of charity, compassion and patronage crucial in the Judeo-Christian ethic.
7. The poor also offer the rich vicarious participation in the uninhibited sexual,

alcoholic and drug-taking habits that they are supposed to have.

8. Poverty helps to guarantee the status of the non-poor – they remain a reliable, relatively permanent measuring rod for status comparison.
9. The poor assist the upward mobility of the non-poor because, being denied educational and other opportunities, they enable others to obtain better jobs.
10. The poor help the economic viability of various businesses and professions such as middle-class civic organisations and the churches so justifying their continued existence.
11. The poor perform cultural factors such as providing their labour on various great building projects or providing the surplus capital to create 'high culture' (e.g. build art monuments).
12. The poor have low culture – artefacts, music, poetry – which becomes adopted and then 'owned' by the rich.
13. The poor serve as symbolic constituencies or opponents for various political groups: vanguards of the revolution for the Left; the spendthrift and dishonest for the Right.
14. The poor, being unable to do otherwise, can be made to absorb the economic and political costs of technological and economic change.
15. Because the poor vote less and participate in politics less than other groups, the political system has been able to ignore them.

The thesis of the functionalists is not that poverty should or must exist but that it does exist because it is useful to a number of groups in society and that many of the functional alternatives to poverty would be quite dysfunctional for more affluent members of society. Gans concludes:

> That social phenomena which are functional for affluent groups and dysfunctional for poor ones persist; that when the elimination of such phenomena through functional alternatives generates dysfunctions for the affluent, they will continue to persist; and that phenomena like poverty can be eliminated only when they either become sufficiently dysfunctional for the affluent or when the poor can obtain enough power to change the system of social stratification.   (p. 288)

Some studies have considered the functional perception of poverty in India. Pandey, Kakkar and Bohra (1982) asked rural and urban, male and female northern Indians the extent to which they believed in the functional nature of poverty. Although the trends were in the predicted direction, none of the analyses reached significance, yet all believed poverty to be functional in India.

Functional theories have, however, been criticised on a number of grounds. It has been objected that functional theories are teleological, and thus incur the logical error of placing the cause of an event after it in time. However, this takes place in any self-regulating system with a negative feedback loop. For example, in a thermostat the behaviour of the system leads to the goal of a certain temperature being attained, though the goal was actually set before this temperature was reached. Homeostatic processes, whereby the body maintains the constancy of its internal environment, operate in a similar way. Teleological explanations are also used in biology to explain the existence of parts of the body in terms of their contribution to the working and survival of the organism. The process behind such functional relationships is natural selection acting on spontaneous mutations in the genes. It has also been objected that functionalism encourages or reflects a conservative bias by emphasising the positive functions of every aspect of the status quo, from the class system to the royal family. Advocates of social change can try to bring about alternative institutions to meet the same needs, or to meet them better, and to avoid areas of dysfunction in society (e.g. groups of people whose needs are not being met). Finally, Coser (1964) objected that functionalists see conflict as dysfunctional, and argued that conflict can have positive functions: for example duelling can allow the free expression of pent-up hostile feelings, and thus preserve a group. Groups can define themselves through struggling with other groups; and conflict can bring about what may be beneficial social changes.

Whether or not functional theories are either necessary or sufficient to explain the perpetuance of poverty in different cultures at different times, they do provide a clear picture particularly of some of the latent or hidden functions of poverty.

## The subcultural theory of poverty

The anthropologist Lewis (1951, 1965) elaborated, clarified and popularised a view that had been in existence for some time. He pointed out that the poorest sections of many societies (English, American, Mexican, French) shared very similar values, interpersonal relations, a family and community structure and had similar spending patterns and concept of time. That is, there appears to be a distinctive pan-cultural, self-perpetuating culture of poor people. The poor form a unique society within society: their beliefs, attitudes and values are passed on from one generation to the next and their life proceeds with different expectations at a different rhythm. The poor are separate and different, not only economically but also intellectually and emotionally.

Part of the appeal of Lewis' work is the careful detail and vivid description. He writes of the characteristics of the poor thus:

> the lack of effective participation . . . in the major institutions of the larger society . . . they have a low level of literacy and education, usually do not belong to labour unions, are not members of political parties, generally do not participate in the national welfare agencies, and make very little use of banks, hospitals, department stores, museum or art galleries. They have a critical attitude towards some of the basic institutions of the dominant classes, hatred of the police, mistrust of government and those in high position, and a cynicism which extends over to the church . . . [they] are aware of middle-class values, talk about them, and even claim some of them as their own, but on the whole they do not live by them . . . on the local community level, we find poor housing conditions, crowding, gregariousness, but above all a minimum of organization beyond the level of the nuclear and extended family . . . [although] there may be a sense of community and esprit de corps . . . people with a culture of poverty are provincial and locally oriented and have very little sense of history. They know only their own troubles, their own local conditions, their own neighbourhood, their own way of life.   (Lewis, 1968: 26)

According to this poverty theory, poor families are likely to be unstable, often headed by females who are less able to respond to the needs of the children. There is usually considerable discontinuity in family life, with marriages dissolving and the make-up of the family changing. These families do not provide the supportive and stable environment that helps children to acquire the skills, education and motivation so that they might work their way out of the cycle of poverty. The poor are also isolated from the centres of decision making about their lives and do not involve themselves in political activities or join groups that might exert political influence.

Because of these experiences, the poor feel cut off from the sources of power in society. The poor tend to be fatalistic, believing (quite correctly) that they have little control over what happens to them and thus become resigned to the degrading and unpleasant conditions in which they live. The culture of poverty is also marked by a present-time orientation – a tendency to seek gratification in the present and not worry about the future. Long-range plans and goals are secondary to pleasurable pursuits in the present.

Despite the popularity and intuitive appeal of the culture of poverty theory, it has come under considerable attack. Some (e.g. Coward, Feagin and William, 1974) have provided data which suggest that the characteristics of the culture of poverty are less common among the poor than suggested by the theory, and that these characteristics may be part of the culture of numerous groups in society rather than simply a result of poverty. Others (Ryan, 1971) have objected to the individualistic, 'blame the poor' aspect of this theory which ignores the lack of opportunity, the discriminations and the prejudice that cause much poverty.

Townsend (1979) has pointed out five problems with Lewis' theory and work:

1. The research method was individual-oriented and uncontrolled:

   Because behaviour was described almost wholly through unstructured individual self-histories, it was inevitable that the patterns of elaborate social organization and in particular the influence upon individuals and communities of values, beliefs and institutions which are nationally or regionally controlled, should have gone largely unexamined and even unremarked. He concentrated on the family and not the subsystems and forces of the wider society as the principal unit of analysis.   (p. 67)

2. Many of the criteria of poverty – apathy, fatalism, inferiority, despair – were formulated in terms of middle-class values, and chosen to contrast with them.
3. The criteria used to distinguish the subculture of poverty were ambiguous, inexact and unquantified. Lewis distinguished between those who belonged to the subculture of poverty and a larger class of those who lived in poverty, but did not state the non-tautological reasons for this separation.
4. The evidence from a number of studies failed to confirm Lewis' findings: 'Much of the evidence presented by Lewis was inconclusive. He emphasized the limited parochial interests and the lack of class consciousness of people with a culture of poverty, and yet large parts of the testimony in his books suggest the contrary' (p. 69).

5. The theory is inconsistent because on the one hand it suggests that poverty is perpetuated by socialisation and social control, but on the other hand suggests that many of the supposed values of the subculture are not accepted by its members. That is, because it can be shown that certain features continue from one generation to another, it does not imply that they have internal (within-group, socialising) causes but could equally be external:

Lewis correctly reported many of the stresses and penalties of life for the poor which affect styles of living. But what he did not do was to distinguish clearly between working-class culture and a subculture of poverty and relate these to the 'structure' of deviance in society. Neither did he begin to disentangle the effects upon behaviour of a simple lack of resources from other cultural influences. (p. 70)

The three theories outlined above – minority group, functional and subcultural – though hotly debated, have contributed most to social psychological ideas and research. This has occurred mainly because each has specified various behaviours which are characteristic of, or describe, the poor and may or may not be responsible for the cause and perpetuation of poverty. This is particularly true of the last theory which, because it appears to point out cognitive and behavioural universals in the poor, seemed to identify the crucial psychological variables that caused poverty.

Psychologists are also interested in taxonomising and forming typologies as a necessary stage in the description of behaviour. Much of the literature concerning poverty consists in describing deprivation in terms of housing, health, education, work and general life-style. More interesting for the psychologist are attempts to differentiate minority groups living in poverty. Townsend (1979) has identified thirteen minority groups as such for a British study:

1. One-parent family: households in which there was a child, one of whose parents was not resident.
2. Woman and adult dependent: households in which there were two or more adults one of whom was an unmarried, separated, divorced or widowed woman who was partly or wholly supporting the other(s) (usually related to her), none of whom was in employment, by means of either income from employment or an unearned income which was larger than that of the dependent(s).
3. Large family: households in which there were four or more dependent children belonging to the same family.
4. Unemployed: households in which there was an adult of under 65 years of age who had been unemployed for eight weeks or more during the previous twelve months, consecutively or altogether.
5. Households affected by the long-term sickness or injury of an adult under 65: households in which there was an adult under 65 who had been ill or injured for eight weeks or more and off work during the previous twelve months, consecutively or altogether.
6. Households in which there was a disabled adult under 65: households in which there was an adult scoring 5 or more according to a special index of disability, or scoring 1 or more and having a disablement condition: epilepsy, mental

handicap, breathlessness or pain in the chest; difficulty in physical movement; having a severe nervous condition (such as depression, inability to concentrate or sleep); inability to read; inability to hear or join in ordinary conversation.

7. Households in which there was a 'borderline' disabled adult under 65: households in which there was an adult scoring 1–4 according to a special index of disability, or having a disablement condition (as listed above), or having disability only for certain times of the year.
8. Households in which there was a disabled child: households containing a child of under 15 years of age who, through illness or disability, had been continuously confined to bed or to the house for at least eight weeks; those with a disablement condition (as listed above); and those attending a special school, training centre, club, day or occupation centre, out-patients' department, etc., for reason of long-term illness or handicap.
9. Households in which there was a severely handicapped adult over 65: households in which there was an adult of 65 years of age or over scoring 9 or more according to a special index of disability, or had been confined to bed or the house continuously for eight weeks or more.
10. Households with low-paid female earners: households in which women aged 21–59 were earning less than £8 gross per week for at least thirty hours' work. This figure was about two-thirds of the median for women.
11. Households with low-paid male earners: households in which men aged 21–64 were earning less than £14 gross per week for at least thirty hours' work. This figure was a little lower than two-thirds of the median for men of this age.
12. Households in which there was a non-white person.
13. Households in which there was someone born in Eire.

Other sociological writers have attempted to describe different categories of the poor, such as, the welfare poor, the marginal poor, the working poor. Some have looked at rural dwellers, minority ethnic groups, the young and the old. However, underlying nearly all these classifications and typologies is the idea of the difference between the deserving and the undeserving poor. Matza and Miller (1976) in attempting a 'sub-employment' conception of poverty have tried to distinguish the reputable from the disreputable poor. The former consist of the following:

1. Unemployed individuals who are willing, able and currently available for work and who have taken definite steps in the last month to find a job.
2. Discouraged workers who want jobs but are not looking because they think no work is available, lack the necessary experience or schooling, are too young or too old, or have other personal handicaps making them unattractive to employers.
3. Currently employed family heads and unrelated individuals whose earnings in the previous twelve months were inadequate to lift their households above the poverty threshold.
4. Other currently employed household heads earning less than a poverty income during the preceding year because of intermittent employment, less than full-time work and/or low wages.

5. Workers employed part-time during the survey week not included in the previous category, who want full-time jobs but cannot find them, have been laid off during the survey week, or have some other economic impediment requiring part-time employment.

The disreputable poor include the dregs (such as beggars, tramps, criminals and prostitutes who have been born into poverty and never left it), the immigrants and newcomers (who, because they have no useful employable skills or financial resources cannot avoid gravitating to slums), skidders (addicts and perverts who have fallen from higher social niches) and the infirm (those who have moved downwards because of age, injury or illness).

Others have drawn up similar typologies but have failed to explain where the types are similar and where different with regard to the causes and consequences of their poverty. These taxonomies have been based on either economic or government classification schemes or sociological concepts and are of not great interest for the psychologist who is more interested in behaviour differences.

## Psychological theories for the causes of poverty

There are many reasons why the obvious joke about psychological theories of poverty being poor theories in psychology are true. Firstly, poverty is a relative economic concept which is too broad and heterogeneous a concept for psychologists. The poor include children, the aged, the unemployed, the handicapped, mentally ill people, migrants, etc., some who have always been poor, others who have recently become poor. That is, there are quite distinct poverty groups like the welfare poor, the marginal poor and the working poor. Because of some (seemingly arbitrary) cut-off point they are all classified as poor yet have very little in common psychologically. Secondly, poverty is almost always a consequence of (or at least a correlate of) some other variable such as socio-economic class, intelligence, etc., or some other set of variables which psychologists are more experienced at measuring and theorising about. Psychologists are highly sensitive to moderating and intervening variables that come between individual and group differences and poverty. Thirdly, and perhaps most importantly, psychology (even social psychology) is not aimed at analysing macro-sociological variables such as poverty and has neither the appropriate level of theoretical and conceptual analysis nor the most appropriate methodological tools for analysing poverty. Social psychology is concerned with the individual and the social and economic system within which s/he is enmeshed so that it may be useful in explaining why some individuals from poor homes remain poor while others do not, but cannot explain the existence of mass poverty over time. Psychological theories and variables have indeed been applied to the poor with a moderate degree of success but they are of necessity never sufficient (and possibly not even necessary) to explain poverty however it is defined. Few, if any, psychologists would be as naive or arrogant as to suggest that poverty can be fully understood or eradicated by psychological factors alone. By concentrating on beliefs, expectations, values and motives, psychology is not asserting the pre-eminence of behavioural over the economic, political or sociological factors, but merely suggesting that they too have an important role to play.

Poverty has been conceived of as either an independent or a dependent variable. When using it as a dependent variable, psychologists attempt to isolate psychological phenomena characteristic of the poor and thought to be a consequence of the deprived conditions under which they have lived. This will be discussed under the heading 'The behaviour of the poor'. When using it as an independent variable, psychologists attempt to ascertain which beliefs or behaviourable variables contribute to an individual's poverty in some theoretical way. However, to establish that a particular behaviour pattern or belief system is associated with poverty does not imply direction or causality. It may be that, as with so many other aspects of human behaviour, there is bidirectional causality between poverty and various psychological phenomena.

There is no shortage of potentially useful psychological variables (individual differences) which may be used partially to explain the existence and maintenance of poverty. It should be pointed out that none of these variables was constructed specifically to explain poverty but other more general aspects of social behaviour, and seemed pertinent to the problem of poverty. Some of the 'theories' seem self-evident, even tautological, while others offer a unique perspective both in the way they explain poverty and in the way they offer insights as to how to 'remove' it. There have also been some attempts to taxonomise poverty. For instance, Rainwater (1970) has offered five perspectives on the poor based on two dimensions: the poor being characterised as weak or strong; and evaluated as virtuous or evil. These kind of taxonomies are, however, more helpful when it comes to social policy rather than to theorising.

A good deal of psychological research and theorising on poverty has concerned children, as early socialisation and learning experiences have been stressed as very important determinants in understanding the psychology of poverty. The primary (parental), secondary (schooling) and tertiary (peer group) socialising agents are thought to play a central role in shaping how poor people think, act and feel. It has been argued that because a child's academic performance depends heavily upon its internalised mechanisms of emotional self-evaluation (Katz, 1970) and that poor children are more self-critical, they tend to underachieve at school. But a good deal of the debate in this area has concerned the hereditability of various traits and skills among the poor. For one school (Jensen and Reynolds, 1982) the role of hereditary factors in determining difference in intelligence is both paramount and proven, whereas other schools of thought have maintained that individual differences in mental abilities are determined primarily by the environment. Although the argument has been applied specifically to intelligence and race, some have attempted to consider whether genetic factors contribute to poverty (Crow, 1970; Vanderberg, 1970). Suffice to say that there is no agreement about the importance of genetic factors in determining poverty, though it is quite reasonable to assume that they have some effect. Part of the problem with the heredity/environment literature (apart from its complexity and political overtones) is the fact that while it may be shown that either or both genetic and hereditary factors determine certain traits and abilities (intelligence, dexterity, strength), it is yet another conceptual step to explain how these traits and abilities relate to poverty.

Perhaps the most interesting psychological work has been done on personality correlates of poverty. A number of factors, many of which are related, have been isolated.

## Time perspective and delay of gratification

A number of researchers before and after Oscar Lewis (1951) have pointed out the present-time orientation and short time perspective in the poor. Allen (1970) has argued that 'the assumption that the poor have shorter time perspective is rather untenable in the light of empirical findings' (p. 247) because of confounded variables (age and ethnic origin with class), weak methodology (projective techniques and story-telling) and equivocal results. Allen (1970) is also disparaging of the more extensive research on postponement of gratification which is a concept akin to impulse control and ego strength. A person's ability to postpone gratification (delay immediate, less valued goals for the sake of later, more valued goals) is supposed to reflect a more mature personality orientation in which the pleasure principle is superseded by the reality principle. In a summary of the extensive literature (much of it his own work) Mischel (1981) notes:

> Two contrasting patterns of delay and impulsivity have been conceptualized as extreme poles. On one end is the individual who predominantly chooses larger, delayed rewards or goals for which he must either wait or work. This person is more likely to be oriented toward the future and to plan carefully for distant goals. He also is apt to have high scores on 'ego control' measures, high achievement motivation, to be more trusting and socially responsible, to have a high level of aspiration, and to show less uncontrolled impulsivity. This extreme pattern resembles what has been called the 'Puritan character structure'. Socioculturally, this pattern tends to be found most often in middle and upper (in contrast to lower) socioeconomic classes, and in highly achievement-oriented ('Protestant ethic') cultures. This pattern of high ego strength is also related to a relatively high level of competence, as revealed by higher intelligence, more mature cognitive development, and a greater capacity for sustained attention.
>
> At the opposite extreme is the individual who predominantly prefers immediate gratification and declines the alternative of waiting or working for larger, delayed goals. Correlated with this is a greater concern with the immediate present than with the future, and great impulsivity. Socioculturally, this pattern is correlated with membership in the lower socioeconomic class, with membership in cultures in which the achievement orientation is low, and with indices of lesser social and cognitive competence.   (p. 47)

As ever, not all the published studies confirm the association between delay of gratification and poverty but the theoretical formulation seems sound and the results encouraging.

## Need for achievement

Since the work of Murray in the 1930s various researchers have been interested in achievement motivation (McClelland, 1961). Achievement is considered an individual motive that includes concern for meeting and excelling various social standards of performance. There is a rich and fairly complex literature on need for achievement: for instance, researchers have distinguished between the motive to achieve success (as measured by TAT stories) from the motive to avoid failure. At the very outset of this research investigators stressed the relationship between this personality disposition and actual behaviour in a variety of settings over time. McClelland (1961), however, extended the concept to a societal level and attempted to find relationships between the achievement level of a society (as measured by, for instance, children's stories) and the economic development of that country.

Many studies carried out on children and adolescents have shown, as predicted, that the need for achievement is lower in the poor and the working class (Rosen, 1959). Similarly, achievement motivation appears to be correlated with upward social mobility. Although the literature in this field is fairly clear (albeit slightly tautological) three problems are apparent. Firstly, there is the ever-present problem of mediating variables such as intelligence, age and race, which have been demonstrated to mediate between achievement motivation and socio-economic states. Secondly, there are very real problems in measuring achievement motivation by the unreliable, and often biased, projective techniques most often employed. Thirdly, although McClelland (1961) has offered an aetiological account of the origin of achievement motivation (see Chapter 11) there is very little work that attempts to assess the direction of causality when it comes to the relationship between poverty and the need for achievement. Pareek (1970) has attempted a conceptual relationship between motivation and poverty. He provided a paradigm for the culture of poverty, reproduced in Figure 5.1. He also noted some of the consequences of low need achievement: disproportionately very low risk taking; interest in chance not control; lack of interest in feedback; seeking the company of friends not experts; and lack of activity and initiative.

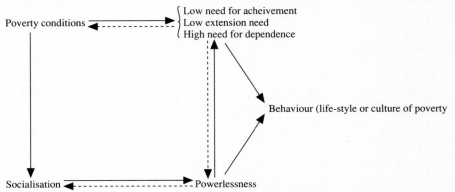

**Figure 5.1** A representation of the culture of poverty. Reprinted by permission of the publisher from Pareek, in Allen: *Psychological Factors in Poverty,* Markham, Chicago, 1970.

## Locus of control, just world and related beliefs

One of the most popular concepts in cognitive social psychology is that of locus of control, that is, general expectancies regarding one's ability to control one's life. People who believe that most life events are consequent upon their actions (behaviour, personality) are said to have an 'expectancy of internal control', while people who believe events in their lives to be controlled by luck, chance, powerful others or powers beyond their control or comprehension have an external locus of control. Numerous studies in the 1960s showed that poor, ethnic, lower socio-economic and other deprived groups had greater external locus of control beliefs than 'normal' groups. However, as in so much of this research, it is unclear whether these beliefs are a cause or consequence of poverty. What is most likely is that there is bidirectional causality and a spiralling effect whereby poverty leads to external control beliefs which in turn help to maintain and increase poverty. Gurin and Gurin (1970) have reviewed the not inconsiderable research on beliefs about expectation and poverty. They conclude:

> Perhaps the overall impression from the expectancy literature we have reviewed is one of complexity, contradiction and tentativeness of our knowledge in this area. . . . Success experience and real changes in opportunities probably can be used to raise the expectancies on low expectancy people. Second studies consistently stress that this be done under conditions where a person feels that the successes come from his own skill and competence. The literature on internal and external control indicates that effects of success and failure are not very reliable when a person feels they do not depend on his own actions. (pp. 97–8)

A related concept is 'just world' beliefs which relate to the idea that the world is a predictable and controllable place in which people get what they deserve. People who hold just world beliefs tend to blame the victim for his/her fate irrespective of the factors causing the problem. Thus the non-poor with just world beliefs see the poor as lazy and undeserving. Furthermore if the poor themselves have just world beliefs (which is a cultural norm; Lerner, 1980) they would tend to derogate themselves with the probable consequence that they lose face and develop a poor self-concept. Once again the direction of causality between just-world beliefs and poverty is not clear.

There are other related beliefs like anomie, the Protestant work ethic (see Chapter 11) and conservatism which overlap with locus of control and just-world beliefs and which operate in much the same way. That is, it may be expected that external locus of control, unjust world, anomie, low Protestant work ethic and non-conservative beliefs contribute to the maintenance of poverty in the poor, while those with the opposite belief system may escape poverty.

## Self-concept, self-esteem and self-worth

Phenomenological theorists have long stressed the importance of the self-concept (a product of social learning) in the determination of social behaviour. Developmental studies have attempted to determine what factors lead to the development, stability and change of the self-concept. Most studies have hypothesised that people from disadvantaged groups (the disabled, the poor, ethnic minorities) will have a more negative self-concept than the general population because of a number of factors – defence against anxiety, admission of inadequacy, reference groups. For Allen (1970) the results remain equivocal. However, a review by Burns (1981) on the psychological literature on the self-concept suggests that it may be a very important factor in helping to explain the origin and maintenance of poverty. For instance, work on the relationship between school children's self-concept and their manifest behaviour perceptions and academic performance shows that successful students are typically characterised by self-confidence, self-acceptance and stable feelings of adequacy, personal competence and personal regard, while unsuccessful students tend to have feelings of uncertainty, low self-regard, self-derogatory attitudes and strong inferiority feelings. The research points strongly to a circular or feedback process which may be generalised to explain poverty; for instance, the process may be represented as in Figure 5.2. This kind of process may also explain why the majority of divorced and separated women perceive themselves as better off than when they were married, even though they in reality have less money (Graham, 1987). A selection of the women's comments exemplify this point: 'Personally I feel better off. Although we've got less money in the family I feel better off because I can control it'; 'Although I have less money it's all mine to allocate where I want . . . I have control now whereas before he used to control me'; 'I know where I am now, because . . . I can control what I spend'. The little money

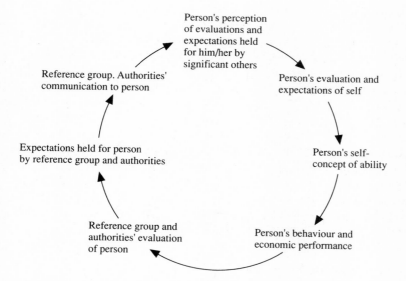

**Figure 5.2**   The circular process of self-concept, behaviour and feedback. Reprinted by permission of the publisher from Burns, *The Self Concept*, Longman.

they do have is their own, under their control and so is probably associated with a greater feeling of self-worth.

Overall the psychological theories are interesting, perhaps necessary, but certainly not sufficient. Most are individual personality theories rather than social psychological theories, which are perhaps not appropriate for understanding the interdependence between the individual and the social and economic system, and the specification of intervening processes. Personality dispositions are clearly important in determining some aspects of poverty, while situational variables clearly predominate in other areas. Most importantly psychological theories need to take into account the well-established problems in social psychological theorising: bidirectional causality, confounding and intervening variables, and the non-linearity (curvilinearity, bimodality) of variables.

## Lay explanations for poverty

As well as explicit, coherent theories for the causes of poverty found in a variety of disciplines (economics, sociology, political science, psychology) there is a fairly considerable literature on lay or everyday explanations for poverty or related phenomena such as begging (panhandling) or homelessness. Some studies are fairly simplistic national surveys where people are asked to attribute poverty to internal or individualistic causes vs. external or societal factors. For instance, a 1945 Opinion Research Survey in America asked a representative sampling 'Why are some of the people always poor?' Relatively few people mentioned economic, political or structural factors such as employment conditions or educational differences; most spoke of lack of effort and initiative, money mismanagement, weak character, or related causes. Other studies have been more restricted in their scope, sample and methodology but have shown similar results.

Perhaps the most thoughtful and careful work on poverty has been the studies of poverty in America. Feagin (1975) asked over 1,000 Americans to rate the importance of eleven reasons why some people were poor in America. Table 5.1 shows his results. More importantly Feagin categorised these explanations into three groups: individualistic (which places responsibility for poverty on the behaviour of poor people), structural (which places responsibility on extreme society and economic forces) and fatalistic (which places responsibility on luck and fate). Furthermore, the results showed various socio-religious, racial, regional, age, income and educational differences. Groups with the largest concentrations of persons giving high priority to individualistic explanations were as follows:

White Protestants and Catholics.
Residents of the south and north-central regions.
The over-50 age group.
The middle-income group.
Groups with middle levels of education.

**Table 5.1**  Reasons given for poverty by 1,000 Americans (per cent)

|  | Very important | Somewhat important | Not important |
|---|---|---|---|
| 1. Lack of thrift and proper money management | 58 | 30 | 11 |
| 2. Lack of effort by the poor themselves | 55 | 33 | 9 |
| 3. Lack of ability and talent among poor people | 52 | 33 | 12 |
| 4. Loose morals and drunkenness | 48 | 31 | 17 |
| 5. Sickness and physical handicaps | 46 | 39 | 14 |
| 6. Low wages in some businesses and industries | 42 | 35 | 20 |
| 7. Failure of US society to provide good schools | 36 | 25 | 20 |
| 8. Prejudice and discrimination against Negroes | 33 | 37 | 26 |
| 9. Failure of private industry to provide enough jobs | 27 | 36 | 31 |
| 10. Being taken advantage of by rich people | 18 | 30 | 45 |
| 11. Just bad luck | 8 | 27 | 60 |

Americans' explanations of poverty

| Importance | Individualistic | Structural | Fatalistic |
|---|---|---|---|
| low | 7 | 18 | 11 |
| medium | 40 | 60 | 71 |
| high | 53 | 22 | 18 |

*Source:* From Subordinating the Poor by Joe R. Feagin, copyright (1975) by Prentice-Hall, Inc. Englewood Cliffs, NJ 07632. Reprinted by permission of the publisher.

In contrast, the groups with the largest proportions ranking high on structuralism were the following:

Black Protestants and Jews.
The under-30 age group.
The low-income group.
The less well-educated.

Feagin (1975) argued that as long as Americans tend to individualise their economic and social problems, attempts at redistributive reform will be impossible. He argues that individualistic views reflect 'false consciousness and mesh well with establishment attempts to maintain the status quo, whereas structural interpretations lend themselves to attempts at counter ideologies and at structural reforms in this society' (p. 126).

Feagin's work was important for a number of reasons. Firstly, his *a priori* classification of explanations into three groups has received fairly considerable backing from factor-analytic studies (Feather, 1974; Singh and Vasudeva, 1977; Furnham, 1982b). Secondly, his study has been replicated in a range of countries: India (Singh and Vasudeva, 1977), Israel (Rim, 1984), Britain (Furnham, 1982b, 1982d), and Australia (Feather, 1974). Thirdly, the variables that apparently discriminated between explanations for poverty (e.g. religion, age, education) have proved equally discriminatory in other studies. Those variables which have shown most discriminatory power with regard to beliefs about poverty have been income and social class, age, rural/urban background, education, ideological beliefs, religion and to a lesser extent sex. Fourthly, he found that explanations for poverty are systematically linked to attitudes to welfare, so suggesting that people hold coherent theories about both the causes of and cures for poverty. Consequently, Feagin's work inspired a great deal of further work in the field concerned mainly with other variables which determine explanations for poverty.

Feather (1974), who replicated this experiment in Adelaide, Australia, was interested in both a cross-cultural comparison and generational differences between parents and their children. He found that Australians were generally less likely than Americans to blame poverty on individualistic reasons, though the pattern of explanations was fairly similar. There were some significant differences in the eleven explanations for poverty offered by the subjects, who were differentiated according to religion, sex, occupation, education and income, though the major differences were between the two age groups (over 75 per cent of the explanations). Younger subjects were less likely to blame poverty on individualistic factors and did not obviously support the Protestant work ethic. However, Feather suggests that other values and beliefs as well as macro-economic factors should also be considered in attempting to predict people's explanations of the causes of behaviour.

> In affluent societies, however, members may believe that there is plenty to go around and that, even though the poor have brought misfortune upon themselves, they should have some part of the plentiful resources that are available. One's reactions to inequalities would therefore depend upon the sometimes harsh economic and social realities of how much is available and whether it can be increased, as well as upon the dominant values, attitudes and modes of causal attribution that have emerged as complex products of one's socialisation.   (p. 215)

The idea that socialisation is important in explanations for poverty was demonstrated by Furnham (1982d), who found that English public-school boys (traditionally from richer middle-class homes) found individualistic explanations for poverty more important than comprehensive-school boys (from poorer working-class homes), who in turn found societal explanations more important. This is consistent with other studies looking at the effects of schooling on values.

A study by Singh and Vasudeva (1977) in India and a very extensive EEC study on the 'Perception of poverty in Europe' (Commission of the European Communities (CEC) Report, 1977) by and large substantiated the findings of Feagin (1975) and Feather (1974) on demographic factors associated with explanations of poverty. The Indian study considered similar age, education and income-related differences but few religious differences. The European study considered how people in the EEC saw and explained poverty. Overall the most common causes of poverty were believed to be – in rank order – poor luck, laziness and lack of willpower and injustice in society. However, there were considerable differences across countries: the Italians and French tended to blame societal factors, the British and Irish the poor themselves, and the Danes fate. Overall the better educated, and the better off most often blamed social injustice, whilst the less well educated and non-leaders tended to blame the poor. An updated near replication of this study reveals some interesting changes over the past decade (CEC 1990). Unemployment now leads the list in most European countries and the attributions of respondents from Ireland and the United Kingdom are less out of line: in 1977 43 per cent of the UK respondents and 30 per cent of the Irish explained poverty with reference to laziness and unwillingness to work; by 1990 the figures had fallen, to 18 per cent and 14 per cent respectively (see Table 5.2).

Across countries, in the most recent survey, the better educated are more likely to blame unemployment, the poorly educated and laziness. Interestingly, those with higher than average incomes are more likely to cite broken families, the social environment and long-term unemployment as explanations revealing some sympathy from among societies' 'winners' not easily explained by a simple self-interest hypothesis.

There are clearly cultural differences in attributional style, yet the rise in long-term unemployment across Europe and elsewhere has had an effect on economic beliefs, which suggests that economic changes, among other things, certainly influence how we explain events and see the world.

Others have related intelligence and personality to explanations for poverty. Rim (1984) found that extraverts and neurotics and the more intelligent prefer societal and fatalistic explanations for poverty in Israel, while introverts non-neurotics and the less intelligent prefer individualistic explanations.

Another variable which has received some attention is political beliefs and

**Table 5.2**  Percentage of people rating explanations for poverty in their own country

|  | Belgium | Denmark | Germany | Greece | Spain | France |
|---|---|---|---|---|---|---|
| Unemployment | 51 | 52 | 43 | 30 | 54 | 66 |
| Alcoholism, drugs | 35 | 44 | 58 | 15 | 41 | 31 |
| Illness | 30 | 51 | 42 | 33 | 16 | 32 |
| Broken families | 30 | 43 | 28 | 26 | 15 | 17 |
| Poor environment | 28 | 6 | 20 | 24 | 28 | 21 |
| Ebbing welfare | 19 | 20 | 19 | 15 | 9 | 17 |
| Laziness | 18 | 15 | 18 | 31 | 9 | 16 |
| Loss of solidarity | 15 | 19 | 11 | 8 | 10 | 22 |
| Education system | 9 | 11 | 7 | 5 | 10 | 17 |
| Too many children | 7 | 3 | 7 | 9 | 18 | 10 |
| Poor area | 8 | 2 | 7 | 13 | 16 | 7 |
| Indifference | 6 | 3 | 5 | 4 | 2 | 10 |

|  | Ireland | Italy | Luxemburg | Holland | Portugal | United Kingdom |
|---|---|---|---|---|---|---|
| Unemployment | 64 | 52 | 38 | 55 | 41 | 60 |
| Alcoholism, drugs | 39 | 37 | 45 | 50 | 30 | 22 |
| Illness | 25 | 32 | 29 | 24 | 37 | 18 |
| Broken families | 33 | 29 | 33 | 41 | 16 | 38 |
| Poor environment | 25 | 26 | 37 | 16 | 28 | 23 |
| Ebbing welfare | 40 | 13 | 7 | 42 | 30 | 33 |
| Laziness | 16 | 19 | 29 | 11 | 9 | 21 |
| Loss of solidarity | 6 | 16 | 12 | 12 | 12 | 12 |
| Education system | 13 | 6 | 12 | 7 | 5 | 11 |
| Too many children | 19 | 19 | 6 | 5 | 25 | 16 |
| Poor area | 13 | 18 | 5 | 4 | 17 | 15 |
| Indifference | 3 | 5 | 5 | 1 | 2 | 3 |

*Source:* CEC (1990, March). Eurobarometer 'The Perception of Poverty in Europe'

poverty explanation. Many have suggested that left-wing people (and post-materi-alists) are more inclined to put down poverty to social causes while the right-wing are more likely to blame the victims. As predicted, Furnham (1982b) found that Conservative (right-wing) voters thought that individualistic explanations for poverty were more important than did Labour (left-wing) voters, who in turn found societal explanations more important than did Conservatives though fatalis-tic explanations showed no difference between the groups and were not rated as important in explaining poverty. Using a simpler questionnaire concerning the attribution of poverty but a more elaborate measure of political beliefs, Pandey, Kakkar and Bohra (1982) found, as predicted, that those politically neutral and right-wingers attributed poverty more to individual habits and ability as well as fate than did the left-wing activists, who in turn attributed poverty in India more to governmental policies and the economic dominance of the few in society. Williamson (1974a, 1974b) has proposed an ideological self-interest theory which predicts a negative correlation between socio-economic status and the perceived motivation of and support for aid for the poor.

Similar research has been carried out in the developing world. Payne and Furnham (1985) investigated national differences in the West Indies. Adolescents from Barbados and Dominica judged societal explanations to be primarily responsi-ble for the cause and persistence of poverty in the Caribbean. However, where there were national differences, it was the Barbadians who were far more concerned with social inequalities and injustices than their Dominican counterparts despite the fact the Dominica is the poorer and less well developed of the two islands. Thus poorer people may be apt to blame themselves for their own poverty. Payne and Furnham suggested that this might be because Barbados has more informative media and that economic inequalities are more exposed.

Most, but not all, of the studies in this area have considered the causes of poverty among unspecified groups. Furnham (1982b) has argued that as different groups in a society are differentially likely to experience poverty, various explanations become salient in explaining these differences. This is also true of different historic periods. Thus Huber and Form (1973) asked a sample of Americans why they thought people went on social security during the Great Depression. Only 4 per cent cited individualistic explanations, yet when asked why people had taken social security during the previous six years, 54 per cent cited individualistic reasons. Similarly Furnham (1982b) asked his subjects to imagine a poor person from one of four groups: black/white; middle/working class and then explain why they were poor. It was established that explanations that may seem salient for one target group are not necessarily so for another. Although there was considerable agreement on the causes of poverty among those groups most susceptible to it, people began to differ radically in the causes of poverty ascribed to groups not usually thought of as poor.

Several more recent studies have confirmed the above findings. Thus Lee, Jones and Lewis (1990) looked at public beliefs about the causes of homelessness. They found beliefs about the causes of current American homelessness emphasised struc-tural forces and bad luck over individualistic factors. Further education, political affiliation and race were significant predictors of these beliefs. Beliefs about the causes of homelessness were also clearly related to perception of the policies needed to deal with the problem.

In two elegant studies Guimond, Begin and Palmer (1989) showed that socialisation in a particular subculture leads quite clearly to the development of person vs system blame ideologies. Thus in their Canadian study the unemployed sample blamed the poor and the unemployed significantly more for their condition than did social science students. Thus the ideology of social groups exerts pressure on members' cognitive/thinking processes; they learn to see the world according to the belief and values of the social group. Hence attributions for poverty are in part a function of the world views of subgroups.

In a recent study Wilson (1991) found beliefs about poverty were affected by exposure to panhandling. That is, the more people on the street are accosted by beggars the more they are likely to regard poverty as a function of personal choice. A natural consequence of all this research on lay beliefs about and representations of the poor has meant that some academics have begun to look at scholarly representations. Thus Bagguley and Mann (1992) have looked at sociological representations of the 'under-class' and find good examples of the same dimensions or distinctions made by lay people.

Finally, although it is not always easy to do so, some attempts have been made to verify public beliefs as to the causes of poverty. Feagin (1975) pointed out that figures available indicated that the public were wrong (or at least they vastly overestimated) the amount of people lying about or having illegitimate children to increase their social security payments. Similarly Goodwin (1973) found that the middle class tended to underestimate the work values (ethic) and life aspirations held by the poor. Indeed a considerable amount of psychological (Allen, 1970) and sociological (Davidson and Gaitz, 1974) research has demonstrated few differences in attitudes, beliefs and values between the poor and those not so badly off. Goodwin (1973) did a path analysis on the relationship between education, age, the work ethic and the perceived motivation of and support for aid to the poor. Naturally those who believed in the work ethic believed the poor to be badly motivated and did not want to support them. They conclude that the work ethic is a fundamental element in popular ideology and that its change could lead to numerous important results.

## Attitudes to the poor and those on social security

A number of studies have attempted to explore the range, structure and determinants of beliefs about the poor as well as which individual difference and demographic factors best predict these beliefs (Vedlitz, 1988). Most of the studies have shown a predictable pattern of findings. For instance studies have shown a weak but noticeable relationship between class and images of the poor, middle class being more negative than the working class (Rainwater, 1968). Similarly Williamson

(1974) noted that older subjects were more negative about the poor than the young, although this could reflect cultural and historical changes. Osgood (1977) noted that rural dwellers had more negative beliefs about the motivation of the poor and were less likely than urban dwellers to support welfare programmes. Some evidence suggests that religious beliefs are related to attitudes to the poor: the more religious the more negative; Protestants more than Catholics are negative about the poor (Feagin, 1975). Other variables which may relate to attitudes to the poor include self-esteem, anomie, interpersonal trust and authoritarianism (Davis, Grube and Morgary, 1984)

A number of studies have been based on the attitude to poverty scale developed by MacDonald (1971b): for instance, attitudes to poverty have been shown to relate to the Protestant work ethic (MacDonald, 1971a), political affiliation (Wagstaff, 1983), birth order (MacDonald, 1971b) and just-world beliefs (Furnham and Gunter, 1984). Thus people who believe in a just world tend to be negative in their attitudes. The results of Furnham and Gunter (1984) are given in Table 5.3.

**Table 5.3**   Just-world beliefs and attitudes towards poverty

|  | Just-world beliefs | | | |
|---|---|---|---|---|
|  | Low | Mid | High | F level |
| 1. By pouring money into poverty programmes we are destroying the very thing that made this a great and prosperous country – competition | 6.14 | 5.87 | 4.64 | 10.63[c] |
| 2. Though I know that their condition is not always their fault, I find poor people unpleasant to be with | 5.35 | 5.75 | 4.80 | 3.83[a] |
| 3. I cannot understand why some people make such a fuss over the disadvantaged state of the poor. Most of them could improve their condition if only they tried | 6.32 | 5.70 | 4.75 | 10.42[c] |
| 4. In this country almost everyone can make it if they try hard enough | 6.28 | 5.62 | 4.10 | 20.25[c] |
| 5. Some people feel that extreme poverty in this country is largely the fault of the poor. By and large, this is true | 6.42 | 6.29 | 5.08 | 12.00[c] |
| 6. Stealing is more excusable among lower-class children than it is among children from middle-class homes | 4.92 | 5.02 | 4.67 | 0.48 |
| 7. Somehow I cannot blame a poor man for hurting a rich man as much as I blame a rich man for hurting a poor man | 3.92 | 4.56 | 4.35 | 0.79 |
| 8. Although we do not like to face it, most people on social security are lazy | 6.17 | 5.62 | 4.83 | 5.89[b] |
| 9. Pouring money into poverty programmes is crippling the national economy and asking too much of people who have worked hard to get what they have | 6.35 | 5.54 | 4.70 | 9.19[c] |
| 10. To solve the population problem and to make life more pleasant for the poor, they should not be permitted to have more than a couple of children per family: that is, there should be compulsory birth control based on income level | 6.07 | 5.81 | 4.77 | 6.57[b] |
| 11. I am in favour of a government-guaranteed minimum annual income – that is, nobody would receive less than a certain income per year | 2.14 | 2.97 | 2.78 | 1.64 |
| 12. Kindness, generosity and love are characteristics found more among the poor than among the wealthy | 3.75 | 4.54 | 4.35 | 1.17 |

[a]$p < 0.05$;   [b]$p < 0.01$;   [c]$p < 0.001$. These scores are the mean on a seven-point agree–disagree scale: 1 = agree; 7 = disagree

In a review, Davis, Grube and Morgan (1984) have pointed out three major shortcomings of the literature on attitudes to the poor. First, most studies have considered how people explain poverty or how the poor behave, but not how respondents felt about appropriate remedies for poverty. Secondly, studies have looked at demographic determinants of attitudes to the poor rather than the influence of personality and general attitudinal variables on specific attitudes and behaviour relating to poverty. They also believe an important gap in the literature concerns the link between prejudice towards minority groups and attitudes towards the poor which has important implications for how beliefs might be changed.

In an attempt to rectify this omission Davis, Grube and Morgan (1984) examined attitudes towards poverty among a large representative sample (N = 2359) in Ireland. They examined the relationship between personality characteristics (e.g. self-esteem, anomie), general social attitudes and beliefs (religiosity, national pride, state efficacy) and attitudes and beliefs about poverty (fatalistic causes of poverty, belief in lack of ambition). In contrast to previous results, poverty was more likely to be attributed to fatalistic causes than to individual traits of the poor. General social beliefs and attitudes to poverty were related to the demographic variables (where age was the best discriminator) and personality variables (where social alienation and authoritarianism were the best discriminators):

> Overall there was a tendency for those who endorsed dispositional causes of poverty also to express more individualistic or dispositional beliefs in general. Thus they were more likely to indicate prejudice towards travelling people, belief in innate tendencies, national pride and national deprecation. . . . The more common poverty was seen to be the greater the likelihood that it was attributed to social, structural, or futuristic causes. Conversely, the less common it was seen to be, the greater the likelihood that it was attributed to dispositional causes.   (p. 160)

Overall the respondents were very positive about improving social welfare benefits. Those with more fatalistic beliefs about the causes of poverty were more likely to consider improving social welfare to be important and familiar, though most respondents believed the idea of improving benefits difficult.

There has been a great deal of public debate and media coverage on the topic of social security recipients. Golding and Middleton (1982), in a thorough, content-analytic study, noted that although welfare news is more extensively covered in the 'quality' media, it is given more prominence in the 'populars', and suggest that it gets widest coverage when meeting news values which stress the importance of crime or political dispute. Furthermore abuse of social security, either by fraud or excessive claiming, is a major theme of news coverage. However, very little empirical work appears to have been done on the public's *attitude* towards social security (welfare) recipients. Some British empirical work has, however, been done. Runciman (1966), as part of a large survey on social inequality, asked people about their attitudes towards government help. He found, as predicted, that both skilled and unskilled Conservatives felt government help in general was sufficient, while both Labour and Liberal voters thought that it was not.

Two more British studies are worth mentioning. Furnham (1983b) examined the effect of sex, education and voting pattern of over 170 normal subjects' attitudes towards (unemployed) people receiving social security benefits. Both education and vote (but not sex) appeared to be important factors in predicting people's attitudes. A factor analysis of the twelve-item questionnaire revealed three clear interpretable factors which indicated that attitudes centred on the difficulty of coping with the amount of benefit provided; beliefs about people being dishonest about their needs and abusing benefit payments; and the loss of self-esteem and stigma associated with being on social security. The results showed that in Britain, just as in America, people not on social security tend to have negative attitudes towards those that are, although they may appreciate some of the problems of the unemployed on social security. Golding and Middleton (1982) reported on a study concerned with social security benefits and claimants in Britain. They found that people generally feel that benefits are too high and too easy to get. Over 60 per cent of the general population and over 50 per cent of those with experience of receiving benefits believed that people on social security can manage quite well. Over half agreed that there is a stigma attached to claiming benefits, yet they thought too much was spent on social security, while less than a quarter believed too little was spent. Nearly half of the sample believed that it would be better to pay low rates and taxes and let people pay for services as they want them. Older, lower-income groups tended to believe that the British welfare system was something to be proud of, yet approximately three-quarters thought that too many people depended on welfare and that welfare made people lazy. Finally, they found that older people and manual workers were most anti-welfare, 'showing the extent to which living on the edge of the welfare state induces fears that are easily aroused by economic recession and that are most easily articulated in terms of the most readily available mythologies' (p. 168).

Furnham (1985c) aimed, in another study, to investigate simultaneously the effects of eight independent variables (five demographic and three 'psychological') on social security attitudes in order to determine empirically which of the independent variables relate to which dimension of attitudes towards social security. Each of the eight independent variables was chosen according to its salience given previous literature: age, sex, education, vote and income; Protestant work ethic beliefs; conservative beliefs and feelings of anomie/alienation. A factor analysis of the attitudes to social security scale revealed four factors similar to those in previous studies. Analysis of variance showed that vote, Protestant work ethic and conservative beliefs most differentiated subjects' attitudes to social welfare. Furthermore, a canonical correlation analysis revealed three significant variates which showed Protestant work ethic beliefs were associated with beliefs about recipients' dishonesty, age with beliefs about the difficulty of coping, and also with the stigma attached to being on welfare.

Not only are factors similar from different studies but so are the misconceptions surrounding social security. As Coughlin (1982) found in America, there is a widespread misunderstanding in the distinction between social insurance and public assistance which may account for some of the more draconian views expressed.

However, he also found a paradox in that while there is widespread belief that social security payroll taxes are too high, at the same time a majority of people think the benefits should be maintained or increased. That is, people can be in favour of reduced taxation and improved social security benefits simultaneously; just as some can and do believe that whereas many social security recipients are idle and dishonest, they may experience both stigma and shame on the dole. Thus people appear to be making in the latter case a distinction between the deserving and the undeserving poor. However, this questionnaire, like all those upon which it is based, does not allow for this distinction to be made. Future work in this field may do well to specify in items the target of social welfare benefits as this may allow subjects to make the distinction between whom they see to be deserving and who not.

Nevertheless there seems to be a universal dislike and distrust of those on social security who are distrusted, stigmatised and patronised. This is most clear in the consistent attacks in the media on 'scroungers', who are seen as the most undeserving of the poor (Deacon, 1978). But one should not imagine that there is no demand for social welfare (Whiteley, 1981). Taylor-Gooby (1983) has attempted to study the contribution of moralism and self-interest to attitudes to social security. He notes that one should distinguish between the various facets of social security. Whereas the general public are in favour of education a health service and benefits for deserving groups, they tend to be against unemployment benefits and council housing. It has been suggested that these values represent the dominant ideology of the society. In a study of 240 British subjects Taylor-Gooby found benefits for the retired, widows, the sick and disabled, care for the elderly, the National Health Service and education receive strong support, while the unemployed, single parents, the low-paid, those in need of day-care for children, child benefits and council tenants receive little support. Although various other beliefs – the work ethic, beliefs in social justice – related to welfare attitudes, social class, income and age were more closely related to welfare beliefs.

## The behaviour of the poor

There is no shortage of findings that have demonstrated that the poor hold different beliefs and behave rather differently from the non-poor. But the establishment of a relationship between poverty and various behaviours is of little importance if it cannot explain how specific economic conditions produce which psychological phenomena that may account for the maintenance of the psychological condition. As yet this literature is rather speculative, though the pattern may be changing. Traditionally research has considered five correlates of poverty: education (where the poor perform badly), housing (where the poor are inadequately housed and overcrowded), families (which are large and unstable), health (where the poor have worse mental and physical health) and crime (where the poor are disproportionately represented).

## Mental and physical health

Perhaps one of the most consistently researched topics in this area is the relation-ship between poverty and mental health in adults (Orford, 1976) and children (Langner *et al.*, 1970), as well as poverty and physical health. Reid (1977) reports data showing that there is a linear pattern with regard to health and social class. The lower one is on the social-class scale (and hence the poorer) the more likely one is to report long-standing illnesses, take 'illness-days' off work, suffer from tubercu-losis, diabetes, influenza, pneumonia and bronchitis, lose all one's teeth in mid-adulthood, consult a doctor, commit suicide and smoke cigarettes.

Cochrane (1983) has reviewed the literature on class differences in mental health. Studies of individual patients admitted to mental hospitals as well as com-munity surveys on the epidemiology both point to the fact that the lower one's social class the more likely one is to suffer mental illness. Two hypotheses for these findings are considered: social causation – social class is correlated (confounded) with a whole range of other variables (work stress, financial strain) which con-tribute to the higher rate of psychological disturbance in lower social groups, social selection – psychiatric impairment prevents people from maintaining the socio-eco-nomic position of their family of origin and they decline into poverty. Despite attempts to do the crucial test between these two hypotheses the results remained equivocal (Dohrenwend and Dohrenwend, 1969), yet the evidence appears to favour the social selection hypothesis. Of course, a major difficulty in this area is diagnosis as it may be argued that the perception of adjustment and maladjustment is relative and evaluative, and often based on the acceptable behaviour patterns of the middle class.

More modern research has tried to relate poverty to specific psychological disor-ders. Thus in Rodgers (1991) survey of psychological vulnerability (i.e. sensitivity to stress) financial hardship emerged as a significant factor for both men and women. Financial problems are apparently a common precipitating factor in the year prior to the onset of agoraphobia (Franklin and Andrews, 1989) and also pre-dispose young males to suicide (Heikkinnen, Aro and Lonnqvist, 1992). The prob-lem here is again that one cannot be certain about the direction of causality.

## Linguistic codes

Another area of research, first popularised by Bernstein (1962) concerns the use of language. It has been suggested that the poor have a different linguistic system compared with the non-poor. Essentially the linguistic code of the poor is restricted rather than elaborated: it is undifferentiated, simple, implicit, lacking in modifiers and aimed at reflecting and reinforcing social structure and routines rather than at conveying information. Although there has been some criticism of this work (Argyle, Furnham and Graham, 1981), a great number of studies have shown a dif-ference in the use of language between the poor and non-poor.

## Personal relationships

It has been suggested that many of the interpersonal relationships (family, work, public authorities) among the poor are perceived and structured in terms of power and authority (Hess, 1970). This stress on power probably reflects the poor's position in society, where they have little or no opportunity to make decisions affecting their daily lives. To have rank or status is to have power. Thus poor parents tend to equate goodness in their children with passive compliance, silence and respect. Techniques of control are based on appeals to norms, rules and status rather than on rational arguments or future consequences of behaviour.

## Dependency

There is a fairly extensive sociological literature on the relationship between poverty and dependency (on public facilities and welfare). The poor become dependent on welfare for a number of interrelated pressures: unemployment, illegitimacy, few occupational skills. Burgess (1969) has noted an adult behaviour pattern including child neglect, illegitimacy, promiscuity, abandonment, marital conflict, drinking and criminal behaviour which characterise the deprived and makes them dependent on welfare benefits. More recent studies have shown that the sex of the head of the family on social welfare is a major conditional variable with regard to poverty (Osmond and Grigg, 1978).

## Work behaviour and attitudes

One of the simplest explanations of poverty is that the poor work less hard than the non-poor; however, studies of both work behaviour and attitudes have yielded few, if any, significant differences (Friedlander, 1966; Cook, 1971; Goodwin, 1973). In attempting to control for other variables, such as ethnic group and sex, Davidson and Gaitz (1974) compared the work behaviour and attitudes of urban poor and non-poor in America. Contrary to the popular view and in accordance with previous literature, the poor were as work-oriented as the non-poor.

This conclusion is borne out by more recent research on the so-called 'underclass'. From a consideration of findings of the 1987 British Electoral Survey and the 1988 British Social Attitudes Survey, Heath (1992) suggests that the attitudes to family life and politics of the poorest groups in society does not differ significantly from those of the mainstream. The poorest groups are more likely to want a job and are less demanding about the conditions of work. Similarly in an American context, Cook and Curtin (1987) conclude that although the 'underclass' are indeed different with respect to some aspects of family life and peer culture, the aspirations and values of the poor are in the main strikingly similar to those of the majority.

## Crime

Strong individual and aggregate level correlations between poverty and official measures of crime are perhaps among the most firmly established of social science empirical generalisations. However calculated, official crime rates are almost always higher among the poor, and poor people are more likely to be arrested and convicted for a wide variety of offences. Yet the precise mechanisms linking poverty to crime remain elusive. (Berk, Lenihan and Rossi, 1980: 766)

Part of the problem lies in matters of definition (of poverty and crime), part in making causal inferences from aggregate data, and part in the large number of intervening and confounding variables.

In addition there are a whole range of findings regarding the behaviour of the poor which attest, in some sense, to the idea that there is a culture of poverty. Studies have shown, for instance, that the poor have a deficit of social skills (Beiser, 1965), greater premarital sexual experience (Kinsey *et al.*, 1948) and a lack of financial savings with an inefficient pattern of consumption.

## Conclusion

What is often error variance for the economist and sociologist (individual differences) is the focus of interest for the psychologist. Thus whereas economists explain and describe poverty in terms of macro- and micro-economic forces, and sociologists focus on class, institutional and social policy aspects of poverty, psychologists have traditionally looked at such things as attitudes to and explanations for poverty, as well as attempting to isolate factors that discriminate between the poor and the non-poor. Whereas the literature on attitudes and explanations is fairly consistent, coherent and complete, research on behavioural differences has been much less successful. Perhaps psychologists' most useful contribution thus far has been in focusing on the structure, determinants and consequences of the beliefs about the causes of poverty. This information can naturally be used to influence these beliefs.

Behavioural variables that psychologists have focused upon (delay of gratification, locus of control belief) are to be found in the anthropological and sociological literature and appear to be necessary but not sufficient variables to be taken into account when explaining poverty. The problem with the research is essentially threefold. Firstly, the findings from the research have often been inconclusive and contradictory, making it difficult to be certain about the relevance of each variable considered. Secondly, because so few of the studies are longitudinal in nature it is not clear whether the discriminating factors found are a cause or a consequence of poverty. What is most likely is that there is reciprocal causation. Thirdly, it may be argued that psychological research operates at an inappropriate level when it comes to poverty in that it focuses on individual behavioural variables and neglects wider contextual and structural variables which are much more important in explaining poverty.

Nevertheless psychologists have an important role to play in poverty research, which until now they appear to have sadly neglected. The sort of questions that would interest a psychologist include: Why is it that some people from identical socio-economic backgrounds, with similar educational experiences, etc. remain in poverty while others escape it, indeed even become rich? Why is it that some comparatively well-off people sink into poverty while others do not? Why is it that people with identical incomes define themselves quite differently – the one poor the other not? How can we change attitudes to and beliefs about the causes of poverty and the nature of the poor themselves? What simple behavioural measures can we use to encourage people with unwise spending habits to budget more carefully?

There are many psychological questions that one can ask with regard to poverty. Yet research in this area remains peripheral, marginal and erratic. Why do some people donate to charities helping the poor, while others do not? How is it that beliefs about the behaviour of the poor are socialised into the members of certain groups? To some extent these questions remain unaddressed.

# Chapter 6

# Wealth

## Introduction

Whereas there appears to be a wealth of social science (if not psychological) studies on poverty – its causes, consequences, definition, explanations (see Chapter 5) – there has been a comparative poverty of studies on wealth and affluence. This is no doubt due to the fact that whereas poverty is considered to be a major social problem, wealth is not. This is despite the fact that many recognised social problems – drug and alcohol abuse, family disorganisation – are associated with increased wealth (Merton and Nisbett, 1976). Of course since Mill and Adam Smith, economists have been interested in wealth and welfare (Carter, 1971), though all have pointed out the difficulties in defining wealth.

Those studies that have been done on the rich appear to have been done primarily by sociologists (Rubinstein, 1974; Abrahamson, 1980) and economists (Galbraith, 1958; Carter, 1971). There have been countless popularist books on the rich and manuals on how to become rich (Biggart, 1983), some more popular and analytic than others (Veblen, 1953).

There is surprisingly almost no psychological, and particularly social psychological, research in this area. Even economic psychologists (Katona, 1977) have devoted very little attention to the rich, or top asset holders as Katona calls them. The only psychologists who have ventured into this area are psychoanalysts who have been intrigued by the desire to amass wealth.

There is, of course, considerable popular interest and writings about the rich, who fall into a number of categories, a few who made their wealth in entertainment and the media (pop and film stars, novelists), entrepreneurial or corporate wealth attainers, and the landed wealth owners. Statistics about the rich reveal how few there are.

Table 6.1 shows two different but comparable estimates. To consider the more recent estimate (Noble, 1981), it seems that in 1980 the top 1 per cent of people

**Table 6.1**   Two different but similar estimates of wealth distribution at different periods of time

(a) Distribution of personal wealth

| % of wealth owned by | England and Wales | | | United Kingdom | | | | |
|---|---|---|---|---|---|---|---|---|
| | 1923 | 1938 | 1950 | 1966 | 1971 | 1978 | 1979 | 1980 |
| | % | % | % | % | % | % | % | % |
| Most wealthy 1 per cent | 60.9 | 55.0 | 47.2 | 33.0 | 30.5 | 23 | 24 | 23 |
| Most wealthy 5 per cent | 82.0 | 76.9 | 74.3 | 55.7 | 51.8 | 44 | 45 | 43 |
| Most wealthy 10 per cent | 89.1 | 85.0 | – | 68.7 | 65.1 | 58 | 59 | 58 |
| Most wealthy 25 per cent | – | – | – | 86.9 | 86.5 | 83 | 82 | 81 |
| Most wealthy 50 per cent | – | – | – | 96.5 | 97.2 | 95 | 95 | 94 |
| Least wealthy 50 per cent | – | – | – | 3.5 | 2.8 | 5 | 5 | 6 |

*Source:*   Noble (1981).

(b) Wealth ownership, 1911–13 to 1970 per cent of total personal wealth (based on mortality rates corrected for social class)

| Proportion of adult | England and Wales Adults aged 25 and over, 1911–13, 1924–30, 1936, 1951–6 (as presented by Lydall and Tipping) | | | | | | Great Britain Adults aged 15 and over, 1960, 1965, 1970 (estimates from Inland Revenue) | |
|---|---|---|---|---|---|---|---|---|
| | % | % | % | % | % | % | % | % |
| Top | 1 | 66 | 60 | 56 | 42 | 39 | 34 | 31 |
| | 5 | 86 | 83 | 81 | 68 | 64 | 62 | 56 |
| | 10 | 90 | 90 | 88 | 79 | 76 | 75 | 70 |
| Bottom | 90 | 10 | 10 | 12 | 21 | 24 | 25 | 30 |

*Source:* 1911–13 to 1951–6, Lydall and Tipping (1961: 92). 1960–70: estimates from *Inland Revenue Statistics* in Polanyi and Wood (1974).

owned 23 per cent of the marketable wealth and the top 5 per cent, 43 per cent of the wealth. Although the pattern of distribution has changed over the last 50 years, it is not so much between the rich and the poor but between the top 1 per cent and the top 5 per cent of the rich. This perceived inequality has led to considerable debate as to how to change this relationship.

# The redistribution of wealth

Although social stratification and economic inequality have long been topics of interest for sociologists, there have been comparatively few empirical studies on people's perceptions of a fair wage and the distribution of wealth. That is, although there are numerous demographic and econometric studies on the actual distribution of wealth and the factors which determine that distribution, there is much less on what people believe to be fair and equitable.

Some studies have shown consistent but predictable differences across cultures (Robinson and Bell, 1978) in beliefs about equity and distributive justice. Indeed equity theory – the relationship between inputs and outputs – is central to a good deal of social psychological theorising. Similarly, the nature and concept of distributive justice is well known in philosophy and ethics. Most researchers in this field have attempted to find general rules of distributive justice in a society while also looking at individual differences in preferences and the rationalisation of observed inequalities.

Alves and Rossi (1978) set about investigating the consensual normative framework for judging the fairness of distributions of earnings in the United States. A large sample were asked to judge to what extent people in certain jobs and households with specific salaries were either under-, over- or equitably paid. Predictably not all characteristics play equal roles in justifying earnings: occupational attainments count more than educational attainments, and husbands' characteristics count more than wives'. As with other findings in this area subjects tended to judge the very richest as overpaid and the very poorest as underpaid irrespective of all other factors. Low income is thought of as unfair despite low levels of merit (occupationally/educationally) while the highest wages could not be justified on any ground. 'Need' therefore appears to play an important role in judgements. Married persons and those with children tend to be rated as underpaid more than unmarried or childless people with identical characteristics and income:

> In sum, respondents were both more generous and more democratic than public policy and the empirical income distribution. The ceilings in earnings represented by the computed social maxima are well below the earnings of the affluent. At the same time fair earnings for persons on the bottom of the occupational and educational pyramid are set higher than poverty-level definitions. Implicitly respondents define an equitable earnings distribution that has a higher mean and a lower variance.   (Alves and Rossi, 1978: 557)

Analysis of individual differences of the respondents showed that higher-status respondents allowed more earnings for additional increments in education and occupational attainment of the hypothetical target people, while low-status respondents give considerably more earnings for each additional child. Thus high-status respondents 'stretched out' the inequality in what they believe to be a fair distribution of earnings while low-status respondents 'shrunk' that inequality.

In a Belgian study aimed at devising a mathematical model to predict attitudes towards the redistribution of wealth (via incomes), Overlaet and Lagrou (1981) found very much the same results as Alves and Rossi (1978) – namely, a desired decrease of the incomes for occupations with 'high' pay, and an increase in income for 'low'-pay occupations, but a maintenance of the income structure. From their study of 161 individuals' judgements of the fair (equitable) income of twelve occupations they were able to devise a regression model which allowed for the calculation of how much each individual favours redistribution, the extent to which an alteration in the income structure is desired, and the reference point used to determine which incomes have to be moderated and which not. Some of their more interesting results suggested that the more a person earns the higher s/he draws the line between high and low incomes. There is a 'preference drift effect' such that as people get used to a high standard of living they consider this level a minimal welfare level. Furthermore the mean income subjects' estimate for themselves is somewhat higher than for the mean of the population as a whole. People then do not use the same criteria in evaluating fairness for themselves and fairness in others.

By and large, studies on the perceived equitable redistribution of wealth are fairly consistent. People appear to favour a reduction in the range (the rich get less and the poor more), an increase in the mean income, but a higher than average income for themselves. Idealism, then, does appear to be tempered by some desire to improve one's lot. Precisely how one may redistribute wealth to fit these many noble sentiments is, of course, not at all clear.

## Attitudes to the rich

Whereas there have been lots of studies on attitudes to poverty (see Chapter 5), there have been very few studies on attitudes to the rich. Those that have been done have nearly always been a response to debates over taxation.

Lewis, Sandford and Pleming (1979) completed a survey in two cities in Britain (Bath and London) of over 200 people in each on their perception of wealth and the wealth tax. Asked whether a wealthy person was one who earned a high income, owned a lot of property and had substantial savings, or both most people chose the second option (property and savings, rather than income). This result seemed independent of age, sex, social class and political preference. They found that 44 per cent of the respondents said that to be rich a person needed an annual income of £15–30,000. However, when asked the question 'What would the total value of a person's savings and possessions need to be before you considered them to be wealthy?', nearly 80 per cent believed it less than £100,000. This is much the same result as that found by Furnham (1983e). Items considered part of a person's wealth included land, antiques jewellery, stocks and shares, but national savings certificates, life assurance policies and pension funds were not considered part of a person's wealth.

Asked what their attitude to a wealth tax was, 27.5 per cent thought it a very poor idea and 18.5 per cent a fairly poor idea, while only 8.5 per cent thought it a very good idea. This response was independent of age, class, sex, marital status, income and home ownership, but not party political preference. Predictably Conservative supporters thought the wealth tax a poorer idea than Labour supporters. The respondents were also asked whether, if a wealth tax were introduced, it should be in addition to, or a substitute for, top rates of income taxation. Most respondents believed that it should be a substitute, but replies depended on whether people were *in favour of* the wealth tax, and least evident for those in favour. Overall it seemed that respondents favoured an additive tax but this trend was most evident for those who were against a wealth tax, and least evident for those in favour. Overall it seemed that the respondents felt *that the wealthy had not worked harder than others,* although they were perceived as more skilful, luckier and having had the benefit of help from others.

Respondents who considered a wealth tax a good idea, or were uncertain about it, were *more convinced* that people who inherit wealth should be taxed more heavily. Respondents who thought the wealth tax a poor idea were *largely undecided*. Those people who considered a wealth tax a poor idea consistently and accountably agreed that the wealthy should keep their wealth and *disagreed* that there should be a more even distribution of wealth in the United Kingdom.

People who considered a wealth tax a good idea or were uncertain *agreed* there ought to be a more even distribution of wealth in the United Kingdom. People who considered a wealth tax a poor idea *disagreed* more that inheritances of property or large sums of money were unfair. People who *were uncertain* whether a wealth tax was a good idea, or were convinced that it was not, *agreed* more that people should be able to pass on their wealth to their children without it being heavily taxed. People who thought a wealth tax a good idea, or were uncertain about it, felt *more strongly* that people who spend their money on lavish entertainments should be taxed more severely than those who save and invest. People who thought a wealth tax a poor idea *agreed* more that the lower paid would not benefit from a wealth tax. The authors conclude:

> Public opinion is notoriously conservative, in that it is resistant to change. It would be very surprising indeed if this survey were to record a demand for the introduction of a new and radical policy especially one relating to an increase in taxation. Consequently some reviewers of the public opinion and attitude literature argue that it is the Government's role to lead public opinion rather than follow it. Nonetheless the Labour party would do well to heed the findings of this investigation as it provides evidence germane to specific proposals such as the wealth tax threshold, whether the new tax should be in addition to or a substitute for the top rates of income tax and an indication of what forms of wealth people feel most strongly should benefit from concessions or better still be outside the wealth tax base altogether. . . . Similarly the Labour party should note that the Introduction of a wealth tax should it occur, would not only be met by the customary degree of indifference but also with antipathy, a reaction which would not be restricted solely to the wealthy.   (p. 54)

Attitudes to the rich may of course differ from one country to another. For instance, in a study of equality, success and social injustice in Britain and the United States, Robinson and Bell (1978) found that the belief that a person has the standard of living that s/he deserves reduces egalitarian attitudes more in Britain than in the United States. This may be due to the British belief that British society is just, in that social arrangements reflect fair rules of competition. Further, while of no importance in Britain, the cultural belief in monetary success reduces egalitarian attitudes in the United States and functions as the belief in the just society does in Britain.

More recent researchers have been interested in attitudes and beliefs about ordinary people themselves becoming rich. Kasser and Ryan (1993), in three studies, examined the hypothesis that values and expectancies for wealth (that is, aspiration to attain wealth and material success) were *negatively* associated with adjustment and well-being. This is indeed what they found: greater aspirations for financial success were associated with interview ratings of lower global adjustment, lower social productivity and more behavioural disorders. Their work tended to confirm the suspicions of psychoanalytic writers who argued that a focus on 'having' and 'consuming' reflects alienation from actualizing tendencies. They conclude:

> One process that could account for the insalubrious effects of financial-success goals is that individuals aspiring for wealth may be more likely to focus on contingent, external goals and fleeting, superficial satisfactions unrelated to inherent needs. Consequently, they may ignore or be distracted from the intrinsic actualizing and integrating tendencies that support personality growth and well-being. Propensities toward relations with others, self-examination, or investment in social concerns may thus be supplanted by materialistic occupations, to the detriment of the self and its development. A related explanation may also be applied: Individuals dispositionally high on broad factors such as neuroticism, or those with lower security and sense of well-being, may be more prone to view money as a means for self-enhancement. A cycle may then be initiated that maintains, or possibly depends on, the original sense of contingent worth. Longitudinal studies and examination of the antecedents of value acquisition may clarify these issues. . . .
>
> Other cognitive theories might attempt to explain the current results on the basis of unrealistic optimism, in effect, that financial success is relatively difficult to realize and, therefore, that high aspirations reflect an unrealistic belief about probable attainment. This explanation seems untenable for three reasons, however. First, analyses examining quadratic effects did not support the possibility than an optimal, moderate level of aspiring for financial success was related to well-being, as might be suggested by work on unrealistic optimism. Second, unrealistic optimism concerns only the likelihood of future events and cannot therefore, explain why ratings of the importance of financial success aspirations related negatively to adjustment . . . unrealistic optimism is generally associated with greater well-being, which of course is inconsistent with the results regarding financial success in these three studies.   (p. 420)

## Psychoanalysis and wealth

As it is pointed out in Chapter 4, psychoanalytic writers have long been interested in money; but some have attempted to explain the drive or need to amass wealth. Fenichel (1947) considered both normal and abnormal drives to become wealthy. He suggests a number of quite different motives:

1. The rational motive, which argues that the more money one possesses, the better one can satisfy one's needs.
2. The power motive, which argues that wealth is a source of power sought by those who are fearful of impoverishment and loss of love: 'The original instinctual aim is not for riches, but to enjoy power and respect, whether it be among one's fellow men or within oneself' (p. 96).
3. The possession motive, which suggests that one accumulates money to regain in fantasy those possessions which one has (faeces) or might lose (genitals).

4. The self-preservation motive, which suggests that one needs wealth to generate wealth and eliminate competitors and hence one consistently strives to keep ahead.

The essay relies a great deal on the association between the anal-period experiences (i.e. potty-training) and subsequent attitudes to and habits of money usage. Because money is equated with faeces one can explain terminology such as 'stinking rich', 'filthy lucre' and understand why the discussion of money and money-related matters are considered indelicate. Furthermore the anal obsessions (cleanliness, orderliness, time-keeping) of famous rich men (such as Howard Hughes) become understandable.

All rational and irrational attitudes to money are seen as arising from unsolved anal erotic conflicts:

> One thinks of kleptomaniacs, or of the women who drain men of their resources, to whom money, which they are always striving to take away, symbolizes a whole series of introjected objects that have been withheld from them; or of depressive characters who from fear of starvation regard money as potential food. There are too those men to whom money signifies their potency, who experience any loss of money as a castration, or who are inclined, when in danger, to sacrifice money in a sort of 'prophylactic self-castration'. There are, in addition, people who – according to their attitude of the moment towards taking, giving, or withholding – accumulate or spend money, or alternate between accumulation and spending, quite impulsively, without regard for the reality significance of money, and often to their own detriment (sometimes unconsciously desired). In the unconscious mental life money can represent not only possessions but everything that one can take or give; therefore it can represent relations to objects in general and everything through which the bodily ego feeling and with it self-regard can be increased or diminished.   (pp. 99–100)

Like all psychoanalytic thinkers Fenichel (1947) draws heavily on medical, anthropological and historical examples. Every psychological event (such as the accumulation of wealth) is explained as the resultant interplay between biological structures and environmental influences (social institutions). But because environmental influences change over time, the drive to accumulate wealth exists only in certain definite social epochs.

Other psychoanalytic ideas are to be found in the chapter concerning the psychology of money.

## Sudden changes of wealth

There is plethora of studies on the negative consequences of unemployment (see Chapter 7) and sudden reduction in wealth that follows from that. Many repeated surveys have been carried out in the United States since 1946. Despite continually rising prosperity, there were considerable fluctuations in the percentage of those who said they were 'very happy'. In 1946–7 the percentage was 38–9 per cent, in the late 1950s it rose to 53 per cent, falling in 1971–4 to 27 per cent, and rising to 35 per cent in the late 1970s. There appears to be very little relationship with economic prosperity when we look at such changes over time, although there is a small positive relationship if rich and poor are compared at the same point in time.

A study of 191 British pools winners, all of whom won £160,000 or more, found that many of them claimed to be a little happier than before, but there were some quite serious problems too. There was hostility and envy from neighbours and relatives; the winners were pestered with requests for money; those who moved house encountered snobbish rejection by middle-class neighbours; and some were more lonely, as a result of giving up work and moving house. At any rate, they had better houses, cars and holidays (Smith and Razzell, 1975), but it is far from clear how many were really more satisfied with life.

Smith and Razzell (1975) interviewed 88 people who had won at least £75,000 at 1957 money values on the football pools, which is equivalent to approximately £1 million in today's money. One of the most striking findings was that sudden wealth typically has very modest effects on most people's lives. They did tend to move to a better house and to buy a better car, but only a tiny proportion of them become reckless with money.

Apart from property, cars and household articles, most of the money won by pools winners tended to be invested. Seventy-seven per cent of the pools winners invested most of their win, usually in stocks and shares, building societies, or local government bonds. The overall picture is one in which the money that had been won was handled in a very conservative and careful fashion. There was not even much of a tendency to splash out on expensive holidays in exotic places. Pools winners were no more likely than non-winners to have had a holiday during the twelve months before being interviewed, and they were not more likely to have gone abroad for their holidays.

While the effects of large pools wins seems rather modest, there are clearly some advantages and disadvantages that are likely to be experienced. On the positive side, the ability to buy whatever one wants is obviously desirable, and some winners took advantage of their win to leave their jobs and set up their own businesses. On the negative side, winning the pools can be a very disruptive event. Most pools winners give up their work almost immediately. Even if they want to keep working, their workmates usually put pressure on them to let someone more in need of money have their job. As a result, pools winners often become bored and turn to drink.

Winning the pools can also be disruptive in terms of social identity. Conflict is produced by the frequent discrepancy between a working-class existence prior to the win and the ability to live in a very comfortable middle-class style afterwards. Many of the winners were aware of this problem, and were unsure which social class they belonged to. Over half of the non-winners were definite about their social class, against only 28 per cent of the pools winners. However, as Smith and Razzell pointed out, sudden wealth typically has an 'amplification effect'; that is to say, it amplifies or exaggerates certain aspects of behaviour that were already present: for example, a very shy and retiring winner stopped work after his win, and so had even fewer social contacts than before.

The impact of sudden wealth on happiness was also looked at by Brickman, Coates and Janoff-Bulman (1978), who selected recent major winners of the Illinois State Lottery, nearly all of whom won at least $100,000, and one-third of whom had won $1 million. The views of these lottery winners mirrored those of the British pools winners in many ways. They mentioned a number of changes in their lives (e.g. financial security, greater leisure time) but nevertheless only 23 per cent of them felt that their general life-style had altered.

The lottery winners were then asked about their level of happiness at three different stages of their lives: before winning the lottery; the present post-win period; and two years in the future. As predicted by adaptation-level theory, the lottery winners did not feel any happier after their big win than before it, and they did not expect to be happier in two years' time. In addition, winning a huge amount of money failed to make the lottery winners any happier than people who had not enjoyed such good fortune.

According to adaption-level theory, the euphoria of winning a fortune in a lottery should increase the winner's adaption level and expectations, and thus make pleasurable events of everyday life seem less enjoyable than they were before. Brickman, Coates and Janoff-Bulman (1978) asked the lottery winners how pleasant they found several activities or events such as watching television, talking with a friend, hearing a funny joke and reading a magazine. The lottery winners derived much less pleasure from these activities than did non-winners.

## The wealth ethic

Though there is a great deal of interest in the Protestant work ethic (PWE) (see Chapter 8) a few have talked about the wealth ethic.

In their scholarly and idiosyncratic analysis of the social psychological effects of unemployment, Kelvin and Jarrett (1985) both dismiss the PWE thesis and propose an alternative. The essence of their criticism is a 'wholly false account of the past' – in fact a myth – whose function is more to inspire the present than explain the past. They suggest that a careful analysis of the English middle classes of the sixteenth and seventeenth centuries does not support the Weberian thesis. They are adamant that the PWE is an explanatory concept of our time, invented to explain the past.

> Ours is also a time in which the media quickly pick up, simplify, and disseminate initially subtle and complex technical concepts. Vague notions of a 'work ethic' . . . have thus become part of everyday language – and in doing so have themselves created expectations in terms of a work ethic. . . . The diffusion of vague concepts then increases the range of phenomena which are perceived to exemplify them – which in turn is taken as proof of the validity of the concepts.   (p. 212)

But Kelvin and Jarrett (1985) are not content to dismiss the PWE as a historically incorrect self-fulfilling prophecy. They suggest that what has been incorrectly historically perceived as the work ethic was in fact the *wealth* ethic:

When one looks at the situation from the very historical perspective which ostensibly gave rise to it, explanations in terms of the Protestant Ethic emerge as little more than an invention of twentieth-century social science, with unwarranted pretensions to an ancient lineage. The ethic, which has truly been predominant and pervasive is not a work ethic but, for want of a better term, a *wealth* ethic. Wealth is (quite correctly) perceived as the basis of economic independence: that is the key issue, and has been for centuries. The ethic; is to make or to have sufficient wealth not to have to depend on others; work is only one means to that end, and certainly not the only one universally most esteemed: not in any class. Provided that one has money enough to be independent, there is no great moral obligation to work, certainly not in the sense of gainful, productive employment. (Kelvin and Jarrett, 1985: 104)

Thus it is maintained that work is normative and not an ethic, and that moral significance does not attach to work, but to not living off others. In other words, not only are Kelvin and Jarrett (1985) disputing the historical, or indeed current, existence of the PWE, but also they believe that the essence of the PWE is the accumulation of wealth often to ensure *independence* and, to a lesser extent, freedom and leisure. Work is only one, and presumably a moderately unpleasant or at least effortful way, of accumulating wealth.

For Kelvin and Jarrett (1985) all people gain numerous satisfactions from work, as well as money and things which money enables them to have and to do. The wealth ethic adherent then condemns the unemployment not for being idle, but for being poor:

In the final analysis, explanations in terms of an ethic rest on the distinction between the 'good' and the 'bad': explanations based on poverty rest on the distinction between the 'haves' and the 'have-nots'. The 'bad' we are entitled to disapprove of, ostracise, punish; the 'have-nots' we know from our most basic ethic we ought to help . . . given our picture of ourselves as fundamentally moral, it is much more congenial to us to attribute our attitudes to the unemployed as 'conditioned' by an ethic, than as motivated by meanness. The inescapable fact, however, is that the 'have-nots' are dependent for their material survival on contributions from others, either in the form of private charity or of provision from the public purse: and resentment at having to feed, clothe, and shelter the bodies of the unemployed poor has long aroused far more public passion than has concern for the salvation of souls of the leisured rich.   (p. 105)

This is an interesting thesis, though support for it is limited. Kelvin and Jarrett (1985) do supply some historical evidence in support of their thesis. However, it is quite possible to re-interpret the evidence they supply in favour of the PWE. For instance, they quote the parliamentary papers of 1884: 'An enormous amount of time is lost, not only by want of punctuality in coming to work in the morning and the beginning again after meals, but still more by the general observation of "It's Monday".... One employer has on Monday only 40 or 50 out of 300 or 400.' Whereas Kelvin and Jarrett (1985) appear to use this as evidence for the fact that the PWE was not found among English working classes during the height of Britain's imperial power, one could equally argue that it was evidence of the PWE in that a group of adherents or believers were in fact chastising a group of non-believers. The fact that there is or was a large element of people who did not endorse the PWE ethic does not invalidate its actual existence!

Equally, however, these criticisms do not invalidate the wealth ethic which may be seen to stress one particular theme in the PWE itself – namely independence. A true wealth ethic would place money in the same place that work holds in the PWE – wealth/money should be pursued for itself and it only should be seen as a desirable product. Possession of wealth, like virtue, may then be flaunted! Furnham and Rose (1987) attempted to measure the wealth ethic and compare it with the PWE. The eight items that they chose are listed in Table 6.2; the means show the extent to which people adore them.

Whether these statements tap in the theme of wealth ethic as outlined by Kelvin and Jarrett (1985) is not yet certain; people seem to agree relatively strongly with certain aspects of it. Yet as predicted when the total score from the wealth ethic was correlated with the PWE score, the correlation was very low and non-significant ($r = -0.09$). They also found that whereas the PWE correlated with numerous other variables such as 'postponement of gratification', 'need for achievement', 'internal locus of control', the wealth ethic did not. Finally, they did find some evidence for the fact that the wealth ethic was multidimensional. The welfare ethics factor analysis also yielded three factors which accounted for above 60 per cent of the variance. The first factor seems to make *financial independence* a desirable goal, while the second stresses the idea of *wealth status*; that is, that money inherited, more than made, is respect-worthy. The third bipolar factor concerns *wealth contentment*, suggesting that lack of wealth causes problems, not wealth itself. Clearly more work needs to be done on the wealth ethic.

**Table 6.2**    Wealth ethic: items from Furnham and Rose (1987)

|  | Mean |
|---|---|
| Provided one has enough money to be independent, there should be no moral obligation to work | 4.36 |
| People work mainly to earn money, and thus work is only a means to an end | 4.96 |
| Money gives one independence and choice | 6.13 |
| Entrepreneurs should enjoy a higher status than the aristocracy with all its wealth (R) | 3.53 |
| Many of the problems in our society are caused through some people having too much money (R) | 4.04 |
| Nobody in their right mind would go back to work after winning the pools or inheriting a great deal (half a million) of money | 3.77 |
| People should be able to retire as early as they wish provided they can be financially independent | 6.02 |
| One should work to live not live to work | 5.52 |

*Source:* reprinted with permission from *Human Relations*
Note: (R) = reversed item
Mean for scale 7 = Strongly agree; 1 = strongly disagree.

# Typologies of the rich

Although psychologists have not paid much attention to the rich, there appears to be an insatiable curiosity among the general (western) public about them. Galbraith has in fact noted that wealth has never been a source of honour in itself, as it must be advertised through obtrusively expensive goods. Hence there are a number of journalistic articles and books about money, the rich, etc. Some, of course, are much better (more insightful, better documented) than others. Many have attempted to classify the rich according to either their motives or their habits recognising that as a group the rich fall into many quite distinct categories.

Wiseman (1974) classified money types into eight different categories which he describes and discusses at some length. However, he does note that it is only the predominant characteristics of a person that means s/he goes into one category or the other, and that overlapping may occur:

> All the categories that I am postulating are open-ended and fluid, but I believe it can be shown that there are patterns in people's money behaviour which can be related to their character make-up, and that there is a sufficiently constant correlation between character and behaviour to justify speaking of money types. (p. 74)

1. *The romantic:* The romantic idealises and overestimates his/her favourite love – money: 'To him money is applause, vindication, approval, the expression of fate's favouritism' (p. 74). These types derive the sort of satisfaction from accumulating wealth as others get from art, religion and scholarship. The romantic is, according to Wiseman, the visionary inventor or pioneering entrepreneur.
2. *The company person:* This type denies the joy of making money, and does so anonymously on behalf of others. They claim they are skilled at making money (for others) and do so out of duty or responsibility. There appears to be guilt when talking about money.
3. *The collector:* Collectors enjoy the mathematics of their money. They enjoy the investing and accounting aspect of money watching it reproduce itself. Closely aligned to Freudian conceptions of the anal personality, this type also denies the source of interest in money.
4. *The hustler:* The hustler does not suffer guilt about his/her desire to accumulate money. They are enterprising, energetic, aggressive, often unethical, pursuers of money. Heroes to some, but swindlers to others, the hustler is somewhat emotionally and socially unstable.
5. *The double-dealer:* As the name implies, they are clever, amoral confidence tricksters. Although not all may be rich, they are psychopathic individuals whose joy is often as much in the defrauding or stealing from another as it is in the money itself.
6. *The criminal:* As the name implies, this person is simply a criminal and a misanthropist. The criminal will do anything for money and appears to be quite unmoved by acts of cruelty or revenge.
7. *The gambler and loser:* The gambler has a real expectation of winning and risks

sums, the loss of which would hurt him/her. This person has the repetitive compulsion to lose (either consciously or not) and so sees rapid rises and subsequent falls in wealth.

8. *The non-player:* This person may have wealth thrust upon him, but does not seek it and indeed often shuns it.

The variety of uses, abuses and symbolism of money makes such typologies useful. Wiseman has noted some of these as well:

There is blood-money and bride-money, conscience money and stolen money, easy money and money that has been earned by the sweat of the brow, money to burn and money as the prize of merit; there is money that is a king's ransom and money that is a whore's pay; there is money to squander and so much money as will make it difficult for its possessor to get into heaven; there is the mistress's allowance and the wife's due; pocket-money, spending money, hush money, and money in the bank; there are the wages of sin and the bequests of rich uncles; there is the price that every man has, and the pricelessness of objects, and the price on the outlaw's head; there are the forty pieces of silver and also the double indemnity on one's own life.

Behind its apparent sameness lie the many meanings of money. Blood-money does not buy the same thing as bride-money and a king's ransom is not the same kind of fortune as a lottery prize. The great exchangeability of money is deceptive; it enables us to buy the appearance of things, their physical form, as in the case of a 'bought woman', while what we thought we had bought eludes us.   (pp. 13–14)

## Wealth and happiness

Psychologists, sociologists and economists, as well as moralists and theologians, have been interested in the relationship between wealth and individual happiness.

Studies done in various countries have shown a very modest relationship between wealth and happiness. An American study in 1983–4 found that income made more difference to positive than to negative affect, and that the positive affects were more marked at the upper end of the income range, while the reduction of negative affect was more marked at the lower end. See Table 6.3, in which positive and negative affect are reports of extent of good and bad moods, on scales from 0 to 1.

There is evidence that money can reduce distress, for instance caused by cold or hunger, and it can add to joy, for example by making possible expensive forms of leisure.

Those people who have larger incomes are a little more satisfied with their incomes, their standard of living, and so on, than other people. However, this is a surprisingly weak relationship – corresponding to a correlation of 0.15 or 0.20 or less in different studies.

Argyle (1988) posed the question if money does not make people happy what makes them satisfied with their incomes. He believes that social comparisons are the major factors.

**Table 6.3**   Income and happiness

| Income | Positive affect | Negative affect |
|---|---|---|
| Less than $2,000 | 0.32 | 0.56 |
| $2,000–2,999 | 0.40 | 0.58 |
| $3,000–3,999 | 0.39 | 0.54 |
| $4,000–4,999 | 0.38 | 0.51 |
| $5,000–5,999 | 0.46 | 0.52 |
| $6,000–6,999 | 0.45 | 0.52 |
| $7,000–7,999 | 0.46 | 0.53 |
| $8,000–9,999 | 0.50 | 0.49 |
| $10,000–14,000 | 0.52 | 0.46 |
| $15,000 or more | 0.57 | 0.46 |

*Source:* Bradburn (1969)

To test the effects of extreme wealth, Diener *et al.* (1985) examined 49 people, most of them earning over $10 million a year, who were compared with 62 people chosen at random from the same areas (controls). Some of the differences are shown in Table 6.4, which includes averages scores for the very rich and the controls, on a number of different self-rating scales. It can be seen that very rich people scored a little higher on a number of measures of happiness, and were quite a lot lower on negative affect. Richer people were more interested in money and scored higher on a factor of obsessional concern with it ('I firmly believe that money can solve all of my problems', 'I worry about my finances much of the time', 'I put money ahead of pleasure', etc), and on a factor of seeing money as power ('I sometimes buy things that I don't need or want to impress people because they are the right things to have at the time', 'I sometimes buy friendship by being generous with those I want to like me', etc.).

There are, of course, many famous biblical quotations warning one about the dangers of materialism and wealth accumulation, such as (1) 'The righteous man will flourish, but the man who trusts in riches will wither' (Proverbs 11.28); (2) 'Keep life free from the love of money' (Hebrews, 13.5); and (3) 'Woe to you that are rich' (Luke 6.24). There are also various teachings about money and the rich which are discussed in Chapter 4 on the psychology of money.

**Table 6.4**   Happiness of the very rich

|  | Very rich | Controls |
|---|---|---|
| % of the time happy | 77 | 62 |
| Life satisfaction | 4.77 | 3.70 |
| Positive affect | 15.35 | 13.97 |
| Negative affect | 4.92 | 7.65 |
| Self-esteem | 0.66 | 0.46 |
| Self-actualisation | 0.71 | 0.55 |

*Source:* Diener, Horowitz and Emmons (1985) 'Happiness of the very wealthy', *Social Indicators Research*.

There are two sorts of studies that are relevant to wealth and happiness: there are studies looking at the relationship between income and job, as well as life, satisfaction. The literature on pay and job satisfaction is by no means unambiguous. Certainly better-paid workers are more satisfied, but pay is confounded with type of job, social status, intrinsic nature of the work, etc.

Studies done in the United States have found no relationship either cross-sectionally or longitudinally for a strong positive relationship between money and happiness. Lane (1983) has proposed three principles to explain this relationship:

1. *Adaptation level theory:* thus although one might feel 'happier' by a recent increase in the standard of living, one soon adapts to this and the positive relationship disappears.
2. *Social comparison theory:* this theory suggests that people's standards of wealth are determined by comparisons with kin, peers, etc., and thus if they all rise together (over time) the relative difference disappears and so as people get wealthier over time they do not become any more happy.
3. *Declining marginal utility of money:* as the supply of money increases other values like freedom and true friendship become relatively more valuable.

Thus the power of any increment of money decreases with affluence. Lane noted that there is always a much stronger relationship between income *satisfaction* and life satisfaction, than between *actual* income and life satisfaction. Furthermore the aspirations and expectations of people, as well as their perceived position with regard to others, is important in predicting happiness. Of course, there are many other social, cultural and economic factors which affect life satisfaction, hence making comparative studies of income and happiness difficult. Thus education, which is associated with greater consciousness of self with particular emphasis on weaknesses and lesser concern for objective circumstances, tends to be associated both with increased income (better-paid jobs often require considerable training) but less satisfaction with self and a special sensitivity to missed opportunities.

Money may make one less worried about some things but more worried about others:

> But the main effect of income is in changing the nature of worries. There is a difference between those who worry about things over which they think they have control, such as their work, and over those things which are less controllable, such as death. Those who worry about relatively controllable things are happier than those who worry about the uncontrollable. Increased income is associated with shifting worry to the more uncontrollable elements of life, perhaps because income is associated with a sense of control over one's fate. Equally important is the shift that income brings in another aspect of substantive worry: from financial, job and health problems to interpersonal and characterological problems, the kind of person one is. As it turns out, this shift helps to explain some of the waning power of money to buy happiness in rich societies. Over the 1957–76 period, the concerns of Americans shifted from role identities, greatly affected by income, to 'a more personalized self-consciousness', where income is less relevant. An increase in national income, like an increase in personal income, shifts the axis of worry to interpersonal dimensions where money has less power to relieve worries. In this sense, personal and

national income first buy happiness through relief of some major worries, but increased income also alters the dimensions of worry toward a field where income loses its significance.   (Lane, 1983: 25–6)

Thus Lane's conclusion is that happiness or life satisfaction is most closely related to self-esteem and belief in one's own effectiveness, neither of which is necessarily related to income. Although money may reduce material worries, concerns with psychological matters, 'Happiness and life satisfaction are too various to be captured in money's golden net' (p. 27). Others have gone further. Fromm (1980) has argued that the pursuit of wealth and happiness is based on two fundamentally mistaken psychological principles: radical hedonism – the aim of life is maximum pleasure which is the satisfaction of any desire or subjective need a person may feel; and that egotism, selfishness and greed, as the system needs to generate them in order to function, lead to harmony and peace. Fromm distinguishes between the mode of having and the mode of being, the former of which confuses material possessions, power and wealth with the latter mode which leads to growth, creativity and satisfaction. Central to this religious/ascetic view is the idea that 'Security, sense of identity, and confidence based on faith in what one *is*, on one's need for relatedness, interest, love, solidarity with the world around one instead of on one's desire to have, to possess, to control the world and thus become the slave of one's possessions' (p. 167). Fromm freely admits that his ideas are not new but found in religious, philosophical and political writings in many countries over various historical periods. The theme of this work is not that money never leads to happiness but that the sole pursuit of money can never lead to happiness. One consistent piece of evidence cited by people who do not believe that wealth necessarily brings happiness is the observation that wealthy men – such as Lord Nuffield in Britain – attempt to attain public honour and social esteem by lavish gifts to universities, etc., which is something the accumulation of wealth alone cannot bring but which is clearly very important.

A second source of information on the relationship between wealth and happiness are studies on people attaining sudden or unexpected wealth. There is, in the sociological literature, the concept of the anomie of affluence. Simon and Gagnon (1976) have extended Merton's formulation of the causes of anomie thus. Anomie results when culturally prescribed *goals,* such as education or material wealth, are dissociated from acceptable *modes* for realising these goals, such as availability of schooling or employment. Basic to any notion of the anomie of success is too easy access to the modes or avenues of achieving the societally determined goals. More people than ever have the possibility of access to these legitimate modes, which leads them to question both their commitment to these goals and the gratifications that they bring. Hence they see the rejection or moderation of the achievement motive (and the desire to accumulate wealth) as an expression of the transition from the anomie of deprivation to the anomie of wealth. Like Merton (1938), they devised a typology of adaptive responses to the anomie of affluence. Briefly they are these:

1. *Optimal conformists:* people who are committed to the major goals of society and experience their realisation as gratifying (upwardly mobile, Conservative).
2. *Detached conformists:* people who find the sources of gratification associated with achievement adequate but are not particularly committed to the goals.
3. *Compulsive achievers:* people totally committed to achievement but lacking a capacity for experiencing the congruent gratifications.
4. *Conforming deviants:* people who have acquired the means of gratification to seek out new (and often illegitimate) modes of gratification.
5. *Detached people:* people who have a dispassionate rejection of both the values of achievement and the gratifications attending it.
6. *Escapists:* people who reject the values of achievement and accept innovative and possibly deviant styles of gratification.
7. *Conventional reformers:* people who combine a desire to replace the major goals of society with an acceptance of the qualities of life that constitute the content and style of a successful life.
8. *Missionaries:* people who wish to replace the major goals of society but also reject the qualities of life associated with current views about success.
9. *Total rebels:* people who desire to replace both the goals of the social order and the quality of life associated with success within that order.

Diagrammatically this typology may be summarised as in Table 6.5.

Abrahamson (1980) examined the effects on lottery winners in American state lotteries. He tried to establish the amount of anomie experienced by the winners a year or so after their win, and also their general commitment to strive for future attainments. He found, as predicted, a positive but small relationship between size of winnings and anomie; however, the larger, indirect effects of large winnings appear to be anomie-reducing. The magnitude of winnings are positively related to gratification permissiveness, and inversely related to future aspirations: 'Thus increased desires do not seem so brutalizing: the appetites, when whetted, do not seem to result in detachment. High anomie is, rather, the price that is paid by those who resist a readjustment in their consummatory styles' (p. 56). It is argued that

**Table 6.5**  Typology of adaptive responses

| Type | Commitment to the goals of society | Gratification by goal, achievement |
|---|---|---|
| 1.  Optimal conformist | Plus | Plus |
| 2.  Detached conformist | Minus | Plus |
| 3.  Compulsive achiever | Plus | Minus |
| 4.  Conforming deviant | Plus | Innovative |
| 5.  Detached person | Minus | Minus |
| 6.  Escapist | Minus | Innovative |
| 7.  Conventional reformer | Innovative | Plus |
| 8.  Missionary | Innovative | Minus |
| 9.  Total rebel | Innovative | Innovative |

*Source:* Simon and Gagnon 'The Anomie of Affluence: A Post-Mertonian Conception', *American Journal of Sociology.* 82. The University of Chicago Press, 1976.

sudden wealth only leads to alienation or anomie when the society is prudish, restrained and respectable and the failure to restrain indulgent impulses may eventually produce a sense of bondlessness and detachment.

In a somewhat atheoretical but interesting study of pools winners in Britain, Smith and Razzell (1974) asked 89 winners a number of questions. They found that people spent their money on such things as property, cars, consumer durables and travel. Nearly 60 per cent invested more than half of their winnings. Of the 70 per cent in full-time employment before their win only 17 per cent remained in full-time employment after. The questions on problems and happiness resulting from the win revealed rather ambiguous results. Winners reported that people in general were more hostile than their relatives and friends to their win (16 per cent vs 8 and 6 per cent, respectively), while relatives were most positive (47 per cent) and other people least (24 per cent). Compared with a control group, twice as many separated from their spouse (8 per cent) and five times as many divorced (14 per cent). However, it is possible that the greater incidence of divorce amongst pools winners is that they can afford to legalise a separation which previously would have been beyond their financial means. When asked if they ever felt lonely, the pools winners tended to be at extremes – more of them claimed never to experience loneliness or to feel it often, while people in the control group tended to cluster in the middle ranges. Thus while a number of winners suffer acutely from the effects of the win, the vast majority adapt themselves successfully to their new situation. Indicators of health suggested that, if anything, the pools winners were healthier than the control group, possibly because of the security that the money brought them. Of course it should be pointed out that most of these winners in fact came from working-class groups where financial insecurity is probably greater.

## Lay explanations of wealth

Despite the paucity of psychological research into wealth and the wealthy, there have been a number of studies on lay perceptions of financial success. Although these have been done in different countries and with very different populations, the results are remarkably similar. Younger, Arrowood and Hemsley (1977) asked a group of Canadian undergraduates to account for how a certain person 'got to be who and what he is'. In the financially successful condition he was described as earning $100,000 per annum; in the average condition he was described as earning $12,000 per annum; while in the failure condition he was described as unemployed. The students viewed the financially successful person as least responsible, and the failed person as most responsible for their condition. The successful person was seen as luckier than either the average or failure person but not more hard-working than the average person. The subjects did, however, believe that if the 'target' person were asked to account for his own success or failure the successful would attribute his achievement to personal and/or situational factors, while failures would attribute their circumstances primarily to situational factors. The authors point out that as the subjects come predominantly from an 'average' background their explanations may serve a self-protective function:

> If one assumes that a high level of observed success functions as a threat to the subject's self-concept or self-esteem, then a conceivable strategy would be to attribute the performance to extrapersonal causes. Such a defensive posture would no doubt serve to minimise feelings of one's own inadequacy or that of one's family.   (p. 513)

In an American study of over 1,000 male workers Vecchio (1981) found that people who expressed external locus of control beliefs were themselves less wealthy, less well-educated, less *satisfied* with their job, and more likely to be black than workers who expressed internal locus of control beliefs. However, a study such as this could not determine whether locus of control beliefs were the cause or consequence of wealth and poverty. In a large British study, Lewis (1981) looked at the relationship between political beliefs/voting patterns and attributions for wealth. Overall the respondents felt that the wealthy had been luckier than others (54 per cent agreement), had received more help from others (60 per cent agreement), rather than having worked harder (26 per cent agreement), although they generally made more skilful use of their opportunities (52 per cent agreement). However, as predicted, more right-wing voters (Conservatives) as opposed to left-wing voters (Labour Party supporters) believed that wealthy people make more skilful use of their opportunities or generally worked harder.

In a similar study on a group of British subjects Furnham (1983e) hypothesised as follows:

1. Conservative voters would find individualistic (effort and ability) explanations for wealth across the general population as more important than Labour voters, who would find societal factors more important
2. A different pattern of explanations would emerge depending on the social class and race of the group from which a wealthy person came.
3. Definition of wealth would differ according to the sex, education and voting patterns of the subjects.

Fifteen explanations for wealth were offered, and subjects were requested to rate them on a seven-point scale (see Table 6.6).

The results support the hypothesis that Conservatives would find positive individualistic explanations for wealth more important than would Labour voters, who in turn find societal factors that maximise inequality more important than do Conservatives. Thus Conservatives believe that rich people are more hard-working and thrifty (have more effort and ability) than do Labour Party supporters. However, the latter believe the rich to be significantly more ruthless and determined than do Conservative voters. That is, Conservatives support individualistic explanations when they portray the wealthy in a positive light, whereas Labour Party supporters support individualistic explanations for wealth when they portray the rich in a negative light.

Similarly Labour voters believe that the rich had better opportunities, and are

**Table 6.6**  Means of the three voting groups for the general expectations for wealth in Britain*

| Explanations | Conservative | Labour | Liberal/other |
|---|---|---|---|
| Individualistic | | | |
| 1. Careful money management throughout life | 2.62 | 3.59 | 3.20 |
| 2. Hard work and great effort among the rich | 1.89 | 2.78 | 1.76 |
| 3. Being very intelligent | 3.78 | 4.35 | 4.58 |
| 4. The rich are ruthless and determined | 4.41 | 3.17 | 4.44 |
| Societal | | | |
| 1. Very high wages in some businesses and trades | 2.34 | 2.25 | 2.58 |
| 2. Being sent to certain schools and universities | 3.91 | 3.60 | 3.61 |
| 3. Better opportunities for people from certain families | 3.49 | 2.57 | 3.15 |
| 4. The taxation system favours the rich | 5.25 | 3.34 | 4.69 |
| 5. Strong trade unions that get higher wages | 4.61 | 4.78 | 4.37 |
| 6. The economic system automatically creates inequality | 4.28 | 2.85 | 2.62 |
| 7. Society rewards those who work hard and take risks | 3.19 | 4.54 | 3.84 |
| Fatalistic | | | |
| 1. Inheriting wealth from parents or relatives | 1.44 | 1.09 | 1.22 |
| 2. Good luck in winning money at gambling | 5.43 | 5.21 | 5.84 |
| 3. Having a lucky break | 2.88 | 3.10 | 3.28 |
| 4. Being born with good business sense | 2.50 | 2.95 | 2.78 |

Note: *Low scores indicate high importance, i.e. the Seven-point scale 1 = Important, 7 = Unimportant
*Source:* reprinted with permission from *Personality and Individual Differences*, 1983, Furnham, 'Attributions for affluence', Pergamon Press.

more favourably treated by the tax and economic system than Conservatives. Yet Conservatives believe more than Labour voters do that society rewards those who work hard and take risks. Liberal and other voters varied considerably, rating explanations similarly to the Conservatives in the individualistic explanations 2 and 4 and similarly to Labour voters in societal explanation 6, and midway between the two in individualistic explanation 1, and societal explanations 3, 4 and 7.

These explanations differed for different groups, however. Thus it was that there appeared to be very little difference between subjects in explaining wealth among blacks, while there was a considerable difference in explaining wealth among the whites. There were only three significant differences (one sex, and two education effects) in explaining wealth among working-class blacks, and no significant interactions. All the subjects believed that luck, business sense and intelligence were the most important factors to account for wealth among working-class blacks. Yet there were a number of differences between the subjects in their explanations for wealth among the middle-class whites, arguably the group most likely to achieve wealth. Apart from one significant sex and two education main effects, there were seven significant vote effects. They paralleled almost exactly the pattern of significant differences found in the explanations for general wealth – namely, Conservatives found positive individualistic explanations more important than did Labour voters, who in turn found societal explanations more important than did Conservative voters.

Two other results were of interest. A factor analysis of the scales revealed the same three economic explanations that had occurred earlier: individualistic, societal and fatalistic. Although there were no significant differences in the estimates of the annual income of the rich the results are interesting in themselves. However the figures in Table 6.7 indicate that subjects appear to believe that the annual income of rich people is about ten times that of the poor, and those able to 'live decently' about two-and-a-half times that of the poor. Similarly the subjects seem to discriminate on a sex basis, though these results are not significant.

These estimates are, of course, crude indices of perceived wealth. Many other variables associated with the target person – age, age of their children, nature of their accommodation, financial commitments, savings, etc. – may be important in estimating their annual income. Yet there appeared to be relatively little variation in the subjects' estimates.

Forgas, Morris and Furnham (1982) did a similar study in Sydney, Australia, though with a larger sample and somewhat different analysis. The first part of this study was based on a content analysis of the answers to the free-response question 'Indicate the six most important reasons, in order of importance, why you think some people are better off financially than others.' They found that by far the most important explanatory category used by subjects were family background variables (inheritance, good schooling), social factors (strong taxation), individual effort (hard work, savings) and luck (gambling).

Subjects made a total of five sets of attribution judgements for wealth, with the target being (1) a person in general, (2) a native-born working-class person, (3) a middle-class person, (4) a migrant middle-class person and (5) a working-class person.

Attributions to external/social causes such as taxation and the economic system were not affected by the target's class and ethnicity: these explanations applied uniformly to all target characters. It is interesting that attributions to internal/individual causes, such as thrift, hard work and business sense, were significantly more likely to be made when the target was a migrant, rather than a native-born Australian. This tends to confirm the common Australian stereotype of migrants as being particularly hard-working and motivated, in contrast with the easy-going, *laissez-faire* attitude of native-born Australians. The third attributional category, family advantages (inheritance, good education, etc.), was significantly more likely to be used as an explanation of wealth in native-born rather than migrant, and middle-class rather

**Table 6.7**  Estimates of the approximate annual income of different categories of people

|  | Estimated annual income (£) | | |
|---|---|---|---|
|  | Poor | Live decently | Rich |
| Single man | 2103.00 | 5349.00 | 21,666.00 |
| Single woman | 2022.00 | 5156.00 | 19,965.00 |
| Man, wife and two children | 3719.00 | 9215.00 | 31,500.00 |
| Single parent and one child | 3007.00 | 7082.00 | 26,218.00 |

*Source:* reprinted with permission from *Personality and Individual Differences*, 1983, Furnham 'Attributions for affluence', Pergamon Press.

than working-class targets. The interaction of class and ethnicity on this variable indicates that family background was mainly seen as an important cause of wealth in native-born middle-class targets. Finally, the fourth attributional category, luck/risk-taking, was significantly more likely to be seen as a cause of wealth in working-class rather than middle-class targets, irrespective of ethnicity.

Certain individual differences in attributions for wealth were also found. The most powerful deterrents were voting preferences, nationality and education. Finally Forgas, Morris and Furnham (1982) found that Australians estimated the necessary income of a 'wealthy' person to be considerably higher than the British estimates of Furnham (1982b). British subjects believed that considerably less income was sufficient for decent living than did Australians, while about twice as much income is necessary to be considered wealthy in Britain than in Australia.

Furnham and Bond (1986) replicated this study in Hong Kong. Although cross-cultural comparisons are notoriously difficult, particularly as it is not easy to ensure equivalent groups, these results were compared to those from Furnham (1983e), who used a large group of British subjects. In all, thirteen explanations were identical (or very similar) in the two studies.

Table 6.8 shows the rank ordering of the thirteen different explanations for the British (Furnham, 1983e) and Hong Kong (this study) group. Because they were rated on a different scale only the rank order scores are shown in Table 6.6. Overall the correlation between the two groups was 0.69, which is significant at the $p < 0.05$ level. There was no clear pattern in either group of the ratings of individualists, above societal or fatalistic explanations. However, what is most interesting between the two groups are the four explanations which showed the greater differences in ranking. The British ranked inheritance second while it was ranked eighth by the Hong Kong respondents, no doubt, because so many wealthy people in Hong

**Table 6.8** Comparisons between the explanations for wealth in a British (Furnham, 1983e) and Hong Kong sample. Number represents the rank order from importance (1) to unimportant (13)

|  | Great Britain | Hong Kong |
| --- | --- | --- |
| 1. Being born with good business sense | 1 | 2 |
| 2. Inheriting wealth from parents and relatives | 2 | 8[a] |
| 3. Careful money management throughout life | 3 | 3 |
| 4. Being very intelligent | 4 | 5 |
| 5. Having a lucky break | 5 | 1[a] |
| 6. Very high wages in some businesses and industry | 6 | 7 |
| 7. Being sent to certain schools and universities | 7 | 12[a] |
| 8. Better opportunities for people from certain families | 8 | 6 |
| 9. Hard work and great effort among the rich | 9 | 4[a] |
| 10. The rich are ruthless and determined | 10 | 9 |
| 11. The economic system automatically creates inequalities | 11 | 10 |
| 12. The taxation system favours the rich | 12 | 11 |
| 13. Good luck in winning money at gambling | 13 | 13 |

*Source:* reprinted with permission from Furnham and Bond (1986) *Journal of Economic Psychology.*
Note: Rank order correlation = 0.69. [a] Items where there is a rank order difference of greater than 4.

Kong are self-made compared to those in Great Britain. On the other hand, the Hong Kong respondents ranked a lucky break and hard work and effort as more important than the British, who believed being sent to certain universities and schools to be important.

Compared to respondents in other cultures – Forgas, Morris and Furnham (1982) in Australia, Furnham (1983e) in Britain, Younger *et al.* (1977) in Canada – these Hong Kong students believed that wealth (and presumably its converse, poverty) is very strongly the result of their own skill, effort, creativity and timing. They appear not to believe that it is the preserve of certain social, political or economic groups acting to deny them access to fair competition. However, it is quite possible that while internal explanations are given for wealth, external ones are given for poverty. Certainly other work in this field would suggest that there is consistency in explanations (tendency for individualistic vs societal explanations) but this has clearly not been tested in this group (Furnham and Lewis, 1986).

The explanations considered most important can probably be explained in terms of the unique social, political and economic climate of Hong Kong. The explanation rated as most important 'Able to grasp opportunities' reflects the free-trade policy of the government which fosters speculation and opportunism. 'Good business sense' was rated third and 'Careful money management' fourth, both of which refer to the importance of adaptability to the changing economic climate. 'Being creative' or innovative is undoubtedly important and was rated fifth. The sixth most important factor was 'Skilful in social interaction', which probably reflects the traditional Chinese belief that work success is dependent on good relations with others, particularly those at work (Jacobs, 1979). The seventh most importantly rated factor was hard work and great effort. Chinese people are widely regarded as diligent and hard-working and it is generally believed that effort is rewarded with material success, as the introductory proverb suggests.

These studies have important implications. What is particularly surprising is the significant and consistent differences between migrant and native-born subjects found here. Migrants to countries like Australia come from a variety of backgrounds, yet they appear to be unified in their belief that individual effort is a significant source of wealth. Migrants are also more likely to be seen by others as having acquired wealth through individual effort, and they have more limited estimates for income levels necessary to be 'wealthy'. The ideology of individual achievement is of course a well-known component of the migrant experience. It is still interesting to note that the Protestant ethic finds its most devout followers not among the predominantly Anglo-Saxon native population, but within the heterogeneous migrant community.

# Conclusion

A surprisingly large number of people have becoming rich as their primary hope and desire. What they define as rich, and how they wish to spend their wealth are very variable. Despite this, there is a surprising dearth of psychological interest in wealth. Those studies that do exist are simply applications of standard social psychological theories – attribution theory (lay explanations of wealth), equity theory (the distribution of wealth) – to the acquisition and distribution of wealth. Those studies which have considered individual differences have usually restricted themselves to demographic factors (age, sex, class, income) rather than considering any psychological factors (social beliefs, attitudes). The fact that wealth is not a social problem does not mean that it does not merit good research.

# Chapter 7

# Unemployment

## Introduction

Research into the psychological consequences of unemployment, like unemployment in the western world itself, tends to be cyclical. The two major periods of research activity followed periods where unemployment increased dramatically – the 1930s, and the late 1970s and the 1980s and 1990s. Most of this research has been done in Australia, Britain, Europe and the United States but there are exceptions (Westin, 1990). The fact that research has been done in two periods nearly forty years apart means that interesting and important comparisons can be made. Jahoda (1982) has noted:

> If it were found that modern unemployment was psychologically less disturbing now than in the past one would conclude that the standard of living to which the unemployed were then reduced – subsistence level and often below – had a greater weight in shaping their experiences than the absence of a job, which would emerge as a matter of secondary importance. If, on the other hand, the modern unemployed showed similar psychological disturbances under unquestionably better living conditions than in the past, economic deprivation would count for less and the absence of employment for more in explaining their experiences. (pp. 15–16)

What is perhaps most striking about the literature is that studies have revealed a substantial amount of similarity whether focused on physical or mental consequences of unemployment, irrespective of where conducted, at what period of time or with what specific population.

This chapter will attempt an overview of the major findings in the ever-growing unemployment literature. Though diverse in terms of where, when and how research was conducted, an attempt has been made to address the topic under broad general headings.

# Early research in the area

Although there has been sporadic research into unemployment for a very long time (Rowntree and Lasker, 1911), the psychological literature dates back to the 1930s, which saw the highest levels of unemployment in most European countries this century (Bakke, 1933; Jahoda, Lazarfeld and Zeisel, 1933; Beales and Lambert, 1934). In a review of the literature, Eisenberg and Lazarsfeld (1938) listed over 100 references from Europe and the United States which had investigated aspects of unemployment. Most of the early literature constituted in-depth case studies of individuals or communities which had suffered unemployment. Many of the themes in these various studies coincided and have been actively pursued today. Two of the most important psychological effects of unemployment that were identified by nearly all the researchers were the sense of social stigma attached to being unemployed, and the suffering resulting from the lack of structure that people experience (Kelvin and Jarrett, 1985).

The most celebrated research in the 1930s is probably the study of Jahoda, Lazarsfeld and Zeisel (1933) on a small Austrian village, Marienthal. Although set in an unrepresentative town (it was a one-factory village in rural Austria), the study is worth considering in some detail for three reasons. First, it is a surprisingly detailed sociography of an unemployed community which has never been repeated since. Secondly, the basic findings from this study were found in other studies in the 1930s (Komarovsky, 1940) and the 1970s and 1980s (Marsden and Duff, 1975). Thirdly, it demonstrated quite clearly a perhaps counter-intuitive finding that has emerged from studies ever since – namely, that unemployment leads more to personal apathy and disintegration than political insurrection or organised revolution.

Fraser (1980) has admirably summarised the findings of Jahoda, Lazarsfeld and Zeisel (1933), which are worth repeating. He lists the findings under seven headings:

1. *Finances.* Despite the fact that wages in the area had already been low, unemployment brought consistent reductions in income. The system of paying unemployment relief and assistance made this a necessity. Unemployment relief was payable for a period of about six months, then discretionary emergency assistance could be provided for a further period of up to a year.

   The maximum relief permissible was 80 per cent of wages in the last week of work; in turn, the maximum emergency assistance possible was 80 per cent of the relief. There were numerous ways in which families failed to be eligible for maximum benefits, but even if they were eligible, within six or seven months of unemployment the most they could receive was slightly less than two-thirds of their previous, generally low, wages. Many families were even worse off. From the figures in the report I estimate, in a necessarily rough and ready way, that the plight of an unemployed Marienthal family of, say, two parents and three children might be compared with that of a similar British family having to live, in 1979, on less than £20 per week, that is, between one-half and two-thirds of the weekly maintenance grant of a university student.

2. *Material aspects of life-style.* Obviously drastic economies of all sorts were absolutely essential. Standard items of food, such as coffee and butter, were replaced by cheaper alternatives. Carbohydrates dominated at meal times. Only 30 per cent of families had meat on at least two days per week, and over 90 per cent of that meat was either horse or rabbit meat. On the day before the fortnightly payments of unemployment benefits, approximately half of the schoolchildren took either dry bread or nothing at all for their lunch at school. Even so, so much of a family's budget had to go on food (perhaps up to 90 per cent) that any other substantial item of expenditure, such as shoe repairs, became a major problem.

3. *Physical well-being.* There was evidence of an overall decline in health standards, despite the equally horrifying fact that there was actually improvement, at least in the short run, in the health of some adults, namely those who had been prone to tuberculosis as a result of their working conditions in the mill. Even the children suffered, despite the willingness of the unemployed families to spend a disproportionate amount of their income on milk for their children. During the study, one-third of the children under 14 were rated as being in poor general health. Only 8 per cent of the children had teeth unaffected by caries. There were signs of an inverse correlation between ill-health and family income.

4. *Emotional state.* There were many specific reports of emotionality, upsets, fearfulness, and the like. Many of the men in particular manifested a blunted sense of time relations. 'Apathy', 'despair', 'depression' were terms frequently used to describe the unemployed. The investigators attempted to classify the overall state of the 100 families for whom they had detailed information. They concluded: 16 families were 'unbroken', that is, they remained positive, even optimistic, in attitudes and emotions; 48 were 'resigned', that is, they had accepted the realities of unemployment but were still coping well with organising the necessities of everyday life; 11 were 'in despair', that is, although still attempting to cope with the necessities of daily living, emotionally they were 'broken'; 25 were 'apathetic', that is, they had given up all attempts to cope either emotionally or practically. Over one-third of the families, then, were regarded as psychologically 'broken'. The emotional well-being of the families showed a positive correlation with the amount of weekly income.

5. *Personal relationships.* In some cases, the crisis appeared actually to have improved marital relations by, for example leaving husbands free to help around the house or forcing them, through financial pressures, to give up drinking. But those were exceptions. The more general picture was one of an increase in minor quarrels and of reports of withdrawal from social relations and friendships. So there was some, though by no means dramatic, evidence of increased interpersonal strains and difficulties. In fact, close personal relationships appear to have held up more effectively than many other facets of individual and family life.

6. *Social interests and activities.* In general, these decreased markedly. Clearly,

some of the decrease, such as visits to Vienna or to the theatre, reflected financial pressures. But almost all formal social organisations experienced a decline in membership and participation, even when financial outlay was not involved. Inexpensive or free informal activities, such as visiting friends or going for walks, also declined in popularity.

The fate of the village library is instructive. Just before the factory closed, the library, fortuitously, had expanded considerably, and its small borrowing charges were abolished. Yet borrowing dropped markedly, mainly in terms of the number of borrowers, but even in terms of the number of books per remaining borrower. The unemployed did not even feel like reading.

7. *Political activities*. The unemployment, poverty and shattered lives led to no increase in political action. Quite the reverse. There had been a history of political involvement in Marienthal, but all three of the major political organisations suffered marked losses in membership. Since membership fees for the unemployed were nominal, it is unlikely that the primary reason for such loss was financial, a point supported by the fact that the cheaper but more political newspaper lost more readers in the village than the dearer but entertainment-oriented one. A striking demonstration of the fact that those who remained politically active tended to be from the minority of people still in work was provided by the Young Socialist Workers, who retained 37 members, of whom only 7 were unemployed: 'When one of their officers lost his job he resigned from his position and decided to give up politics entirely' (Jahoda, Lazarsfeld and Zeisel, 1933: 41).

# Theoretical approach to unemployment

The complexity associated with, and the applied nature of, the findings in the area of unemployment has meant that few orthodox psychological theories have been applied to this research. Some investigations have argued that one cannot and should not develop a theory of unemployment as distinct from a theory of employment, while others have attempted to develop various specific theories that seek only to explain a limited number of findings in this area. Thus for some, unemployment is simply a stressor much like any other stressor. However, others have attempted more refined theory development.

## Jahoda's functional deprivation theory

M. Jahoda (1979, 1981, 1982) has tried to interpret the experience of unemployment in terms of a framework that is partly derived from Freudian theory. Freud and his followers consider work a means whereby the individual learns about reality. Transactions with reality are mediated by the ego instinctual urges, internalising social norms and the demands of the environment: this mechanism is the ego and many of the functions of the psychoanalytic ego are similar to the function that Jahoda attributes to work. According to Jahoda, work imposes a time structure, enlarges social experience to complement close family attachments, unites the individual with collective purposes, provides identity and enjoins activity. These functions are called the latent function of work and together with the manifest function, income, provide the basis of psychological experience.

These functions are very general and not easily amenable to quantification. How much time structure, social purpose and identity is necessary? It is also questionable whether all types of employment satisfy these functions. Time structure is certainly imposed but is unlikely that all employment provides a sense of collective purpose, rational and informative social relationships and a positive sense of identity.

This 'deprivation theory' has had it critics. Fryer (1986) has offered three kinds of criticism:

1. *Pragmatic:* the theory is very difficult to test.
2. *Methodological:* one cannot be sure which or how the deprivations are caused by unemployment; people not deprived do not necessarily enjoy, appreciate or acknowledge this state.
3. *Empirical:* the theory does not take into account change over time or individual differences in reacting.

Fryer (1986) argues that the latent function theory has not been properly verified and that some of the observed consequences of unemployment need a different theory. He feels that individuals develop towards self-determination and autonomy and that behaviour is determined as much from within as from external demands. That is, some unemployed people take part in creative and autonomous activities and appear to cope with lack of work fairly well.

In a sense Jahoda (1982) argues that people are deprived while Fryer (1986) argues that institutions impose things on people (like stigma). Whereas the former underlays individual choice and personal control, the latter tends to underplay social identity and interdependence of people at work. Clearly both are right but prefer different emphases.

## Warr's vitamin theory

An alternative model has been proposed by Warr (1987) called the 'vitamin' model, which assumes that mental health is influenced by the environment in a manner analogous to the effect of vitamins on physical health.

> The availability of vitamins is important for physical health up to, but not beyond, a certain level. A low level of intake, vitamin deficiency gives rise to physiological impairment and ill-health but after attainment of specified levels there is no benefit derived from additional quantities. It is suggested that principal environment features are important to mental health in a similar manner: their absence tends towards an impairment in mental health, but their presence beyond a required level does not hold further benefit. In addi-

tion, however, certain vitamins become harmful in a very large quantities. In these infrequent cases the association between increased vitamin intake and health becomes negative after a broad range of moderate quantities. (pp. 9–10)

Thus, for instance, up to a point vitamins C and E improve health but then have no further effect, while A and D in moderation increase health but in excess are bad for people. Thus pay, physical conditions and interpersonal contact may be like vitamins C and E, while control, job variety, clarity and workload might like vitamins A and D.

For Warr (1987) there are nine basic vitamins, the benefits of work or the principal features of the environment:

1. Opportunity for intrinsic and extrinsic control.
2. Opportunity for skill use.
3. Externally generated goals.
4. Variety.
5. Environmental clarity.
6. Availability of money.
7. Physical security.
8. Opportunity for interpersonal contact.
9. Valued social position.

The vitamin model also seeks to avoid the limitations of perspectives in terms of environment 'stress'. Aspects of job or other settings have sometimes been approached from the standpoint that they may be defined as stressful, giving rise to feelings of strain. This perspective can accommodate many types of investigation, but it is limited by its emphasis upon the negative aspects of environments. Furthermore, the notions of stress and resulting strain are liable to become over-inclusive. (p. 283)

Warr (1987) is aware of a number of problems with this approach. Firstly, that his list of nine vitamins may be enlarged (subdivided) or reduced (reclassified). Secondly, that when looking at the relationship between these features at work and mental health it comes progressively more difficult to define the latter, which has itself many different components and conceptualisations. Thirdly, there is a paucity of empirical evidence in favour of certain features of the model and by definition a plethora in others. Fourth, that the model is exclusively a situation- or environment-centred model in that it looks at the effects of job characteristics on mental health and not at individual differences.

## Feather's expectancy-valence theory

The studies by Feather and Barber (1983) and Feather and Davenport (1981) have interpreted the degree of negative affect during unemployment in terms of expectancy-valence theory. It assumes that a person's actions are predictable from the perceived attractiveness (positive valence) or avertiveness (negative valence) of expected outcomes. Individual behaviour and cognitions are a function of the attractiveness of valued outcomes and expectation about the instrumentality of certain behaviours in achieving these outcomes.

Feather (1992) noted:

> Within the framework of expectancy-value theory a person's actions are related to the expectations that the person holds and subjective values (or valences) that are associated with alternative instrumental actions and their possible outcomes. The subjective values (or valences) may be positive or negative, signifying attractive or averse events or outcomes. For example, a person may perceive that travelling a long distance to his or her job is aversive but that working at the job itself is attractive. The expectations encompass beliefs about whether a particular action can be performed to some required standard that defines a successful outcome and also beliefs about the various positive and negative consequences that may follow the outcome. An unemployed person, for example, may have a strong expectation that he or she can perform (e.g. by addressing the question asked at the interview and by presenting self in a favourable light). The unemployed person may also hold the expectation that succeeding at the job interview will have positive consequences, the major one being getting the job. The outcome may in turn be linked to other consequences that have positive or negative subjective value (e.g. getting a salary, having to do a lot of shift work).    (pp. 317–18)

Thus, Feather and Davenport (1981) found that depressive affect in the unemployed was greatest for those who perceived employment as very attractive and had high expectations of obtaining a job. The framework could be applied to more complex behaviours if there was an associated theory of work values and a theory linking work values to expectations and behaviourial intentions. Attribution theory has also been used by Feather and his associates to explain variations in depression and depressive affect. This type of theory specifies that the amount of depression displayed by the unemployed will depend on the extent to which the individual attributes unemployment to external causes (e.g. economic factors) or internal causes (e.g. ability). Feather and Davenport (1981) did show that those who were not depressed were more likely to attribute unemployment to external attributions.

## Bakke's theory of tasks, income and personal control

O'Brein (1986) who made a close study of the early research on unemployment has spelt out Bakke's early theories. Bakke (1993):

> described the distress of the unemployed in terms of past work experience, loss of income and reduced personal control over life satisfactions. His theoretical comments were not stated formally but tended to be consistent in emphasizing that task experiences and money shaped personality. He also argued that personal control, as an internalized belief system, was one of the central personality dimensions determined by tasks done in work and leisure. His writings appear to be useful for current research because the concept of personal control has been frequently studied by social and clinical psychologists. Much

of the research has been based on Rotter's concept of internal–external control and individual variations in internal/external control have been shown to predict a wide range of behaviours. By linking unemployment experiences to personal control, Bakke's is able to provide a theoretical mechanism for understanding patterns of unemployment behaviour (O'Brien, 1986: 243)

Researchers and reviewers (Fraser, 1980; Furnham, 1982a; Kelvin and Jarrett, 1985), including Jahoda herself (M. Jahoda 1979, 1981, 1982), have been impressed more by the similarities than the difference in research findings on current unemployment. This is not to say that research is no different now – for instance, very little of the early work was concerned with how people explain the causes of unemployment, unemployment among women, youth unemployment, etc. Furthermore the early research was more concerned with physical deprivation and hardship consequent upon employment, whereas current research has focused more upon psychological (clinical, social) aspects of unemployment. Samples are more representative, methods more sophisticated, analyses more powerful, but the essential nature of the results remains the same.

O'Brien (1980) made a close study of the early research and came to the following conclusion:

This brief review of the general response to unemployment indicates that it is a mistake to accept the conventional interpretation of the psychological effects of unemployment in the 1930s. Some of the unemployed did progressively lapse into a permanent state of despair and apathy. However, most accepted their disappointment with resilience. They tried to do what they could to obtain jobs and maintain their families within the constraints imposed by little money and poor health. They were not idle, if this means regular inactivity and laziness. They experienced stress, boredom, anger and despair. But most were not broken by these experiences. Those who suffered most tended to be those with prior vulnerability and those who had lost most in economic terms. These generalizations reflect, in my judgement the conclusions reached by the majority of writers. Their conclusions, admittedly, are only as good as their methods. In many cases their methods were open to bias because they were not able to assess the degree to which all of the determinants of behaviour in unemployment were present in their samples. Nevertheless, these studies are all that we have to go on. Although there may be doubts about the basis for their conclusions, it should be possible to give a balanced account of what these conditions actually were.

It is a distortion to say that they found that the loss of job activities led to distress and psychological damage if what is meant is that the job activities were essential for the maintenance of psychological health. Few of the unemployed regretted the loss of unsatisfying work. They did regret the loss of income, a regular time structure and social status. It appears to have been underrated. The role of past work experience has also been underrated. The extensive work of Bakke illustrated how work could shape personal orientations of unemployment. It suggested that much of the apparent inactivity and negative mood of the unemployed was not a function of job loss alone. It was also a function of past work experiences which left people feeling they lacked control of their lives. Unemployment just placed extra restrictions on people who were already unhappy and unable to develop their own personal resources. (pp. 195–6)

# Nature and function of employment and unemployment

One way to attempt to understand why the experience of unemployment is so psychologically detrimental is to attempt to understand the motivational functions of work. The question posed is, therefore, 'What are the beneficial aspects of work, the absence of which leads the unemployed to experience so much difficulty?' M. Jahoda (1979, 1981), following Merton (1957), distinguished between manifest and latent consequences of employment. The manifest aspects of work are simply earning a living, while the latent consequences are unintended by-products of the purposeful action that is necessary to achieve the manifest consequences. The distinction is not unlike that made by Herzberg (1966) in his two-factor theory of job satisfaction. Hygiene (maintenance or dissatisfaction) factors relate mainly to the extrinsic, manifest aspects of employment, while the motivating (satisfaction) factors relate to the intrinsic, latent aspects of employment. While the unemployed quite demonstrably miss the manifest consequences of work such as a (possibly) high standard of income, what is most distressing to them are the latent functions. The latent functions of work include the following:

1. *Work structures time:* Work structures the day, the week and even longer periods. The loss of a time structure can be very disorienting. Feather and Bond (1983) compared the structure and purposeful activity among employed and unemployed university graduates. They found, as predicted, that the unemployed were less organised and less purposeful in their use of time, and reported more depressive symptoms when compared to the employed.

2. *Work provides regularly shared experiences:* Regular contact with non-nuclear family members provides an important source of social contact. There is a vast literature on social-skills deficits which suggests that social isolation is related to disturbed mental states (Trower, Bryant and Argyle, 1978). There is now a growing interest in the social support hypothesis, which suggests that social support from family and friends buffers the major causes of stress and increases coping ability, so reducing illness (Gore, 1978). If one's primary source of friends and contacts is work colleagues then the benefits of social support are denied precisely when they are most needed. There are also a wealth of studies in organisational psychology which suggest that one of the most frequently cited sources of job satisfaction is contact with other people (Argyle, 1983).

3. *Work provides experience of creativity, mastery and a sense of purpose:* 'Both the organisation and the product of work imply the interdependence of human beings. Take away this daily experience that efforts must be combined, and the unemployed are left with a sense of uselessness, of being on the scrap heap' (M. Jahoda, 1979: 118). Work, even not particularly satisfying work, gives some sense of mastery or achievement. Creative activities stimulate people and provide a sense of satisfaction.

A person's contribution to producing goods or providing services forges a link between the individual and the society of which he or she is a part. Work roles are not the only roles which offer the individual the opportunity of being useful and contributing to the community but, without doubt, for the majority they are the most central roles and consequently people deprived of the opportunity to work often feel useless and report that they lack a sense of purpose. (Jahoda, 1979: 313)

4. *Work is a source of personal status and identity:* A person's job is an important indicator of his personal status in society – hence the often amusing debates over job titles such as sanitary engineer for street cleaner! Furthermore it is not only to the employed person that the job gives certain status but also to his/her family. The employed person therefore is a link between two important social systems – family and home. An unemployed person has lost employment status and hence identity. Not unnaturally there is a marked drop in self-esteem following unemployment.

5. *Work is a source of activity:* All work involves some expenditure of physical or mental effort. Whereas too much activity may induce fatigue and stress, too little results in boredom and restlessness, particularly among extraverts. People seek to maximise the amount of activity that suits them by choosing particular jobs or tasks that fulfil their needs. The unemployed however, are not provided with this possibility and have consistently to provide stimulation to keep them active.

A number of points should be made about this list of the functions of work. Firstly, it is not exhaustive and the functions are not mutually exclusive. Secondly, it is possible that other, even more obvious, functions could be mentioned, such as providing an income. Thirdly, these latent or manifest functions of work can be provided by other social institutions such as societies, clubs, etc., which provide a source of unpaid work. Finally, nothing actually prevents the unemployed from seeking out some of the benefits of work, such as creating a stable time structure to their day, though this may be difficult particularly for those most likely to be unemployed (school-leavers, unskilled labourers).

Another way of understanding the benefits of employment – and by implication the frustrations of unemployment – is to look at the extensive and exhaustive literature on job satisfaction. There are, of course, a number of theories of job satisfaction (Herzberg, Mousner and Snyderman, 1959; Vroom, 1964; Maslow, 1970), but all have focused on certain specific factors. The following list is not exhaustive, nor are the factors in rank order as these differ from one job to another.

Those attributes are defined as follows:

*Skill-variety:* the degree to which a job requires a variety of different activities in carrying out the work; which involve the use of a number of different skills and talents of the person.

*Task identity:* the degree to which the job requires completion of a 'whole' and identifiable piece of work; that is, doing a job from beginning to end with a visible outcome.

*Task significance:* the degree to which the job has a substantial impact on the lives or work of other people; whether in the immediate organisation, or outside it.

*Autonomy:* the degree to which the job provides substantial freedom, independence and discretion to the individual in scheduling the work and in determining the procedures to be used in carrying it out.

*Feedback:* the degree to which carrying out the work activities required by the job results in the individual obtaining direct and clear information about the effectiveness of his/her performance.

When jobs are high on all these attributes they lead individuals to experience their work as meaningful and capable of providing them with experience, responsibility and knowledge about the actual results of their work activities. The attributes are also used to diagnose the motivation potential of a job.

A very large number of studies have been done using this measure; they show that job satisfaction is significantly related to the attributes, separately and in combination.

Argyle (1983) on the other hand has divided the causes of job satisfaction into a number of categories: intrinsic (variety, autonomy, use of skills and abilities); hours of work; incentive conditions (pay, occupational status, promotion prospects, security); work group (cohesiveness, popularity, size, opportunities for interaction); supervision (consideration, participation in decision making); the company (size and structure, participation in management); and individual differences (age, intelligence, personality, orientation to work). Some of these sources of satisfaction apply only to the employed but others equally to the unemployed, to the extent that they do not have them.

Although it has been challenged (Hulin and Blood, 1968; Guion and Landy, 1972), Herzberg's two-factor theory perhaps gives the best insight into the sources of job satisfaction (as opposed to dissatisfaction) which are denied to the unemployed. These look very much like the list of the functions of work given above but include others as well: opportunity for achievement, opportunity for recognition, the work itself, responsibility, advancement, and personal growth. It is the consistent emphasis on intrinsic factors associated with job satisfaction, rather than extrinsic factors, that suggests that the unemployed are likely to suffer most from not being in work. However, the work on job satisfaction has one more important feature of relevance to unemployment. Jobs that lead to a high degree of dissatisfaction may be more unpleasant or unhealthy for the individual than unemployment under good conditions. Warr (1983) has differentiated between 'good' and 'bad' jobs and 'good' and 'bad' unemployment in terms of nine variables that have proved discriminating in previous research (Table 7.1). Thus it may be that if a person leaves a bad job s/he may adapt well to good unemployment. There are many examples of this. The point made here is that just as not all jobs are satisfying, so not all unemployment is unsatisfying. Depending on the job, the person and the society's reaction to unemployment, it may be possible to experience beneficial

**Table 7.1** Factors discriminating between jobs

|  | 'Good' jobs have | 'Bad' jobs have | 'Good' unemployment has | 'Bad' unemployment has |
|---|---|---|---|---|
| 1. Money | more | less | more | less |
| 2. Variety | more | less | more | less |
| 3. Goals, traction | more | less | more | less |
| 4. Decision latitude | more | less | more | less |
| 5. Skill use/development | more | less | more | less |
| 6. Psychological threat | less | more | less | more |
| 7. Security | more | less | more | less |
| 8. Interpersonal contact | more | less | more | less |
| 9. Valued social position | more | less | more | less |

*Source:* 'Work, jobs and unemployment', *Bulletin of the British Psychological Society*, 1983, 36.

aspects of unemployment. Indeed some have argued that the central ethic must move away from work to post-industrial self-fulfilment through the growth of the informal or free economy (Pym, 1980).

The importance of the nature of the job, or organisational climate, was demonstrated in a study by Friedlander and Greenberg (1971) of the hard-core unemployed in a period of low unemployment. They examined 478 hard-core (people who find it difficult to hold down a job) unemployed people's biographic and demographic backgrounds, their attitudes to work, the organisational climate in which they were placed and the effect of a two-week intervention programme. The only correlate of work effectiveness and behaviour was the degree of supportiveness of the organisational climate in which the person was placed. Hence the authors concluded that the social structure or climate in most organisations may be more a cause than a cure for the hard-core unemployeds' work behaviour.

Over the years there has been a steady accumulation of studies of what Warr (1987) calls the jobless environment. Warr and Payne (1983) have looked at actual changes in behaviour following job loss. These authors looked at social-class differences in specific behaviours after job loss which were grouped as: domestic work (household chores, shopping, cooking), domestic pastimes (radio, television), other pastimes (smoking, window shopping), book reading (library visits, extramural classes), recreations (sports, hobbies), entertainment through money (drinking, cinema) and social contacts (church, political meetings). Apart from entertainment through money (a set of behaviours which declined), many forms of behaviour appeared, not unnaturally, to increase after job loss. The middle-class group tended to report a significantly greater increase in book reading, and the working-class a greater increase in other/pastimes, but a greater reduction in entertainment through money. Furthermore several significant associations between change in behaviour and general health were noted; for instance, a reduction of entertainment through money was moderately associated with lower well-being for the middle class, but not the lower-class respondents. Many of these results are in accordance with other studies, such as a reduction of drinking (Smart, 1979) but, contrary to older studies which found that apathy associated with unemployment led to a reduction in church and political party attendance (Bakke, 1940), there was no reduction (or increase) in this study.

In another study with a larger population, Warr (1984) focused on age and length of unemployment as mediating variables in self-reported behaviour after job loss. The same 38-item scale subdivided into seven categories was used. Just over a third of the activities changed with length of unemployment: all forms of domestic work increased as did other pastimes and social contacts. Entertainment through money, however, declined. Nearly half of the behaviourial changes were age-related, particularly domestic work, other pastimes and recreations, many of which were curvilinear. Predictably, sitting around at home and watching television (not for study) were highly correlated with mental maladjustment. Warr does point out that the results probably illustrate that there is no overall difference in the *amount* of a person's social contact between periods of employment and unemployment, but that the *content* and *location* of encounters and the *range* of people met are reduced after becoming unemployed.

Warr and Jackson (1984) examined the age and length correlates of unemployment among nearly 1,000 men. Psychological distress, financial and labour-market commitment were greatest amongst the middle-aged men. There was a positive relationship between length of unemployment and mental and physical illness; and the probability of having an unemployed wife was found to be negatively associated with the length of unemployment. They conclude: 'Age and duration are themselves not causal variables; they stand as proxies for processes and states which require elucidation' (p. 84).

In a useful summary Warr (1987) looked at the experience of the jobless in terms of his nine factor model. However, he does believe that the experience of joblessness is different for middle-aged men, teenagers, women, the long-term unemployed and those unemployed people who regain their jobs.

## Stages and cycles of reactions to unemployment

A number of attempts have been made to understand the way in which the unemployed adjust over time to their new circumstances. Because so little research in this area is longitudinal (it is nearly all cross-sectional) there is more speculation than research with regard to transitional stages or phases for the unemployed. Those longitudinal studies which do exist (Warr, Jackson and Banks, 1982) have not investigated the reactions of the unemployed over a very long period (being usually less than one year) hence the long-term effects of unemployment are not clear.

There is, however, no shortage of theories concerning how the unemployed may react to unemployment (Harrison, 1976; Hopson and Adams, 1976). Because unemployment involves the reactions to *loss*, the extensive literature on grieving and bereavement (Parkes, 1975), divorce (Levinger and Moles, 1979) and migration (Furnham and Bochner, 1985) has been seen to be relevant. Researchers in all these areas have relied on early neo-psychoanalytic researchers (Bowlby, 1969) for their ideas.

Before examples of these stage-wise descriptions are considered it is perhaps worth noting that all stage-wise descriptions have their problems. Firstly, stage-wise models are descriptive rather than explanatory – they simply describe the typical pattern of response over time. Secondly, they rarely specify what factors determine that a person moves on from one stage to another or remains fixated in one stage. All stage-wise models are linear, but it is quite possible that patterns of reactions are cyclical: that is, there are erratic progressions and regressions. Further crucial individual differences and moderating variables are ignored in these descriptions which are by definition general. Finally, the more stages a theory has the more vulnerable it is to disproof. Hayes and Nutman (1981) have reviewed a number of stage-wise, approaches. These include Hopson and Adams' (1976) seven-stage approach, the four stages of Harrison (1976), three of Hill (1978) and five of Briar (1977).

Clearly, although there are some obvious similarities between these theories, there are also important differences. Hayes and Nutman (1981) summarise their review thus:

It appears that the transition can be viewed in terms of three broad stages. Within the first of these is an initial phase of shock and immobilization, followed by a phase characterized by renewed hope, optimism and a tendency to minimize or deny that there has been a change. The second broad stage seems to include a period in which the idea that 'things will turn out all right in the end' is shaken and the individual's identity comes under pressure. This stage often appears to be associated with depression and withdrawal. The onset of this stage is characterized by an acceptance that there has been a change and by a 'letting go' of the past, and during this second stage the individual gradually begins to search for and test out new relationships between self and situation. If unemployment is prolonged and if re-call to the lost job fails to materialize then the individual must find and internalize a new identity. This process of readjustment is characterized in the third and final broad stage irrespective of whether the individual successfully re-enters the world of work in a new work role or continues in a state of unemployment.

It is as though the period of disorganization and crisis unfreezes both the individual and his or her family and helps them to search for and find new values and standards better suited to the present. (pp. 18–19)

**Table 7.2** Stage-wise theories of reactions in unemployment

| Hopson and Adams (1976) | Harrison (1976) | Hill (1977) | Briar (1977) |
|---|---|---|---|
| Immobilisation | 1. Shock | 1. Trauma/denial | 1. Shock |
| Minimisation | 2. Optimism | 2. Depression | 2. Optimism |
| Depression | 3. Pessimism | 3. Adaptation | 3. Self-blame |
| Acceptance of reality | 4. Fatalism | | 4. Depression |
| Testing | | | 5. Inertia |
| Search for meaning | | | |
| Internalisation | | | |

*Source:* Hayes and Nutman (1981).

# Unemployment and health

For over a decade a considerable amount of research has been done on life changes and discontinuities in experience and their effects on mental and physical health. A vast literature surrounds the relationship between life events and illness which has shown that a range of physical illnesses are related to social stress. Many scales have been developed to measure these life events, which include the Social Readjustment Rating Scale (Holmes and Rahe, 1967) which ranks both being fired at work and retirement highly, and the Cochrane and Robertson (1973) Life Events Inventory which ranks unemployment and retirement amongst the most stressful of items.

The work on life stresses is extensive yet equivocal. The exact nature of the causal link between personal distress and psychological disturbance is, however, unclear and many intervening variables have been hypothesised. There are also widely different models and explanations for the relationship, including Rahe's Optical Analogy (Rahe *et al.*, 1974), which posits a series of filters and lenses which are between exposure to stress and the reporting of symptoms, and Robertson and Cochrane's (1976) value change model which suggests that people with the new as opposed to the traditional value systems will be more aware of and sensitive to social stresses and pressures and less able to cope with them.

Yet researchers have noted that as unemployment is a major life event, it may explain the fact that unemployed people are by and large less healthy, well adjusted and happy than their employed peers. There are three sorts of data which show this relationship:

1. There are a number of archival studies which have looked at such things as the relationship between unemployment and social problems over a specific period. For instance, Boor (1980) examined the relationship between unemployment rates and suicide rates in eight countries between 1962 and 1976. The question that was addressed was whether social and psychological conditions associated with relatively high suicide rates were also associated with relatively high suicide rates in these countries during these years (*not* whether unemployed persons were more likely to commit suicide than employed people). There were significant positive (between 0.53 and 0.79) correlations between annual variations in suicide and unemployment rates for the United States, Canada, Japan and France, but no significant relationship for Germany, Sweden and Italy. Great Britain, however, showed the opposite pattern (−0.59). Annual variations in the suicide rates of females and males were highly intercorrelated but not associated differentially with unemployment rates, and showed similar patterns within the various age subgroups, thus indicating that cultural factors associated with levels of unemployment had similar effects on the suicidal behaviour of male and females. Boor explained the unpredicted British findings thus: the rate of unsuccessful suicides did actually increase during this period primarily due to the reduction of carbon monoxide in the domestic gas supply. Similarly, Schapiro

and Ahlburg (1983) found a significant positive relationship between unemployment and suicides for males in the United States over the period 1946–76. That is, a 1 per cent point increase in the unemployment rate precipitates over 300 additional suicides per annum. In Britain Krafchik (1983) found a strong positive correlation between unemployment and vagrancy (measured by admissions to the poor law casual wards) in the 1930s.

2. There is extensive research on macro-economic factors and mental health at the University of California (Catalano and Dooley, 1977, 1979; Dooley and Catalano, 1977, 1980). Catalano and Dooley (1979) argued that recent analyses of annual archival data suggest that admission to mental hospitals is significantly associated with previous macro-economic changes, but that this relationship is modified by two important intervening variables: stress in day-to-day life and mental depression, both of which vary with economic change. However, as they point out, it is not clear whether economic changes serve to uncover existing untreated cases or to provoke symptoms in persons previously normal. Their results, however, indicate that the relationship between economic change and recourse to in-patient mental health facilities was due more to the uncovering than to the provocation of behaviourial disorders. Their other research in metropolitan communities has found significant time-series associations of monthly unemployment rate with depression (Catalano and Dooley, 1977), of absolute change in employment in the basic economic sector with stressful life events (Catalano and Dooley, 1979) and various psychophysiological symptoms associated with low-income respondents (Dooley and Catalano, 1979).

   In a review paper Dooley and Catalano (1980) propose a model (given in Figure 7.1) that attempts to explain economic change as a cause of behavioural disorder. They believe that this model may help mental health planners to anticipate increases in economically caused symptoms and to identify the subpopulations most likely to be affected.

   The life-event hypothesis has also been supported by work on low-income families. Thoits and Hannan (1979) compared an income-maintenance and a control group's psychological distress. One hypothesis was that increase in or stabilisation of income would facilitate the experimental subjects' ability to cope with life crises, which in turn would reduce their psychological distress relative to the distress levels of the control subjects (resources hypothesis). The second hypothesis was that re-adjustments following from a change in income will raise the psychological distress levels of experimental rather than control subjects (life-event hypothesis). Their results were consistent with the latter life-event hypothesis, namely that *any* change (positive or negative) in life circumstances is distressing. Thus promotion as much as unemployment may be seen as leading to psychological problems.

3. There are studies concentrated exclusively on the mental/physical health and psychological well-being of unemployed people (Kasl and Cobb, 1970). Banks

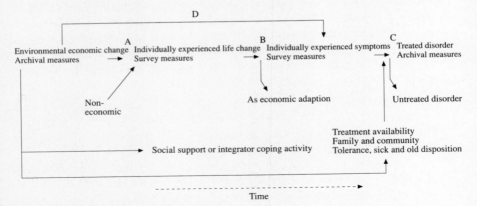

A = Cause of life-events by economic change.
B = Cause of symptoms by stressful life-events.
C = Translation of experienced symptoms into demand for service.
D = Possibility that economic change might affect individual symptoms without mediating life change.

**Figure 7.1**   Hypothetical intervening variables between environmental economic changes and treated disorder. Reprinted by permission of the publisher and authors from Dooley/Catalano, 'Economic change as a cause of behavioural disorder', *Psychological Bulletin 87*, copyright 1980 by the American Psychological Association.

*et al.* (1980) compared the mental health (as measured by the General Health Questionnaire) of employees in an engineering firm, recent school-leavers and a group of unemployed men. They found, as predicted, that the unemployed group (and women more than men) had scores indicating lower mental health, but that these scores were unrelated to age, job level or marital status. Similarly Warr (1981) has suggested that the unemployed's mental health deteriorates because they are denied many of the positive features of work (money, activity, variety, temporal structure, social contacts, status and identity within society). Warr notes that a variety of studies looking at such things as depression, anxiety, life satisfaction, minor psychiatric morbidity, self-esteem, and positive and negative affect, consistently show the unemployed to be less well adjusted. However, this research has, so far, not answered the following important problems. What other features influence the strength of the association between employment status and psychological health? What is the sequential or longitudinal pattern of reaction to unemployment over time? What sort of people thrive in unemployment? Others (Liem and Rayman, 1982) have suggested that researchers need to con-centrate more on mediating *processes* than on the outcome of unemployment: 'We need to know how the costs of unemployment are incurred, what material, and social factors moderate their effects, and what conditions exacerbate them' (p. 1122). One area of research that they note is the effects of unemployment on children – for instance, the effects of a family history of job loss on the child's adjustment, view of the world of work, and so on.

Data from the British General Household Surveys (Arber, 1987) show that both unemployed men and women reported having considerably worse health than those employed. For instance, men between the ages of 30 and 39 reported having had twice as many long-standing illnesses as the employed. When subjective health reporting was analysed, more than twice as many unemployed as employed reported that their health was 'not good'. Although self-reported health has been regarded as rather unreliable, such 'perceived health' measures have been shown to be fairly good predictors of mortality (Kaplan and Camacho, 1983), at least confirming their clinical significance.

The most consistent relationship found in cross-section at aggregate level is between unemployment and cardiovascular disease (Carstairs and Morris, 1989). This would be consistent with hypotheses based on stress (or psychological distress) as a pathogenetic factor.

Also there is interest in the relationship between unemployment and suicide or suicide attempts (parasuicide). Platt (1984) has reviewed some 100 studies on this relationship, showing that the unemployed are grossly over-represented among those attempting or actually committing suicide. In terms of relative risk, the association is so strong that it could hardly be explained solely on the basis of selection. In a recent study by Platt and Kreitman (1990) in Edinburgh the relative risk of parasuicide for the unemployed compared to the employed was seen to have decreased somewhat since 1970, but was still at a level of ten to one for both sexes. Since suicide and parasuicide have been increasing at an alarming rate in many western countries, including Norway, its relationship to unemployment should be a matter of great public health concern.

Beale and Nethercott's study from a British general practice was able to demonstrate that the consultation rates and out-patient referral rates increased significantly compared to control for 80 men and 49 women who lost their jobs when a meat factory in Calne closed down in 1982 (Beale and Nethercott, 1985). The increase occurred even prior to the actual closure, and it also affected family members of the laid-off workers. Numbers and average length of sickness certifications were also demonstrated to increase in these workers when they were threatened by job loss.

Furnham (1983a) looked at the mental health (as measured on the Langner index) of five groups depending on their employment status: full-time employed, part-time employed, unemployed, retired and students. Although there was no age or sex differences in the total mental health score, there was a significant difference between the five employment groups' total score, with the full-time employed having the lowest (best-adjusted) score, the retired and students having moderately high scores, and the unemployed and the part-time the highest scores.

On the basis of previous findings, one might have expected the part-time employed's adjustment score to be higher than that of students, which in turn would possibly be higher than that of retired people. Yet the part-time employed people's score was almost as high, and not significantly different from that of the unemployed. There could be many reasons for this. Firstly, people seeking full-time work may take a part-time job which they do not like and which is not well paid, simply as an interim measure. Secondly, people with other commitments (family, handicapped relatives, etc.) may only be able to take a part-time job which, because of travelling and other stress, is too much for them and leads to mental distress. Thirdly, some part-time work is very casual in that it is for very short periods only, thus instead of giving the benefits of work, it does the precise opposite. Certainly future studies on the part-time employed would do well to tease apart these various hypotheses by asking subjects to stipulate clearly why they have chosen part-time employment, how long they intend to be in the job, and what the hours are. With the prospect of increased job-sharing, the importance of part-time employment is likely to rise.

The importance of longitudinal studies cannot be ignored. To establish a relationship between unemployment and psychological distress tells one nothing of causation, merely of correlation. It is possible that the less psychologically adjusted are prone to unemployment or are indeed unemployable! Only careful longitudinal research can decide whether and how unemployment leads to psychological problems.

Iverson, Sabroe and Dansgaard (1989) examined hospital admission prior to and after a Danish shipyard closure, showing that the risk of admissions due to cardiovascular disease increased, compared with controls subsequent to job loss. However, admissions due to accidents and diseases of the digestive system decreased, suggesting that the occurrence of some occupation-related conditions might have decreased when the workers were no longer exposed to previous occupational hazards. A one-year longitudinal study by Westin and Norum (1977) showed that the occurrence of new doctor-assessed health problems increased in the first year subsequent to job loss, and outweighed the number of improvements in health. Improvements were most often due to less musculoskeletal complaints in those who had suffered much physical strain in their jobs.

In a two-year follow-up study of 1,083 pupils in the last year of secondary school, Hammersmith (1986) found that unemployment led to increased psychological as well as psychosomatic symptoms. While still in school, fear of becoming unemployed was rated third highest, only surpassed by fear of war and fear of something (terrible) happening to their closest family. Among 1,669 adolescents in Nottingham in 1984, fear of becoming unemployed was actually rated as a prime source of anxiety more often than war (Gillies, Elwood and Hawlin, 1985), suggesting that the effects on health of unemployment may extend also to those who are still only at risk of unemployment.

The social and private costs of unemployment naturally lead to various social policy considerations. The financial, psychological and medical costs of unemployment are borne not only by individual workers but also by their families and communities. Liem and Rayman (1982) have suggested a statutory minimum period of notification before workers can be laid off and the creation of a system of medical insurance which is not tied solely to current employment, 'nevertheless the primary assumption informing overall policy on unemployment should be that job loss brings costs to personal health and the quality of family and community life. This premise, together with the social ethic of ''the right to work'' should figure centrally in the formulation of unemployment policy' (Liem and Rayman, 1982: 1121). They also note that one of the most important policy recommendations arising from their own work is to create a medical insurance scheme *not* tied solely to current employment.

Liem and Atkinson (1982) have noted that joblessness should be thought of as happening not only to individuals but also to families. In their research they found that two or three months after their husbands became unemployed, wives in families with continuing unemployment were significantly more depressed, anxious, phobic and sensitive about their interpersonal relationships than their counterparts in employed (control) families. They conclude:

> Consequently, to the familiar criticisms of official Bureau of Labour Statistics procedures for estimating the nation's unemployment rate we would have to add the short-sightedness of assuming that joblessness only happens to individuals. In terms of serious consequences of being without work the impact of unemployment probably exceeds by a factor of two or three that group of Americans who are counted as unemployed.   (Liem and Atkinson, 1982: 19)

Other social policy implications may be found in studies concerning unemployment and the handicapped which shows that unemployed handicapped people suffer more problems than employed handicapped people (Markova, Lockyer and Forbes, 1980), and that in times of high unemployment the handicapped are *more* likely to be unemployed – that is, employers discriminate against them.

Another important source of data on the relationship between unemployment and health concerns studying the characteristics of unemployed people admitted to mental hospitals because this helps to unravel the direction of causality. Fruensgaard *et al.* (1983) investigated the psychosocial characteristics of a group of unemployed patients consecutively admitted to a psychiatric emergency clinic in Denmark. They found that alcohol abuse was registered in two-thirds of their sample of 70, and about half were found to be habitual neurotics with a tendency to antisocial behaviour while intoxicated. However, only 4 per cent had *never* suffered from a mental disorder requiring treatment prior to their unemployment. Indeed, 41 per cent had previously been admitted to a mental hospital, and 60 per cent were on sick leave prior to unemployment. Despite the fact that this sample was hardly typical and that there were other potential causal factors giving rise to mental disease in addition to unemployment, it was noted that anxiety, depression, neurasthenic and psychotic illnesses were accentuated by or commenced with unemployment.

In a follow-up study Fruensgaard *et al.* (1983) found that in most of the sample there had been a drop in alcohol and drug abuse and an improvement in mental health. Most importantly they found that those who succeeded in getting work and/or those who had favourable employment experiences were 'stronger' than those who did not get employment and had had a significantly lower frequency of previous admission to the psychiatric department and of sick leave prior to unemployment:

> In addition, the duration *of* their actual unemployment was shorter and therefore probably less of a strain. . . . Furthermore, there was an extremely significant correlation between a favourable course with regard to employment and both improvement of the general mental condition and improvement of the interpersonal relations.   (p. 135)

Thus it seems that the relationship between mental health and unemployment is bidirectional. The mentally unstable are less likely to find employment than the mentally stable, but lack of employment accentuates the problem, whereas employment does the opposite.

Other attempts to understand the relationship between unemployment and health have been phenomenological. Fineman (1979) has looked specifically at psychosocial stress induced by managerial unemployment. He interviewed twenty-five unemployed managers and also gave them a battery of tests. Predictably they had high GHQ (General Health Questionnaire – a measure of mental health) scores indicating psychological disturbance almost twice the national average, yet their 16 PF (a measure of personality with sixteen dimensions) scores fell within the normal range. Whereas some managers seemed highly stressed by unemployment, others seemed to enjoy it. What appeared to characterise the high-stress group was prior high personal involvement in the job, belief in personal competence, domestic problems, symbiotic failure in job applications and learned helplessness. Low-stress cases, on the other hand, perceived their problem in low-threat terms, had previous low job involvement, strong belief in personal worth and a direct, confronting (as opposed to avoidance, passive) approach to problems. From his rich but unquantifiable data Fineman draws a number of conclusions. Stress in unemployment arises from the interaction of four factors: (1) an individual's perception of the environment; (2) personality, experienced threat and behaviour in response to threat: (3) direct confrontation is the only form of behaviour which can involve mastering the problem of stress; and (4) a stressed person needs to be encouraged to examine his/her perception of environmental demands.

Swinburn (1981) also attempted to look at the psychological impact of unemployment on managers and professional staff. In the interview study she questioned subjects on their feelings about being unemployed, the problems of structuring time, and their job search process. She found that although the experience of unemployment varied according to individual circumstances, certain trends were apparent. Many (50 per cent) reported initial shock and fear/uncertainty about the future, but as few as 10 per cent reported shame, or loss of status and self-respect. Although the negativity of their initial reactions appeared less than reported elsewhere, they appeared to pass through the various hypothetical stages much more slowly.

In a study of the effect of social support in moderating the health consequences of unemployment Gore (1978) interviewed 100 married men who previously had been regularly employed but had suddenly been made redundant. The men were interviewed five times over a two-year period. She was particularly interested in the effect of supportive and affiliative relations with wife, friends and relatives on the unemployed man's illness symptoms. She found that the rural unemployed, because of the ethnic ties and concern in a small community, had a higher level of support than the urban unemployed. In addition the unsupported unemployed had significantly greater levels of cholesterol illness symptoms and emotional response than did the supported. The author argued that these results demonstrate not so much that support buffers the effects of life stress, but rather a low sense/level of social support exacerbates life stress. Unemployment, in large part, means the inability to make instrumental accomplishments. Thus it might be interpreted that this loss in the absence of a continuing sense of self-worth maintained through supportive relationships contributes to negative health responses. In this research it is impossible to point to specific behaviours of others which ameliorate life stress, that is, the buffering effect. It thus makes more sense to explain the more negative responses of some terminees as the exacerbation of the unemployment experience by a low sense of social support.

Finally, it should be pointed out that not all studies of unemployment and health are retrospective. Jenkins *et al.* (1982) carried out a prospective study to examine the effects of the threat of journalists' promised redundancy on minor psychiatric morbidity. Each subject was tested three times: two months prior to closure (one month after receiving notice of redundancy), immediately after redundancy notices were revoked and work continued under a new proprietor, and then three months after the threat of redundancy had been removed. Despite various methodological problems, it was unambiguously demonstrated that subsequent to the withdrawal of redundancy notices, there was a considerable reduction in minor symptomatology.

Hepworth (1980) looked at moderating factors in the relationship between unemployment and mental health. She found that length of unemployment was inversely correlated with mental health and well-being; semi- and unskilled men were less well adjusted than those of higher occupational status and that the best predictor of the unemployed's mental health was whether or not they felt their time was occupied. In a re-analysis of this data Brenner and Bartell (1983) found that with the passage of time a reciprocal process takes place in which mental health affects subjective wellbeing and the proportion of time occupied. The authors suggest that there may well be a 'critical period' immediately following job loss in which time adaptation may or may not occur. Poor adaptation leads to a vicious circle which results in increased negative effects with time.

Many writers have noted a change in the self-concept and identity in the unemployed. In their review of the psychological effects of unemployment in the 1930s Eisenberg and Lazarsfeld (1938) note the development of apathy, depression, fatalistic beliefs, lowered self-esteem, resignation and self-doubt among the unemployed.

As Kelvin and Jarrett (1985) have noted, in a society whose socio-economic structure is defined in terms of its divisions of labour, the unemployed are defined by what they are *not* – not integrated within that structure. This means that the unemployed person's position is highly ambiguous as saying what a person is *not* rather than what he is, and does not tell us much of what s/he is. It is only on the explicit and often unjustifiable assumption that once they find work that they will once again have an identifiable place in society.

It has been argued that the self-concept is a schema which locates the individual within the social environment and shapes his/her interaction with it. Hence becoming unemployed causes psychological dislocation and disorientation which induces a modification of the self-concept. Tiffany, Cowan and Tiffany (1970) administered the Tennessee Self-Concept Scale to two comparable groups, one in work and one not, and found that the profile of the unemployed group reflected a lower level of self-esteem. The unemployed had significantly less faith or confidence in themselves, and saw themselves as less desirable, doubted their worth more and felt more anxious, depressed and unhappy than the employed group. This pattern has been studied by Allerhand *et al.* (1969), Hodgson and Brenner (1968) and Teahan (1969), all of whom found lower self-esteem in the previously unemployed compared with the previously employed. Briar (1977) has also noted a desire for secrecy and a distancing in the unemployed which appears to be a means of protecting themselves against being labelled failures and 'self dependent'.

Of course, one problem plagues the self-esteem and unemployment literature, and that is correlation and cause. It is possible that those with low self-esteem and a poor self-concept are more susceptible to unemployment rather than unemployment reducing self-esteem. Of course, what is more probable is that both occur together, exacerbating each other. Only longitudinal work can actually determine the direction of causality.

## Youth unemployment

Since the early 1970s, when the problem became most acute, there have been several important studies of youth unemployment (Baxter, 1975; Roberts, Duggan and Nobel, 1982; Mair and Raffe, 1983). Many of these have looked at the same factors (health, self-esteem, causal explanations) that have been investigated in the adult population, but some have been quite specific to young people. The late 1980s and 1990s have seen a flood of studies, many of them longitudinal, which have been published by active groups (Winefield and Tiggerman, 1989, 1990; Winefield, Tiggerman and Winefield, 1991, 1992).

The underlying causes of increased youth unemployment are of course manifold. They include demographic factors (change in the birth rate and an extension of the school career), micro- and macro-economic changes (change in technology, different productivity agreements) and educational and training factors (the relevance and appropriateness of education). Changes in youth unemployment are naturally associated with changes in adult unemployment but move with a greater amplitude. It has been calculated that if the unemployment rate for males rises by 1 per cent, the unemployment rate for males under 20 (excluding school-leavers) rises by 1.7

per cent (Makeham, 1980). Compared with other groups, young people change jobs more often or start without jobs, hence as the recession deepens and recruitment is cut young people are among the most vulnerable.

## Psychological adjustment

Some studies have looked at the emotional, social and psychological adjustment of unemployed school-leavers. Using a questionnaire developed from the ideas of the neo-psychoanalytic thinker Erikson, Gurney (1980b) looked at over 400 unemployed Australian school-leavers. It was hypothesised that having a job helps school-leavers to clarify their perception of their identity, and not being able to get work leads to a confused perception of self or no change due to a moratorium. The hypothesis was confirmed for females but not for males. Furthermore the unemployed males showed a significant shift towards the mistrust pole of the first dimension of *trust–mistrust,* and the employed of both sexes shifted significantly on the *industry–inferiority* subscale. He concludes, 'it seems reasonable to conclude that unemployment has the effect of inhibiting development in school-leavers, rather than inflicting trauma as is sometimes popularly supposed' (p. 212). Gurney (1980b) also found that over a four-month period after leaving school, self-esteem increased only for those young people who obtained work.

Donovan and Oddy (1982) investigated the social and emotional development of a small but carefully matched group of employed and unemployed school-leavers. They found that school-leavers who were unemployed were more depressed and anxious, had lower self-esteem and poorer subjective well-being, were less well adjusted socially and showed a higher incidence of minor psychiatric morbidity than school-leavers who had acquired jobs. They also found a significant interaction between employment status and gender on the locus of control scale: unemployed males tend to be more external than employed males, whereas these differences were minimal for females. They write: 'Certainly the apathy and hopelessness frequently associated with unemployment could be linked to an increased tendency to attribute events to uncontrollable forces' (p. 24). Similarly Feather (1982) found both male and female young unemployed people had higher depression scores, lower self-esteem and Protestant work ethic scores, and reported that good and bad outcomes to everyday events were less important to them compared with employed male subjects. He notes:

> These results therefore indicate that both lower self-esteem and less effort to find a job were associated with increasing time out of work. They also show that the active pursuit of employment tended to be more frequent among those with higher self-esteem, stronger Protestant ethic values and higher levels of concern about positive and negative events (lower apathy). But frequency of job search was lower among those unemployed who reported more depressive symptoms. These findings may imply a sort of reciprocal determinism in which the state of continued unemployment has effects on the person, and the person so modified by his or her experience, begins to behave in ways that alter the probability of finding a job. (p. 320)

Stafford (1982) examined the impact of the Youth Opportunities Programme, devised to offer 16–18-year-olds opportunities for training and work experience to increase employment prospects, on young people's employment prospects and psychological well-being. She found a significant improvement in employment prospects after participation in the scheme, which also acts as a buffer against any detrimental effects of unemployment. However, the beneficial effects of the programme do not last, and the detrimental effects of unemployment return for those ex-trainees who remain unemployed.

Other studies have noted the medical and psychological health costs of being unemployed. In Britain, Banks *et al.* (1980) gave 647 recent school-leavers the General Health Questionnaire (GHQ, a self-administered screening test for detecting minor psychiatric disorders). There was a large significant difference between those unemployed (3.78) and those employed (1.27), but no significant sex differences. Further analysis showed that although the unemployed scored higher on the GHQ this relationship was moderated by their motivation to work, such that unemployed with a high motivation to work scored higher than those with lower work motivation. Similarly in an American study Greenberger, Stenberg and Vaux (1981) compared the health and behaviourial consequences of 16–18-year-old school children who had part-time jobs compared with those who had never worked. Although they recognised the potentially positive influence on adolescents, their work concentrated on the costs of job stress. Their study focused on self-reported frequency of psychological and physical health symptoms, school absence, and the use of cigarettes, alcohol, marijuana, and other things. The results indicated that the working youths (especially boys) reported fewer somatic symptoms than the non-working youths, and that even boys who worked under stressful job conditions report fewer somatic and psychological symptoms than do boys who hold less stressful jobs. However, the results did show that exposure to job stress is related to alcohol and marijuana use for both boys and girls.

The authors proposed four explanations for their finding that work is associated with fewer symptoms in boys but more in girls: differential selection (hardier boys are likely to take more stressful jobs), differential attributes (hardier boys are likely to remain at stressful jobs while those less sturdy are likely to leave), differential reporting about health (boys who work under stress are less likely to report health problems than are girls) and sex differences in socialisation (boys are led to expect more stress than girls).

Other studies have been concerned with the effect of youth unemployment as rapid labour turnover and delinquency. For instance, Baxter (1975) studied chronic job changes in the early 1970s. Job changers tended to be less intelligent, more neurotic, from poorer homes and less socially and occupationally skilled than their counterparts who did not change jobs so rapidly. However, Raffe (1983), in a study of employment instability in young people, found that although instability was generated more by occupational than personal factors (unstable jobs not unstable workers) their chances of finding new employment depended on personal factors more than on their earlier occupational experiences. Similarly Raelin (1981) found that early career unemployment is not a critical factor in retarding personal economic growth, relative to educational background and first job experience, but does have negative job-attitudinal consequences. Young males who are early entrants in the labour force and who spend the bulk of their work in part-time employment do as well economically and better occupationally in their later work experience than full-time youth.

Milham, Bullock and Hosie (1978), in a study of over 1,000 boys in approved schools, found that employment experiences were a crucial factor in promoting economic and social well-being. Though the authors were careful not to draw causal links between unemployment and delinquency, they did find that regular work did build up offending boys' confidence, changed their job aspirations, enhanced their self-perceptions and remotivated their interest in numeracy and literacy.

The problem with nearly all the studies on youth unemployment and psychological adjustment is that one cannot infer cause only correlation. That is, it is quite possible that poor psychological adjustment leads to a young person being unemployed rather than the other way around. The only study that attempted a longitudinal analysis of the problem, however, yielded ambiguous results. Warr, Jackson and Banks (1982) interviewed two cohorts of recent school-leavers over a two-year period, but measures of psychological stress and self-esteem were found to be correlated with the duration of unemployment for young men. In one cohort of women the young people appeared to be better adjusted the longer they were unemployed, apparently because of their reduced commitment to the labour market along with a stronger personal involvement in family matters. The authors offer two compatible explanations for their puzzling findings: that the association between well-being and length of unemployment may differ between age groups (older people with more commitments may experience greater distress); and secondly, that longer periods of unemployment than those studied in this study (over a year) lead to distress.

Similarly Banks and Jackson (1982) interviewed two age cohorts of young people up to two-and-a-half years after leaving school to investigate the association between unemployment and risk of minor psychiatric morbidity. They found a positive relationship between unemployment and morbidity after controlling for sex, ethnicity and educational qualifications. Further longitudinal analyses showed that the experience of unemployment was more likely to create increased psychological symptoms, rather than the reverse. More recently Jackson *et al.* (1983) studied longitudinally two cohorts of young people in the first three years of their working lives. They found, as predicted, that psychological distress is higher for the unemployed than for the employed and that changes in employment status lead to changes in distress score. Furthermore this relationship is moderated by the person's commitment to work: the more committed suffer more from the experience of unemployment.

More recently there have been a number of Australian longitudinal studies with young people in Australia. For instance, Winefield, Tiggemann and Winefield

(1991) looked at four groups of young people who are 'psychologically' equivalent while at school. Some were unemployed, others students, some in jobs they liked and others in jobs they disliked. Their analysis, over an eight-year period, showed clearly that the satisfied employed and the students showed higher self-esteem, less depressive effect, less external locus of control (fatalistic) beliefs and fewer negative moods than either the dissatisfied employed or unemployed. Other measures of such things as social alienation, hopelessness, psychological distress and life satisfaction revealed similar results. A careful analysis of the results showed that the results were due to the satisfied employed and students getting 'better' over-time, rather than the other two groups getting worse.

Similarly O'Brien and Feather (1990) looked at four similar groups of school-leavers that they had tested earlier: unemployed, students, those in good and those in bad employment. When the school-leavers who got good jobs were compared with the unemployed group it was clear that the former had lower depressive affect, higher life satisfaction, higher internal control and higher personal competence. But there was little difference between the unemployed and 'poorly employed' group. Thus the relative effects of employment and unemployment upon adolescents and young people depends extensively on the quality of the experienced unemployment.

## Attribution and expectation about employment and unemployment

Although there have been some studies of adult explanations of unemployment (Furnham 1982c, 1983b), considerably less work has gone into establishing young people's beliefs about, and actual attempts at, getting a job. Feather and Davenport (1981) tested their expectancy-valence theory on young people. A person's actions are seen to be related to the expectations that a person holds *and* to the subjective values of the outcomes that might occur following the action. They found, as predicted, that higher motivated, more depressed unemployed youths blamed stable external factors for unemployment and rated the attractiveness of work more highly than less depressed youths. Although incompatible with learned helplessness theory, the results supported their theory, which assumes that positive motivation to seek employment is identical to the multiplicative combination of expectancy of success in getting a job *and* the perceived net attractiveness of unemployment. They note:

> One might assume that work will have stronger positive valence for individuals with strong Protestant ethic values than for those people for whom these values are weaker. If this assumption is valid, then it follows that people with a strong Protestant ethic value will be more persistent in their efforts to get a job and that they will suffer more negative effects if they fail to obtain employment   (p. 337)

Gurney (1981) in fact examined the attributions for the causes of unemployment in both employed and unemployed groups of school-leavers. In a first study he attempted to discover, among a population of Australian school-leavers, whether the unemployed differed in their attributions of employment from those who succeeded in getting work; and secondly, whether any differences were antecedent to, or consequent upon, unemployment. Subjects were asked to ascribe the ability to get work either to internal or external factors to the job seekers, and to fill out a simple eight-item scale devised by the author. He found that unemployed males attributed both getting *and* not getting work significantly more to external factors, as had been found previously, but there were no differences in the female groups. Gurney suggested that the lack of differences among the female groups may be due to their lesser defensiveness and need to blame external factors for being unemployed. In a second longitudinal study students were given a twelve-item attribution for getting jobs questionnaire prior to leaving school and then approximately four months later. He suggested that:

> The unemployed may believe themselves powerless to change the circumstances of their lives (external locus) but the fact that they are without work whereas others are not and that they remain so, may lead them eventually to see themselves as responsible for their condition (internal attribution) with consequent self-blame and self-derogation. (Gurney, 1981: 34)

The results showed that prior to leaving school the groups did not differ, yet later it was not the unemployed who changed their attributions, but the employed who shifted significantly towards a more internal set of causal ascriptions. Overall Gurney (1981) seemed unable to account for his 'counter-intuitive and unexpected' findings suggesting perhaps that subjects of this age have their self-esteem based on numerous other things such as parental evaluation and peer-group approval, rather than exclusively on work, which is more often the case with adults.

In a rather different study Dayton (1981) looked at the way in which young people looked for a job. He set out to determine what job-seeking approaches were being used by young people and what factors they found positive and useful (aids) and what negative and worthless (barriers) in a job search. Using a population of 250 young Americans, Dayton found they regarded their own positive personal attributes (personality, flexibility, academic ability) as the most important aids in their job, and external factors (labour unions, welfare and unemployment insurance, government training programmes) as least important. Employment success and satisfaction were correlated with careful analysis of which job suited them best, the assemblance of a placement file, letters of recommendation, and a CV, combined with persistence in the job search.

Research within the framework of attribution theory would, however, lead one to make a number of predictions about school childrens' expectations and beliefs about getting a job (Furnham 1982a, 1982c, 1983e). For instance, people more prone to unemployment, and the unemployed themselves, tend to make more external attributions for the causes of unemployment in contrast to those in jobs and unlikely to become unemployed. Furthermore studies have shown that external attributions are to some extent protective of self-esteem in the context of achievement Harvey, Ickes and Kidd 1975). Hence Furnham (1984b) predicted that females more than males and working-class subjects more than middle-class subjects (for whom unemployment is statistically more probable) will be prone to make more external attributions about getting a job. Further it was suggested that these attributions will also be reflected in the number and type of job search strategies adopted by young people and the barriers and aids that they consider operate in job-hunting success. In this study Furnham set out to examine sex and class differences in 240 British school-leavers' attributions about unemployment, the most and least useful job search strategies, and which school course they believed most and least useful in getting a job. The results of the four different parts of this study suggest that, overall, attributions about getting a job are frequently internal (that is, to personal attributes or abilities) rather than environmental or societal factors. Confidence, perseverance and qualifications were all considered to be primary factors responsible for success in finding employment, yet this is moderated by the belief that jobs are not currently available (a fact which is attributed to the government). Yet failure to get a job was rarely attributed to the personal shortcomings of the job-seeker him/herself. Thus these results tend to support the well-established, attributional finding that success is attributed to internal factors and failure to external factors.

Where there were significant sex differences it was found that females were more external in their attributions than males. This conflicts with Gurney (1981), who found that unemployed males were more external in their attributions about employment than employed males, but that there were no differences between employed and unemployed females. However, the extensive locus of control literature has shown that where sex differences exist in generalised locus of control beliefs, females are more external than males. Similarly class differences tended to show that working-class subjects tend to place more emphasis on structural or external factors (Furnham, 1982c). Again this is to be expected and is in accordance with previous literature on the topic (Furnham and Gunter, 1984).

The results on the aids and barriers confirm the findings of Dayton (1981), who found that the subjects saw their own personal attributes as the greatest aids and external factors as the biggest hindrances. Similarly, regarding strategies, class and sex differences showed that the middle class tended to rate all job-hunting strategies as more useful than the working class, and girls showed less faith in following up specific job choices than boys. The subjects all stressed the importance of summer and after-school work for experience, but tended to rely on personal contacts rather than direct approaches to employers. It would be interesting to compare these beliefs with those of employers, who may have quite different beliefs concerning which factors make an applicant more employable.

The belief in the usefulness of 'A' level (twelfth-grade) courses revealed that both males and females believed science courses (and English) were the most useful in getting a job, although females tended to opt for arts courses and males for sciences at 'A' level. Females also believed that arts courses were more useful than science courses, so providing a rationalisation for the choice. However, a study such as this was unable to determine whether females chose arts subjects and then felt it necessary to justify their choice, or whether they actually believed them to be most useful *per se* and hence selected them accordingly. It is of course also possible that when candidates select a particular course they do so for many reasons, only one of which is its usefulness for getting a job. Further, the believed importance of science courses may reflect recent government pronouncements and support for the 'hard' sciences, rather than the arts or social sciences. These results also indicate that attributions are to some extent a function of the expectation of work.

Feather (1983) examined causal attributions and beliefs about work and unemployment among Australian adolescents in state and independent schools. The results were analysed for school and sex differences. State-school children tended to blame economic factors, physical appearance and interview inadequacy more than independent-school children, 80 endorsing societal or external explanations. As predicted, children from the independent schools (of higher socio-economic status), as opposed to those from state schools, had higher expectations of obtaining employment, higher internal attributions of controllability over their own lives, and were more likely to see work as attractive. Also female students tended to have lower expectations about finding employment, when compared with their male peers. These results were explained in terms of the current economic situation in Australia, socialisation forces in the family, the schools and in peer groups (middle-class children have experience of reward for effort and individual competition; working-class children have lower expectations).

In a more detailed study, Feather and Barber (1983) investigated correlates of depressive reactions associated with unemployment in a sample of young unemployed male and female Australians. From studies on depression and attributions three hypotheses were tested and some support was found for each. They were: depressive effect about unemployment is associated with high job expectations, with the rated importance of having a job and with external attributions for the causes of unemployment. General depressive symptomatology is associated with low expectation of getting a job, low self-esteem, internal attributions about the causes of unemployment and perceived uncontrollability or helplessness about changing things. Depressive symptoms are associated with an unsuccessful employment history. Overall, the findings indicated that attributional variables accounted for only a relatively small proportion of the variance in depression:

> In future investigations of the psychological damage that unemployment may cause, it is important to assess a range of other variables as well, especially those that relate to the personal and social costs of not having a job and the different ways in which people learn to cope with negative outcomes.   (Feather and Barber, 1983: 193)

Winefield, Tiggeman and Winefield (1992) reported a longitudinal study of attribution for employment in young people. Young people who resigned from or were dismissed from their job (for whatever reason) were asked why. It was hypothesised and demonstrated that those who gave internal attributions for their unemployment would show lower self-esteem and those who gave external attributions would show greater hopelessness than those who gave internal causal attributions.

It seems then that it can be healthy to attribute job loss to external factors, though if this persists it may be unhealthy in the long run.

## Education about unemployment

Because it has become so widespread, various researchers have argued for some sort of education about the problems and prospects of unemployment. Some (Stirling, 1982) have gone so far as to suggest that we need to prepare school-leavers for unemployment, arguing that because as many as a third of school-leavers in Britain (in 1982/3) may experience unemployment they need to know what to anticipate and how to cope. Furthermore high levels of youth unemployment have produced a questioning of and disenchantment with the whole education system (Hargreaves, 1981).

Dancy (1978) argued that young people need to be educated in all aspects of job-sharing and to be encouraged to have a new definition of work, to include not only paid employment but a variety of other activities. To this end he believes a careers education programme should involve such topics as the mechanics of collecting benefits, the acquisition of job-seeking skills, the experience of unemployment, leisure and community roles, the politics of the right to work.

Watts (1978) also considered the implications of school-leaver unemployment for careers education in schools. He argues that careers educators have not seriously dealt with the problem of unemployment because they do not feel competent to tackle it effectively; they are aware of its highly political and emotional overtones; it might affect deleteriously the work ethic within and outside the school; and the teachers feel instinctively hostile to the concept of preparation for unemployment. A number of possible curricular objectives are listed, including equipping children with employability, survival and leisure skills. Four alternative aims are described depending on whether one is focusing on change in society (to help students see unemployment as a phenomenon resolved by social and political measures), change in the individual (to maximise students' chances of finding meaningful employment), status quo in the society (to reinforce students' motivation to seek work) and status in the individual (to make students aware of the possibility of unemployment and how best to cope with it). Many of the educational responses and strategies are dependent on whether one believes unemployment to be voluntary (aversion to the will to work), cyclical (cycles of recession and expansion) or structural (a major change in the relationship between capital and labour). These solutions may include a deeper inculcation of the work ethic, job creation schemes, etc. Careers education is seen as the education of central life interests and personal growth and development, rather than the matching of people to (non-existent) jobs.

As a practical measure Lavercombe and Fleming (1981) attempted to identify (by using attitude measures) school children at risk of longer periods of unemployment and hence in particular need of support, information and skills. Although they found that their measures did not predict which pupils would take longest to find jobs, they believed all pupils should be prepared for unemployment. Their results suggested that employers have little confidence in what teachers report concerning expected examination results, attendance records or attitudes to school, authority or work when selecting among young applicants.

Fleming and Lavercombe (1982) in a study of twenty-nine professionals working with young people found that they varied considerably in their topics and approaches. The sort of topics discussed by the professionals in schools were: whether work itself is the major basis of self-respect and how the unemployed can compensate; how to spend one's leisure/free time; the mechanics of claiming supplementary benefit; possibilities of continuing education; and the politics of unemployment. In talking with unemployed school-leavers after school the professionals believed their primary role was giving support while being as honest as possible. They also believed that their activities helped combat boredom and anxiety, to help them get a job; and to facilitate personal development. The professionals who believed that there was a chance of returning emphasised job-seeking and -keeping skills, while those who were more pessimistic about the future of work concentrated on developing survival skills for the unemployed. This seemed a basic division among the professionals, some of whom believed their job was primarily to help young people get a job, while others believed it was to help young people cope and amuse themselves because they would never have a job. Not surprisingly many of the professionals seemed depressed and exhausted by a job that confronted so starkly the discrepancy between young people's aspirations and the lack of jobs available.

Coffield (1984) has considered the future for the whole of education in a world without jobs. He suggests that young people are learning to live with unemployment, with moving in and out of jobs and with government schemes. Furthermore he notes how the education system and particular schools should be willing to adapt their curriculum for new circumstances. He proposed a new organisation formed by schools, universities and colleges of education that would translate research findings into industrial terms, and vice versa; give educational institutions rapid and reliable feedback on the general and specific skills needed by young workers at the beginning of their careers; and use latest research findings to update educational curricula. Thus 'a return for a steady stream of articulate, literate and numerate young workers and managers with the appropriate skills, local industry would pay to keep both the university and local schools in the vanguard of progress' (p. 41).

## Explaining the causes of unemployment

A number of writers have suggested that people out of work for long periods of time tend to offer fatalistic explanations for the causes of their own and others' unemployment (Jahoda, 1979b; O'Brien and Kabaroff, 1979; Hayes and Nutman, 1981).

Furnham (1982c) set out to examine differences in the explanations for unemployment in Britain as a function of whether people were employed or unemployed as well as their age, sex, education and voting pattern. It was hypothesised that more unemployed people would find societal (external social economic and political factors) and fatalistic (luck, chance, fate) explanations important for unemployment than employed people, who would find individualistic explanations (internal dispositional and personality factors) more important. It was also hypothesised that Conservative (right-wing) voters would find individualistic explanations for unemployment more important than employed Labour voters, who would find societal factors more important. The results showed a predictable pattern of differences between the employed and unemployed, the former believing more in individualistic explanations and less in societal explanations than the latter. However, whereas there were few sex and age differences, education and vote revealed numerous differences in explanations for unemployment. As is the case with explanations for poverty (see Chapter 5), Conservatives found individualistic explanations for unemployment more important than did Labour voters, who in turn found societal explanations more important than did Conservative voters. It was suggested that the results confirm the theses of a number of writers in the field (Tiffany, Cowan and Tiffany, 1970) that unemployed people will be more external in their attributions for the causes of unemployment than employed people, though this is only a matter of degree. Furthermore, according to Hayes and Nutman (1981) and others, this pattern should increase the longer a person remains out of work. Yet the overall national unemployment figures would probably affect this relationship. As unemployment grows, even employed people tend to offer societal and fatalistic (external) explanations for unemployment partly as a defence against becoming unemployed themselves.

Using much the same questionnaire, Furnham and colleagues have conducted various cross-cultural replications: for instance, Furnham and Hesketh (1989) set out to compare lay explanations for unemployment in two comparable samples in Great Britain and New Zealand, two countries that, although separated by more than 15,000 miles, have much in common historically, politically, culturally and economically. If Kelvin (1980) is correct in maintaining that people find unemployment more acceptable (less personally blameworthy) as it rises in the population as a whole, it may be predicted that the British – whose unemployment rate at the time of the study was about 12 per cent – would endorse societal rather than individualistic explanations more strongly than New Zealanders, whose unemployment rate at the time of the study was about 4 per cent.

Overall the results of the study support this finding. The British, whose unemployment rate was nearly three times that of New Zealanders, tended to rate societal factors as more important, whereas the reverse was true for the individualistic factors. This pattern was clear in both the uni- and multivariate analyses.

Later Payne and Furnham (1990) compared the causal attributions for unemployment among a large mixed group from the Caribbean island of Barbados. There were clear sex, age and education differences, but, curiously, employment status appeared not to relate to attributions.

Despite slight differences in the factor structure emerging from these various studies on explaining unemployment, it certainly appears that the threefold struc-

**Table 7.3**   Means and F levels for the explanations for unemployment offered and unemployed subjects

| Explanations | Employed | Unemployed | F level |
|---|---|---|---|
| **1. Individualistic** | | | |
| Unemployed people can earn more money on social security | 5.21 | 5.31 | 0.17 |
| Lack of effort and laziness among unemployed people | 5.13 | 4.21 | 1.72 |
| Unemployed people do not try hard enough to get jobs | 3.15 | 4.21 | 13.22[a] |
| Unemployed people are too fussy and proud to accept some jobs | 4.89 | 4.57 | 1.67 |
| Poor education and qualifications among unemployed people | 4.40 | 3.55 | 12.94[a] |
| Unwillingness of unemployed to move to places of work | 4.32 | 5.51 | 10.60[a] |
| Inability of unemployed people to adapt to new conditions | 4.77 | 4.38 | 3.44[c] |
| Lack of intelligence or ability among the unemployed | 5.46 | 4.76 | 9.70[b] |
| **2. Societal** | | | |
| The policies and strategies of the present government | 2.05 | 2.33 | 1.48 |
| The policies and strategies of previous British governments | 2.82 | 2.85 | 0.06 |
| Inefficient and less competitive industries that go bankrupt | 3.38 | 3.45 | 0.10 |
| An influx of immigrants have taken all available jobs | 5.32 | 3.92 | 29.09[a] |
| Trade unions have priced their members out of a job | 4.37 | 3.85 | 4.83[c] |
| Overmanning in industry which has occurred for too long | 3.53 | 3.93 | 2.93 |
| Incompetent industrial management with poor planning | 2.94 | 3.46 | 5.98[b] |
| Weak trade unions that do not fight to keep jobs | 4.80 | 3.58 | 26.05[a] |
| **3. Fatalistic** | | | |
| Sickness and physical handicap among unemployed people | 5.14 | 3.74 | 29.32[a] |
| Just bad luck | 5.73 | 5.27 | 4.63[c] |
| World-wide recession and inflation | 2.19 | 2.57 | 3.69[c] |
| The introduction of widespread automation | 3.70 | 3.09 | 6.14[b] |

*Source:* Furnham, 'Explanations for unemployment in Britain', in *European Journal of Psychology*, (1982c)
Note: [a] $p < 0.001$, [b] $p < 0.01$, [c] $p < 0.05$. Following scale: important, 1 – unimportant, 7.

ture (individualistic, societal, structural) proposed earlier holds up.

More recently Furnham (1982a) looked specifically at the relationship between Protestant work ethic beliefs and attitudes towards and explanations for unemployment. Most of previous research has concerned the relationship between work ethic beliefs and paid work. However, Furnham (1983a) looked at the relationship between work ethic beliefs and unemployment. As predicted, subjects who strongly endorsed the work ethic endorsed negative individualistic explanations for unemployment and were, by and large, more against welfare payments than subjects who did not strongly endorse these beliefs. This confirms MacDonald's (1971b) finding that protestant work ethic believers were proponents of the ethics of social responsibility, which tend to blame people rather than 'the system' for the source of their difficulty. It also confirms other findings which suggest that these beliefs (as measured by any of the Protestant work ethic scales) are part of a general conservative attitude pattern. These results are also in accordance with studies of lay beliefs about economics (poverty, wealth, unemployment taxation, social security, etc.), which suggest that there are coherent lay 'theories' about such matters. Thus a high

Protestant work ethic scorer is likely to explain poverty in terms of idleness and poor money management, wealth in terms of hard work, honesty and saving, unemployment in terms of laziness and lack of effort, and s/he is likely to be against both taxation and social security (Furnham, 1982a: 283).

Although most of the research on explanations for unemployment has been stimulated by other work within an attribution theory context, other conceptual frameworks have been put forward. Moscovici (1981) has argued that social representations (set of concepts, statements and explanations originating in daily life in the course of inter-individual communication) in fact determine people's attribution about such things as unemployment benefits. Whereas attribution theory is concerned with the way individuals attribute causes to events that belong to their experience, the theory of social representations concerns how groups or individuals create a stable world in which diverse, unfamiliar or unpredictable behaviours are given meaning and become familiar and predictable. He maintains that people gather information, classify it into certain categories *and then* attempt to explain it. He believes that attributions follow from social representation and not the reverse.

> I am convinced that the theory of attribution will become more fruitful and less mechanical as soon as it recognizes the importance of the content of representation and its social character. Any reduction to cognitive patterns and constructs, by eliminating the extraordinary richness of collective thought, its rootedness in a well defined setting, and by flattening all social relation into interaction between two individuals, converts an important problem into a mere academic exercise.   (p. 208)

He in fact illustrates his point by reference to unemployment:

> Some think of the unemployed person as lazy, unlucky or as incompetent in looking for work; others consider him to be the victim of economic downturn, of social injustice and the contradictions of the capitalist regime. The former attribute the cause of unemployment to the individual, to his way of facing the world, and the latter to the general situation, to the individual's class affiliation and to the way in which the world treats him. Obviously this divergence is due altogether to their respective social representations. One representation gives precedence, under all circumstances, to personal responsibility, individual effort, and individual solutions to the problems of society; the other leads to a sharp awareness of social injustice and social responsibility, contemplating collective solutions to individual problems.   (pp. 107–8)

La France and Cicchetti (1979) were concerned with social-class and employment-status determinants of the perceived responsibility and blame for economic success and failure. Four groups of subjects (middle-class employed, middle-class unemployed, working-class employed, working-class unemployed) were asked a series of questions about a stimulus figure that they had read about. They found that subjects were more concerned with praising the successful job-seeker than with blaming the unsuccessful. The middle-class subjects distinguished significantly more between success and failure than working-class subjects, assigning more responsibility to the former and less to the latter. The middle class also believed personality to be more influential than the working class. Overall employed subjects assigned more responsibility to the stimulus person and saw luck as being less influential in the successful outcome than did the unemployed. Nearly all of the studies in this section on explanations for unemployment used a limited and unrepresentative sample and a structured questionnaire. However, more recent studies have considered a free-response interview format with large, representative samples.

In a free-response study Lewis and Furnham (1986) asked 450 people how they believed unemployment could be reduced. Many different answers were given, such as lowering the retirement age, increasing job creation schemes, increase public spending, etc. Most people gave answers which implied a stimulation of the economy, a number for the redistribution of jobs, yet about 15 per cent could provide no answer at all. When the sample was given six closed questions it was found that over 90 per cent of them believed that the level of unemployment in Britain was unacceptably high, while 66 per cent argued that the government should spend more money in order to reduce unemployment. There were some interesting and predictable sex, age and employment history differences: for instance, women were against sacrificing their jobs if their husbands were unemployed but did favour job-sharing and reducing working hours; similarly younger people seemed more liberal than older people in that they did not believe in curbing immigration or in women giving up jobs.

Using a large and representative sample, Lewis, Snell and Furnham (1987) asked 900 British people to explain the causes of unemployment. Content analysis using thirteen economic codes revealed that 28 per cent of the explanations concerned falling demand for goods, 23 per cent the rate of inflation, 18 per cent government policy and 17 per cent high wage demands. Curiously, there were very few demographic differences, though many were investigated (sex, class, age, housing, trade union membership). These explanations (many of which defied coding) were reclassified into the three categories used by Furnham (1982c): 78 per cent of the explanations were societal, 24 per cent fatalistic and only 7 per cent individual. What was particularly striking about the explanations offered for unemployment was the fact that so few were purely economic – that is, lay explanations for economic phenomena are often normative, moralistic and socio-political as well as economic.

## Women's unemployment

Even less research has been devoted to unemployment among women than to the effects of employment on well-being, self-esteem, etc. (Spitze and Waite, 1981; Faver, 1982).

In a review of work and well-being in women, Warr and Parry (1982) found that the association between employment status and psychological well-being is mediated by a woman's occupational status, the quality of her non-occupational environment, and the quality of her employment relationship. In certain circumstances psychological well-being is significantly associated with having paid employment – in single rather than married and working-class rather than middle-class women. Although there appears to be a paucity of good research in this area, the results seem to indicate that work outside the home is not generally as important to the well-being of women as it is of men. Indeed various studies have shown deleterious effects of work on physical and psychological health (Zimmerman and Hartley, 1982). In a study of the lives of women managers, Cooper and Davidson (1982) found that, compared with men, women have major additional stresses to cope with, and that often their home life obstructs rather than supports their careers. Similarly Faver (1982) found that a women's labour force participation is partially a function of the interaction between career and family task demands and values.

Warr and Parry (1982), who looked at depressed mood in working-class mothers with and without paid employment, compared the depressed mood scores for matched full-time employed, part-time employed and non-employed mothers, and found a large significant difference indicating that the former were least depressed and the latter most depressed. They also looked at various other variables such as their attitude to employment, strain in coping with domestic and paid work duties, the amount of social support they received, and their child-care demands. Overall the strain in coping variable was the most predictive of depressed mood in that employed mothers with high interaction strain have mood scores similar to those without paid employment and part-time employees with high strain have particularly high depressed mood scores. The smallest associations with depressed mood were child-care demands. The authors are conscious of the experimental shortcomings of their and others' work, especially in the need to control for various important demographic variables.

Leeflang, Klien-Hesselink and Spruit (1992) argued that women's situation with reference to the labour market is more complicated than men's and that substantial hidden unemployment often exists among women. They reviewed nearly twenty recent studies on unemployment among women as well as reporting on their own study. The results do suggest that unemployments' adverse health affects exist equally for men and women, and the impact of unemployment shows far more similarities than differences between men and women. Surprisingly perhaps risk factors and 'paths' leading from unemployment to ill-health are the same for registered unemployed men and women. The same may not be true of those unregistered as unemployed, though they may be very hard to track down.

## Conclusion

This chapter has attempted to review the now voluminous literature on unemployment under selected headings. Of course, there are other topics; for instance, there have been a few studies on personality differences between the employed and the unemployed. Hartley (1980) set about exploring the popular myth that unemployed managers possess fewer characteristics traditionally associated with managerial ability than employed managers. Contrary to this belief, a group of unemployed managers were significantly more outgoing, conscientious and imaginative than a group of matched employed managers. There was no evidence that the unemployed were more shy, tender-minded, forthright, apprehensive, conservative, tense or anxious than the employed managers. There are of course macro-economic and organisational factors associated with unemployment and the author concludes from her data that researchers need to get away from conceptualising the 'problem' of unemployment strictly in individualistic terms.

Finally, there has also been some work on value systems of the unemployed which deserve mention. Penner and Rokeach (1969) hypothesised that there would be certain changes in salient variables as a result of changes in employment conditions. They contacted four groups: temporarily unemployed subsequently employed; actually unemployed subsequently employed; temporarily unemployed still unemployed; and actually unemployed still unemployed. For the first group the value 'broadminded' became significantly more important and 'polite' less important, which was also true of the second group. For the unemployed groups the terminal value 'equality' became less important especially for the third group, possibly because they were more concerned with their own well-being. The fourth hard-core group rated 'salvation', 'tender' and 'polite' as more important and 'patient' as less important over time. In Australia, O'Brien and Kabaroff (1979) found that, compared with employed workers, the unemployed had poor physical health, lower work values and higher external control orientation, and made more use of community-helping agencies. The work value differences showed that the unemployed tended to desire less influence, interaction and pressure in their work compared with the employed.

Research on unemployment is scattered across a wide number of disciplines: economics, education, psychiatry, psychology (clinical, educational, occupational and social) and sociology. Although some results are equivocal and others contradictory, various themes and established findings emerge. For instance, studies on the psychological consequences of unemployment tend to point in the same direction, namely that unemployment causes stress, a lowering of self-esteem and a change in expectations. Similarly the work on attributions and explanations has revealed consistent findings. Taken together, they show a vicious circle for those who are unemployed. Loss of work leads to lowered self-esteem, and possibly mental and physical illness and low expectations for getting work. These in turn lead to poor or maladaptive job search strategies, so confirming beliefs. Hence we find self-fulfilling prophecies or reciprocal determinism (Feather, 1982a).

Although research in this area is comparatively recent, difficult and expensive, there is no excuse for poor research which only leads to unreliable, unconfirmed and ambiguous findings. Researchers need to be more specific in the individual difference, organisational and macro-economic factors which together influence unemployment. For instance, three categories of individual difference factors need to be considered: (1) psychological differences in personality, self-concept, beliefs and skills prior and subsequent to unemployment; (2) there are demographic differences in age, sex, religious and ethnic group, schooling, class, etc., which condition expectations and coping strategies; and (3) there are work experience differences in that some people have had some or all or none of the work experiences possible: full-time, part-time, voluntary, none. Similarly there are a number of organisational differences which have to be considered such as its size, structure, social support, manning levels, etc. Finally, gross macro-economic factors, such as the inflation and unemployment rate, levels of social security and unemployment benefit, must be taken into consideration.

# PART IV
# Morals and the market

# Chapter 8

# Fairness, ethics and the 'greens'

Adam Smith spoke of the market being run by an 'invisible hand' (1776/1937: 423): 'Led by an invisible hand to promote an end which was no part of his intention. Nor is it always the worse for society that it was no part of it. By pursuing his own interest, he frequently promotes that of the society more effectively than when he really intends to promote it.' This chapter considers whether 'the invisible handshake' is a better metaphor: economic actors are not solely guided by base self-interest; instead there are inherent notions of fair play, of give and take, which turn economic transactions into social encounters. An 'invisible hand-shake' is good for business too; it builds bonds between people; shoppers develop loyalties and no longer compare prices; retailers develop trusting relationships with wholesalers. It works because economic relationships are part of society and culture, a social economic person could not survive in the real world without learning the social rules. Naked self-interest is generally frowned upon: retailers raising the prices of air-conditioning systems in a heat wave may be doing the economically rational thing but they should not expect to be liked for it as they will probably be seen as behaving 'unfairly'.

The chapter is divided into four parts: the first deals with 'norms of fairness' regarding prices and wages (Kahneman *et al.* 1986) and the allocation of scarce health resources (Hessing and Elffers, 1986; Lewis and Snell, 1996; Elster, 1991); the second with business ethics; the third with 'green' consumerism and energy conservation; the fourth with ethical purchasing and ethical investing. (For philosophers 'ethics' and 'morals' are not one and the same: 'ethics' are rules and justifications for conduct; 'morals' are distinctions between good and bad, right and wrong. 'Eating people is wrong' is a moral statement, 'because it offends the sanctity of the human body and treats humankind as if of equal status to animals' is an ethical statement with other moral implications. The current authors are not so rigorous in their usage of the terms and trust this causes, at most, only slight irritation.)

## Is it fair?

Consumer protection acts of various forms are firmly in place in many of the advanced industrial nations of the world. In an oft-quoted speech to Congress on 15 March 1962, J. F. Kennedy spoke of the right of consumers of both public and private goods as: (1) the right to safety; (2) the right to be informed; (3) the right to choose; and (4) the right of redress. If you buy a children's toy you have the right to assume that it is safe for children to play with – a consumer could reasonably expect a manufacturer to alter the way a teddy bear is made if a child could easily remove its eyes, exposing a long, sharp, securing pin. It is reasonable to expect that a child's nightdress will not ignite on the slightest exposure to a naked flame. You have the right to know the constituents of foodstuffs – how much preservative and colouring they contain, what proportion of the ingredients are 'natural' or the result of chemical manufacture. The right to choose restricts the development of monopolies and cartels. And finally the right of redress legitimises a proper complaints procedure.

What is considered fair (even right), however, not only includes the interests of consumers but covers the views of employers and producers as well. A pertinent paper published by Kahneman, Knetsch and Thaler (1986) will be considered in some detail. Imagine the following case: A hardware store has been selling snow shovels at $15. The morning after a large snow storm, the store raises the price to $20. Is this fair or unfair? In telephone interviews with residents in Toronto and Vancouver, 82 per cent of respondents (N = 107) considered it unfair for the hardware store to take advantage of the short-run increase in demand due to the snowfall (Kahneman, Knetsch and Thaler, 1986).

Take another case, shared economic beliefs about profit seeking involving employers and employees:

> A small photocopying shop has one employee who has worked in the shop for six months and earns $9 per hour. Business continues to be satisfactory, but a factory in the area has closed and unemployment has increased. Other small shops have now hired reliable workers at $7 an hour to perform jobs similar to those done by the photocopy shop employee. The owner of the photocopying shop reduces the employees wage to $7.

Is this acceptable? Is this fair? Eighty-three per cent think that it is not (N = 98). However, these fairness ratings are radically changed when the question is slightly altered to read: A small photocopying shop has one employee.. [as in the question above] ... The current employee leaves, and the owner decides to pay a replacement $7 an hour. Now 73 per cent thought the employer's action acceptable (N = 125).

Kahneman, Knetsch and Thaler felt that results such as these showed that the 'stickiness' of wages, their resistance to changes in macro-economic circumstances, a common but not easily explained phenomenon, is partly due to participants' shared notions about what is fair and acceptable. To take other examples, it seems acceptable for a firm to raise prices as well as the size of these price rises, if, for example, the firm experiences an increase in the cost of materials. But if the cost of materials falls there is no corresponding requirement, in terms of what people deem to be fair, for the firm to reduce its prices by the same amount as the reduction in the firms costs; the firm only needs to pass on part of these gains to be seen as fair. Furthermore it is not acceptable for the firm to increase prices because of shortages of a desired commodity, according to Kahneman, Knetsch and Thaler (p. 735):

> Conventional economic analyses assume as a matter of course that excess demand for a good creates an opportunity for suppliers to raise prices, and that such increases will indeed occur. The profit seeking adjustments that clear the market are in this view as natural as water finding its level – as ethically neutral. The lay public does not share this indifference.

## Medical ethics

There are many people, both 'experts' and lay people, who believe that the medical services are goods like any other and are most efficiently supplied in a 'free' market without government interference (Green, 1986). The consumers are the patients, the suppliers; doctors, nurses and pharmacists. Problems arise as so often demand exceeds supply: for instance, there are more people needing a kidney transplant than can have one. How are these scarce resources to be allocated? In a 'free' market system of consumer sovereignty the answer is straightforward: people prepared to pay the (high) price head the queue. In most developed countries the 'free market' system has been amended, there is a feeling that allocation purely on the bases of wealth is somehow unfair and inequitable. This is an area of economic activity where input from moral philosophers, social policy analysts, psychologists, sociologists and political scientists has been considerable. Has the inclusion of moral considerations improved the allocation of these precious resources? Would a market without such 'interference' be more efficient? These are big questions and the literature too is huge (Donaldson and Gerard, 1993): we limit ourselves, for illustration, to the cases of kidney machine allocation and organ transplantation.

There are many 'psychological' factors of importance in the transplant equation: both potential donors and participating doctors have their fears (Hessing and Elffers, 1986; Lewis and Snell, 1986). In Britain and the Netherlands (as well as several other countries) there is an 'opting-in' scheme, where members of the public carry signed cards, stating their willingness, in the event of death, to donate various organs, usually including kidneys. It appears that the main reason that people give for not carrying cards is the fear that death may be declared prematurely if they were to (Hessing and Elffers, 1986). There is a reluctance too for doctors to enquire of relatives at an extremely delicate time whether or not organs can be removed. It is plausible that doctors need to be reassured that the views of the 'general public' will be sympathetic before making an approach and there is evidence that feelings (both of doctors and potential donors) are volatile: in October 1980 the BBC put out a documentary programme 'Transplants: are the donors really dead?', in the following three months the number of kidney transplants undertaken fell sharply; conversely in 1984 when the British government launched a kidney donor card campaign through television advertisements and posters the average monthly donation of kidneys increased from 149 to 212 (Lewis and Snell, 1986).

Are there important 'psychological' as well as 'rational' influences in medical decision making? Just as Kahneman, Knetsch and Thaler found in the settling of fair prices and wages, are there norms of behaviour which govern who should or should not receive dialysis or a kidney transplant beyond those which are purely rational (or medical)?

In his paper Langford (1992) initially described a simple model made up of only two components, namely 'medical prognosis' and 'medical emergency'. Discussing the case of the allocation of kidney dialysis machines, medical prognosis requires that kidney machines should go to those patients to whom it would be of the longest-term benefit. This is tempered by 'medical emergency', those patients who would die in the very near future if not immediately given dialysis.

The dilemmas change depending on the medical service discussed but it is certainly true in the case of kidney transplantation that a patient receiving a kidney who would otherwise imminently die (a medical emergency) has a poorer prognosis than a 'fitter' patient receiving a transplant (Elster, 1991). For every decision of this kind there are opportunity costs: the doctors and others involved in the decision have to consider not only the needs of the individual patient but what benefits are foregone by giving a particular treatment to *this* patient (possibly at a high cost) rather than *that* or *those* patients. 'Efficient' decisions based on medical prognosis are stymied by 'inefficient' decisions based on medical emergencies.

Doctors are human; they are not rational calculating machines. They want to do what is right and their decisions are influenced by the available repertoire of relevant considerations situated within the medical profession, feelings of justice and fairness perceived by patients, the wider public and, last but not least, the considerations of hospital managers. Doctors, including consultants, inevitably develop a sense of obligation to individual patients, what Klein (1977) refers to as 'ethical individualism', the sense of obligation to *this* individual patient. Klein continues that this individualism is generally linked with a tendency to underestimate opportunity costs, the greater kudos in the medical profession of treating acute conditions rather than chronic conditions and too great an emphasis placed on prolonging life (quantity) rather than on quality of life.

Elster (1991) identifies three norms of behaviour which influence decisions: the norms of compassion, of thoroughness and just deserts. The norm of compassion is similar to Langford's (1992) notion of 'medical emergency' and Klein's observations about 'ethical individualism', the tendency to give transplants and other expensive treatments to dangerously ill patients, a norm which Elster relates to Tversky and Kahneman's (1981) 'certainty effect' in their studies of heuristic decision making. Burgoyne *et al.* (1994), have also shown in their studies of 'lay' opinions about prioritisation that many people feel market considerations should have little or no impact in a medical emergency.

In the United States and the United Kingdom people have very thorough eye tests, the justification being that people with serious eye diseases would not otherwise be identified; but this ignores the cases that go undetected because the patient never makes an appointment with the optician at all. Although similar to the concept of opportunity costs, Elster gives the eye-test case as an example of the norm of thoroughness. In the realm of transplants, thoroughness creates a commitment whereby those who have received a transplant that has failed may even get another, when the chances of success are even smaller than the first transplant (but where success, should it happen, is greatly acclaimed). Economists would think of this in terms of 'sunk costs', spilt milk that should not be cried over, but once a transplant has been given and failed it is difficult for decision makers to behave as though nothing has happened.

There is now a large empirical literature on 'just-world beliefs' and 'just deserts' (see Furnham, 1988). This recommends that judgements about who deserves a transplant go above and beyond purely medical concerns, even, at times, curbing the norm of compassion. The waiting list for liver transplants is much longer for problem drinkers than more sober members of the population. This is not surprising, perhaps, given that many liver failures are due to excessive alcohol consumption. The question is whether the differences in waiting for the two groups is justified in terms of eventual success or failure of these transplants? Additionally should past behaviour (which cannot completely predict future behaviour) be punished to the extent that, quite literally, boozing of heroic proportions becomes a capital offence? Maybe some feel that is what patients in some sense 'deserve': but what about an excessive consumption of coffee and pancreatic failure, should such people be placed below those with a preference for tea?

Most economists prefer to distance themselves from subjective consideration in medical decision making and to generalise (and this is not straightforward, as the literature is huge) are concerned instead with the change in health status resulting from the receipt of medical care compared to the next best alternative (Williams, 1985). As an explanatory example let us take 100 patients with heart problems who are treated with drugs; that is to say, are 'medically managed' with no surgical intervention. An evaluation would then take two things into account: the first is the 'quality of life', varying from perfect health (point 1) to death (point O); the second is duration of life. Our 100 patients can be presented in Figure 8.1 for the quality of life profile AB. If the cohort were instead treated with by-pass surgery the results might be as follows:

10 died producing, compared with medical management $-0.1 \times$ the area OAB 'qualys' per patient case.

30 stayed on AB, there being no gain for surgical intervention over 'medical management'.

60 moved to profile AC producing $+0.6 \times$ the area ABC 'qualys' per patient.

A calculation can then be made of the expected output of by-pass surgery measured as quality-adjusted life years as follows:

$$-0.1 \times OAB + 0.6 \times ABC \text{ per case.}$$

This then has to be translated as a cost per 'qualy'. Some procedures may produce

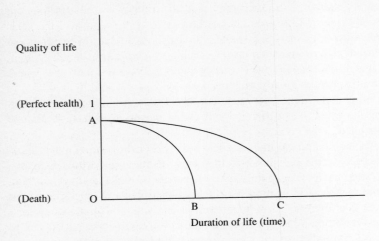

**Figure 8.1**   Quality adjusted life years.

substantial gains but at exorbitant costs. Tables can be drawn up comparing the relative merit of different medical procedures and funds can then be allocated in an efficient manner.

This is all fine and dandy as far as it goes but there are of course numerous problems. How, for example, is quality of life to be measured? It has often been the case that this has been decided upon by doctors and consultants proxying 'patient experience' based on their judgements of, in particular, pain and activity restriction of typical patients. But, as most researchers in this area recognise, this in itself is not ideologically and morally neutral; recent work by psychologists is concerned with developing more sophisticated quality of life measures which take the views of patients into account (Fallowfield, 1990). The 'qualys' also tend to treat individuals as the same; the assessment is concerned more with the overall performance of medical procedures than with which medical procedures are best for particular kinds of patients. This more disaggregated analysis is of course technically possible; one could compare the quality-adjusted life years of patients of different ages and between patients who smoked and those who did not, for example; results which might reveal that it is more 'efficient' to treat younger non-smokers with by-pass operations than the rest. However, many economists shy away from such calculations, perhaps for good reason, as it implies that one person's life is in some ways worth more than another's and such questions are not easily resolved within a single discipline.

## A compromise?

In his initial and simplest model, Langford suggests that if two individuals are equal in terms of prognosis and acuteness of their illness the only fair thing to do is to choose between them based on a lottery. 'Logical' and 'rational' as this may be, 'lay' people tend to find the idea of a toss of a coin for a life morally repugnant. Although he quotes no evidence, Langford reckons that people would be affronted if a young mother with dependent children lost out in this grim race to an 80-year-old recluse. It should not, however, be assumed that moral approval or disapproval is universal; they are culturally bound and determined.

Langford offers a compromise between deontological and utilitarian ethics: the former referring to self-evident rules which are not led by the consequences of action; the latter by the belief that the ultimate good is the greatest happiness of the greatest number. The deontological line directs that medical prognosis should be the dominant (if not exclusive) rule governing decision making and that equality should be maintained in all other respects. The compromise that Langford puts forward is that some discrimination should take place but this should be of the least offensive kind. The 'offensive list' includes discrimination on the grounds of sex or race but not, interestingly, age. This main 'inoffensive' criterion is 'irreplaceability': there can be no real substitute for a mother for her children; she is irreplaceable to them in a way that, say, a heart surgeon is not irreplaceable to his/her patients, unless no-one can do the surgeon's job. 'Irreplaceability' is bound to be open to argument and the author recognises the rules of discrimination will change over time and be different for varying cultures, that the criteria should be known and open to public debate.

## Business ethics

From Harvard Business School to the Stockholm School of Economics ethics is being taught to students as part of the curriculum, a move that presumably Milton Friedman would deplore, as according to him the corporation has no responsibility beyond serving the interests of its stockholders. The corporation's only responsibility is to 'use its resources and engage in activities designed to increase its profits so long as it stays within the rules of the game, which is to say, engages in open and free competition, without deception or fraud' (Friedman, 1962: 133).

Why 'business ethics' now? One reason is that the image of business has been tarnished in high places: the 1980s and 1990s have seen a comparatively large number of court cases dealing with insider trading and fraudulence, which have grasped public attention. New laws have been introduced in many countries which can lead to heavy fines for transgressors. It is as well to train managers in the law, and how it might change in the future: there is a fear among business corporations of further government intervention regulating business practices. There is an incentive for businesses to be seen to be putting their own houses in order. Last, with the rise and rise of the consumer movement (and private litigation), companies, big companies in particular, can no longer be politically neutral, environmentally naive or unaware of the possible harmful effects of their products. It seems as though almost all consumables in the United States carry some kind of health warning, ojectile qualities of champagne corks is brought to a would-be reveller's ....on. More seriously perhaps companies who manufacture cosmetic products tested on live animals, produce aerosols with dangerous CFCs, or (in the recent past at least) invest heavily in South Africa (or are supportive of other 'oppressive' regimes) do so at their marketing peril. This does not mean that Harvard and other business graduates will become saints overnight; they may see ethical or environmental aspects as just another characteristic to be used in marketing. Some consumers may not be fooled so easily; it could even be that 'genuineness' rather than cynicism is an optimal corporate strategy.

A logical extension of this theme is that corporations, rather than being neutral, may in the future feel socially responsible in taking positive, even politically normative, steps to improve the world (Stone, 1994). However, teaching foreign countries the 'American way' of doing business might be viewed as smacking of a kind of imperialism. There are practical issues too associated with whether, from a management point of view, one takes various rules of the market as fair and reasonably 'universal' or whether certain values are culturally 'relative'. For those managers shy of taking their part in world affairs there are still the problems of international economic social skill. What is appropriate in Tokyo may not be the usual practice in New York and London (Rosansky, 1994).

There is now quite a large literature on business ethics – recent examples include Harvard Business Review's, *Ethics at Work* (Donaldson, 1992); there is even a *Journal of Business Ethics* (Davis, 1991). The main research areas are product design, product functions and safety, pollution of the environment, employee relations, marketing and distribution policies, gifts and bribery, taxes and charges, accountancy practices and financial practices generally.

For our current purposes special attention is paid to two articles which specifically relate to the themes of this chapter: the first is concerned with fairness in consumer pricing and the role of the law (Kaufman, Ortmeyer and Smith, 1991); the second with the ethics and economics of product policy decisions (Menezes, 1991).

Kaufmann, Ortmeyer and Smith report two case studies of legal prosecutions in the United States of May's department store and a housing development company GDC (General Development Corporation) for defrauding and deceiving customers. Both prosecutions were successful. It seems that in 'the land of the free' the emphasis has changed from *caveat emptor* (buyer beware) to *caveat venditor* (seller beware): the economist's belief that a fair price is simply one that a consumer is prepared to pay is insufficient in the eyes of some consumer law.

When is a sale not a sale? In June 1989 the Colorado section of the departmental chain store May's were charged by the Attorney General's Office of engaging in deceptive advertising practices. Since 1986 (although there were some later 'improvements') the firm's policy was to advertise a range of goods at a 'regular' or 'original' price (a reference price) for ten days at the start of a six-month selling season, thereafter the goods were discounted (to varying degrees), returning only to the 'original prices' in the last ten days of the six-month selling period. Evidence was presented for the prosecution that 97 per cent of a sample of 5,340 household

## Love, sex and automobiles

We are in love with the automobile. It is going to be very hard to end the affair. Is the greening of the car industry a possibility? Car manufacturers supply the goods: a recyclable auto that looks good, accelerates quickly, yet uses energy sparsely and pollutes little. The impossible dream? Does something have to go?

Why do we love the marque of a Rolls Royce, a Mercedes, even the chirpiness of a tiny Fiat? Look at the facts. Today there are around 400 million cars in the world. Arguably automobiles impose the greatest negative externalities of any product: through mountainous consumption of fossil fuels; approximately 250,000 people die every year in motor accidents; carbon monoxide pollution as well as other gases and metals fill the atmosphere; look at congestion on the roads, disfigurement of the landscape. The list could go on (Ekins, 1992).

The car lobby has been strong, perhaps too strong. The infrastructure of railways in the United States and in other countries has been lost. The railway depot is a hypermarket now.

For Sachs (1983) in a well scripted article, car ownership is symbolic and full of cultural meanings which make for a very special product. Consequently on page 349 he asserts: 'a transition to a low energy society or, for that matter, to a low speed society consequently implies a rearrangement of cultural meanings' (Sachs, 1983: 349).

Historically, and more than vestiges remain, car ownership is associated with an independence of spirit, going where you want to go at your own speed and time; you quite literally do not have to keep to the rails, share space with strangers. And what a lot a car can do for you. It can give you speed, rivalry, power, thrills. You can exercise control and skill, feel virile, even omnipotent. If is a form of self- and social identification: 'Car driving is the most conspicuous but not the sole case in which we learn to appreciate and need an identity that is energy driven' (Sachs, 1983: 352).

Are some people, owners of the largest cars, secretly pleased to announce just how few miles to the gallon their car can achieve? There are 960 different brands and types of car available in present-day Germany alone, and there remains a strong correlation between a person's position in the social and economic hierarchy and the size and horse power of that person's car. It is there for all to see but only seen with such clarity when one considers the possibilities (or lack of them) for change.

With ever more sophisticated models coming out every year we are spurred by a possessive narcissism. We are no longer spectators: we can take part 'in society's great project; striving for refined technology means bringing technical progress within reach, taking history home' (Sachs, 1983: 352).

All this said the number of people who say they drive mainly for enjoyment has fallen in the last thirty years. Most of us drive because we feel we have to; the alternatives are unattractive. Ironically what has most damaged the image of the motor car is its success. Distinctiveness is dwindling. You can rarely drive your car fast; there are too many other people attempting to do the same. Driving has become an amalgam of mild exhilaration and all too familiar frustration.

Will the future yield social cachet associated with the ownership of small energy-efficient cars? If so, how is one to indicate that one could have afforded and purchased a Cadillac but chose not to?

Gender issues have not been developed very much in this area of research. Could it be that much of what we have said so far applies mostly to men, that women might prefer people and the arts to hunks of metal? I (Alan) could identify at least 100 different motor cars by name; my wife Sandie, fewer than ten. I see roses in our garden; my wife sees a botanical lexicon – all in Latin. According to Claxton, Ritchie and McDougall (1983), women are much more supportive of active environmental programmes, especially those referring to the restricted use of motor cars. Yet overall it is a habit difficult to break. According to Uusitalo and Djerf (1983), as a result of time series data for 1970–9 of several European countries as well as the United States, increases in gasoline prices have had little effect on driving intensity and car stocks (over this period at least) have continued to rise. The authors argue that only gasoline increases twice that of percentage increases in real disposable income are required if price is to have a desirable environmental effect on consumption. When various policy options are put to consumers, people are generally much keener to reduce energy consumption in the home than accept consumer restrictions on automobile use (Claxton, Ritchie and McDougall, 1983). There is a suspicion too that tax levies on gasoline are less for environmental reasons and more to line treasury coffers (Lavik and Lunde, 1991).

Dholakia, Dholakia and Firat (1983) are of the opinion that while financial incentives (or for that matter disincentives) are important, their effects are short-lived: economists and psychologists need to work together, not apart or in opposition. Taxes on gasoline touch the rational economic person's pocket but not their psyche.

Dholakia, Dholakia and Firat (1983) quite rightly stress the importance of political–economic structures to decision making when considering private individual consumption (say, in the personal use of a motor car) compared to public collective endeavours (riding on a train or a bus): 'Quite simply, the private individual consumption pattern provides greater opportunities for capital accumulation compared to any other pattern under conditions of monopoly capitalism' (1983: 239). In the United States, they continue, socialisation effects are such that children expect car and house ownership almost as a right; it is an essential part of their life-style, of being American: 'The American dream is today a generalized cultural pattern transmitted intergenerationally much in the same way American language is' (1983: 240–1). With the emancipation of the old Eastern bloc, the American dream is becoming even more widespread. If we are not careful things could get even worse and the notion of post-industrial society could become an alien one.

So what of the future? All is not gloom, you might say. A look at contemporary motor car advertising reveals that while sex is not quite out, safety features, catalytic converters and the like are definitely 'in'. Whether these initiatives are driven by consumer demand, fear of government intervention or marketing strategy is another matter. But at the current state of play manufacturers and consumers are trying to have their cake and eat it: turbo-charged vehicles with catalytic converters; diesel engines with fuel injection, otherwise they do not go fast enough.

Governments have tried a number of measures: taxes on gasoline; fines for manufacturers of large fuel-inefficient cars; road tolling; not providing parking spaces for cars with fewer than three passengers; improving public transport. But policy, however well meaning and informed, is little use without changes in consumer attitudes, beliefs and values. Public transport could be made more attractive by providing discounts at stores in return for free advertising – the public and private sectors could work together in ways beneficial to all (Geller, Winett and Everett, 1982). But whatever the incentives, the mould has to be broken, the belief that public transport is mostly for lower socio-economic groups and ethnic minorities. Will riding on a bus ever be the chic thing to do?

And in answer to the question 'Would you forgo your car to live in a car free city?' the answer must surely be yes but only if everyone else does.

Catch a bus? I do not have the energy.


## Turn out that light! The economic psychology of household energy consumption

The household sector accounts for over a third of all directly consumed energy in the United States. This is where we bring environmental questions right home.

Heberlein and Warriner (1983) report on a field study of 700 residential electricity consumers in north-eastern Wisconcin, conducted over three years. The particular interest was the use of on- and off-peak electricity which was differentially priced, in three different conditions, in ratios of 2:1, 4:1 and 8:1. The higher price ratios did indeed reduce peak electricity usage but the authors report that 'psychological commitment' has a higher impact, surprisingly, than price. Commitment changed behaviour even at low differentials (it is worth noting that the 'commitment' measure was of the Fishbein type and consequently was highly focused; as we have noted before, more generalised attitude measures are not in themselves closely associated with specific environmentally aware behaviours).

The Heberlein and Warriner study underlined the importance of knowledge factors: people often underestimated the price ratios. It seems likely that the price differences need to be made very clear to consumers in their bills as well as the reasons for the price differences. There will, however, be a conflict of interest. Why precisely would a private utility company, responsible to its shareholders to maximise profit, actively encourage a reduction in consumption? One can imagine such bizarre happenings as governments paying companies to persuade their consumers to buy less of their product! Or stranger still, offer financial incentives to consumers to, in effect, spend less on electricity.

In a longitudinal panel study of 1,000 household respondents in Canada, consumers were asked to assess the relative acceptability of a variety of household environmental programmes put forward by environmental experts (Claxton, Ritchie and McDougall, 1983). Consumers favoured schemes where they did not have to make personal financial sacrifices but where costs were borne by government. (This is an interesting result in itself as it suggests that paying increased taxes to find environmental programmes is acceptable while making 'personal' financial sacrifices is not; it depends on how the proposal is 'framed'. More likely perhaps is that consumers believe that environmental policies can be financed from existing revenue.)

Information programmes were the most popular ('how to' books and so forth) – whether they are effective or not is another matter. Consumers also welcomed information labels on household appliances, switches and boilers but were lukewarm about grants for insulation costs. Overall, consumers prefer 'soft options' to heating regulations, for example, imposed by government. Very similar results have been recorded by Olsen (1983) in a study of 900 mail respondents in the state of Washington, 83 per cent of respondents favouring schemes involving financial incentives and only 9 per cent favouring various price increases.

In a democracy it matters not only whether a scheme is a good one in terms of potential energy savings, equity across different income and consumer groups, administrative efficiency and feasibility but also whether it is acceptable to consumers, as ultimately it is they who will make or break a scheme.

Dholakia, Dholakia and Firat (1983) quite rightly point out that there are important structural elements in contemporary capitalist societies, especially the United States, which restrict what politicians and consumers can do. People have generally moved out of the cities and often live a long way from their work in widely dispersed residential areas, making long journeys by car almost inevitable. Because of the large number of individual household units it is difficult to envisage how heating can be 'shared' as it is in an apartment block. Dholakia *et al.* argue that sharing and co-operation is difficult in a society governed by individualism, and, on page 237, that 'energy use and energy conservation behaviours must be seen within the context of a broader consumption pattern which is socially determined'.

Dholakia *et al.* and Dillman, Rosa and Dillman (1983) all emphasize the importance of equity. They argue that increases in utility prices can be accommodated by discretionary changes in the life-styles of middle to high socio-economic groups while they produce involuntary changes for the poor. Grants to improve, for example, household insulation are more likely to be taken up by the middle class. With the exception of grants it is poorer people who have often been more responsive to environmentally motivated price increases as 'Their conservation behaviour may, in fact, be non-voluntary and jeopardize their own welfare' (Dholakia, Dholakia and Firat, 1983: 236).

Can we break away from selfishness, learn to co-operate and share resources? Mosler (1993) in a fun experiment derived from the ideas of Hardin (1968) (The tragedy of commons) offers a hint of optimism. Respondents took part in a computer simulation acting as a fisherman fishing a lake, with a limited stock of fish, along with twenty-four other fishermen in separate boats (unbeknown to the respondents, their behaviour was computer-simulated). Respondents 'play' with real money and are asked to earn as much as they possibly can. If each fisherman catches 2 per cent of the fish stock in any given year the stock will remain stable as it is assumed that the fish can cope with a 50 per cent attrition rate (i.e. 25 x 2 per cent). Two per cent is enough to make a profit. If individuals go above 2 per cent and others follow everyone loses as there will be no fish left. Participants are invited to join an interest group called 'fishing in moderation'. If one joins, this information is publicly displayed on the computer screen. There were 100 participants altogether. The simulation of public commitment (interest group membership) encouraged co-operative behaviour, attitudes having no statistically significant main effect; public commitment is even effective among participants with low environmental consciousness.

Mosler argues in the more general part of the paper that change is possible so long as there is mutual trust and that behaviour is open to verification by others and is publicly visible. I will not free-ride if you do not, but I have to be sure. The problem is there is evidence that people who have low scores on Rotter's interpersonal trust scale (Rotter, 1967) actually increase their use of resources when resources are already overexploited, while those with high scores reduce theirs (Messick *et al.*, 1983). Similarly undergraduates trained in economics are more likely to 'free-ride' compared to undergraduates in other disciplines (Frank, Gilovich and Regan, 1993).

There are many dilemmas and ironies in our attempts to reverse the exploitation of planet earth. Individuals are more prepared to make sacrifices the better off they are and the better off they hope to become! Interestingly the 'market solution' to environmental problems, with a minimal amount of government intervention is likely to be favoured by right-wing governments yet it is right-wing consumers, because of their cynicism about human nature, who are least likely to think that people will make co-operative, environmentally desirable choices of their own free will.

## 'Ethical'/'social' investing

Are people prepared to put their money where their morals are? To an extent this is self-evident when one considers charitable giving, although the amount overall is large it is a small part of most individuals' 'spending' (Hodgkinson and Weitzmann, 1990). The central question here is whether people want to *make* money morally. Could such actions lead to a better world? As an example we concentrate on 'social' or 'ethical' investments (Lewis and Cullis 1990; Cullis, Lewis and Winnett 1992; Lewis and Webley 1994).

In the United States alone around 20 per cent of all investments are 'social' investments. The criteria used to define these investments vary a good deal (Dominic and Kinder, 1984; Bruyn, 1987). Exclusions, however, are common: not investing in companies with poor pollution records, companies that manufacture tobacco or nuclear weapons, companies with large investments in 'oppressive' regimes (in the recent past South Africa has been a prime example). What we can call 'proactive' ethical investments are less common, that is, investing in companies that recycle paper and plant new trees, or in wind-powered energy stations. It is clear that ethical investments are expanding in the United Kingdom and other countries as well and, although a much smaller sector than the United States, they provide the opportunity to examine whether this part of the market will develop in the same way. Surely here is a case where people's values and beliefs have economic consequences that cannot be explained away.

Unravelling the ethical dilemma requires both a psychological and an economic perspective as well as an appreciation of both supply and demand. People's preferences (for which read attitudes, values, beliefs, moral commitments) are treated as exogenous in economic models; only if all else fails might they be alluded to with the comment that economists know nothing about preferences, that this is a job for a psychologist. Why then has ethical investment increased? A natural explanation for a social psychologist is to say that there has been a value shift, people are now more aware of and concerned about the environment and want to do something about it, an explanation based in one way or another on consumer demand. Economists have nothing against consumer demand except that here one wants to say that preferences have changed and that will not do for economists. Economic attention is turned instead to investigating performance of ethical unit trusts: if they are performing well then it is obvious that people will choose them be they righteous, ethical or satanic. This is question 1.

## Does investing ethically pay?

An ethical or social portfolio must be a restricted one where companies are chosen for characteristics other than financial performance. All portfolios are restricted in the sense that one cannot invest in everything: one chooses, usually on the advice of a broker, a selection of investments that one hopes will do as well (and perhaps even better) than the average performance of all shares. It is difficult enough to achieve this without having to exclude whole industries, countries, even continents of the world.

What do the results show? In a highly technical area there are naturally disagreements, but few would argue that ethical funds perform better than others; instead the consensus is that they perform on a par with others or marginally worse (Dominic and Kinder, 1984; Luther and Matatko, 1991).

Risk is the second major aspect of the investment decision for economists. There should be few significant differences between social investments which employ exclusions, whereas proactive social investments may well be riskier.

So where do the economists go now to explain matters? The answer is to look at supply.

## Supply and authenticity

How is the consumer to choose between investments, all of which are behaving adequately? A marketing manager's strategy is to differentiate his/her product from others. Seen this way, an advertising claim that 'profit does not have to be a dirty word' can sell 'ethicalness' as just another characteristic reducing morality to the level of packaging. This kind of scepticism naturally leads one to consider whether these 'social' investments are really ethical at all. Many trusts have responded to this by forming advisory boards consisting of the great and the good, including environmentalists and respected senior journalists. There even exist organisations specialising in fitting investments to personal preferences while at the same time testing the authenticity of those investments (e.g. 'Good Money', see Lowry, 1991 in United States; EIRIS, in the United Kingdom). Closer inspection suggests a kind of moral pragmatism operating where exclusion, say in investments in South Africa, does not exclude investments in companies who have money in other companies who invest in South Africa and so on. Fund managers are aware that their trusts must perform well. Total exclusions make this difficult: it is relatively common to find that investments, for instance, in weaponry may be allowed as long as they make up less than 5 per cent of the portfolio, that is, certain avenues are restricted not excluded. The fact that these funds may marginally underperform suggests that investors are prepared to put their money where their morals are but only when the cost is low (additional pertinent evidence for this claim is presented later in this chapter). Nevertheless there is a case for a broader utility function encompassing moral commitment.

## Preferences and people

It would be relatively uncontentious to claim that there has been a growth in environmental consciousness throughout industrialised societies. In one CBS poll for the *New York Times* (1990) in response to the unequivocal statement 'Protecting the environment is so important that requirements and standards cannot be too high, and continuing environmental improvements must be made regardless of cost' a significant majority of 79 per cent agreed and only 18 per cent disagreed; in 1981 the results were 45 per cent and 42 per cent respectively (Kirkpatrick, 1990). But how meaningful is such a result? What would happen if it had financial implications for you and me right now? It is not always easy to separate rhetoric and good intentions from actual behaviour; most of us like to view ourselves in a favourable light. And as Margaret Thatcher, the former prime minister of Britain, was keen on saying, the point of the biblical story of the Good Samaritan was not only his generosity but the fact that he had the money (what she would make of the story of the widows' mite is a moot point). During much of her period of office (she claimed) income tax was cut and public expenditure curtailed, while charitable giving went up year after year, Conservatives making much of the inverse relationship between the public provision of goods and individual morality. In a poll conducted by Mintel (1991) young people were found to have more positive green attitudes than other groups, a sympathy that was not linked with replies to questions about ethical investing. It seems that the young simply do not have the money: there are more important things than investments on their minds.

Those now in their forties believe the 1960s to be a special time, a time of the anti-Vietnam movement, of peace, of love, of post-industrialism. It seems plausible that we are not continually open to societal influences, that there are critical periods, the 1960s may have been one, the depression of the 1930s another. It is useful to imagine preferences as being like 'clay' rather than 'putty'. The children of the 1960s, with their families growing up and mortgage commitments lessening, may now, for the first time, have the money to put with their beliefs.

Until now we have gone on as though investment decisions were individual decisions made in a vacuum. This of course is nonsense. Not all of us need share a burning desire to put the world to rights; life is simply not like that. We may, however, have sympathies which can turn into action when the costs are relatively low. Because some of us are more motivated than others 'zealots' can get things done (Bruyn, 1987). Institutional investments, trade unions, pension funds, even university accounts can be invested ethically because of the tenacity of just a few people, and when talking about pension funds we are talking about very large sums of money (PIRC, 1990).

There are special, honourable people around, most of us can name a few, but we at present have no personality profile of the 'average' individual ethical investor. Are they just like you and me? Or are people who are prepared to lose money, even relatively small amounts, eccentrics whose economic impact is likely to be small? These are crucial research questions for the future.

## A pilot survey and an experiment

Two apt pilot studies have been conducted by Lewis and Webley (1994). In the first, a hundred of the more wealthy home owners in Bath, were interviewed about their perceptions of ethical and green investments, whether they themselves would favour them, how they thought they performed compared to other investments, whether they would invest a windfall in a green and ethical investment even if one could make more money elsewhere. In the second study eighty four undergraduates took part in computer simulations of investment decisions which were compared to their preferences towards environmental and ecological issues.

Most of the respondents in the interview studies were in professional occupations: solicitors, accountants, dentists; there was even one stockbroker. There were sixty-two males and thirty-seven females. Most of those interviewed were investors, although few invested ethically. It was hoped that the study would tell us something about the 'average' investor compared to those already committed to 'green' and other concerns. In replies to open-ended questions twenty-four of those 'average' investors had some vague notions that ethical investments have something to do with 'avoiding immoral things' or 'doing good'. Fourteen people specifically mentioned ecology, the environment and the 'greens'. The largest category of replies (thirty-five people) mentioned exclusions, which indeed characterise most of these investments, citing South Africa often together with the embargo on armaments, tobacco and alcohol. Mentions of the environment rose to twenty-five altogether as these were spoken of in connection with exclusions. Generally those who spoke of exclusions had more articulate views on the subject.

In closed questions where respondents were asked to rate their agreement (or disagreement), on five point scales, as to whether a set of five characteristics were and should be characteristics of ethical investments, some additional information concerning salience was generated. 'Pollution' and 'nuclear weapons' were at the top of both lists, exclusions of 'nuclear power' at the bottom of each. Exclusion of investments in South Africa no longer have the power they once did; they are perceived as still very much in evidence but now less pertinent.

Next, respondents were asked:

> You have received a windfall gain of £1000, would you invest 'all of it', 'most of it', 'some of it' or 'none of it' ethically if the portfolio had all the characteristics you hold to be desirable and performed just as well as any other investment.

(An annual return of 10 per cent; a realistic if slightly optimistic figure at the time of asking.) Figure 8.2 suggests that even among 'ordinary investors' ethical investments are viewed quite favourably, 56 people out of 100 saying they would invest all or most of the windfall gain. But what is also clear when the question is altered so that the return on the investment varies from 9 to 8 per cent and finally to 5 per cent compared with the original 10 per cent on the all-share index is that investment is price-elastic and enthusiasm falls away steadily.

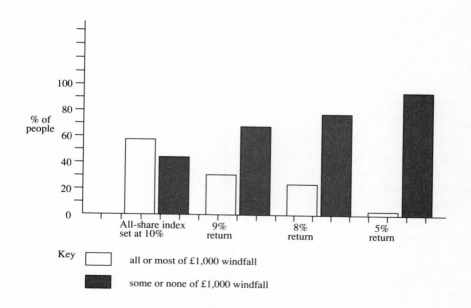

**Figure 8.2** Preferences for ethical investments with varying returns.

# A simulation

In the Lewis and Webley (1994) simulation eighty-four undergraduate students studying a wide range of subjects first took part in a practice session each on a personal computer. Participants were presented with information about the past performance of five shares. Each participant was 'given' £40,000 ($60,000) and asked to invest as little or as much as they liked in the shares over a period of 'quarters'. When participants had got used to using the keyboard and the graphical displays depicting changes in share prices, they were deemed ready to begin and received the following instructions:

> You have just inherited £40,000 from your uncle. You decide to invest in Scottish Equitable Unit Trusts, as this enables you to manage your investments whilst spreading the risks across a number of companies.
>
> Scottish Equitable have five trusts; (1) Global, (2) European, (3) UK Blue Chip, (4) Far East, (5) Ethical. A brief description of the investment policies of each is given in a leaflet. You may invest as little or as much as you like of the £40,000 in as many of the different funds as you like. You will be able to change your investments quarterly.
>
> Uninvested money stays in the bank where it earns an interest rate of, on average, 5 per cent.
>
> In order to help you with your investment decisions, each quarter you will be given some political or economic news (on teletext) and a graph displaying movements of unit trust prices and the *Financial Times* all-share index.

The teletext information was in a form common to that available on British Television. The information was a mixture of real economic and political news and fabricated, but hopefully believable, information. The leaflets provided four or five lines on each of the investments. For the ethical trust, it read:

> The Ethical Unit Trust covers companies with significant business activity in health care and companies who take an active interest in green issues (e.g. maintaining forests, protecting the ozone layer, recycling waste through the sensitive use of land, reducing acid rain, through energy conservation, reducing pollution etc.).

Participants were placed in three groups: in the first the ethical trust performed above average but nevertheless behind the 'Global' share; in the second group the ethical trust performed in line with the *Financial Times* (*FT*) all-share index; in the third the ethical trust performed badly, performance deteriorating during the period of the simulation.

The performance of the unit trusts was the same for all groups; the Far East and European trusts performed roughly in line with the *FT* index, the UK Blue Chip showed a slow but steady increase, the 'Global' trust was the 'star' performer.

After the simulation participants completed a twenty-item 'green' attitude scale with a seven-point response format from 'strongly agree' to 'strongly disagree'. The items covered general issues (e.g. 'I am worried about the ozone layer'; 'To go a short distance I would rather use a bike than a car'), pollution (e.g. 'All cars

ment of Mrs Thatcher was to attract the votes of skilled and semi-skilled manual workers with aspirations to 'higher things', workers who would 'traditionally' vote Labour. Conversely it is not uncommon for middle- and high/middle-income earners with greater than average numbers of years in education to vote Labour – the 'champagne socialists'. The attraction of the self-interest hypothesis is its flexibility and adaptability: it has so much (perhaps too much) rope that it can lasso any economic and social phenomenon and brand it with its explanation. So why do comparatively wealthy people support a mixed economy? Easy? With a dash of sociology we can come up with the idea that state benefits, especially at times of high unemployment, quell unrest, make the upheaval of the status quo less likely, keep middle- and high-income earners cosy and safe and relatively free of guilt.

It seems highly plausible that economic and political beliefs are closely linked, in such a way that one informs the other: for example, Furnham (1987) has shown that adolescent pupils in fee-paying 'private' schools are more likely to favour lower taxes and reductions in public spending, vote Conservative, have parents or guardians with higher than average incomes and be more likely to blame individuals who 'fail' in the economy and praise those that 'succeed', compared to adolescents in schools funded entirely by the state. Even among 7–12-year-olds children from wealthier backgrounds are more aware of, and are more articulate about, income inequalities (Emler and Dickinson, 1985): for instance, they are prone to explain that doctors earn what they do because their job is very important to other people and they have to spend many years in training; 'working-class' children were more likely to explain income differences in terms of luck or fate, or just the way things are.

We are all of us embedded in a culture; each of us is part of history. Our fiscal preferences are not only determined by income, by values, by aspects of our schooling but by the socialisation process writ large; by whether we are citizens of the United States of America, or Britain or Sweden. While the United States, Britain and Sweden are all democracies, their fiscal histories contrast: the status quo, the fiscal preferences that any individual might hold in any of these three countries 'without thinking about it', will be dependent on these fiscal and politico-economic histories. Sweden is still one of the highest taxed nations in the world, the United States one of the least, the United Kingdom somewhere in between. Reflected in this is a large public sector in Sweden, with the resulting expectation among Swedish voters that the state will provide, and provide generously, for crèche facilities, health, education. In the United States things are very different; taxes are comparatively low but tax antipathy remains high. For a citizen in the United States it is one's own country that counts not what happens in Sweden; it seems 'natural' that health care should be provided by 'private' insurance plans.

But history can never be static and the 1990s have witnessed major fiscal change, yet to some extent these changes have come as a surprise. Throughout the 1980s the Reagan administration in the United States and Margaret Thatcher's in the United Kingdom led a crusade of fiscal conservatism. In Britain, voters began to see privatisation programmes, for health, gas, electricity and telecommunications, reversing the trends of most post-Second World War UK governments (Bartlett, 1992). In the United States many states legislated to make fiscal expansion through, for example, an increase in state property taxes, only possible where majorities, sometimes two-thirds majorities, in fiscal referenda approve of them. The collapse of the old Soviet bloc was an enormous surprise; less spectacular, but a surprise none the less, has been the weakening of the public sector of that bastion of the mixed economy, Sweden, with reductions in income taxation and government spending. Conversely the Clinton administration dares to propose that private insurance schemes may not, after all, be the most efficient, nay the 'fairest' way to distribute the scarce resources of health care. We have histories, yes, but what constitutes fiscal wisdom is not enshrined in stone.

## Give or take? charity or taxation?

As we have said, the role the state should take in the provision and distribution of welfare is a political and moral question. A central idea of 'welfarism' is that state bureaucracies, acting as 'benevolent dictators', distribute goods on the behalf of consumer/voters. If we do not approve of the taxation and public expenditure policies of government, of how much or how little they spend on health, education, police and the armed forces, we can simply register our disapproval by not voting for them at the next election. If politicians want to stay in a job it is in their best interests to take account of the wishes and preferences of consumer/voters especially as elections approach. But is this enough? One of the reasons fiscal referenda have been introduced in some states of the United States of America has been precisely because, some have argued, governments have not been responsive enough and have been more interested in feathering their own nests, resulting in an increase in the size of the administration and a decrease in efficiency. Advocates wishing to see a reduction in the size of the public sector have not always had their way as a result of fiscal referenda, however; as voters become more aware of and interested in the fiscal connection between taxes and spending they sometimes become keener on expenditure programmes rather than becoming more 'fiscally conservative'.

In the United States, United Kingdom and other advanced democratic countries the size of the public sector appeared to be growing at least until the late 1970s; such that political commentators began arguing, especially in Western Europe, that some countries would become neo-communist by default, without the mandate of the electorate. As we have seen, leading political 'actors' such as Ronald Reagan and Margaret Thatcher have reversed these trends (or at the very least stemmed the tide); even Sweden, one of the most heavily taxed nations in the world, has experienced fiscal cut-backs in the 1990s.

With a state 'take-over' at one extreme one must also consider the reverse: a society and an economy with little or no state intervention; where, for example, provision for health and welfare would be financed by private insurance contributions and charitable donations. We concentrate here on the role of charity.

In Britain politicians such as Enoch Powell, a stalwart of the conservative right most prominent in the 1960s and 1970s, have nevertheless left a legacy of the argument that health and welfare services provided by the state detracts from a sense of moral responsibility and obligation among individuals; responsibilities are 'handed over' to that state instead. For commentators of this persuasion what at first sight might appear to be corporate benevolence becomes corporate malevolence, creating a 'dependency' culture; a culture where, for example, senior citizens are no longer viewed as the responsibilities of families but of governments: 'Please find Grannie a home; you surely can't expect us to look after her' goes up the cry from relatives.

Margaret Thatcher, the former Prime Minister of the United Kingdom, was fond of eulogising about the inverse relationship between the level of taxation and charitable contributions; a government committed to reducing taxation, far from being immoral was depicted as returning freedom to individuals, in the form of increased income, to express their moral preferences by giving freely to charities of their own choice instead of being 'coerced' by government making welfare and other expenditure decisions on voters' behalf. Power was being returned to the people, so the rhetoric rang, thus ending a period of individual moral disenfranchisement. Mrs Thatcher, particularly at party conferences, was able to quote successive increases in charitable contributions across the United Kingdom concurrent with a symmetrical fall in the total burden of taxation (as you can imagine, these figures and this relationship were contested by those who did not share Mrs Thatcher's enthusiams).

Let us for the time being imagine that there *is* an inverse relationship between tax burdens and charitable contributions; the crucial question then becomes: if we were to rely on volunteerism could we guarantee that money would go to the right places (which also begs the question of whether state bureaucracies do this successfully in any case)? Certainly when the fiscal preferences of the electorate are sought there are marked similarities between the attitudes of voters in the United States and many other western democracies: provisions for health care, education and care for the elderly are popular whereas some social security payments to the 'undeserving poor', say single-parent families or 'scroungers' who make themselves unavailable for paid employment, are not. Funds for 'foreign aid' almost always come bottom of the charts. If volunteerism took charge there is the chance that the more visible and 'deserving' would do well; hospitals, paediatric oncology units and the like – while the less attractive ones perhaps would not, for example, the mentally ill. Would it be acceptable to see a donkey sanctuary flourish at the expense of AIDS victims? Probably not. But it would be our responsibility, in terms of where we put our charitable contributions, to decide.

The new market in several countries in Europe where public expenditure has been curtailed is one where there is increased competition between charities, where charities for hospitals and schools are competing vigorously with the more 'traditional' famine and animal welfare agencies. Who are and who might be the winners and losers? Where do charitable contributions roost?

*The Financial Times* of 14 December 1993 makes interesting reading in its listing of the top twenty fund-raising charities in the United Kingdom. Children's charities do particularly well, Save the Children coming top with voluntary income exceeding £70 million (approximately $105 million) and Dr Barnardos eighth (£34 million, $51 million), the National Society for the Prevention of Cruelty to Children, (NSPCC) twelfth (£30 million, $45 million). The Cancer Research charities do well too, filling fifth and sixth places and Cancer Relief seventeenth. Guide Dogs for the Blind and the Royal National Institute for the Blind raise over £50 million ($75) between them. The National Trust, responsible for the protection and upkeep of historic buildings and areas of natural beauty, are second; the Royal National Lifeboat Institute third. An even more peculiar British result perhaps is that the Royal Society for the Protection of Birds (RSPB) appears in the top twenty (almost £22 million, $33 million) and the Royal Society for the Prevention of Cruelty to Animals (RSPCA) attracts more money than does the equivalent charity for children (NSPCC). No charities dedicated to funding provision for mental health appear in the top twenty.

Barnett and Saxon-Harrold (1992) opine that charitable contributions may actually be falling in the 1990s due to a 'compassion fatigue' following the successes of Band Aid and other initiatives of pop stars. Does it follow from this that a responsible government should take over and not allow matters of such import to be decided by the popular whim of public opinion and sentiment? Problems arise because individual benevolence is much affected by the buoyancy of the economy. In optimistic times people give generously; but could it not be the case that welfare payments are most needed when times are hard? This of course is a political point as well as a debating point in contemporary economic theory, that is, whether a government should spend or curtail the money supply in times of recession (Keynesianism vs Monetarism). Certainly there are individual differences among those who give to charity, charitable contributions being closely associated to the number of years in education, an association replicated in the United States (Hodgkinson and Weitzmann, 1990).

Older and less educated people are more likely to consider that charities are run inefficiently; those on relatively low incomes and Conservative (Republican) Party voters are strong believers in self-sufficiency.

For most relatively stable democratic economies the status quo remains powerful: just as in the United States there is a reluctance for governments to play a larger part in provision of health care (although this is on the agenda for the Clinton administration of 1994) in Britain, with a tradition of greater public sector intervention, Mrs Thatcher or no Mrs Thatcher, the majority of the electorate still look to the government, rather than charities, to take care of the needy (Barnett and Saxon-Harold 1992: 199).

## Tax evasion

Tax evasion is a moral question. Besides simply breaking the law, we can harm others and create inequities by evading taxes. Just as some motorists obey speed limits to avoid getting pulled over and fined by patrolmen and women, others comply because they think it is morally right, that driving at lower speeds reduces the likelihood of injury to motorists and pedestrians alike. The first group of motorists would drive faster when the patrols were off duty, the second perhaps would not. If, as some economic theoreticians would have us believe, we are motivated almost entirely by self-interest, almost everyone would evade taxes if it were not for the provisions of revenue-auditing procedures and subsequent fines. The truth is, and also the mystery, in many western democracies most people most of the time comply, voluntarily, with the requirements of tax systems. How can this be? Do people recognise that if they pay less tax this in effect means that others will pay more; that evaders will still receive the benefits of public expenditure without paying their fair share? There should be more research on why people comply but most of it concerns explanations for evasion and a brief review follows.

Paying taxes is never popular, even when the taxes are seen as legitimate and the government expenditure they will finance as highly desirable. So it comes as no surprise that many people try to reduce the amount of taxes they pay. Given the unwelcome imposition of a tax, one can simply break or ignore the law and hope to get away with it (tax evasion); compromise, which might involve extensive discussions with one's accountants and negotiations with the tax authorities about the meaning and applicability of particular regulations; or comply with the rules. The latter may involve compliance in substance or compliance in form, where laws and regulations are obeyed and the spirit of the law ignored (tax avoidance).

Nearly all research has focused on tax evasion and we shall do the same, while noting that tax avoidance may stem from the same psychological roots as evasion and raises fundamental questions about the interaction of law and economics (see McBarnet, 1992). The obvious and simple question to ask at the outset is how prevalent tax evasion is. Though the question is straightforward, the answer is not. In discussing avoidance and evasion James and Nobes (1992) are content simply to say that 'there are no accurate estimates of their importance'. Cowell (1990) is rather more constructive and concludes from a summary listing of all the main studies that the underground economy accounts for about 2–10 per cent of GDP in western economies. Three main methods have been used to produce these estimates of the extent of evasion: monetary methods (where the size of the hidden economy is predicted by otherwise unexplained changes in the demand for money), discrepancy methods (where differences between statistics from different sources on the same economic phenomenon are compared) and direct methods (which have used official records and surveys). Most interesting to us are the various surveys that have been carried out. In some cases these have been highly imaginative. Aitken and Bonneville (1980) and McCrohan (1982), for example, report on the use of the 'locked-box' and the 'randomised response' techniques. The 'locked box' technique involves the use of a box like a ballot box in which respondents put their completed questionnaires. This is felt to reassure respondents that their questionnaires will remain confidential. The results revealed that 13 per cent said that they sometimes under-reported income and 4 per cent said that they made more deductions than they were really entitled to. The randomised response technique gave much higher figures (21 and 16 per cent respectively). Here respondents answered questions about either tax cheating or another topic at random. Which questions were answered was not known but the overall replies to the tax-cheating questions could be inferred through a comparison of the findings with a subset of respondents who answered questions only about the other topic. It is probable that the randomised response method gives more accurate results than the locked box method (as under-reporting of evasion is more likely than over-reporting) but even this technique is probably affected by under-reporting. Kazemier and van Eck's (1992) view is that survey research in general is not actually very good at providing estimates of the size of the hidden economy but that it is ideally suited to uncovering its structure.

Aggregate information about the extent of evasion is anyway only the beginning. We really need to know how, how often and how much people evade. Kinsey (1984) concludes from her thorough review of the survey literature that under-reporting income is the most popular form of tax evasion (as in the Aitken and Bonneville study), and that not filing tax returns at all is used by comparatively few people. The evidence also suggests that most tax evasion by the employed is financially not very significant. Detailed Dutch data reveal that most non-compliance detected by careful auditing is for small amounts (Elffers, Robben and Hessing, 1991, report that the mean tax correction was roughly £300) and British data paint a similar picture (Brown *et al.*, 1984, conclude that only on second jobs was there a non-trivial amount of evasion and these second-job earnings averaged only £18 per week). One needs to bear in mind that here we are talking about employees; measurement of compliance has consistently revealed businesses to be less compliant than individuals and small businesses to be the least compliant of all. Dumais, Kinney and Ricci (1991) report, for example, that small businesses are responsible for 36 per cent of the income tax reporting gap in the United States. Small businesses probably also evade taxes differently: in her study of over 400 small American businesses Hite (1991) reports that more companies admitted knowingly claiming more deductions than under-reporting income; overall 38 per cent admitted non-compliance over the past five years.

## Models of evasion

So why do some individuals and apparently many small businessmen and businesswomen evade taxes? The simplest answer (and one that lies at the heart of economic models) is that people are greedy, that they are motivated by economic gain. The classic economic model (Allingham and Sandmo, 1972) assumes that the decision to evade is influenced by the benefits of evasion (which will be determined by factors such as the tax rate) and the costs (the probability of detection and the penalties of fraud). This suggests that if detection is likely and penalties are severe few people will evade taxes. The evidence for this very plausible proposition is surprisingly thin on the ground. Kinsey's (1984) review of the literature suggests that a high probability of detection is more of a deterrent than heavy penalties: Hessing *et al.*'s (1992) varied empirical work revealed that for occasional and habitual evaders deterrence has no effect at all. Tax evasion is more than just a simple gamble and recent economic models (described in more detail in Webley *et al.*, 1991) have faced up to the challenging task of incorporating social factors. Benjamini and Maital (1985) and Cowell (1990) have, for example, tried to take into account social psychological variables like stigma and reputation by making the utility of evasion partly a function of the size of the underground economy (the idea being that as this increases the stigma of evasion drops). This analysis implies that in a heterogeneous population members of some groups will generally evade while members of others will generally be honest. More recently Cowell (1992) has incorporated the notion of equity into an economic model of tax evasion, an analysis that focuses attention on whether individuals are able to alter perceived inequity by their own actions.

Turning away from economic models, it is somewhat surprising to discover how many sociological and social psychological models of tax evasion have been proposed. A thorough description of these is given by Hessing *et al.* (1988); here we will concentrate on three that are particularly relevant to the theme of this part of the book.

The first approach (that of Vogel, 1974) has had a lasting impact, not least on the stream of Swedish research on tax evasion that has appeared over the last twenty years. Vogel presented a theoretical framework which specified three objective factors (the individual's exchange relationship with the government; social orientation; opportunities for evasion) which have both direct and indirect effects on tax attitudes and evasion. There is strong evidence that these factors are important and in survey investigations opportunity has often been identified as the most important explanatory factor. But it is Vogel's typology of taxpayers that is particularly interesting. This is based on Kelman's (1965) distinction between internalisation, identification and compliance. Compliance is behaving as an authority requires without changing one's beliefs. A compliant taxpayer is one who pays taxes because s/he fears the consequences if s/he does not and not one who believes that it is morally right to pay taxes. Identification involves a change of beliefs to be akin to an admired person; so if a friend evades taxes and you respect him/her you may evade taxes yourself. Internalisation involves a genuine change of beliefs such that belief and behaviour are in line. By combining these distinctions with two kinds of taxpayers' behaviour (compliant and deviant), Vogel derived a sixfold classification of responses to the tax system. Conformist internalisers will pay their taxes in full because they believe that it is morally right to do so: deviant internalisers will evade taxes for the same reason (a good example would be some poll tax protesters in the United Kingdom). Conformist and deviant identifiers pay taxes (or not) because of the behaviour of their reference group. Conformist compliers pay taxes because they fear the consequences if they do not; deviant compliers evade taxes because they believe that the likelihood of being caught is low.

Regardless of the success of this particular classification (and Vogel had some difficulty fitting his respondents into these categories), this is an intriguing attempt to make the moral dimension of taxpayer behaviour more salient and to deal with individual differences. Moral rhetoric is common among compliant taxpayers: witness the assertion of one interviewee that 'I'm an upstanding citizen of this country so therefore I believe that [paying taxes in full] is the right thing to do' (Webley, Robben *et al.*, 1991). Rhetoric and reality probably diverge, though: the evidence that there is a hard core of moral non-evaders is not compelling. Isachsen, Samuelson and Strøm (1985) carried out a survey of 700 Norwegian taxpayers and were able to classify only 15 per cent of these as moralists. Whether this group was included or not made little difference when modelling the decision to evade, which suggests that the true moralist is a rather rare character.

The second approach we will consider is that of Smith and Kinsey (1987). They describe this as a conceptual framework rather than a model but in any case it is helpful in a number of ways. First, they make a distinction between the process and content of decision making and claim that most research has inappropriately concentrated on the latter, that is, the actual decision to cheat. As they emphasise (a point reiterated by Groenland, 1992), people do not take a single decision to evade. Through a series of actions (forgetting 'on purpose' a payment, mentally redefining some earnings as somehow not the business of the internal revenue, etc.) people will end up evading or not. They present a flow chart which displays the factors that shift individuals from their habitual behaviour into consciously taking a decision. These include a range of things that make taxation more salient: tax reform, changes in economic circumstances, etc.

If people shift from their habitual response and consciously take a decision to evade or not, they are considered to weigh up four kinds of factors: material consequences, normative expectations, socio-legal attitudes and expressive factors. Material consequences and normative expectations are the province of the standard economic models and some of the earlier social psychological theorising on tax evasion (e.g. Lewis, 1982), which applied Fishbein and Ajzen's (1975) theory of reasoned action to this area. Smith and Kinsey add two things to our understanding of these factors: first, they emphasise the importance of celerity (the promptness with which consequences occur); and second, they make the point that the private nature of taxpaying limits the impact of normative expectations – informal sanctions for evasion can have little effect, since all the evader has to do is keep quiet. If there is little to fear by way of shame, internal sanctions (i.e. guilt) may play a more important role for some.

The other two factors (socio-legal attitudes and expressive factors) are less often included in models of evasion. Attitudes towards government spending and attitudes towards the tax system as a whole are considered to be the most significant. As many individuals do not recognise the connection between taxation and government spending, attitudes towards the latter are seen as having indirect effects on attitudes towards the system, which themselves have indirect effects on material consequences. Expressive factors are rather different: these are simply the subjective costs and benefits involved in paying taxes, such as the irritation caused by incomprehensible tax forms.

Smith and Kinsey's model has two distinct merits. It provides a picture of the taxpaying process and it gives us some testable hypotheses. But is the picture of the process correct? Does taxpaying consist of a web of interconnected decisions extending over a long period of time? The only empirical study that we are aware of that takes this idea seriously is Carroll's (1992) diary study of 100 Boston tax-payers. The participants in this research, interviewed at the beginning and end of the tax 'season' (presumably January and April), kept daily diaries of any tax-relat-ed thoughts and behaviour and had to think aloud in the presence of a research assistant when they were completing tax forms and doing preparatory work. The sample was predominantly white and middle class and over half of them reported evading taxes over the past three years. The analysis is incomplete but revealing in a number of ways. First, the majority of diary statements that involved comparisons were concerned with tax refunds, an issue of some significance in the United States and one which we will consider when we discuss our final model of evasion. Thus one respondent wrote:

> I made $1,500 more in 1987 than in 1986 and in 1987 I will only be paying about $6 more in taxes. . . . In spite of actually having more money during the year, I still rather miss the large tax refund check. . . . Still feels like a loss.

Second, the measures of non-compliance used give apparently inconsistent results. Many of the respondents said that they had under-reported income or made too many deductions but none the less reported that they had paid what they legally owed. This led Carroll to divide his sample into three groups: the honest taxpayers, the pseudo-cheaters (who misreport in various ways but believe that they have paid what they owe) and the classic cheaters. Membership of the pseudo-cheater group was predicted by diary comments about saving time in the tax process, which sup-ports the idea that people may justify cheating on the grounds that the whole proce-dure is too complex. One participant, for example, chose a quick way to complete a form rather than the exact way, as, although the latter allowed more interest to be deducted, it was extremely complicated. He reports:

> I felt somewhat guilty but also somewhat smug and justified since I perceived I wasn't even getting my 65% interest deduction . . . and that I was probably penalizing myself because I did not want to bother with filling out the incredibly complicated Part III of Form 8598

One suspects that many pseudo-cheaters are actually real cheaters, albeit in a small way, who would be able to construct a plausible defence of their behaviour both to themselves and the tax authorities if challenged.

Third, at least for this sample, taxpaying did not seem to be the private act that Smith and Kinsey describe. Overdeducting was predicted by the usefulness of rela-tives and friends as sources of information and the diaries make clear the social nature of some evasion. This reinforces the notion that tax decisions are an interconnected web, with the proviso that some of the thread is social. 'Had dinner with friends, discussed tax write-offs. Specifically day care expenditures, they hike it up to what they feel is acceptable'; 'What I will always do is try to get money back. My friends and I talk about this and all agree. We can't see what the government is doing for us and we have no control over how the money is spent.' These diaries obviously provide a rich data set, though Carroll acknowledges that they are difficult to code reliably and anyway may not adequately reflect people's thought processes. None the less, they do encourage us to see taxpaying as a series of decisions and incidents, a view of economic acts that can usefully be applied to other areas.

The final approach to be considered is that of Weigel, Hessing and Elffers (1987), who treat tax evasion as defective behaviour within a social dilemma. A social dilemma (sometimes referred to as a 'social trap' or the 'tragedy of the commons') involves a potential conflict between what is best for an individual and what is best for the group. The prototypic example is an open common where an individual benefits if s/he alone grazes more animals but where everyone will suffer (as the quality and amount of grass is reduced) if most or all people do this. Similarly an individual may benefit if s/he evades taxes but the whole system will break down if too many people do this. This social dilemma aspect of the tax system became very apparent to many people in the United Kingdom during the brief lifetime of the Poll Tax, as a considerable part of the annual increase in this tax was caused by the very large percentage of non-payers in some areas. This only served to increase resentment and the percentage of non-payment in subsequent years, which made the system economically (as well as politically) non-viable.

Social dilemma research has concentrated on the motivational orientation of individuals (whether they are co-operative, individualistic or competitive) so it is unsurprising that Weigel, Hessing and Elffers incorporate individual differences into their model (see Fig. 9.1). But this is only part of the theoretical framework that they propose, which specifies two kinds of variables: instigations and constraints. These are found both in the individual and in the social setting. Thus financial strain (the amount of tax owed) is a situational instigation and its psychological counterpart is personal strain; lack of opportunity is a situational constraint and perceived opportunity is its psychological counterpart. In each case the variables mirror each other: for each objective social condition (such as being self-employed with lots of deduction possibilities) there is a parallel subjective condition (a personal estimate of the evasion options).The social force is filtered through psychological conditions.

Hessing and Elffers (1985) have also discussed the general conditions under which central attitudes, peripheral attitudes and norms will predict behaviour in a social dilemma and have stressed the importance of the distinction between private and public acts. Their very plausible claim is that central attitudes will be more important in determining private acts whereas norms will only have an influence when a behaviour is public and visible. Evasion, of course, is a private act but it is frequently measured in a public way using self-report. This implies that self-reported evasion may be predicted by rather different variables (e.g. norms) than actual evasion.

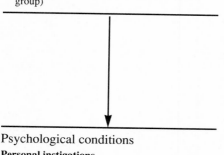

## Social conditions

**Situational instigations**
1. Financial strain (amount of tax owed after withholding)
2. Social norms (emphasis on individual wealth as a measure of success within reference group)

**Situation constraints**
1. Opportunity (occupational rating regarding the probability of cash receipts, withholding at source, etc.)
2. Legal controls (probability of apprehension and punishment for reference group)
3. Social controls (number of evaders in reference group)

## Tax-evasion behaviour
(unreported income, unwarranted deductions, failure to file a return)
1. Self-reports
2. Behavioural outcome measures
3. Behavioural simulation measures

## Psychological conditions

**Personal instigations**
1. Personal strain (estimates of difficulty meeting tax obligations and perceived unfairness of tax laws and authorities)
2. Personal orientation (self-serving versus community orientation)

**Personal-constraints**
1. Perceived opportunity (subjective estimate of opportunity to evade)
2. Perceived risk of punishment (certainty and severity)
3. Intolerance of tax evasion (attitudes and moral beliefs about the propriety of tax evasion)

**Figure 9.1** A social psychological model of individual income tax-evasion behaviour (adapted from Weigel, Hessing and Elffers 1987: 229) Examples of the variables in the model are included in brackets.

Tests of this model have been reasonably successful, although Hessing and Elffers' research has exposed the extraordinary measurement problems encountered by work in this area. Elffers, Weigel and Hessing (1987) provided the first test, with a unique study which combined self-reported measures of evasion with official data on individuals. They used a very complicated procedure to guarantee confidentiality and studied two carefully audited groups from an initial sample of 3,500: one group consisted of individuals who had evaded tax for two years, the other of individuals who the tax authorities were certain had made accurate returns for two years. The cumbersome procedure resulted in a rather low response rate (23 per cent) but the participants were representative of the original categories, for example in terms of the amount of money evaded. The remarkable finding of this study was that there was a negligible correlation between self-reported and officially documented evasion: 69 per cent of the evader group denied evasion and 25 per cent of the supposedly honest group admitted some misrepresentation of income or deductions. One would have expected both the self-report and official measures to be fairly accurate, as the evader group had had to pay back taxes for two years in a row and the criteria used for the official classification were very stringent. One possible conclusion from this is that evasion is not so much a behaviour as a judgement about behaviour, and judgements of actors and observers are notoriously discrepant. As anticipated, different variables predicted the two indices of evasion: peripheral attitudes and social norms correlated with self-reported behaviour but were unrelated to officially documented evasion and central attitudes (alienation, competitiveness) showed the reverse pattern.

Kinsey (1988) followed this up with a secondary analysis of an IRS-sponsored survey. Obviously she could not match the variables used by Elffers, Weigel and Hessing exactly and did not have access to official records but she used reasonable proxies for both the independent and dependent variables. For example, those respondents who reported having to pay more taxes as a result of an audit were treated as 'officially documented' evaders. The results were similar to those of Elffers, Weigel and Hessings. The attitude and social norm measures did not correlate with self-report evasion but were predictive of self-reported audit outcome. The reverse pattern was found for one of the central attitude measures (tolerance of illegal behaviour).

Webley, Robben, Elffers and Hessing (1991) also provide some support for the Weigel *et al.* model, using experimental measures of tax evasion. Early experiments in this area (e.g. Friedland, Maital and Rutenberg, 1978) involved respondents being given a monthly net income which they then declared, with various factors (fine rates, audit frequencies and the like) being investigated. But a number of critics have pointed out that the purpose of these experiments is transparent and so Webley *et al.* devised a more involving set-up implemented on a microcomputer in which the participants take a variety of decisions (pricing, advertising, hiring personnel) as well as declaring income. Some of their studies focused on correlates of evasion and they found that the measures which predicted evasion in an experiment were similar to those found to predict officially documented evasion, though the pattern of results was not as clear-cut as the Elffers, Weigel and Hessing study.

Elffers, Robben and Hessing (1992) have taken the logical next step and carried out a study in which self-report, officially documented, and experimental measures of evasion were obtained from the participants. Yet again there was a negligible correlation between the first two measures: unfortunately it was also true that neither correlates with the experimental measures. Triangulation in this case has certainly not led to researchers homing in on the target. This result has led Elffers *et al.* to suggest that tax evasion consists of three independent conceptual aspects that are measured by three independent measures, an excessively gloomy view of the matter, in our opinion. As Groenland (1992) has observed, 'tax evasion as an act does not really exist. Instead, tax evasion exists as a fact in retrospect.' He advocates a dynamic approach, which he argues will then enable us to see the coherence among the various measures used to date. Whatever the merits of this suggestion, it is certainly better than allowing measurement problems to guide our conceptualisation, which is a bit like talking in terms of candle time, water-clock time and watch time.

The substantive findings of this study are of some interest and are reported in Elffers (1991). Self-reported tax evaders were different from non-evaders in that they had more positive attitudes towards evasion, believed evasion was more prevalent among their friends and that people approved of evasion and perceived more opportunities for evasion. But their financial situations were similar, there was no difference in opportunities for evasion and their social orientation was similar. We suspect that these differences were largely produced by a self-presentational concern for consistency. When one looks for differences between those defined by the authorities as tax evaders and non-evaders there are almost none. Honest taxpayers are slightly more positive about the way in which they are treated by the tax authorities and are slightly less competitive; but to all intents and purposes the social psychological picture of evaders and non-evaders is the same. Why? As Elffers points out, the evaders in this study are nearly all minor cases and would not have been classified as evaders using the stringent criteria used in the Elffers, Weigel and Hessing study. As they are not habitual evaders, it is not surprising that there are no clear differences.

This is an appropriate place to leave the area of tax evasion. Although we know a great deal more than we did a decade ago, it is still extraordinarily difficult to come to a clear conclusion. It is clear, however, that simple economic models are inadequate, yet so too are the social psychological models we have described. The measurement problems have not been solved, though we have a better grasp of the issues involved. The challenge now is to develop concepts and measures that can cope with the kind of behaviours described by Elffers (1991: 209):

> Taxpayers are wrestling with an ambiguous task, worrying about making errors, worrying about how to minimise their tax liability, forgetting things, overcomplying, undercomplying, constructing, reconstructing and sometimes misconstructing their fiscal situation.

If we were to add, in true postmodernist spirit, 'deconstructing their fiscal situation', the enormity of this challenge becomes all too apparent.

## Reducing tax evasion

The kind of academic self-doubt and uncertainty expressed above emphatically does not mean that we are unable to recommend to policy-makers ways of reducing tax evasion. Six broad ways of achieving this have frequently been proposed. These range from the clearly economic to the more psychological: increasing penalties and the chance of detection, lowering tax rates, decreasing the opportunities for evasion, simplifying tax rules, influencing the attitudes and norms of taxpayers and improving the relationship between taxpayers and the tax authorities.

As indicated above, for criminal behaviour in general penalties are less of a deterrent than the probability of being caught. A large number of studies have found that evaders make lower estimates of the probability of detection than non-evaders (e.g. Grasmick and Scott, 1982), whilst people in general considerably overestimate the chance of being audited. The evidence is that being audited *per se* has a minimal deterrent effect (Long and Schwartz, 1987; Kinsey, 1992) but that being contacted by the tax authorities about unreported income does decrease the likelihood of future evasion (Kinsey, 1992). Remarkably enough, in Holland being caught evading actually predicts future evasion; rather than acting as a deterrent, detection acts as an incentive! (Hessing *et al.*, 1992)! It needs to be borne in mind, however, that in the Dutch system the effective probability of being fined for every-day evasion is zero: the authorities can, under certain conditions, levy a fine proportional to the back-taxes evaded but this is extremely rare and usually all an evader has to do is pay what s/he should have paid in the first place. On balance, it is probably better for the tax authorities to enhance their ability to identify evaders (for example, by requiring taxpayers to supply information that can be cross-checked with other sources) than to increase the penalties for evasion, especially given the difficulty of proving intent to evade in the courts.

Economic models imply that the higher the tax rate, the more worthwhile is evasion. On this basis, lowering tax rates should reduce the incidence of evasion, but there is actually no evidence for this. Elffers (1991) points out that in Holland people only have the vaguest idea of the tax rate that applies to them. Similarly Lewis (1978), in a study of 200 UK electors, found that people consistently underestimated their marginal tax rate (by 11 per cent on average), although the 1988 tax rate changes in the United Kingdom seemed to have brought about a more accurate perception (Calderwood and Webley, 1992). Wahlund's work (see below) suggests that people take some time to notice tax rate changes and that anyway such changes have no effect on evasion. More importantly, there is actually no evidence that people who are subject to higher rates of taxation actually evade more. So although there may be good reasons why a reduction in tax rates is a good idea, reducing tax evasion is not one of them.

With the proposal that the opportunities for evasion should be reduced we are on firmer ground. The vast majority of survey studies reveal that greater opportunity is associated with admitted evasion and it has been reported as the most important explanatory factor in many investigations (e.g. Slemrod, 1985; Witte and Woodbury, 1985). Experimental work in a wide range of countries suggests that opportunity does have a causal role (Robben *et al.* 1991) and its apparent significance is not just a consequence of those who are predisposed to evasion seeking out jobs where the opportunities are greatest. But Elffers (1991) casts some doubt on whether opportunity is really a measurable concept; as he puts it 'There is no more opportunity to slake a thirst in a room with three taps than in one with a single tap.' This leads him to argue that governments need radically to abolish opportunity rather than limit it, which brings us neatly to the idea of simplification.

The popular image of nearly all tax systems is that they are too complex and bur-densome, as is illustrated by the 'Cathy' cartoon where she dials the tax authorities hotline and shouts 'I want the home phone number of the lunatic who says it should only take 56 minutes to fill out my tax form'. This complexity results in many errors on tax returns (Long and Swingen, 1988, estimate that there are simple math-ematical or clerical errors on one in six US federal income tax returns) and encour-ages non-compliance. So simplification can reduce evasion in a variety of ways. It can abolish opportunity, make the taxpayer more aware of what s/he is doing (so s/he is less able to conceal the evasion from him/herself) and enhance the perceived fairness of the system, as honest taxpayers are more likely to believe that others cannot be abusing it. Simplification has been an important aim of tax reform in the 1980s (see below) but in practice turns out to be difficult to achieve as it conflicts with other aims (e.g. the desire to deal with special cases and to have a progressive tax system). The poll tax (a single-rate tax levied on all local residents introduced in the United Kingdom in 1989 and 1990) was incredibly simple but even that was made more complicated with exemptions (e.g. for nurses and students) and transi-tional arrangements.

It seems reasonable that the authorities would wish to influence the attitudes and norms of taxpayers, although the evidence presented above suggests that these are more closely related to self-reported evasion than to officially documented evasion. Hasseldine and Bebbington (1991) report, for example, that the New Zealand gov-ernment heavily advertised their tax reforms and the taxpayer advisory service in an attempt to improve taxpayers' perceptions of the Inland Revenue and so reduce non-compliance. But is this effort worthwhile? McGraw and Scholz (1991) had two groups of taxpayers view one of two videotapes. The first emphasised the norma-tive principles which underlay the Tax Reform Act and stressed the importance that Americans place on the norms of social responsibility and how these are related to taxpaying. The second was an edited version of a commercial video, which empha-sised the use of legal strategies to minimise one's tax liability. The participants were interviewed at home two weeks to one month after viewing the videos and again six months later. McGraw and Scholz also obtained aggregate tax return information for each group. The results showed that the videos had predictable and persistent effects on tax attitudes but that this had no effect on compliance, either as measured by self-report or the official tax return data. Although this is only one study, it certainly does not encourage governments to increase their persuasive efforts.

Lastly we come to the question of whether it is desirable to improve the relation-ship between taxpayers and the tax authorities. Feeling that the tax system is unfair is certainly associated with self-reported evasion though it is possible that per-ceived inequity is an after-the-fact justification for evasion rather than a real motive for it. The experimental evidence that equity is a relevant factor is equivocal. But whatever the real state of affairs it seems evident that good relationships between taxpayers and the authorities will enable the system to work smoothly and may facilitate effective tax reform (see below).

## Tax reform

A number of western countries introduced major tax reforms during the 1980s. In most cases this involved the introduction of measures to broaden the tax base while simultaneouly flattening the structure of rates. Although these tax reforms do have some things in common, it is worthwhile to provide some details for those countries where the effects of the reforms have been investigated by economic psychologists.

The stated aims of the US Tax Reform Act of 1986, which arguably initiated the most extensive changes since the inception of the federal income tax system, were to increase the simplicity, fairness and efficiency of the tax system. Simplicity was to be achieved by increasing the standard deduction, restricting other personal deductions and reducing the number of tax brackets. This was expected to have the effect of reducing the number of people who made tax returns by 6 million and reducing by a third the number who had to fill in more complicated itemised returns. Fairness (both horizontal and vertical equity) was to be achieved by placing limitations on claims for losses (thought to be abused by high-income taxpayers) and eliminating the preferential treatment of capital gains, interest payments on loans, etc. Efficiency was to be achieved through minimising economic distortions introduced through tax policy (e.g. through lower marginal rates).

The conventional wisdom was that the Tax Reform Act would produce 'lower taxes for most individual tax payers, no taxes for the working poor, higher taxes for those with tax shelters and higher taxes for business' (Dildine, 1987).

For the Dutch, the initial goal of reform was simplicity, although in the parliamentary process a second theme (base broadening and a general rate decrease) was introduced and came to be the dominant features of the reform (de Kam, 1992). The number of tax brackets was reduced from nine to three and a large number of tax deductions were abolished. National social security premiums were integrated with income tax.

In Sweden the main aim was to affect economic behaviour (to stimulate work and saving and reduce tax evasion). Marginal rates were reduced (in some tax brackets by up to 30 per cent) as were the maximum value of tax deductions (from 85 to 50 per cent). In the United Kingdom the aim was to reduce the disincentive effect of high tax rates. The number of tax brackets was reduced and the highest rate of tax sharply reduced (to 40 per cent).

What were the effects of all these reforms? For some insight on the American experience we can consider the work of Scholz, McGraw and Steenbergen (1992), who carried out a panel study of 471 New York taxpayers. This sample was interviewed twice, in January 1988 and in summer 1988. Scholz *et al.* deliberately over-sampled individuals filing more complex returns so the sample was older, better educated and better-off than the average tax payer (mean age = 49, modal income between $25,000 and $50,000). They investigated three hypotheses: first, that those whose taxes increase the most are the most likely to consider the tax unfair and to be more likely to cheat (self-interest); second that the attitudes of those an individual discusses tax with will have an important impact on his/her tax schema; and third, that individuals who see the government as legitimate will view legislation more favourably and be more willing to comply with new legislation even if it imposes costs on the individual.

Overall, there turned out to be a very weak linkage between the objective impact of the tax reform (the actual change in tax due) and subjective responses. Other influences appeared to play a major role in shaping reponses to tax reform. In particular, prior attitudes of the individual towards the state and the attitudes of others with whom the individual talks influenced evaluations and attitudes. New laws like the Tax Reform Act seem to be given the benefit of the doubt by those who trust the political system and believe the tax system to be relatively fair. On the other hand, new laws are condemned by taxpayers perceiving the system to be less legitimate, regardless of any possible benefits the law may bring to them.

Kinsey (1993) reports similar findings. She compared people's tax opinions in 1990 with those in 1985 and found no overall differences in the perceived unfairness of personal tax burdens. However, there was a decline in perceived unfairness for those respondents who reported low levels of tax avoidance (presumably those who tended to see the system as legitimate) but an increase in perceived unfairness for those who sought out tax avoidance opportunities.

The Swedish experience was rather different. Wahlund (1989, 1992) reports a series of studies using telephone interviews, questionnaires and secondary data (tax return forms, public statistics) which explore the question of whether the Swedish tax reform had an effect on tax evasion and saving. Attitudes and behaviour were measured at four different points in time: December 1982 (just before the start of the tax reform), May 1983, December 1983 and June 1984. In total over 1,500 men were interviewed by telephone on the basis of a structured questionnaire. In addition a mail questionnaire was sent to all respondents and was answered by 81 per cent of them. Old-age pensioners and women were excluded from the surveys and only those people with a job were included in the analyses, which necessarily limits the conclusions that can be drawn.

None the less it is clear that the considerable changes in the tax system did not produce correspondingly large changes in behaviour. The cuts in marginal tax rates were only partly perceived, not at once and not at the same time by everybody. The average actual marginal rates decreased by about 4 per cent in 1983 and then 3 per cent in 1984. In 1983 the decrease was barely noticed by people and by 1984 the average perceived marginal tax rate had dropped by 2 per cent. The percentage of individuals admitting different types of tax evasion did not change significantly between the first and the last survey. It is possible that this may be because changes in various factors cancelled each other out. So although opportunities to evade taxes decreased and tax evasion was seen as increasingly risky, attitudes towards tax evasion became more lenient. There was also no increase in saving at the macro level. However, people save for different reasons and if the results are looked at at the micro level it is clear that different saver types did react to the tax reforms (Wahlund and Wärneryd, 1988). Wealth managers (who most resemble 'economic man') reduced their debts. They continued to increase other types of saving. The 'goal-directed savers' increased their saving, both by increasing their regular saving and by reducing their loans. 'Buffer' savers (who save to have a buffer for unexpected outlays) reduced their saving. The 'cash-managers' increased their debts and decreased their saving.

For an employer's perspective on tax reform, we can turn to the work of Eling (1992). She carried out a three-measurement panel study of the reactions of three different kinds of organisation: corporations, business income taxpayers and non-profit-making institutions. Overall it was clear that the tax reform was not warmly welcomed, nor did experience of it increase enthusiasm. Eling reports that the non-profit institutions were the least negative about the reforms but, as de Kam (1992) comments, this could be a consequence of a more positive view of the tax system found in such organisations.

So what can be concluded from all this material? We would suggest that in general single reforms are probably less important than the cumulative impact of tax and other policy changes over time. Taxation is not that salient to individuals and so it probably takes some time for any changes to be known and take effect. The situation is complicated by two factors. First, the measures introduced by governments serve a variety of policy ends and are rarely consistent. So despite the efforts of reformers in the United States and Holland, personal income tax has probably become more complicated overall during the 1980s. Second, the ideal of greater fairness has probably not been achieved as taxpayers have taken diverse steps to limit the effects of reforms on their own financial position.

## The Poll Tax

Single reforms may in general be less important than the cumulative impact of policy changes, but the recent attempt to reform the local taxation system in the United Kingdom certainly did have major effects and has certainly increased the salience of taxation in the United Kingdom.

The Poll Tax was first mooted in 1986 as a way of dealing with the deficiencies of local authority rates (property taxes). Rates were widely seen as unfair and as a poor way of raising revenue by the authorities themselves. From the Conservative government's point of view the importance of the Poll Tax was that it would increase local accountability, since almost half of the electorate paid no rates. Ultimately, given the Conservative view that Labour-controlled authorities tend to be profligate spenders, this would have the effect of weakening Labour support. In other words, the motive underlying this tax reform was not to improve the tax system (to make it simpler, fairer or more efficient by reducing fiscal illusions) but was party-political (Cullis, Jones and Morrissey, 1993a).

The government's response to the public opposition to the Poll Tax was completely rational: only two years after the tax was introduced all individuals received a fixed subsidy of £140 financed out of an increase in VAT. Essentially this amounts to replacing a visible tax with a much less visible one. Ultimately, of course, the Poll Tax was withdrawn and replaced by the Council Tax. As Cullis, Jones and Morrissey (1993b) put it:

> The description of events [from the Green Paper, through the anti-Poll Tax protests and Thatcher's resignation to the introduction of the Council tax] is consistent with the accusation that governments will pursue their own interests if they feel they enjoy a monopoly position. When the Conservative Government faced increasing competition – their market becoming more 'contestable' – they increasingly retreated from the more extreme ideological principles that underpinned the Community Charge.

The Poll Tax episode is interesting as it highlights the possibility of 'moral' tax evasion (or tax resistance). We might expect to find considerable numbers of those Vogel called deviant internalisers among those refusing to pay their poll tax. However, the exploratory analysis by Bowles and Jones (1993) suggests that economic factors (such as the unemployment rate, the proportion of the population claiming benefits and the level of the Poll Tax locally) are all significant predictors of the percentage of the tax collected in London boroughs and that there is no evidence of a 'Labour Party effect', despite the allegations by many Conservative MPs that Labour MPs and local authorities encouraged tax resistance. The possibility, however, that Labour voters and people with less belief in government legitimacy are more likely to evade cannot be ruled out, as the authors agree.

## The social construction of tax evasion

The experience of the Poll Tax makes it obvious, notwithstanding the conclusions of Bowles and Jones (1993), that we need to place our understanding of tax evasion and fiscal policy within a political and cultural context (Lewis, 1982). One person's tax evasion may be another's legitimate political protest: and quite what is and what is not tax evasion is 'socially constructed', at least in part, by political elites and tax officials. It follows from this, and this is especially apt when considering tax reform and ways of reducing tax evasion, that the beliefs of policy makers and tax inspectors are central: just as crime depends on the interactions of criminals, the police and the judiciary, tax evasion depends on much more than just the activities and beliefs of taxpayers. As we have seen there are competing explanations for economic behaviour, the explanations one favours influences how one views the world, whether these are 'lay' theories or more rarefied ones put forward by economists, criminologists, social psychologists. If as a tax official one agrees that the model of rational economic man is actually true all one will see are a world full of taxpayers evading tax at every opportunity; that the enculturation of officialdom requires a shared understanding, often implicit, about the nature of the job and 'what taxpayers are like'. One can envisage a culture of taxpayers also who have implicit codes of practice of 'honour amongst thieves', of not evading too much, of not embarrassing their accountants and most important of all having shared notions about what tax officials are like and what tax officials think of them. The rules of the game, the game itself, is decided upon by the players.

It is unlikely that the differing approaches of economists and social psychologists can be morally neutral as each influences the 'facts'. Just as treating people like criminals encourages people to act like criminals, treating people as narrow-minded, individualistic utility maximisers encourages people to fit the bill.

Presently the Inland Revenue and HM Customs and Excise are being encouraged to treat taxpayers as customers, to provide a service rather than to impose. These changes require a change in culture, a belief in encouraging good behaviour rather than pursuing and punishing bad. It is a delicate balance, which varies between nations, between the carrot and the stick, especially when the mule, every now and then, can sack the muleteer.

## More on fiscal policy and illusions

In 'free' economic systems the economy is driven by consumer demand. When public services are provided the link to consumer demand for public goods is less direct; there may be a line of communication via fiscal referenda but the more usual route is through more infrequent visits to the ballot box. As a result of this comparative lack of communication government departments may 'overproduce' and become inefficient. As a partial remedy to this a kind of 'quasi-market' system has been set up in the United Kingdom where, for example, schools are allocated funds from the state according to whether they can attract pupils and in terms of examination results; schools are encouraged to compete with one another. Such competition is likely, say the supporters of such schemes, to increase the efficiency of delivery and the quality of the 'education product'. Further the role of the consumer, parents and pupils is enhanced; theirs is a voice to be heard. What might be the consequences of greater consumer involvement in the public sector? On first examination there is a lot to be gained: it could be taken as an extension of democracy; but in the case of the United Kingdom does this bear close scrutiny? Numerous non-conservatives would point to the demise of local authorities and the increased centralisation of power. And what of the United States? Are fiscal referenda a gain for democracy or do they offer just another obstacle to change; more mud to clog radical wheels. It is not just cynics who ask if this increased use of the market for the provision of 'public goods' really did empower the people would governments try quite so hard to sell the idea? It could follow that a well-informed electorate might actually favour more government intervention and be less likely to be manipulated by political parties seeking power. Much has been written about 'fiscal illusions' (Wagner,

1976; Goetz, 1977). One theory goes that voters/consumers of public goods under-estimate tax burdens and overestimate the benefits of public service expenditure (Wagner, 1976). If this has empirical validity it would mean that public goods (hospitals, schools and so forth) would appear to be being provided at less cost than they really are and it is certainly true that in the United States voters believe that local services are cheaper (and central government services more expensive) than they really are (Hewitt, 1986). The idea of fiscal illusions would explain in a *post hoc* way why government expenditure as a proportion of GNP has generally risen in many western democracies up to and including the mid-1980s. Given the methodological preferences of economists, it is unsurprising that these 'fiscal illusions' have rarely been explored directly. Work by economic psychologists such as Wahlund (1989) in Sweden, Lewis (1978) and Lewis and Cullis (1988) in the United Kingdom, has shown that under certain circumstances at least half of the hypothesis is probably true: people underestimate their total tax burdens. This does not accord with the popular rhetoric of exorbitant tax and wasteful government spending, so how does it come about? The explanation seems to lie in the comparative 'visibility' of taxes. Taxes on income are highly visible, especially in countries like the United Kingdom where people employed by others receive wage or salary information with the amount of income taxation already deducted, this figure appearing on the invoice/pay slip. Taxes on goods and services are hardly 'invisible' yet it seems taxpayers underestimate just how widely spread these taxes are and the amount of revenue they accrue together (in the United Kingdom these taxes account for about 31 per cent of total tax revenues, very close to the average for OECD countries). So in part it is the centralisation of tax collection which may be the key to the explanation: more centralisation, more visibility. It is no great intellectual leap then to anticipate what a government, needing to raise taxes but also wishing to maintain voter popularity, would do – increase taxes on goods and services and spread them, at least in the first instance, thinly. Fiscal policy is a tool governments use in controlling the economy. Broadly speaking, the accepted wisdom is that increases in taxation are anti-inflationary and tax reductions inflationary or a method to 'rejuvenate a sluggish economy', whatever the appropriate rhetoric is. This is not intended to sound sardonic. To make the point it is useful to think of fiscal policy (and economics as a whole) as having three components: analytic 'fact', empirical hypothesis, rhetoric (and ideology). The relationship between taxation and work makes these three components clear. For any individual income taxation can have either, theoretically, a 'substitution' or 'income' effect: logically, income taxation can be a disincentive to work effort or an incentive. The 'income effect' conceptualises that a higher tax rate (at the margin) has the effect of encouraging people to work more, as income is reduced and people, consequently, need more money to pay for things. The 'substitution effect' assumes that as income tax rates rise the individual is encouraged to work less hard, as in the theoretical trade-off between work and leisure, leisure becomes more attractive and less expensive compared to income that could otherwise have been earned. Therefore the analytical facts lead us to two equally plausible but logically contradictory possibilities.

The empirical results cover a number of different methodologies varying from the secondary analysis of aggregate statistical sources reporting on the number of hours worked and wage rates (e.g. Cohen, Rea and Lerman, 1970; Hill, 1973); large-scale field experiments such as the New Jersey Negative Income Tax experiment (Kershaw, 1972); and studies employing interview and social survey techniques (Fields and Stanbury, 1970; Wahlund 1989; Calderwood and Webley 1992). This is not the place for a critical analysis of these results (samples have too often over-represented professionals and managers) but it can be said with confidence that the results reveal that there is no clear-cut winner between the incentive and disincentive contenders and if anything the conclusion must be that taxation has little or no effect on work effort. Having dealt with the 'facts' and the experiments, what about the rhetoric? A frequent comment is that 'taxation stifles work effort and initiative.' It is one of life's unquestionable facts, or so it is presented by right-wing politicians wishing to reduce the 'burden of taxation' and 'set the entrepreneurial spirit free' which is incidentally 'the only way to provide "genuine" jobs and bring us out of recession'. The idea that the effect of income taxation on the quality and quantity of work is neutral is one that dare not speak its name outside academia for fear of popular ridicule. Many, perhaps most, claims in economic policy are contentious, but as soon as an explanation becomes 'common sense' it is hard to challenge. Keynes is becoming more and more an historical figure: reduce employment, curtail a recession by increases in public expenditure, what an idea! The past is indeed a foreign country, they do things differently there. Contemporary rhetoric extols the virtues of a smaller public sector and lower taxes, a rhetoric that has claimed the minds of the citizens of the United Kingdom, even of Sweden, and with it the re-arrangement of tax principles: at the very least, a change of priorities. Tax principles include those of simplicity, equity, ability to pay, efficiency, flexibility, compatibility and certainty (Brown and Jackson, 1978; Sandford, 1978). The principles of ability to pay and efficiency are the ones most germane to our current discussion. The principle of ability to pay is founded primarily on the notion of equality of sacrifice. But how is this to be determined? Should taxation be regressive, proportional or progressive? A regressive tax is one where wealthier individuals pay a smaller proportion of their total income in tax compared to those less well-off even though the actual amount may be greater. For example, person A, someone with a gross taxable annual income of £100,000, may have a total tax bill of £50,000 (50 per cent) and person B, with a gross taxable annual income of £20,000, a bill for £12,000 (60 per cent). A proportional tax would mean, for example, that persons A and B would both pay 50 per cent: that is, person A, £50,000, and person B £10,000. Is this equality of sacrifice? The final option is a progressive tax, where person A pays a higher proportion than person B, perhaps 60 per cent (£60,000) compared to 40 per cent (£8,000). The choice between them is not only technical but based on philosophical and political notions of social justice (John Stuart Mill favoured proportional taxation). Ideology comes into it as well: the right favours regressive taxation and the left progressive taxation. The preference for progressive taxation is linked to the belief that the purpose of fiscal policy is not only in controlling the economy but as a means for redistributing wealth, to reducing income inequalities. The principle of efficiency is of great interest to economists. Taxation can be viewed as inefficient in the sense that it distorts the supply of labour, the pattern of consumption and, in a more general sense, freedom of choice and taxpayer satisfaction. However, it must be remembered that principles of efficiency also incorporate normative aspects. A distortion of the market in terms of consumption, say, may nevertheless be desirable when the consumption of private goods produces social and environmental costs for everyone. The consumption of leaded petrol is an example where differential gasoline taxation may be used to encourage consumers to buy unleaded gasoline instead. Skirmishes between the principles of efficiency and ability to pay abound. The 1960s and beyond in the United Kingdom and Sweden in particular more often than not saw the ability to pay as victors of the battle but not the war: the principle of efficiency is now king even in the lands of the north. Alongside this has grown the belief that principles of efficiency are technical, positivist principles not normative, value-laden ones. Consequently a shift towards taxes on goods and services and away from income can be justified in terms of the reduced administrative costs of collection with scant regard to the fact that more 'indirect taxes' are regressive, incur higher costs for those on lower incomes and if anything increase income inequalities.

## Finale

Ordinary people have fiscal preferences. These preferences are neither random nor simply explained by narrow self-interest hypotheses: there is a 'public sector economic mind' to be explored. People are not solely driven by their own immediate concerns but have some sense of the welfare of others and the appropriate role of the state in its distribution. A spirit of communitarianism, even though the politics of individualism has had the upper hand in recent years, is far from dead.

There is a case that rhetoric and 'lay public sector explanations' interact both with public economic policy (and possibly the discipline of economics itself); that on occasion the predominance of one economic explanation over another may be led not by empirical 'facts' but by ideology and 'commonsense' opinions.

# PART V

# Work ethics and economies in transition

# Chapter 10

# The Protestant work ethic

## Introduction

It has long been pointed out that psychology has two rather different traditions: experimental, which is concerned with general laws of behaviour; and correlational, which is concerned with individual differences in behaviour. One of the most interesting questions for the psychologist interested in economic behaviour concerns which individual factors determine economic beliefs and behaviour. Traditionally psychologists have considered different types of individual difference factors: demographic (age, sex, class), personality (introversion, anxiety) and belief (political, social) variables, attempting to explain how, which and when individual differences are important in explaining and describing economic behaviour.

What is clearly important in this area is to delineate which of the myriad of possible variables explains most of the variance. This chapter is a review of the psychological literature on a concept that has been described as one of the most parsimonious for predicting economic behaviour (Furnham, 1984b). It is furthermore a concept that straddles all the social sciences and one which has commanded an extensive literature: the Protestant work ethic (PWE) as specified by Weber (1905; Davies, 1992).

Weber's theory was introduced into psychology by McClelland (1961), who offered a social psychological explanation for the link between Protestantism and capitalism. The theory is simply that PWE ideas and values determine child-rearing practices which foster independence, delay of gratification and mastery, which in turn lead to the children acquiring strong achievement motivation. These high achievers in turn become successful entrepreneurs and create an expansion of business. McClelland's approach extended previous research on individual achievement to the macro-societal level. In a lengthy historical and conceptual review he found relationships between the achievement level of a society (as measured by the content of children's literature) and the subsequent growth or decline in capitalism and industrialisation in that society. For instance, he found that from 1500 to 1800 achievement motivation in England rose and fell with the level of coal imports. In a further study of forty nations, he found a correlation of 0.53 between achievement motivation in 1925 and the growth in the electricity supply. Cross-cultural work in thirty cultures has documented the relationship between PWE-type beliefs and achievement (Fyons *et al.*, 1983). McClelland has subsumed the PWE concept into the need for achievement (nAch) concept, which he saw as a basic dimension of personality. Indeed, results from studies on high achievers are similar to those from studies on people with high PWE beliefs: high achievers tend to do their best to obtain monetary and other rewards in laboratory games and tasks; they set themselves high but realistic targets; and are optimistic about the outcome, etc. Work on type-A behaviour would suggest that PWE beliefs, need for achievement and control, and type-A behaviour patterns are all linked (Furnham, 1983d). Furnham (1990b) has identified nine psychological and four attitudinal correlates of the work ethic (see Table 10.1). Although each overlapped with the PWE, clearly there was enough unique variation left for it to be worthwhile to retain the concept.

Despite the fact that McClelland's work has spawned a great deal of research on nAch, it has been criticised for having very poor measurement techniques and equivocal findings. Furthermore, the nAch concept has concentrated on only some aspects of the PWE belief such as hard work, productivity and frugality, while ignoring others such as asceticism. Nevertheless the suggestion that nAch is a stable disposition resulting from early socialisation in the PWE probably encouraged other researchers to operationalise and attempt to measure PWE beliefs as an important individual difference variable in its own right. However, it has not been until comparatively recently that psychologists (primarily occupational and social psychologists) have actively pursued research using the PWE concept. Although psycholo-

**Table 10.1**   Nine psychological and four attitudinal correlates of the work ethic

| Components of the PWE | PWE |
|---|---|
| Traits | |
| 1. Achievement motivation | +++ |
| 2. Authoritarianism | ++ |
| 3. Beliefs in a just world | + |
| 4. Conservatism | ++ |
| 5. Personal control | +++ |
| 6. Postponement of gratification | ++ |
| 7. Social values | ++ |
| 8. Type-A behaviour pattern | + |
| 9. Entrepreneurship | + |
| | |
| Attitudes | |
| 1. Leisure | +++ |
| 2. Money | ++ |
| 3. Time | +++ |
| 4. Success | +++ |

Note: The + sign indicates the strength rather than the direction of the relationship.

gists have been interested (and probably ignorant) in the origins of PWE and of the criticism of Weber's thesis, they have recognised the behaviour pattern of the typical high PWE believer. However, it is quite possible that PWE behaviour, as described by psychologists, has become independent of PWE beliefs as described by Weber. Scholars conversant with Weber's original thesis may, however, take issue with psychologists for not having read thoroughly or understood the PWE concept. That is, it may be argued that scales devised to measure the PWE might measure some aspect of a person's belief system and behavioural patterns but definitely not what Weber himself had in mind. Hence the use of the term PWE by psychologists may be challenged. Most of the research on the PWE has been concerned with devising a valid and reliable measure of PWE beliefs, and seeing how these beliefs related to variable aspects of work and non-work. Some work has, however, also been done on demographic attitudinal and personality determinants of PWE beliefs.

## Measurement of the Protestant work ethic

A number of self-report scales have been devised to measure the extent to which a person believes in the Protestant work ethic. Those often used in research include the pro-Protestant Ethic Scale (Blood, 1969), the Survey of Work Values (Wollack *et al.*, 1971) and the Protestant Work Ethic Scale (Mirels and Garrett, 1971). Furthermore other self-report scales concerning beliefs about work have subscales measuring such things as the work ethic (Buchholz, 1976). A problem with all these scales is that they are derived from either divergent interpretations or a very narrow reading of Weber's original works. Where high intercorrelations exist between scales they may simply be due to extensive item overlap between the different measures. Thus although they may all be measuring much the same thing, it may be inaccurate to describe it as PWE belief in the Weberian sense.

Perhaps the first attempt to devise a self-report measure for PWE beliefs was the work of two sociologists, Goldstein and Eichborn (1961), who used a simple four-item scale which had been used earlier in unpublished work and shown to have a coefficient of reproducibility of 0.91. In their research using this measure they found that high PWE beliefs were found to be related to individualism and asceticism, but no longer necessarily predictive of systematic, rational, economic behaviour. The sociologists Hammond and Williams (1976) also developed a PWE scale (unworldly ascetic and spirit of capitalism) but provide little evidence of the validity or reliability.

Another short measure is the Pro-Protestant Ethic scale (Blood, 1969), which has two four-item subscales (pro- and non-Protestant ethic). The scale was initially tested on a group of over 400 airmen and passengers and appeared to show reasonable factor structure and validity statistics. Later research by Wanous (1974) showed that the scale had a reasonable reliability coefficient, while Greenberg (1978) found evidence of the scale's construct validity. Cook *et al.* (1981) report on four recent studies which used this measure.

The survey of Work Values scale (Wollack *et al.*, 1971) is the longest, but perhaps the least used of these measures, though it has been used by Stone (1976). It is a 54-item scale, with nine items covering each of six areas: activity preference, job involvement, pride in work, social status of job, upward striving and attitude towards earnings. The first three subscales supposedly measure intrinsic aspects of the Protestant ethic, while the latter three subscales measure extrinsic aspects. A correlational, discriminant and factor analysis all lend support to the various components of the scale.

A similar multidimensional scale is Buchholz's (1976) long questionnaire measuring beliefs about work. He developed a scale which has five indices: the work ethic, the leisure ethic, the organisational belief system, Marxist-related beliefs and the humanistic belief system. Although some factor-analytic work was done on the original item pool, no descriptive statistics have been provided. The scale has been used by Dickson and Buchholz (1977, 1979) and Buchholz (1978).

The Protestant Ethic Scale (Mirels and Garrett 1971) is perhaps the best known and most widely used of the three scales. It is a nineteen-item scale developed on three large student samples, and it appeared to correlate in a logical manner with a number of other measures. Later work by Kidron (1978) revealed reasonable reliability coefficients, while Lied and Pritchard (1976) report five recent studies which have used this measure though there are many more (Furnham, 1990). Ray (1982) has developed an eighteen-item Eclectic Protestant Ethic scale, which was constructed 'to give some alternative to the rather pugnacious tone of the Mirels and Garrett items and because that scale has virtually no control against acquiescent response set' (p. 131). The author also attacks the Blood (1969) scale, as he found no significant negative correlation between the two subscales. He found that his new scale was significantly correlated with church attendance, religious belief and the Mirels and Garrett (1971) and Ray (1970) scales, and in a number of studies he demonstrated its reliability. These scales are shown below.

Few attempts have been made to compare these scales. An exception is Waters, Bathis and Waters (1975), who administered the Blood (1969), Wollack *et al.* (1971) and Mirels and Garrett (1971) scales to 165 students. All of the six subscales from the Wollack *et al.* (1971) scale correlated with the other scales, though they ranged from 0.24 to 0.49. The Blood (1969) scale correlated 0.70 with the Mirels and Garrett scale (1971), which is encouraging. A factor analysis of the Protestant ethic scale yielded two factors, intrinsic (work-related) and extrinsic (reward-related), and the Blood (1969) and Mirels and Garrett (1971) scales loaded substantially on both factors (see Table 10.2).

There appears to be renewed interest in the measurement of the PWE. This has taken two forms. Some have developed new scales: thus Ali (1988) has developed and tested an Islamic Work Ethic scale; Wayne (1989) also developed a new PWE scale to examine the relationship between PWE beliefs and contemporary work ethics and values. Others have attempted to do psychometric work on the current scales (Furnham, 1990; Tang, 1993a).

Although there has not been a great deal of psychometric assessment on these

**Table 10.2** Questionnaires used to measure the Protestant work ethic

| Scale | No. of items Total | Reversed | Response scale | Reliability | Validity | Studies in which scale was used |
|---|---|---|---|---|---|---|
| Protestant Ethic Scale (Goldstein and Eichhorn 1961) | 4 | 0 | Agree–disagree (1 or 2) | None | None | None |
| Protestant Work Ethic Scale (Mirels and Garrett, 1971) | 19 | 3 | Agree–disagree (7 to 1) | 0.67[c] 0.79[d] 0.70[c] | Cc Pd | Merrens and Garrett (1975) Greenberg (1978) Kidron (1978) Furnham (1982a, 1983a, 1984a, 1985b) |
| Pro-Protestant Ethic Scale (Blood, 1969) | 8 | 4 | Agree–disagree (6 to 1) | 0.70[c] | Cc Pd | Aldag and Brief (1977) Rim 1977, Amerikis, Field, Bederais and Leadbetter 1977 Filley and Aldag (1978) |
| Spirit of Capitalism Scale (Hammond and Williams, 1976) | 6 | 0 | Agree–disagree (+3 to –3) | None | Cc | None |
| Leisure Ethic Scale[f] (Buchholz, 1977) | 8 | 2 | Agree–disagree (7 to 1) | None | Cc Pd | Buchholz (1977), Dickson and Buchholz (1977, 1979), Furnham (1984b, 1985) |
| Work Ethic Scale[f] (Buchholz, 1977) | 7 | 0 | Agree–disagree (7 to 1) | None | Cc Pd | Buchholz (1977), Dickson and Buchholz (1977, 1979), Furnham (1984b, 1985) |
| Eclectic Protestant Ethic Scale (Ray, 1982) | 18 | 9 | Agree–disagree (5 to 1) | 0.82[c] | Cc Pd | Ray (1982) |
| Australian Work Ethic Scale (Ho, 1984) | 7 | 1 | Agree–disagree (4 to 1) | 0.76[c] | Cv Cc | Ho (1984) |

*Source:* reprinted with permission from the *Protestant Work Ethic*, Routledge 1990.

Note: [a]Although the first questionnaire had no evidence of validity, the others provided evidence of at least three types; concurrent (Cc), predictive (Pd), and convergent (Cv).
[b]This list is not exhaustive.
[c]Spearman-Brown.
[d]Kuder-Richardson.
[e]Cronbach's alpha.
[f]Buchholz's leisure and work ethic scales are typically combined in one question.

self-report measures, they appear to be moderately reliable and valid measures of the same thing. Certain criticisms may be levelled at them, however: they may have more items in favour of the work ethic than against it; all the scales appear sexist in their language; many appear to be multidimensional but provide only one total score; too often they have been validated on students alone; and the extremeness of many of the items may induce various artificial response sets. Nevertheless it should be pointed out that they are probably no better or worse than numerous other measures in this area of work beliefs, attitudes and behaviour.

# The protestant work ethic and work

Most studies using the PWE concept have not unsurprisingly looked at the relation-ship between the PWE and paid employment/work. Most of these have looked at the relationship between the PWE and job satisfaction, but some have looked at actual work behaviour. For example, Blood (1969), using his own scale, found that the more a worker agreed with the ideals of the PWE the more s/he will be satisfied in his paid work and life in general.

Aldag and Brief (1975) also looked at the relationship between the PWE (as measured by the Blood scale) and certain work values (affective responses, per-ceived task dimension, perceived leader behaviour, and higher-order need strength). The results confirmed the findings of Blood (1969). The Pro-Protestant scale was positively correlated with internal work motivation and growth satisfaction as well as higher-order need strength. On the other hand the non-Protestant scale was nega-tively correlated with general satisfaction, external work motivation, supervisory satisfaction, growth satisfaction, skill variety, task identity, task significance, auton-omy, feedback from job, leader consideration and high order need strength. Certainly the results supported the hypothesis that adherence to the PWE is associ-ated with strong higher order needs, which are perhaps the main alternatives of work attitudes.

Similarly Kidron (1978) found as predicted a positive relationship between the PWE and moral and calculative commitment to the work organisation. This rela-tionship held over all three organisations tested: an insurance company, a hospital and a personnel department. He concluded that although the PWE is associated with stronger moral identification with the organisation for which one works, it need not necessarily indicate a willingness to remain in a given system. Others, however, have found that this relationship is by no means clear, in that other vari-ables are more powerful moderators of this relationship. Armenakis *et al.* (1977) attempted to identify whether the PWE or an individual's need strength would be most useful in identifying those textile workers who demonstrate a positive rela-tionship between job characteristics and job satisfaction. Strong endorsers of the PWE showed positive correlations between job satisfaction and the job characteris-tics of autonomy, task feedback and friendship. Yet weak endorsers also showed the same positive correlations:

> It may be concluded then, that the moderator variable individual need strength is more discriminating than is PWE. . . . Therefore, being able to identify individuals as being strong PWE does not enable one to predict satisfaction any more accurately than being able to identify individuals as being weak PWE.   (p. 1153)

Stone (1975, 1976) also found a positive relationship between job scope and job satisfaction, but neither the PWE nor any of its subscales (as measured by the Wollack *et al.* (1971) scale) appeared to moderate the job scope/satisfaction rela-tionship. Ganster (1980) also found no direct relationship between PWE beliefs and job satisfaction. He attempted to test the moderating effects of the PWE, growth need strength, nAch and arousal-seeking tendency on task design relationships on 190 college students. He found that none of the individual difference variables moderated the objective scope/satisfaction relationship, although nAch did moderate the perceived scope/satisfaction relationship.

Earlier studies too found the PWE to be only a moderately useful predictor variable of job attitude. Wanous ( 1974) found higher-order need strength, followed by the PWE and lastly urban–rural backgrounds are good predictors of reactions to job characteristics. However, as he noted:

> The fact that higher order need strength yielded the clearest results seems reasonable because it is closest to the employee reactions it moderates. Thus, it is also not surprising that the PWE showed moderate usefulness as a moderator and urban/rural background the least because each is increasingly farther removed from on-the-job attitudes and behaviour.   (p. 622)

Other studies have looked at the relationship between PWE and actual work behaviour. Merrens and Garrett (1975) suggested that as the PWE holds that hard steady work is itself worthy, and unwillingness to work is seen as a symptom of absence of grace or as sinful, high PWE scorers would perform better on tasks designed to provide low motivation and interest levels. As predicted, they found high PWE scorers spent significantly more time participating in a boring repetitive task than low PWE scorers. Ganster (1981), however, failed to replicate this result and concluded that Merrens and Garrett's task was not representative of real jobs and that their experiment may well have induced apprehension, evaluation and hence biased the results. Greenberg (1977) found that high PWE scorers' performances improved and low PWE scorers' performances declined when given negative performance evaluation. He also found that, when told a co-worker was superior to them at a task which brought them unearned rewards, high PWE scorers performed at a high level and felt neutral about the task, whereas low PWE scorers performed poorly but liked the task. In a later study Greenberg (1978) found that belief in the PWE among train commuters correlated positively with the relative frequency of working compared to not working while commuting, perception of commuting as an extension of work rather than leisure, and a preference for working rather than commuting. Greenberg (1979) has also shown that endorsing of the PWE is related to perceived fairness in using various equity inputs. In one experiment high PWE scorers were shown to distribute money to hypothetical workers in proportion to their total productivity by taking into account both the quantity and duration of work, while low PWE scorers paid only according to duration ignoring quantity. It was also found that high PWE scorers believe it fairer to base reward on performance when differences were attributed to internal rather than external causes, while the reverse was found for low PWE scorers.

The profile of the PWE believers is of an independently minded, hard-working individual who is prepared to persevere at a task to achieve desirable ends. The fact that PWE believers are higher in individualism implies that they are more likely to be competitive than co-operative. Furnham and Quilley (1989), in fact, used two versions of the well-known prisoner's dilemma game to investigate the co-operation/competition strategies of PWE believers and found that, as predicted, high PWE scorers tended to be more competitive than low PWE scorers. They argued that these results are most important for further work on the PWE. Many studies have shown, for instance, that the PWE is associated with a strong desire to succeed, persistence at work tasks and a strong resistance to cheating (Eisenberger and Shank, 1985). Yet, as this study demonstrated, the competitiveness associated with an endorsement of the PWE can be disadvantageous. In this study, because of their competitive rather than co-operative tactics, high PWE scorers actually achieved lower scores, thus winning least reward. What PWE high scorers therefore need to do is to be able to distinguish those solutions in which competitiveness is the best strategy from those in which it is the worst. However, given the often replicated finding that PWE beliefs are closely associated with inflexible and simple conservative thinking, it is possible that co-operative strategies are fairly antithetical to PWE beliefs in general and, indeed, may threaten them. In this then may lie the Achilles' heel of PWE beliefs, namely the idea that competition as opposed to co-operation is the best strategy.

The literature on the PWE and work belief and behaviour is therefore inconsistent. The PWE does not appear to be the major determinant of job satisfaction, though it does appear to predict certain quantitative and qualitative aspects of work behaviour. By and large, PWE believers had to work harder and be more satisfied with extrinsic aspects of their work and PWE beliefs appear to be closely associated with strong higher-order needs. However, considerably more and better research needs to be done in this area if firm conclusions about PWE beliefs as measured by self-report inventories and work behaviour are to be established.

## The Protestant work ethic and unemployment

Whereas most of the previous studies have concerned the relationship between the Protestant work beliefs and paid work, some studies have looked at the relationship between these beliefs and unemployment. Furnham (1982a) asked subjects to rate the importance of various explanations for unemployment in Britain, as well as their agreement with various statements about social security (welfare) payments to the unemployed. As predicted, subjects who strongly endorsed the Protestant work ethic belief stressed negative individualistic explanations for unemployment and were by and large more against welfare payments than subjects who did not strongly endorse these beliefs. This confirms MacDonald's (1971a) finding that PWE believers were proponents of the ethics of social responsibility which tend to blame people rather than 'the system' for the source of their difficulty. It also confirms other findings which suggest that the PWE is part of a general conservative attitude pattern (Mirels and Garrett, 1971; MacDonald, 1972; Beit-Hallahmi, 1979; Furnham, 1984). These results are also in accordance with studies of lay beliefs about economics (poverty, wealth, unemployment, taxation, social security, etc.), which suggests that there are coherent lay 'theories' about such matters (Feagin, 1972; Feather, 1974; Forgas, Morris and Furnham, 1982; Furnham 1982a, 1982b, 1982c). Thus a high PWE scorer is likely to see poverty in terms of idleness and poor money management; wealth in terms of hard work, honesty and saving; unemployment in terms of laziness and lack of effort; and is likely to be against both taxation and social security (Furnham, 1983f). Nearly all of the analysis in Furnham's (1982a) study confirmed this view. The only exception being that of two fatalistic explanations for unemployment which, contrary to expectation, high PWE scorers endorsed more than low scorers. Research into locus of control and the PWE (Mirels and Garrett, 1971; Waters, Bathis and Waters, 1975) would suggest that they are related, yet, as MacDonald (1972) has found, this is only true for males and not females. Further, in a study of the unemployed themselves Feather (1982a) found that young unemployed Australians had lower PWE scores than a comparable employed group. His results also showed that the active pursuit of employment tended to be more frequent among those unemployed with strong PWE values. He also found a confirmation of the results of Furnham (1982a and 1982c) a difference in attributional style of unemployed compared with employed people in that the former tend to blame bad events on stable recurrent aspects of the self that are outside the personal world and to externalise good events by attributing them to certain external factors that might not occur again (e.g. interaction of others, etc.). Shamir (1985) examined over 400 adults in Israel, all of whom had been unemployed. Contrary to his hypothesis, however, he found that individuals with a high PWE turn to non-work activities more frequently while the unemployed derive more psychological benefits from such activities than individuals low in PWE beliefs. Thus it appears that PWE beliefs contribute to, rather than hinder, coping strategies useful while unemployed. There may be some sort of 'spillover' principle where stable, intellectual, and motivational coping styles associated with the PWE in the occupational role get transferred to non-work activities.

> In summary, the results of this study raise some doubts concerning the claim that a reduction in the PWE would automatically lead to coping better with unemployment. In fact, the opposite might be true. Rather than fighting the Protestant work ethic, a more realistic strategy would be to harness it and channel it to non-employment related work and to other non-work activities which have the potential for answering individuals' need for activity structure, social meaning an intellectual stimulation.   (p. 334)

In a related study, Shamir (1986) tested various hypotheses about the psychological well-being of unemployed individuals focusing on the moderating effects of the PWE. Contrary to predictions, the PWE did not moderate the relationship between employment status and psychological state, though various methodological problems could account for them. Thus Shamir (1986) concludes: 'There is also no evidence in our study that the Protestant work ethic hinders the processes of coping with unemployment in any way or that individuals who 'free' themselves of the ethic find unemployment easier to bear' (p. 36).

Furthermore, using the same data, Shamir (1987) was able to demonstrate that people's belief in, and adherence to, the PWE is not influenced by their change in work status in and out of work. This implies both that the PWE is a relatively stable dispositional factor but also that the experience of unemployment does not lead to work inhibitions.

Shamir's work would appear to indicate that PWE beliefs do not adversely affect people who are unemployed, indeed they may even make adjustment to worklessness better. However, it should be pointed out that these results are based on a limited sample of middle-class Israelis. It is quite probable that other variables as well as the PWE mediate between unemployment and psychological reactions such as class, self-esteem, attributional style, coping strategies, etc. In fact the studies on young people – school-leavers – have tended to examine those other factors and, as a result, come up with a rather different set of findings concerning the moderator effects of the PWE. Kelvin (1980) has set the relationships between PWE beliefs and unemployment in temporal perspective: 'What is happening in our time is precisely such a shifting of the attribution of responsibility for being unemployed from an internal personal level to the exterior situational level, this is not so much a cause as a manifestation of the end of the Protestant Work Ethic' (p. 309). However, the studies of Feather (1982a, 1982b) and Furnham (1982a) would suggest that this is only true of the unemployed and/or those with low PWE beliefs. Thus, because of the stress on the virtue of hard work (doctrine of calling) and personal control over one's life (doctrine of sanctification) PWE believers are intolerant of, and unsympathetic to, the poor, the unemployed and the disadvantaged. They are seen as non-elect, idle and damned, rather than the hard-working successful and elect. The unemployed, however, or those less concerned with PWE, tend to be sympathetic to the unemployed simply because they believe and attribute the causes of their plight to external social factors, rather than lack of individual effort.

## The Protestant work ethic and individual differences

The way in which the various Protestant work ethic scales have most often been validated is by correlating them with numerous personality and individual difference measures. It has been suggested that PWE beliefs are closely related to a number of other psychological variables. These can be divided into two groups: personality and belief variables, and demographic variables, the former having received more attention than the latter.

### Personality variables

Since Mirels and Garrett (1971) suggested that PWE beliefs may be considered a personality variable (that is, a stable disposition), a number of studies have correlated individual difference measures with one or other measures of the PWE. A wide variety of personality measures have been used, but in different studies (with different populations, and often different PWE measures) the results have been remark-ably similar. For instance, when comparing the locus of control scale with the PWE, Mirels and Garrett (1971) found a significant correlation of −0.30; Waters, Bathis and Waters (1975) −0.35, Lied and Pritchard (1976) −0.41; and McDonald (1972) −0.23. Similarly two studies which have used the California F scale found similar positive correlations between it and PWE beliefs: Mirels and Garrett (1971) 0.51, McDonald (1972) 0.44, and Joe (1974) 0.38.

Other related measures have shown a similar pattern. Mirels and Garrett (1971) found a significant correlation between the PWE and morality conscience and guilt, while Lied and Pritchard (1976) found a significant correlation between the PWE and restraint. MacDonald (1971a) found that endorsement of the ethics of social responsibility correlated with the PWE indicating that proponents of the ethics of social responsibility tend to blame people rather than the 'system' for the source of their difficulty.

In a later paper MacDonald (1972) looked at the relationship between the PWE, beliefs about the poor and human values. He found, as predicted, that the PWE was significantly related to negative attitudes towards the poor and opposition to a guar-anteed minimum annual income. Further he found that such values as 'comfortable life, equality, an exciting life and pleasure were negatively related, and ambition, self-control and salvation, positively related to the PWE'. He suggests that the con-struct of the PWE may 'be valuable to those who are concerned with identifying and subsequently altering the attitudes and dispositions that militate against the suc-cess of our nation's poverty programs' (p. 121).

In a study comparing PWE beliefs with established measures of personality, Rim (1977) found that men whose PWE scores were above the median tended to be more intelligent, less extravert and less neurotic than those below the median though the very opposite was true for women. He offers no theoretical interpreta-tion of these results. Few other studies in this area appear to exist.

Despite the variety of measures correlated with the PWE beliefs there appears to be coherence to these results. Studies on the psychology of conservatism (Wilson, 1973; Joe, Jones and Miller, 1981) have noted a number of character-istics of the conservative person which are strikingly similar to those with PWE beliefs: religious fundamentalism, pro-establishment politics, insistence on rules or punishments, pro-militarism, preference for conventional art and insti-tutions, an anti-hedonistic outlook, an intolerance of minority groups and a superstitious resistance to science. Indeed Furnham and Bland (1983) have demonstrated that PWE beliefs are consistently and significantly related to more general conservative social attitudes and conclude that it would be unlike-ly that PWE beliefs would change without the other beliefs doing likewise. The high PWE believer then is likely to be conservative in his views, have an inter-nal locus of control, and to be concerned with self-control. He is likely to hold values that are concerned with achievement and ambition, but be against plea-sure and relaxation. The PWE believer thus favours an ascetic rather than an aes-thetic life-style.

## Demographic variables

A number of studies have attempted to establish demographic determinants of current beliefs in the PWE. Beit-Hallahmi (1979) found that PWE scores were significantly related to religious self-identification (Catholics and Protestants had higher scores than Jews and agnostics), ethnic background (white groups had higher scores than black groups), political self-identification (Conservatives had higher scores than Liberals and leftists) and religious beliefs (people with conventional beliefs and high church-attendance figures scored more highly than those with unconventional beliefs or poor attendance figures) but not to socio-economic status. He concluded:

> The results may be interpreted as indicating that the PWE is separate from what is commonly referred to as 'achievement motivation' and that the PWE can be more correctly regarded as an attack towards work. . . . The Protestant Ethic should be regarded as an orientation, toward the place of work in one's life and society, which is related to a great extent to social background variables.   (p. 266)

Ray (1982) found that his PWE scale predicted both church attendance and religious belief but was not related to education or self-assigned social class. As Beit-Hallahmi (1979) had found, PWE beliefs did not discriminate between Protestants and Catholics: 'We now have some reason to believe that the Protestant ethic as such has perhaps run its course, in any way to say that the spirit of enterprise or the worship of work is now dead is only to say that all religions have come to share these attributes to an equal degree. The Protestant ethic in substantive terms is certainly not yet dead, it is just no longer Protestant' (p. 135).

Some studies have found that PWE beliefs are related to age: for example, Aldag and Brief (1975) found a significant correlation between PWE beliefs and age; but neither Buchholz (1978) nor Furnham (1982a) found a significant relationship. Similarly there appears to be no sex differences in PWE belief (Furnham 1982a). Thus there are no simple patterns in the relationship between demographic variables such as age, sex and class and PWE beliefs. Although there is a tendency for older, lower-middle-class people with a Conservative outlook to endorse PWE beliefs more than younger, middle-class or radical people, many other variables mediate this relationship. Most importantly perhaps, is the feeling that the PWE does not now discriminate between Protestant and other Christian believers. Hence one finds some writers who have dropped the term Protestant and simply talk of the work ethic.

# Change in the Protestant work ethic

Furnham (1990) has argued that those who have thought about distribution of PWE beliefs in society have usually come to one of five conclusions:

> The PWE never existed, it is a myth that it even existed in this, or any other cen-

tury. Either it existed for a small elite for a certain limited period of time, or else is a completely historical myth.

The PWE is dead, dying or on the decline – for some this is to be lamented, for others it is to be welcomed.

Depending on the nature of the job and the biography of the worker, the PWE is on the increase for some and decrease for others – for meaningful, interesting, involving, autonomous jobs, and for people with ambition and enthusiasm the PWE is on the increase whereas for boring, repetitive jobs, and people more interested in an easy life the PWE is on the decline.

The PWE is alive, well and even flourishing – this suggests that not only is the PWE not declining it is, as a belief system, actually on the increase.

The PWE has changed, metamorphosed into a new ethic which is a natural successor of the PWE, and shares some of its original features.

Kelvin (1980) has considered the future of the PWE and its relevance to social psychology. With the inexorable decline of the PWE, rising unemployment and a decline in the central significance of work, Kelvin sees major cultural changes:

> The outcome of that change will be the acceptance of being unemployed as an essentially normal rather than deviant condition, like maternity or retirement rather than like poncing or recidivism. With this will come financial provision for the unemployed at comfortable levels of subsistence and the acceptability of unemployment and the provisions for the unemployed will greatly reduce the significance and status attached to work. (p. 306)

Kelvin (1980), however, does not see the complete disappearance of the PWE but its transformation. Examples of this are cited such as the enthusiasm for do-it-yourself and home improvements which are seen as late twentieth-century descendants of Victorian working- and lower-middle-class self-improvement literature. The do-it-yourself enthusiasts favour economy, work and independence, all of which are core values of the PWE. Further the distinction between work and leisure will no doubt be softened. Thus for Kelvin there will be a steady decline in the PWE (at least in richer, western countries) though it may go through a number of transformations. Whereas religious beliefs may have been seen to lead to the development of the PWE, changes in the economy and the rise of structural unemployment are seen to lead to its decline and transformation. Indeed there are numerous popular calls for the end of the PWE which is seen at best to be inappropriate and at worst malicious in its consequences.

Furnham and Bland (1983), however, are not as convinced as Kelvin regarding the future of the PWE. They argue that because PWE beliefs are such an integral part of general conservative beliefs and values in general one can only expect them to decline, if conservative beliefs do likewise. As there is no reason to suppose conservative beliefs will go into decline, there is no reason to suspect PWE beliefs also to do so. Though these beliefs may not change, their manifestations in such things as do-it-yourself, professional and trades work may undergo some change. Following from McClelland's analysis, therefore, if people still socialise their children in the traditional middle-class values of independence, mastery training, saving and achievement they will develop as adults beliefs that are similar to PWE beliefs. Unless of course their early primary socialisation experiences are changed by later secondary socialisation experiences in school or ordinary life, there can be no reason to expect the decline of the PWE.

If indeed social welfare, taxation and other social benefit policies change radically in a country, it is possible that the experience that people have as a result of these changes will lead them to alter their PWE beliefs (in either direction). Psychologists, however, on a preliminary reading of a complex sociological and historical concept, blandly set out to 'measure' it. What is needed before empirical work proceeds is a careful conceptual analysis of the origin and maintenance of work beliefs and attitudes.

## Can the work ethic predict economic development?

It is the dream of some psychologists to be able to identify and measure an individual difference variable (i.e. PWE beliefs) which, if measured in small or large populations, is able to predict micro- or even macro-economic variables. Is it possible that PWE beliefs could be used to predict a country's or region's economic development? First, there are numerous practical problems to be considered if such a task is to be undertaken.

Which measures of PWE beliefs to use?
Who to sample?
Which economic variables should be considered?
Which intervening or moderating variables should be taken into consideration?
What actual relationship (linear, curvilinear, etc.) should one predict?

For instance, one measure of the PWE may have more predictive validity than another; some influential groups' PWE scores may be related to economic variables whereas the beliefs of other groups are not predictive; some economic variables like saving, gambling or investing may be predictable from PWE scores whilst others, like the growth of the money supply, may not; PWE scores may be moderated by class, age and sex such that when these variables are 'partialled out' no remaining influence is noticeable; and finally to expect a simple linear relationship between (multidimensional) PWE beliefs and (any) economic variables is surely naive.

Despite these formidable empirical problems, it may indeed be possible to investigate the relationship between PWE in a group, region and country at some specified point in time and relate to some economic variables. But can PWE beliefs predict economic behaviour? There are indeed a number of reasons why it is unlikely that PWE beliefs predict economic development. First, as Weber pointed out, it is necessary that certain industrial, bureaucratic or formal structures are in place that support entrepreneurial work. Without various economic, legal and commercial practices, the enterprise of individuals may not flower. Taxation systems, accounting principles and legal constraints may help or hinder PWE beliefs and practices. Thus in some countries or regions, moderate to low PWE beliefs may be greatly facilitated by legal and economic systems that led to economic development, while in other regions or countries high PWE beliefs on the part of individuals are thwarted by inappropriate or absent systems. Second, it seems that PWE beliefs decline after significant developments have been reached. Thus after the 'economic miracle' in Germany observers report that its young people now openly and explicitly reject the PWE of their parents which may have played a part in the recovery. One therefore needs a historical appreciation and base rate measures of the PWE to establish its effects on the economy. Furthermore one needs to look at the factors that influence economic variables – that is, growth may be greater in developing countries for historic reasons that have nothing to do with its citizens' work beliefs or behaviour.

Third, PWE beliefs are usually held by minorities in most cultures. Therefore the size, power and influence of these minorities are as important as the absolute level of beliefs that they hold. For instance, it has been observed in various Central European countries like Hungary or the former Yugoslavia that the reason for substantial differences in the economic development and personal wealth of certain groups is due to their propensity for work and their beliefs in the PWE. However, ethnic and geographic reasons appear to prevent those people from having an influence over the country as a whole.

Fourth, inherent in traditional PWE beliefs is strong risk aversion and conservatism. Most wealth creators and entrepreneurs have at certain stages of their life to take risks which may be deeply antithetical to the PWE. In this sense it may be argued that PWE beliefs predict poor economic development because if a group has not the courage to venture certain changes they will inevitably fall behind in beneficial developments. On the other hand, if people with enterprise are not carefully supported by those with strong PWE beliefs their courage and foresight may not be realised.

Fifth, it has been argued that PWE beliefs are multidimensional. Hence two people or groups may attain equal results by scoring similarly high and low on different dimensions, but because the scores are summated they appear equivalent. It may also be that some of these PWE dimension are related to economic variables and others not. Indeed it is possible that, of those that do predict economic development, some are positive and others negative. Therefore by obtaining only a gross, single, average score the differences between difficult factors are ignored and their predictability is significantly reduced.

Finally, the sort of people from whom PWE beliefs are obtained tend to be unrepresentative, being educated and articulate. There is frequently a bias in data gathering because the people interviewed have to be literate, insightful and helpful.

Although it is unlikely that psychological variables alone can account for or predict economic variables, however, it is possible that they do account for some unique variance. McClelland's (1961) pioneering work was perhaps too optimistic (see Gilliard, 1989), but laid down the idea of a model for psychological as well as sociological, historical and economic variables actually having a direct effect on economic development.

## Conclusion

More than a decade of intensive work on the PWE beliefs construct has confirmed its place as an important individual difference variable related to human motivation. Psychologists have chosen to conceive of and measure the PWE as a coherent, bipolar belief system similar to the locus of control or just-world belief constructs. Indeed there is a striking similarity between PWE and other individual differences (rather than dispositional) variables such as locus of control and just-world belief systems in both their antecedents and determinants. However, as in the above two related concepts, no attempt has been made to delineate the aetiology of the beliefs in individuals or the socio-cultural specificity of these beliefs. Considerable effort has gone into devising valid, reliable and robust self-report questionnaires that measure PWE beliefs, and many exist. However, as in the locus of control construct it is probable that PWE beliefs are multidimensional as Weber (1905) initially suggested – including beliefs about work and leisure, pleasure and indulgence, success and failure, control and fate. Yet the present scales appear to concentrate on only a few of these dimensions and provide a simple single score. This may account for the fact that studies on the PWE and beliefs are equivocal as beliefs need to be subdivided into their various components. Most of the research on the PWE has concerned PWE beliefs and work, where it has been found to be an only moderately useful predictor of behaviour, values, job satisfaction, etc. However where the PWE beliefs have been examined in relation to poverty, unemployment or mental illness, it has also been shown to be a more useful discriminatory variable. Perhaps the fact that the construct has been called the Protestant work ethic has led psychologists to concentrate on the relationships between PWE beliefs and aspects of work, rather than looking at a range of related areas such as leisure, economic behaviour, health, etc.

The research relating PWE beliefs to other personality variables has been limited but is encouraging. However, little or no work has looked at the aetiology and determinants of these beliefs, their stability over time or their cultural specificity. If the PWE beliefs are to be conceived of as a personality dimension, as Mirels and Garrett (1971) suggest, there is room for a great deal of further empirical and theoretical research in this field.

Finally there remains some confusion as to whether one should talk about the PWE, the work ethic (Buchholz, 1976) or the Protestant ethic (Ray, 1982). The term PWE implies that the concept has been borrowed from the writings of Weber, which is clearly not the case, as few psychologists appear to have read his many works in detail or paid much attention to the metaphysical aspects of PWE beliefs. The PWE beliefs and behaviours as defined and measured by the many PWE scales appear to be concerned with work values, beliefs and needs and more particularly 'a person's continuing commitment to paid employment' (Cook *et al.*, 1981: 132). Just as it was pointed out that the Holy Roman Empire was neither Holy, nor Roman, nor Empire, so it could be claimed that the PWE is neither exclusively Protestant, nor about only work, nor exclusively concerned with ethics. It may therefore be more accurate to talk about work values and beliefs rather than the PWE itself.

In that the PWE seems such a good predictor of work, non-work and socio-economic beliefs and behaviours, it seems that economic psychologists would do well to concentrate on it as an individual difference variable of great importance and relevance.

# Chapter 11

# Economies in transition: the new Europe

The changes which are happening or might happen in the more than twenty countries of the old Soviet empire are the most important set of political, social and economic transformations since the emergence of the independent third-world countries from the dissolution of the West European empires. All of the new former communist states claim that they want to use markets as the main co-ordinating devices for their economies. This does not mean that the mode of production need be capitalist, but in most of the countries it is the clear intention that it should be. Even in those where it is not, there will be a major expansion in capitalist spheres of influence. In the absence of counter-revolutions it seems likely that in even the most non-democratic and authoritarian of these states capitalist relations will eventually flourish and form a significant part of the way the economy is organised. These societies have chosen a market system because they want the economic benefits which they think it will generate, just as they have chosen or pay lip service to democracy because it seems a more attractive way of organising the polity, or at least it is the system used by the more successful market economies.

In the short run the economic impact of the abandonment of central planning has been a fall in production of anywhere from 4 to 60 per cent (see Table 11.1), a rise in inflation and in the CIS the emergence of hyperinflation, and an increase in unemployment – in the case of the former East Germany effectively to almost 50 per cent of the workforce. Now the extreme results reflect extreme circumstances. The largest output falls have happened to countries at war – especially Georgia, Armenia and Azerbaijan, or in civil war in the cases of Moldova, Tajikistan and again Georgia or under economic blockade as with the Baltic states. The most extreme inflations, in Russia and the Ukraine, reflect either a divided political and economic authority or a paralysed economic transition where the fear of change is matched by a reluctance to increase the taxation of a shrinking tax base. The highest levels of unemployment are either the result of war and subsequent dislocation, as in Georgia and Armenia, or are caused by the overwhelming demand and supply

**Table 11.1** Changes in real output in former communist states 1990–92 (real GDP changes %)

|  | 1990 | 1991 | 1992 | Cumulative 1990–92 |
|---|---|---|---|---|
| Albania | −10 | −30 | −8 | −42 |
| Armenia | −9 | −12 | −50 | −60 |
| Azerbaijan | −12 | −2 | −30 | −40 |
| Belarus | −3 | −3 | −11 | −16 |
| Bulgaria | −9 | −12 | −8 | −26 |
| Croatia | −9 | −29 | −11 | −42 |
| Czechoslovakia | 0 | −16 | −7 | −22 |
| Estonia | −4 | −13 | −26 | −38 |
| Georgia | −12 | −25 | −30 | −54 |
| Hungary | −4 | −12 | −5 | −20 |
| Kazakhstan | −2 | −8 | −13 | −22 |
| Kyrgyzstan | 3 | −5 | −25 | −27 |
| Latvia | 3 | −8 | −44 | −47 |
| Lithuania | −5 | −13 | −35 | −46 |
| FYR Macedonia | −11 | −11 | −15 | −33 |
| Moldova | −2 | −12 | −21 | −32 |
| Poland | −12 | −7 | 1 | −17 |
| Romania | −7 | −14 | −15 | −32 |
| Russia | −4 | −11 | −19 | −31 |
| Slovenia | −5 | −9 | −7 | −20 |
| Tajikistan | −1 | −9 | −31 | −38 |
| Turkmenistan | 2 | −1 | −5 | −4 |
| Ukraine | −3 | −14 | −14 | −28 |
| Uzbekistan | 4 | −1 | −14 | −11 |

*Source:* reprinted with permission from EBRD *Economic Review; Current Economic Issues* July 1993.
Note: For the newly independent states of the former Soviet Union, except Estonia, Latvia, Lithuania, Kyrgyzstan and Russia estimates are for real net material product. For Russia, the 1990 and 1991 figures are for real NMP, while the 1992 figure is for real GDP. For Croatia and FYR Macedonia the figures in the table cover real GSP (the value-added concept of the former Yugoslavia).

shocks of take-over by a dominant and vastly more efficient neighbour, as in the case of East Germany.

For our purposes the key points to note are that the transition has already been and will continue to be extremely costly in economic welfare, and that if the shift to a market system is to happen and they are to more than recoup those losses, then most individuals and many of their institutions need to change their economic culture. That means that their objectives may change, as will the ways they form those objectives, and try to achieve them. To work at its most efficient a market system requires individuals to respond to price signals by changing behaviour. Profit opportunities need to be seized and loss-making activities abandoned. Workers must be happy with these principals, if not exactly with every impact they have on their own welfare.

Bearing the short- to medium-run costs of transition obviously requires considerable political consensus or, alternatively, repression, and the relative failure of many states to make significant and rapid progress reflects their lack of the former and their inability or unwillingness to use the latter. But just as consensus building in a newly democratic system is made difficult by the lack of familiarity with its institutions and operating characteristics, so running a market system is hindered by the fact that under communism it was anathematised.

In this chapter we look at the developments in the transitional economies in the light of their history, and particularly in the light of how communism influenced individuals' economic behaviour. The legacy of that influence is paramount in understanding present behaviour and perhaps in determining the ultimate fate of the transition. There are four further sections. In the next we look at the economic mind under the old regime, and indicate some of its influence on the transition. We then look at some recent evidence of this influence in the results of social surveys. This is followed by an examination of the conflicts between individualist and collectivist attitudes in running the economy during transition. A concluding section summarises the arguments and evidence.

## The economic mind under the old regime

Although there was some diversity in the final years of communism, to all intents and purposes the economies which may now be in transition were carbon copies of each other. The methods of economic organisation, economic policy and of course economic ideology were required to be copies of Soviet practice, and more or less to the end that is exactly what they were. So, for example, although there were political differences between the Soviet Union and Romania from the 1960s onwards, the impact of Romanian communism on individual Romanian economic behaviour was insignificantly different from that of Soviet communism on its own citizens.

The ideology of the system obviously owed much to Marx, though the influence of Lenin and of Lenin's interpretation of Marx was of decisive importance. After Stalin Soviet leaders spoke increasingly infrequently about long-term economic end states, and long before Brezhnev's death it was clear to almost everyone that communism as opposed to 'actually existing socialism' (in practice Stalinism tempered by Brezhnevian sloth, corruption and some humanity) was a very distant dream. The system described itself as being in a state of socialism – in transition on the way to communism. Under communism the distributive ideal was 'from each according to their ability, to each according to their need'. Under socialism this was replaced by 'from each according to their ability, to each according to their contribution'. So socialism in the Soviet interpretation was a transitional state which, because of economic failure, became a terminus – but at least one where effort was in principle to be rewarded.

For Marx the key to distribution was the ownership of capital. This ownership allowed capitalists to expropriate the surplus of the economy for their own purposes, and so dominate the polity and society. So under communism there could be no significant private ownership of capital or paid labour outside of the state system.

After the 1989–91 revolutions these facts had crucial impacts on the form of the privatisation process and on the stock of entrepreneurial ability which was available to transform the system.

None of these ideological influences required a planning system of the type which came into existence. Certainly some planning was indicated, but worker self-mangement, self-employment and various collective and co-operative arrangements would have been possible. In practice, in the late 1920s for reasons of control Stalin chose the command system – sometimes called central planning, the administrative economy or the military economy. This system was a mixture of planning and priorities, where plan fulfilment in physical terms was paramount. In the production sector money was passive – in that its possession did not entitle the holding firm to access to goods. That could only be arranged if those goods had been allocated as inputs in the physical plan. The financial plan was simply a mirror of and a checking device for the physical plan. Organisations were arranged hierarchically under ministries, and information flowed up and down formal vertical channels. Horizontal information flows across administratively separate hierarchies were absent or informal. This placed a premium on connections, for managers who generally struggled to fulfil inconsistent and frequently revised orders.

Lenin saw a major task for the Communist Party in teaching a largely peasant society the disciplines of industrial labour. He, and after him his party, believed in the superiority of factory work over artisan or peasant labour. To be a member of the industrial proletariat was, according to official doctrine, the highest form of labour force participation. In ideological terms only belonging to the vanguard party, which led the proletariat, lay above it. So peasants were collectivised – though only on state farms did their ideological status equal that of industrial workers. Artisans were starved of inputs and reduced to the very margins of the workforce, and generally everyone became rather too much like soldiers – without orders nothing happened.

The individual at work came to rely not just on orders to work, but on the factory for housing, leisure activities, health services, social security, and in larger enterprises for shops, consumer goods and crèche facilities. As services were generally badly underprovided in the wider community, and the range of services increased with the size of the factory, jobs at large plants were especially sought after. Losing such a job was often a family disaster. As the inadequacy of the social infrastructure has continued into the transition, so workers' reluctance to leave such plants is understandable.

Away from work the pervasive nature of controls exerted a profound influence on economic activity, of whatever degree of legality (Katsenelinboigen, 1977). For example, in practice the demand for artisan services could not be met by state-owned workshops or the few individuals permitted to continue their trade. Consequently moonlighting using stolen inputs was common. Again this reinforced the importance of connections in sustaining a reasonable life-style, but also often involved association with criminal or semi-criminal activities. As income from work was rarely of significant size, those who possessed substantial assets were generally assumed to have acquired them illegally. Almost always such popular suspicion was correct. Thus under the old regime a citizens' most vivid experiences of a market economy were likely to be tinged with fear or distaste. Even the most common experience of free markets – the peasant markets for agricultural produce which flourished quite legally in most towns – was accompanied by some socially undesirable implications, because prices were generally significantly higher than in the state food shops and consequently these markets were less frequented by the poorer sections of the community.

So from the viewpoint of the successful conditions for transition the old regime had, most deliberately, equipped its citizens with a set of behavioural characteristics and psychological predilections exactly antithetical to the introduction of a market economy. The strengths of the old system – its ability to concentrate resources on a limited range of priority tasks, its provision of full, indeed over-full employment, existence of actively stable prices, its provision of crèche facilities for most children and the virtual guarantee of an adequate if low standard of living – were of no or of marginal weight in the balance in deciding the fate of communism. Relative to the west, it had failed to deliver more than a modicum of prosperity and in the process had choked all political and much individual dissent. Yet in looking back at the momentous choices for change made by the electorates during these revolutionary years it is hard not to believe that most thought change would be relatively painless – or, as a Slovak friend put it, 'They voted for West German living standards – but expected to achieve them with Slovak work practices.' Those habits of thought and action inherited from communism, as well as the understandable disillusion with the costs of transition, need to be borne in mind when we look at the emerging evidence of how their economic minds are coping with the shock of transition.

## The economic mind in transition: evidence from social surveys

Our evidence on changes and continuities in the economic mind under transition comes from two sources – opinion surveys and case studies. Neither is comprehensive or definitive. Our intention is to illustrate the range of responses to change and to point up some of the more obvious problems in interpretation. We begin with some social survey results.

The collapse of communism allowed and encouraged a rapid increase in social attitude surveys. It may also have encouraged more candid replies by interviewees. In the west some noteworthy survey sources have been the Centre for the Study of Public Policy, University of Strathclyde, the Roper Center, University of Connecticut, and the Mirror Center, Washington, DC. As an example of the type of evidence which was collected soon after the revolutions we could take the Centre for the Study of Public Policy's 2,500 sample study of Bulgarian and Czechoslovak attitudes.

A key aspect of this study is its evidence on attitudes towards money makers. This is summarised in Table 11.2. It is clear that there are substantial differences in attitudes towards entrepreneurs in the two countries. In part this reflects their different histories, and in part their different conditions. In both countries there is a strong identification of money making with political connections through the old nomenclature. That reflects reality. Much, if not most, of the old ruling bureaucratic class is still in a position of influence throughout the area. They rapidly metamorphosed into more voter-friendly forms but generally retained their positions through their connections, and through the unique ability to make the system function. Access to their networks of connections and permissions is especially important in view of the highly regulated nature of even the post-revolutionary economy. In extreme but very common cases this access has been used for spontaneous privatisation, where managers and bureaucrats have conspired to shift state assets into the private sector and into their own control.

The fact that respondents in Bulgaria associated money making more with political connections, taking advantage of people, and dishonesty, than did Czechoslovaks, reflects the fact that corruption in Bulgaria was and is almost certainly more pervasive and severe than in Czechoslovakia. Of course once such a negative image of entrepreneurship is established this would account for some of the discrepancy between the two groups of interviewees on the favourable perceptions of entrepreneurs. But another important factor is undoubtedly the history of the two states. Before communism Czechoslovakia, or at least the Czech lands, were heavily industrialised and very strongly market-oriented, while Bulgaria was largely a peasant society with a high degree of emphasis on production for self-consumption.

But in both societies non-recorded transactions were significant adjuncts to the official economy; as Rose (1991: 24–25) puts it:

**Table 11.2**  Images of money makers

|  | Czechoslovakia (% saying applies) | Bulgaria (% saying applies) |
|---|---|---|
| *Favourable* | | |
| Intelligent | 63 | 40 |
| Work hard | 55 | 35 |
| Help make economy grow | 55 | 30 |
| Average | (58) | (35) |
| *Unfavourable* | | |
| Political connections, nomenclature | 71 | 79 |
| Taking advantage of other people | 66 | 85 |
| Dishonest | 57 | 77 |
| Average | (65) | (80) |

*Source:* reprinted with permission from State and Market Surveys, Centre for the Study of Public Policy, University of Strathclyde.

The deprivations and distortions of a centrally planned economy have strengthened social exchange outside the immediate household as the best means of securing many goods and services. The obligation to help other people – and the right to make claims on others – has created an extensive network of exchanges beyond the nuclear family.

Economies in transition have larger unofficial economies, partly because of breakdown in control mechanisms and partly because in their move from the state to the private sector a high proportion of the labour force has disappeared from official view.

Of course, in addition, with the drop in real wages the incentive to look for extra work has increased: for example, in Bulgaria during 1991 consumer prices increased by 334 per cent, but wages rose only by 120 per cent; in the Czech Republic in 1991 average industrial wages rose by 16.7 per cent, but consumer prices by 56.7 per cent (EBRD 1993). Given the higher standard of living in Czechoslovakia, it is thus not surprising to find that the survey found that 76 per cent of the Bulgarian sample, but 56 per cent of the Czechoslavakian said that regular jobs often do not provide sufficient funds to purchase necessities. Over two-thirds of households produced goods for themselves and a majority of households engaged in socio-economies not involving cash payments.

Taking 'uncivil' paid illegal jobs as a whole (and not just those involving foreign currency) a seventh of Bulgarians and a third of Czechoslovakians participate. It is as though households need a portfolio of economic activity to survive, both official and unofficial. Making connections becomes a necessity and often foreign currency is required to obtain services which should otherwise be 'free', such as treatment by the doctor or to obtain familiar goods like cars and television sets.

A household with a portfolio of economic activities is the norm rather than the exception: if one of the aims of a market economy is to increase official market activity then certainly the 'old' economic mind will work against this – with resulting losses in tax revenue. And from the actors point of view a continuance of such diversity *is* rational – while state industries close and a free market is introduced job opportunities will be as quickly lost as found; a household would be foolish to put all its double-yokers in a single basket.

Holding a portfolio of jobs creates some flexibility in income sources, yet ironically it can lead to lower geographical mobility, for the would-be migrant has to replace a whole network of income opportunities. Only 23 per cent of the Czechs and Slovaks and 15 per cent of the Bulgarians were prepared to move to another town or country in search of work. This seems low, but it needs to be borne in mind that under the old regime such moves required government permission, and though many moved without it, accommodation was and is difficult to obtain. As new laws on the sale of land and property are enacted, the pattern, frequency and attitude towards mobility will change, but given the present general shortage of housing of a reasonable standard this is not likely to happen quickly.

In 1991 the Times Mirror Center completed a massive quantitative sample of 13,000 personal interviews in nine European nations and three of the former

Soviet republics. The results add substance to the image projected so far. In the new democracies political pluralism was greeted more enthusiastically than economic reforms, especially in 'European' Russia and the Ukraine. The 'old' political regime was rejected by the majority but free-market capitalism of the US type was only favoured by minorities: Bulgaria (12 per cent), Czech (14 per cent), Russia (17 per cent), Hungary (23 per cent), Poland (23 per cent), although there was more support in Lithuania (47 per cent). Respondents in Czechoslovakia, Hungary, Poland, Bulgaria, Russia, the Ukraine and Lithuania were all asked whether a list of activities ranging from farming and the running of food stores to the provision of health care and education should be run by the state or be private. As one would expect from previous results, the state was still seen as the appropriate provider of welfare and the appropriate manager of 'public' utilities like electricity. Only 11 per cent or less said that health care should be run mainly privately across the countries; Lithuania being an exception (27 per cent). Over 80 per cent in Russia, the Ukraine and Lithuania believed that electricity supplies should be managed by the state. More surprising, given the legacy of Stalinism, is the lack of enthusiasm for the privatisation of the media; in most countries the most popular option was some combination of state and private control for newspapers, that the state should run radio and television and, perhaps most surprising, the majority across all the 'new democracies' favoured state control of the telephone system, rising to over 70 per cent support in Czechoslovakia, Bulgaria, Russia, Ukraine and Lithuania. What becomes a challenge when viewing the tables of results is to find an activity where private sector provision was seen as the best option. There was majority support for privately owned restaurants in Czechoslovakia, Hungary and Poland and for shops in Czechoslovakia. The most prominent support for private enterprise was in farming: Lithuania (56 per cent), Poland (62 per cent), Ukraine (74 per cent) and Russia (75 per cent). Heavy industry and mining have large majorities in all the countries sampled advocating continued state control.

The Central and Eastern Europe economic mind will, if a market economy is to work, have to accept some unemployment and be prepared to see prices rise in shops. Majorities in all the seven countries realise that the days of full employment are over but have very mixed feelings about free floating prices. It follows that 'profit', while not a dirty word, is certainly a tarnished one; almost as many people feel that the profits of privately owned businesses should be limited as those that feel people should be allowed to earn as much as they can. There is notably a similarity between the new democracies and the United States, not shared by other European democracies on incentive salary schemes compared to fixed salaries. Sixty-three per cent or more favoured incentives schemes in the new democracies, rising to 79 per cent for the Ukrainian sample and even 86 per cent for the Lithuanians. Yet such schemes are favoured by only a small majority of US citizens (53 per cent). The United Kingdom, France, Spain, Italy and Germany all have majorities favouring fixed salaries. Here as elsewhere the question wording may be at fault, and respondents from Central and Eastern Europe may have taken it for granted that incentive schemes were the most common form of payment in the Western European nations.

Elsewhere in the current volume we have looked at 'lay explanations' for social problems, how they are caused and how they can be assuaged. Embracing the market economy would entail a move away from collectivist and societal explanations towards individualistic ones. When asked why some people do not succeed in life, there were no clear majorities from among Russian and Ukrainian respondants as to whether this was due more to society's failures than to personal weaknesses. As with so many answers the Lithuanains seem closer to the western democracies – 58 per cent attributing causation to personal frailty. There appears to be a slightly higher degree of what Furnham (1988) would term 'fatalism' in the new democracies, where respondents are more likely to agree that 'success in life is pretty much determined by forces outside our control' made evident in the comparison, for example, of Hungary (67 per cent agreement), Poland (66 per cent), Bulgaria (73 per cent) with the United Kingdom (51 per cent) and the United States (40 per cent). Again, in terms of their past this was largely true, and the speed and disruption involved in the transition can have done little to change their views.

Optimistic pointers for the future were the enthusiasms of the Lithuanians, the initial exultations of the newly united Germans (for what appeared to be sound economic reasons), and the embracement of captialism especially by the young and better educated (Tzszka and Sokolovska, 1992). Time will tell whether this optimism was well founded, and whether people can wait for the rewards a market economy can bring. Meanwhile in the last months of the Soviet Union it was only 'one cheer for capitalism' and, as the Director of the Soviet Center for Public Opinion and Market research put it:

> The economic and political difficulties experienced by the population are coupled with a troubled state of consciousness, the destructive traits of which are pessimism, nostalgia for the past, uncertainty and fear for the future. People are exhausted by the scarcity of goods, inflation, crime, and the decay of central and local authority.  (Zaslavskaya, 1992).

Nothing that has happened since, objectively or subjectively has yet required a revision of this assessment.


## Individualism versus collectivism: some case studies

The first noticeable change in the economic transition was the rapid growth of small businesses, mostly in the retail and distribution sectors. Such a development is a direct challenge to the previous collectivist attitude, yet if growth is to occur it will almost certainly have to come from this sector. Small businesses can be innovative, not only in the sense of filling gaps in the market, but also in experimenting with new management practices and structures. Jone Pearce, in a series of articles, has examined the management mind, the legacies of communism and the need for change, with special reference to Hungary and Czechoslovakia (Pearce 1991, 1992; Branycizki, Bakacsi and Pearce 1992).

In the past (and to a very limited extent in the present), business practices in Hungary and Czechslavakia differed considerably from those in the west. The main task of managers was to fulfil a plan in quantitative terms. Quality was a secondary issue, and because the system was supply-driven, the consumer was generally not a prime consideration. Profitability was planned profitability – not a reward for seeing a gap in the market. Labour turnover was similar to that in market economies, and dismissal for disciplinary reasons little different. But redundancy for lack of demand and restructuring was very rare, and it was the manager's job to find the worker a new job. Notions of efficiency in a western sense were largely absent.

Incentive schemes, within terms of salaries and promotions, in the not atypical Hungarian case seem odd as well. Managers have been appointed often because they are reliable party members, which does not in itself make them good managers (or for that matter, bad ones). And in present-day Hungary many large companies have been slow to become privatised or attract foreign capital. Old party members who could see the writing on the wall, colloquially known as 'parachutists', secured for themselves senior management positions before the demise – they are still there.

Making progress depends on who you know, on connections that have been made, on private deals and favours struck. This is not perhaps what an outsider would expect of a communist or post-communist organisation. According to Pearce, this has placed too much emphasis on personal relationships at the expense of institutional trust and corporate allegiance. (As a metaphor it is as though Central and Eastern European citizens trust individual politicians while distrusting the system, while citizens of the United States are more likely to distrust politicians (and take inordinate interest in their public humiliation) while saluting the flag and the democractic system.)

Distributing jobs by personal favour and private political recommendation is bound to cause discomfort in the workplace. Pearce has some sympathy with the idealised version of Weberian bureaucracy as a superior alternative to such 'corruption': promotions and salaries should be determined by publicly agreed guidelines and rules. But there are apparent contradictions here. The popular vision of a state-run industry *is* one governed by rules and hierarchical structures, stymied by such rules and structures. Listening to managers talk, another story unfolds: the major job of the manager is securing credits, material and labour, all requiring bargaining of an interpersonal, often secretive kind – there are no procedural guidelines for processes such as this. Furthermore many of those enterprises are still state-owned, the pace of formal governmental privatisation programmes has been snail-like, while elsewhere the Hungarian economy is rapidly privatising. As wages are comparatively low in the state sector, managers are faced with labour shortages. Discretionary bonuses are common, although, as with so much else, the guidelines for such payments are unwritten, with the result that wages are bargained for on a personal basis with management, which creates all sorts of felt inequities and injustices. As was discussed in an earlier section, many workers have a portfolio of jobs

to make ends meet, so bonuses are necessities not extras, and consequently very little can be done without personal deals being struck.

Labour is now not scarce, though capital is. Pearce details the case of a state-
owned glass-manufacturing company with an operating profit attempting to attract
foreign capital. Although making a profit, the company is overstaffed by Western
European standards, and coupled with this is a large debt incurred before the revolution which makes the company less attractive. This is a revealing case study of
markets in transition: how can management reduce the workforce, how can it be
done fairly, in a way that will not further alienate the rest of the workforce, by managers with next to no experience of laying people off? Pearce shows that it can be
done, but it requires considerable imagination from the participants. Two committees were formed: the first comprised heads of departments and union representa-
tives, whose jobs was to produce agreed procedural guidelines for laying people
off; the second committee was set up to hear appeals. Without the committees in
1991 staffing levels had already been reduced from 2,000 to 1,850 by voluntary
redundancy, early retirement and other 'soft' options; the committees became necessary, and were recommended by a Hungarian consulting company, when a foreign consultancy recommended a further reduction to 1,160 employees using western staffing models. Between July and August 1991, 350 people were laid off using
the committees, without major interruptions in production – in the past firing just
one person could result in group protest.

Collectivism and social solidarity is still strong in the minds of these people, as
revealed by the criteria used by the committees. People were not appraised solely
according to their productive contribution to the company, attendance record and
skill level but also by 'irrelevant' social welfare criteria: no one with a large family
was to be laid off, nor anyone with an unemployed spouse.

In the process of enterprise transition, departments taken for granted in western
democracies have had to be virtually invented, including human resource departments (less fashionably called personnel departments) free from political control,
and marketing departments. The strain on managers and workers alike has been
considerable; change is almost invariably stressful, and the nature and number of
changes that have to be made, nearly simultaneously, will stretch people to breaking point and beyond. It is little wonder that, for some, the bad old days perhaps
were not so bad after all, but the price for resisting change may be dire. Pearce and
Branyiczki (1993) describe the fate of a famous Hungarian porcelain factory, established in 1777, which previously sold 80 per cent of its products through the
Hungarian state network and a few of its own shops. In 1990 many of the factory's
900 workers were the third generation of their families to work there. The factory
owned apartments and worker's hostels in the area. But then three changes
occurred: energy costs rose fourfold; consumers stopped buying luxury goods as
economic depression struck; and tastes changed, as people came to prefer plain
porcelain to the previously produced hand-painted versions. The factory failed to
adapt and is on the brink of insolvency: the managing director, recently trained in
western management techniques and keen to lay off a group of old party para-

chutists and administrators, was himself fired as the threatened employees organised themselves against him.

The best way to handle change is to have a cadre of managers, a nucleus from which organisational change can spread – the porcelain manager was too isolated (Tushman and Romanelli, 1985; Gersick, 1991). There have been successes such as the Advertising Agency, one of only two in Hungary until the reforms of the 1980s with major contracts for state-owned enterprises. By 1990, 2,000 advertising companies had been established and state-owned clients were not paying their bills. Due to some highly industrious individuals, forming a persuasive cadre, the company survives after securing a partnership with a multinational advertising agency. While some managers and workers keep their heads down, the enterprising ones found themselves working twelve hours a day, having their competencies and self-esteem challenged and making painful changes.

## Managing change

On managing change a gaggle of authors are saying much the same thing – an economic (and political) system is bounded by culture (e.g. Etzioni, 1988; McIntyre, 1992; Wight, 1992). One cannot change one without the other: the 'shock treatments' advocated by economic advisers such as the Harvard economist retained by Solidarity, Jeffery Sachs, will cause unnecessary conflicts because they ignore social mores, attitudes and practices. It is of great concern that economists (although they often go out of their way to deny it in their academic articles) should involve themselves in normative debates, of telling people what they 'ought' or 'should' do, not so much because they are doing it but because they are doing it without proper recourse to social history, sociology, anthropology and psychology – as though the humanities and most social sciences were of no account. Culture and economic systems grow and evolve; they cannot be built or restructured rapidly. An economy of a particular type, for example a command economy, is not a single system but more a portfolio of economies, an aggregation of personal 'unofficial' agreements and understandings. Similarly a capitalist economy takes many forms but is always tempered by government intervention, by bounded rationality, 'satisficing' principles and the fairness considerations of economic actors (Simon, 1957; Kahnemann, Knetsch and Thaler, 1986).

As if this ahistorical and asocial advice were not enough, there is strong evidence that the unfettered kind of market system is not to be wholeheartedly recommended. McIntyre (1992), for one, argues that among the economies showing the greatest growth in the last 100 years, namely Sweden, Japan and Korea, there are relatively narrow pay differentials and in the cases of Japan and Korea these are societies which reward and respect group rather than merely individual performance. It is also worth reminding ourselves that social surveys suggest that respondents in Central and Eastern Europe would have preferred and still prefer a controlled movement towards a Swedish style mixed economy rather than the shock treatment received by some, albeit not all of these economies in transition. To quote McIntyre:

> The 'new democracies' are being directed onto a path which no countries have success-fully followed, after the free-market and minimal government experiences of the United Kingdom and the United States during the early phases of the so-called industrial revolu-tion of the 18th and 19th Centuries. Even the 19th Century, classical liberal economic policy was more talked about than followed and now it appears to be anomalous. Unfortunately consideration of neither the subtle facts of advanced capitalist institutional differentiation nor their connection to performance seem to be playing a significant role in contemporary discussions of systems design in eastern Europe.   (McIntyre, 1992: 4)

And Voskamp and Wittke (1991):

> recent work in economic history is making it increasingly clear that successful cases of industrialization (for example nineteenth century Germany and twentieth century Japan) were not simple copies of a dominant standard of international efficiency. Instead success involved the adaptation of exogenously developed models of industrial organization to local political, economic and social conditions (markets, social structure, educational system, and mentality).   (Voskamp and Wittke, 1991: 342).

We as authors are engaged in speculation; perhaps even as you read this book events will have changed which either substantiate or repudiate the views currently being put forward in the community of economic psychology and socio-economics. Nevertheless there is great concern, a concern that will continue, about the rise of individualism and the demise of communitarianism. The thrust of neo-classical economics is individualistic, based on rational *individual* economic actors. The power and influence of economists have increased; they not only describe the eco-nomic world, they aid and abet in shaping it and the economic mind alongside it. The adoption of the neo-classical paradigm is virtually world-wide. And as Wight (1992) puts it:

> privatisation of state-owned enterprises, and other efficiency enhancing measures have become the new focus of economic development . . . the transition to market economies could lead to frustration and ultimate repudiation, however, if the central value of the community – as opposed to the individual – is ignored in the rush to modernize.

The rise and rise of individualism has been a consistent characteristic of most western democracies if the social survey evidence is to be accepted (Glen, 1990). Glen makes a useful distinction between 'liberal individualism' and 'conservative individualism', 'liberal individualism' refers to a lessening of allegiance to institu-tions such as the church and the family, a diminution of social identification as a function of sex, race and colour; on the other hand 'conservative individualism' is the freedom to choose in the marketplace, freedom from the interventions of the state. The worry for commentators such as Wight (1992) is that while the move towards the 'freedom' of individualism is understandable in the new democracies, do we want these countries simply to import selfishness and acquisitiveness, and to loose sight of communitarian values? Even if one concentrates solely on economic interests a market cannot work without trust and at least some consideration for others mixed with an incentive to satisfy one's individual desires. If it were simply based on self-centredness the system would soon fall apart. The strong version of this view is Etzioni's statement that 'The more people accept the neoclassical paradigm as a guide for their behaviour, the more the ability to sustain a market economy is undermined' (Etzioni, 1988: 250).

There is now a vast literature on attitude change and attitude structure in social psychology. Unfortunately a lot of it is itself individualistic and is not as illuminating as it might be in this context. What can be said with confidence is that people do not change their attitudes at the drop of a hat, at least not those which are salient, and that the way attitudes are assessed, measured and recorded is of some importance. Contemporary wisdom recommends, at least in European social psychology, that attitudes are not the possession of individuals; they are social and 'owned' by groups and societies – they are not the invention of a contemplative soul in a garret. Most people seek social approval, and attitudes expressed in a social context – on the street, on the bus, in casual conversation – are attitudes which, to some degree, are shared by others. People, both as individuals and cultures, have a repertoire of attitudes and beliefs – some deeply held, others not, some for public consumption, others hidden – that can be contradictory or apparently contradictory: we can both like and dislike the same person, we can agree that tobacco seriously damages health but continue to smoke, to welcome capitalism and reject it. Citizens of Central and Eastern Europe were never totally, unambiguously communist, nor will they ever be totally capitalistic – alternatives to communism were present in protean form but needed other people to articulate them, to give them form. As Kuran (1992) explains, even during the Stalinist terror campaigns families and friends shared 'private' thoughts. But it is well-nigh impossible to develop a deep understanding in secrecy. While people are now free to think, they do not necessarily know what to think with – it is quite a different thing to say in reply to a questionnaire that you believe agriculture should be privatised and to have an articulate view of an unfamiliar economic system. Besides answers to survey questionnaires we need to delve into the private views of citizens as well as their 'public' views, the things that they hold dear as well as the things they will let go, researchers need to listen to people talking, to try and get inside their heads, to see economies in transition from participants point of view.

## Conclusions

In this chapter we have argued that the costs of economic transformation in the former communist states are, and will continue to be, immense. We have stressed that a key, if not *the* key, to success is a change in the economic mind of the citizens of these states. Yet we have shown that the legacies of communism include an economic mind set which is largely antithetical to that needed to drive a market system.

We traced the impact of the old ways of thinking, as well as some changes in those habits in the results of opinion polls, and in some case studies of worker and managerial change. We stressed that these economies and their economic actors have had experiences very different from those of the citizens of developed democratic states. The process of economic restructuring has barely begun, and the socialisation of citizens into market economy psychological responses is in its infancy. It is clear that it will take at least a generation. It is not clear that in all countries it will succeed.

# PART VI

# Conclusions

# Chapter 12

# Digestif

## The deconstructed economic mind

This is not the place to review all that has gone before but it is the place to consider where we might go from here. We have confidence that economic psychology and the 'greens' have an important future. Economic minds will have to change; any progress must be psychological as well as technological. Similarly the political upheavals of Central and Eastern Europe will stretch human adaptability to its limits. In social psychology and beyond, interest in 'lay explanations' shows no signs of abating. Studies on economic socialisation will continue to contribute essential data for developmental psychology. Last but not least (although coverage in the present volume is not as great as it would be in a text with a less 'social' emphasis) is the contribution to cognitive psychology and decision-making research. In all these fields contemporary research is becoming more qualitative and contextual in orientation.

The growth of economic (social) psychology forms part of the greater growth of information world-wide. Alan Lewis gave a paper at the Economics Department of the University of Connecticut not so long ago and in the discussion that followed an overheard comment from an economist in the audience ran: 'What really worries me is that I might have to know some of this.'

The main audience for our book comprises social psychologists, allied social scientists and educated 'lay' people in the private and public sectors; but economists have a place in the stalls too. If nothing else, the message that a broader utility function needs to be considered is at least getting through. Nevertheless and besides not wanting to do more perhaps unnecessary work, economists can feel threatened. Economists, after all, have a well-worked-out research programme, some economists even believe that there is not much more to be found out and indeed within the methodological and epistemological limits that the mainstream discipline sets itself there may even be some truth in this view. Any moves towards a more behavioural analysis will be cautious ones and the fodder of economists with a behavioural orientation, such as Earl (1983), Baxter (1993) and Frank (1988), is easier to swallow and digest than the richer and more varied fare of psychologists writing primarily for psychologists. But there are exceptions to this rule: the work of Kahnemann and his colleagues in particular *is* psychological but has direct relevance to 'unsolved' problems in economics such as 'stickiness of wage rates' and savings ratios. There is a tendency to recognise that social surveys have a usefulness in the 'new economics' as do carefully controlled experiments (Smith 1991; Hey, 1992).

The view that scientific progress in economics can be achieved by mainly technical means is still commonplace: the discipline is simply not ready to embrace the postpositivism of our age; it could after all just be a fashion and many economists would feel self-conscious in new clothes. There is a danger after all in going too far along the path (if indeed it is one) of social constructionism and a normative economics: yes, we can change the world but only part of the world and its working can be known; there are some things 'out there' which are more than our social constructions of them. Economists do not want to let go of research, particularly deductive research, which is theory-led; economic psychology, they feel, is too inductive and unfocused in comparison.

The three of us were all originally trained as social psychologists, Alan in the depths of South Wales, Paul and Adrian at the London School of Economics. Our PhD theses were on reciprocal communications, children's understanding of deception and person/situation interactions respectively. We have moved a long way since then, although traces of our original interests are no doubt still apparent in the earlier chapters of this book. But although we may sometimes stress other aspects of our identities (Adrian is fond of portraying himself as a personality and individual differences man, Alan and Paul prefer to be known as economic psychologists), being social psychologists is very important to us. So, as well as regularly attending conferences of organisations like SASE (Society for the Advancement of Socio-Economics), SABE (Society for the Advancement of Behavioural Economics) and IAREP (International Association for Research in Economic Psychology), we still, when straightened university budgets permit, attend social psychology conferences. And what we hear at these conferences is strikingly different. SASE has a mission; it is out to change the world (particularly America) in theory and in practice. This strong streak of idealism means that SASE conference papers are, sometimes, long on rhetoric but short on data. IAREP (and SABE) members, by contrast, are nearly always empirical. The data may not always have been collected by the time of the annual gathering but the defining characteristic of papers given on these occasions is data or the promise of data, mostly, but not always, of a quantitative nature. Social psychology conferences (at least those held in Britain) are another matter. Here we hear talk of discourse, rhetoric, ideology and power; of social constructivism (and deconstruction) and of the crisis in social psychology that we thought had been overcome in the early 1970s (Parker, 1989).

These contemporary movements in social psychology have had a notable impact, albeit perhaps a delayed one, on research into economic behaviour and it is to these issues that we devote this last chapter. What we say here may seem impossibly out of date in five years' time (perhaps it will then be time for *The Renewed Economic Mind?*) but to conclude without some signposts to the future and some meditations on epistemological issues and methods would be evasive: and, as might be inferred from our discourse in Part IV, we take moral issues seriously.

## Rhetoric

McCloskey (1990), for one, is of the opinion that there is now a 'crisis in economics' and that the study of rhetoric is the best way to develop an alternative, postmodern approach to economics. McCloskey's aim has been to deconstruct, demystify and debunk the 'pretensions' of mainstream economics. This work has much in common with writings on the sociology of scientific knowledge (SSK) (Bloor 1976). SSK has, for example, explored the claims of physics (Collins and Pinch, 1982), health economics (Ashmore, Mulkay and Pinch, 1989) and most recently macro-economic modelling (Evans, 1993).

To summarise, the claims of SSK are that what scientists actually do in generating scientific 'facts' is rather different from what one might at first suppose: the 'facts' do not stand or fall according to empirical validation (or falsification); instead what constitutes acceptable knowledge is decided upon by social agreement and belief, rejected theories and findings falling from grace through ridicule, for being unfashionable, even by undermining the credibility of researchers. In SSK the scientists are viewed as a tribe with languages and rites of passage all their own: physicists, medics, economists are not trained, they are 'enculturated' in a belief system and way of looking at the world, which to outsiders is far from commonsensical. For Evans (1993) economists, and in his case well-known macro-modellers, maintain their boundaries from attack from these outsiders, yet, perhaps surprisingly, are prepared to admit, at least to Evans, that economic data are capable of sustaining alternative hypotheses, have 'interpretative flexibility', even that macro-models of the economy are highly inaccurate.

Much of the literature in SSK, including that focusing on economics, has pushed Humpty Dumpty off the wall but has done little or nothing about putting him back together again. The work of Klamer (1983) is a little more optimistic, placing emphasis on 'commonsense' economics and the belief that the ideas of 'ordinary' economic agents influence economic behaviour and in turn the economy; which has considerable overlap with the research on lay explanations reviewed in our earlier chapters. Klamer quotes Robert Lucas, a distinguished colleague of Becker's, on the differentiation of the 'science' of economics and being a 'person', or 'ordinary economic actor': 'In my house we don't use words like "marginal" everyday. I don't find the language of economics to be useful to think about individual decision problems. I never pay my children to do their jobs. I try to use family loyalty or an exchange system: you help me, I'll help you' (Klamer, 1983: 48).

There has also been recent research (not necessarily in the SSK tradition) on the economic decisions of politicians and the media. Most interesting has been the work of Emmison (1983), who carried out a content analysis of newspapers and magazines to explore the metaphors employed, and Rae and Drury (1993), who have looked specifically at reasoning and rhetoric in 'quality' newspapers. Emmison carried out a qualitative content analysis of twentieth-century newspapers and magazines in an attempt to discover when the term 'the economy' entered public discourse. He found that although there were many references to the idea of 'economy' prior to the 1930s, these all used the term in the sense of a frugal and careful use of resources. An example would be 'railway companies are acting out of motives of economy rather than passenger safety' (*The Times*, 1840). In the 1920s the expression 'the economic system' appears, which although today is sometimes used synonymously with 'the economy' was then used as an alternative term for capitalism; in other words, a particular mode of production. 'The economy' is first used in a modern sense in the 1930s. What is particularly interesting is that initially the dominant metaphorical usage is passive (the economy has things done to it) but in the postwar period there is a change to more active metaphors and an increasing anthropomorphism. Contrast these quotations: 'The British national economy has been converted from one based on competitive free enterprise into one whose strategic centres are controlled' (*Economist*, 1940); 'Since the US economy came through the first quarter full of vigour, expressions of doubt about its health have all but disappeared' (*Time*, 1957); 'We were too optimistic about what we or the economy, working in partnership could perform' (Australian PM Fraser, in *National Times*, 1979). Here the shift from passive object to active partner is well illustrated.

Emmison's claim is that this change in the usage of the term 'the economy' is not just a socio-linguistic curiosity, but that it has ideological implications. The current usage treats the economy as a super-person who is on no one's side, an entity who has to be taken for granted, who is part of an arrangement that cannot be challenged. In other words, current usage legitimises capitalist arrangements by reifying them.

Rae and Drury put forward a similar argument. They examined a sample of articles published in *The Financial Times* and *The Guardian* in the final quarter of 1990, an eventful period which saw the fall of Mrs Thatcher the former prime minister of the United Kingdom. They describe the various rhetorical strategies that the newspapers use to make a case for, and that government ministers use to problematise, the existence of a recession. For example, the newspapers used the device of juxtaposing news-telling with reported speech, as in:

> On a day marked by job losses, corporate collapses and a profits fall at ICI, John Major the current British Prime Minister told the Commons 'I can certainly confirm that output is slowing and has been slowing over the period of the last two months.'

Government ministers introduce definitional considerations and present the recession as a bureaucratic matter, as Major does when he says 'As to whether it is wi, in the normal definition of recession, which is, of course, why my officials and sub sequently I, use that term, it is a matter we shall soon see.' This is essentially saying that an answer to the question 'Are we in recession?' simply depends on what defini- tion you use and the reference to officials suggests that the issue is a technical one.

Rae and Drury go on to analyse the metaphors used by newspapers when dealing with the recession. They claim that two main groups of metaphors are present in the material: those which present the recession as something that can hit, cut or bite ('With recession biting deeper analysts expect an intensification of the burger wars with consumers hungry for bargains'), and those which use movement imagery ('The CBI yesterday urged the Government to haul the economy out of recession'). Weather metaphors are also popular, such as 'the hurricane of high interest rates' and 'Fiat and Olivetti battening down the hatches for recession'. These metaphors are deployed in arguments which construct the economy and the recession as some- thing separate, as a thing in its own right (as is evident in the 'biting' extract), a ten- dency which Rae and Drury point out is also shown by researchers, commentators and politicians. This could be merely linguistic (though we can talk about being ill as well as having an illness, we cannot say that we will 'be' a recession) but, like Emmison, Rae and Drury argue that the discourses they describe are ideological. They present a situation of exploitation as legitimate by reifying current economic and social relationships as natural. As they put it 'Like commodity fetishism, the discourses . . . collapse contigent, social processes (the economy) and relationships (between people and capital) into natural and necessary ones'.

One does not need to accept these Marxist interpretations, but this kind of analy- sis forces us to consider the bases of our own constructions of the economy and its processes.

## Identity, communication and economic behaviour

The idea that economic behaviour has an important communicative function was most famously put forward by Veblen (1899/1979), who claimed that there was a general tendency for conspicuous consumption, that is, the deliberate purchase of expensive goods purely to display wealth. The notion that economic behaviour is essentially expressive or communicative has been developed by Douglas and Isherwood (1980), as we briefly described in Chapter 4, and most recently by McCracken (1990), Lunt and Livingstone (1992) and Dittmar (1992).

McCracken talks about symbolic consumption and treats products as a kind of language through which people communicate and construct notions of self. Thus:

> The meanings of consumer goods and the meaning creation accomplished by consumer processes are important parts of the scaffolding of our present realities. Without con- sumer goods, certain acts of self-definition and collective definition in this culture would be impossible. (p. ix)

McCracken reports a series of studies on how people decode clothing. Respondents were presented with slides of people in various outfits (conventional, conventional items in unusual combinations, idiosyncratic items) and asked what they could tell about the target figure on the basis of their clothing. With the conventional outfits people responded instantly whereas the other two kinds of slides caused people interpretative problems. From these findings, McCracken concluded that although products may well be communicative, the rules of combination which apply to language do not apply to consumer goods. Separate clothing items do not convey bits of information, but the whole ensemble conveys a message. If material goods are a relatively poor form of communication why then are they used for communicative purposes at all? Part of the answer is that they are particularly good at expressing social category membership and so help maintain the status quo. This makes this form of communication ideological, in that it supports current economic and social relationships.

Lunt and Livingstone base their analysis on a social constructionist perspective; that is, they assume that people act according to their perceptions of social and economic reality and that this reality is based on shared belief systems. It is these ordinary understandings that make economic life meaningful and enable people to locate themselves in relation to others; hence Lunt and Livingstone's focus on lay accounts, beliefs and explanations. We have considered the details of their findings on debt and savings in earlier chapters; here, we just want to deal with their more general perspective. Their conclusion is that people now have to construct and continually reconstruct their identities within two opposing discourses about consumerism. One discourse sees the consumer society as progressive, as providing opportunities, as empowering people: the other sees it as regressive, as trapping people in a materialist treadmill. This can be seen very clearly in people's comments about the second-hand market. Second-hand goods were described by some people as symbolic of poverty and an outmoded class system, but for others buying second-hand goods was a way of resisting the consumer culture. One respondent gives an insight into both perspectives:

> When I have been involved in working in jobs with people who collect the wage packet at the end of the week and then go and spend it in shops, I have always been confronted with the attitude that they would never do as I do – get things from skips, jumble sales or second-hand shops. They have none of the pride I have in preserving something that would otherwise have gone to waste. Their pride is in having something produced for them, brand new, untouched by human hands.   (Lunt and Livingstone, 1992: 148)

Dittmar (1992) provides a complementary insight into the importance of identities in economic behaviour. As she makes clear, the symbolic meanings of possessions are crucial both in expressing one's own identity and in perceiving the identity of others. Thus men and women not only prefer different objects, but relate to their possessions in different ways: men have activity-related, functional and self-oriented concerns, whereas women see their relationships with possessions in a symbolic and relational way. So a man's motorbike might be seen as a means of transport (functional) and as differentiating him from others. The most important objects for women, on the other hand, tended to be sentimental possessions which symbolised their relationships with others. Possessions are also a powerful cue: students who read different descriptions of an individual in which material possessions were varied systematically came to very different conclusions about the individuals personal qualities. Wealthy individuals were seen as more forceful and in control of their environment but also as lacking warmth and expressiveness.

The three contributions we have discussed here are just part of a movement which draws together traditional consumer research and other disciplines like social psychology, sociology and anthropology: in this context we could also have considered the work of Belk (1988) and Solomon (1983). What makes them valuable is that they draw our attention away from decision-making processes and force us to take the social and emotional aspects of goods seriously.

## Postmodern economic behaviour

In March 1992 one of us attended a symposium entitled 'The future of economic psychology', where the speakers had been invited to reflect on trends in the discipline and their hopes for the future. The most entertaining talk (or rather performance) was given by Fred van Raaij, who walked on stage with a ghetto blaster and proceeded to stun the audience with slides of postmodern architecture and art, interspersed with ironic commentary and witty remarks. A permanent record of this talk (sadly without the pictures and the music) can be found in van Raaij (1993). In this paper he characterises the postmodern condition and sketches the relevance of this for consumer behaviour. So what is postmodernism? Dr Criminale, the eponymous hero of Malcolm Bradbury's (1992) book, summed it up in his keynote address:

> The postmodern condition . . . was something more than a post-technological situation, a phenomenon of late capitalism, a loss of narratives. . . . What it most resembled, he said, was his own situation now – jet-lagged, culture-shocked, stuffed with too much in-flight food and too much vacant in-flight entertainment, mind disordered, body gross, thoughts hectic and hypertense, spirits dislodged from space and time, baggageless, without normal possessions.

Put another way, the postmodern era is the period of the information revolution, of globalism, of fragmented culture: there are no dominant ideologies anymore and pluralism is everywhere. This can be neatly seen in architecture. Modern architecture had a message, be it functionalism, minimalism or formalism; postmodern architecture does not: the keywords here are irony, parody, lost innocence, hyperreality.

How does this relate to economic behaviour? Van Raaij describes the four major postmodern characteristics of consumption as fragmentation, hyper-reality, value realisation later in the consumption cycle and paradoxical juxtapositions of opposites. We will describe these briefly.

Fragmentation applies to both the demand and the supply side. Many modern

...sion programmes offer fragmented bits of entertainment, information and music; mass production produces more varieties and personalised versions of products: consumers opt for multiple life-styles which are dependent on the product domain. There is no longer one dominant style but many genres and postmodern consumers are encouraged by marketing to switch images, to have many selves and self-images. Associated with this fragmentation is an increased individualisation.

Hyper-reality refers to simulations of reality. Instead of dealing with the 'real', consumers are increasingly part of the hyper-real: DisneyWorld and museums which create 'staged authenticity' are good examples, but so too are the Balinese religious ceremonies that have become detached from their cultural background and become a tourist spectacle.

The traditional view was that value is created by production and destroyed in consumption, later modified to the notion that value is created in the exchange of goods. For the postmodern consumer, identity is created and maintained by consumption rather than by production and thus value is realised through usage, that is, much later in the consumption cycle.

Perhaps the most important characteristic of postmodern consumer culture is its paradoxical nature. Anything can be combined with anything and 'anything is at once acceptable and suspect.' The Benetton advertisements which showed a dying AIDS patient are a good example of postmodern marketing. The market legitimises everything.

For those studying economic behaviour the postmodern condition is a challenge both to theory and to methodology, though we should remember that for those in the non-western world talk of 'an *embarras de riches* and an *embarras des choix*' (van Raaij, 1993: 542) rings a little hollow. Consumers who are self-conscious parodists fond of ironical twists are not easy to study; it is certainly hard to imagine what one would make of a questionnaire filled in by such an individual. The kind of reflexive theory one would require to explain their behaviour boggles the imagination. But these are challenges for the future.

We hope that the intellectual nourishment that we have provided is of better than in-flight standard and that the reader has been stimulated, but not made hypertense. And we remain optimistic that more imaginative research will make a real contribution to dealing with some of the social problems facing us.

# References

Abdul-Muhmin, A. G., Nyhus, E. K. and Rønqvist, M. (1993) 'What is the residual: saving or consumption?', in S.V. Malakhov (ed.), *Economic Psychology and Behavioral Economics* Moscow: Academy of National Economy.

Abrahamson, A. (1980) 'Sudden wealth, gratification and attainment: Durkheim's anomie of affluence reconsidered', *American Sociological Review*, 45, 49–57.

Abramovitch, R., Freedman, J.L. and Pliner, P. (1991). 'Children and money: getting an allowance, credit versus cash, and knowledge of pricing', *Journal of Economic Psychology*, 12, 27–46.

Adams, J. (1965) 'Inequality in social exchange', in L. Berkowitz (ed.), *Advances in Experimental Social Psychology*, vol. 2, New York: Academic Press.

Aitken, S. and Bonneville, E. (1980) *A General Taxpayer Opinion Survey*, Washington, DC: CSR.

Aldag, R. and Brief, A. (1975) 'Some correlates of work values', *Journal of Applied Psychology*, 60, 757–60.

Ali, A. (1988) 'Scaling an Islamic work ethic', *Journal of Social Psychology*, 128, 575–83.

Ali, A. (1993) 'The islamic work ethic in Arabia', *Journal of Psychology*, 126, 507–19.

Allen, V. (1970) *Psychological Factors in Poverty*, Chicago: Markham.

Allerhand, M., Friedlander, F., Malone, J., Meadow, H. and Rosenberg, M. (1969) *A Study of the Impact and Effectiveness of the Comprehensive Manpower Project of Cleveland*, Department of Labor.

Allingham, M. G. and Sandmo, A. (1972) 'Income tax evasion: a theoretical analysis', *Journal of Public Economics*, 1, 323–38.

Alves, W. and Rossi, P. (1978) 'Who should get what? Fairness, judgements of the distribution of earnings', *American Journal of Sociology*, 84, 541–63.

Amerikis, A., Field, H., Holly, W., Bedenan, A and Ledbetter. B. (1977) 'Human resource considerations in textile work redesign', *Human Relations*, 30, 1147–1156.

Angus Reid Group (1992) *Canadians and the Environment*, Vancouver, BC: Angus Reid Group.

Antaki, C. (1988) *Analysing Everyday Explanations*, Beverly Hills: Sage.

Arber, S. (1987) 'Social class, non-employment and chronic illness: continuing inequalities in the health debate', *British Medical Journal*, 294, 1069–73.

Argyle, M. (1983) *The Social Psychology of Work*, Harmondsworth: Penguin.

Argyle, M. (1988) *The Psychology of Happiness*, London: Routledge.

Argyle, M., Furnham, A. and Graham, G. (1981) *Social Situations*, Cambridge: Cambridge University Press.

Armenakis, A., Fields, H., Bederan, A. and Ledbetter, B. (1977) 'Human resource considerations in textile work redesign', *Human Relations*, 30, 1147–56.

Ashmore, M., Mulkay, M. and Pinch, T. (1989) *Health and Efficiency: A sociology of health economics*. Milton Keynes: Open University Press.

Axelrod, L. and Lehman, D. (1993) 'Responding to environmental concerns: what factors guide individual action?' *Journal of Environmental Psychology*, 13, 149–59.

Ayllon, T. and Azin, N. (1968) *The Token Economy: A motivational system for therapy and rehabilitation*, New York: Appleton–Century–Crofts.

Ayllon, T. and Roberts, M. (1974) 'Eliminating discipline problems by strengthening academic performance', *Journal of Applied Behaviour Analysis*, 7, 71–6.

Bagguley, P. and Mann, K. (1992) 'Idle thieving bastards? Scholarly representations of the "underclass"', *Work Employment and Society*, 6, 113–26.

Bakke, E. (1933) *The Unemployed Man*, London: Nisbett.

Bakke, E. (1940) *Citizens without Work*, New Haven: Yale University Press.

Banks, M. and Jackson, P. (1982) 'Unemployment and risk of minor psychiatric disorder in young people: cross-sectional and longitudinal evidence', *Psychological Medicine*, 12, 789–98.

Banks, M., Clegg, C., Jackson, P., Kemp, N., Stafford, E. and Wall, T. (1980) 'The use of the General Health Questionnaire as an indicator of mental health in occupational studies', *Journal of Occupational Psychology*, 53, 186–94.

Barnett, S. and Saxon-Harrold, S. (1992) 'Interim report: charitable giving' in R. Jowell, R., Brook, L., Prior, G. and Taylor, B. (eds). *British Social Attitudes* (ninth Report), Aldershot: Dartmouth.

Bartlett, W. (1992) 'Privatization and quasi-markets in public sector delivery in the UK', in F. Targetti (ed.), *Privatization in Europe: West and east experiences*, Aldershot and Vermont: Dartmouth.

Baxter, J. (1975) 'The chronic job changer: a study of youth unemployment', *Social and Economic Administration*, 9, 184–206.

Baxter, J. (1993) *Behavioural Foundations of Economics*, New York: St Martin's.

Beale, N. and Nethercott, S. (1985) 'Job loss and family morbidity: A study of factory closure', *Journal of the Royal College of General Practitioners*, 35, 510–14.

Beales, H. and Lambert, R. (eds) (1934) *Memoirs of the Unemployed*, London: Gollancz.

Bean, L. H. (1946) 'Relation of disposable income and the business cycle to expenditures', *Review of Economics and Statistics*, 28, 199–207.

Becker, G. (1976) *The Economic Approach to Human Behaviour*. Chicago: University of Chicago Press.

Becker, G. S. (1992) 'Habits, addictions and traditions', *Kyklos*, 45, 327–46.

Becker, G. S. and Murphy, K. M. (1988) 'A theory of rational addiction', *Journal of Political Economy*, 96, 675–700.

Behrend, H. (1988) 'The wage-work bargain', *Managerial and Decision Economics*, special issue, 51–7.

Beiser, M. (1965) 'Poverty, social disintegration and personality', *Journal of Social Issues*, 1, 56–78.

Beit-Hallahmi, B. (1979) 'Personal and social components of the Protestant ethic', *Journal of Social Psychology*, 109, 263–7.

Belk, R. W. (1984) 'Three scales to measure constructs related to materialism – reliability, validity and their relationship to measures of happiness', *Advances in Consumer Research*, 11, 291–7.

Belk, R. W. (1985) 'Materialism: trait aspects of living in the material world', *Journal of Consumer Research*, 12, 265–80.

Belk, R. W. (1988) 'Possessions and the extended self', *Journal of Consumer Research*, 15, 139–68.

Belk, R. W. and Wallendorf, M. (1990) 'The sacred meanings of money' *Journal of Economic Psychology*, 11, 35–67.

Bellack, A. and Hersen, M. (1980) *Introduction to Clinical Psychology*, Oxford: Oxford University Press.

Beloff, H. (1957) 'The structure and origin of the anal character', *Genetic Psychology Monograph*, 55, 141–72.

Benjamini, Y. and Maital, S. (1985) 'Optimal tax evasion and optimal tax evasion policy: behavioral aspects', in W. Gärtner and A. Wenig (eds), *The Economics of the Shadow Economy*, Berlin: Springer.

Benzion, U., Rapoport, A. and Yagil, J. (1989) 'Discount rates inferred from decisions: an experimental study', *Management Science*, 35, 270–84.

Bergler, E. (1958) *The Psychology of Gambling*, London: Hanison.

Berk, R., Lenihan, K. and Rossi, P. (1980) 'Crime and poverty: some experimental evidence from ex-offenders', *American Sociological Review*, 45, 766–86.

Berlyne, D. (1960) *Conflict, Arousal and Curiosity*, New York: McGraw-Hill.

Bernstein, B. (1962) 'Social class, linguistic codes and grammatical elements', *Language and Speech*, 5, 221–40.

Berthoud, R. and Kempson, E. (1990) *Credit and Debt in Britain: First Findings from the PSI survey*, London: Policy Studies Institute.

Berti, A. and Bombi, A. (1979) 'Where does money come from?', *Archivio di Psicologia*, 40, 53–77.

Berti, A. and Bombi, A. (1981) 'The development of the concept of money and its value: a longitudinal study', *Child Development*, 52, 1179–82.

Berti, A. and Bombi, A. (1988) *The Child's Construction of Economics*, Cambridge: Cambridge University Press.

Berti, A., Bombi, A. and de Beni, R. (1986) 'Acquiring economic notions: profit', *International Journal of Behavioural Development*, 9, 15–29.

Berti, A., Bombi, A. and Lis, A. (1982) 'The child's conceptions about means of production and their owners', *European Journal of Social Psychology*, 12, 221–239.

Biggart, N. (1983) 'Rationality, meaning, and self-management: success manuals, 1950–1980', *Social Problems*, 30, 298–311.

Blasi, G. (1990) 'Social policy and social science research on homelessness', *Journal of Social Issues*, 46, 207–19.

Blood, M. (1969) 'Work values and job satisfaction', *Journal of Applied Psychology*, 53, 456–9.

Bloor, D. (1976) *Knowledge and Social Imagery*, London: Routledge.

Böhm-Bewark, E. von (1891) *Capital and Interest*, trans. W. Smart, New York: Strechert.

Boor, M. (1980) 'Relationships between unemployment rates and suicide rates in eight countries, 1962–1976', *Psychological Reports*, 47, 1095–101.

Boustead, E., Cottee, K., Farquhar, R., Jonas, R., Walter, J. and Webley, P. (1992) 'The perceived value of a new coin', *Journal of Social Psychology*, 132, 143–4.

Bowlby, J. (1969) *Attachment and Loss*, London: Hogarth.

Bowles, R. and Jones, P. (1993) 'Nonpayment of Poll Tax: an exploratory analysis of tax resistance', *International Review of Law and Economics*, 13, 445–55.

Bradburn, N. (1969) *The Structure of Psychological Well-Being*, Chicago: Aldine.

Bradbury, M. (1992) *Doctor Criminale*, Harmondworth: Penguin.

Brandstätter, H. (1992) 'Individual differences: should economic psychology care about them?', paper presented at the IAREP colloquium, Frankfurt.

Brandstätter, H. (1993a) 'Should economic psychology care about personality structure?', *Journal of Economic Psychology*, 14, 473–94.

Brandstätter, H. (1993b) 'Personality structure as a determinant of saving behaviour', paper presented at the IAREP colloquium, Moscow.

Branyiczki, I., Bakacsi, G. and Pearce, J. (1992) 'The back door: spontaneous privatization in Hungary', Annual of Public and Cooperative Economics, 63 (2), 303–16.

Brenner, S. and Bartell, R. (1983) 'The psychological impact of unemployment: a structural analysis of cross-sectional data', Journal of Occupational Psychology, 56, 129–36.

Briar, R. (1977) 'The effect of long-term unemployment on workers and their families', Dissertation Abstracts International, 37, 60–2.

Brickman, P., Coates, D. and Janoff-Bulman, R. (1978) 'Lottery winners and accident victims?' Journal of Personality and Social Psychology, 36, 917–27.

Brown, C. V. and Jackson, P. M. (1978) Public Sector Economics, Oxford: Martin Robertson.

Brown, C. V., Levin, E. J., Rosa, P. J. and Ulph, D. T. (1984) 'Tax evasion and avoidance on earned income: some survey results', Fiscal Studies, 5, 1–22.

Bruce, V. (1989) 'Human factors in the design of coins', The Psychologist, 12, 524–7.

Bruce, V., Gilmore, D., Mason, L. and Mayhew, P. (1983a) 'Factors affecting the perceived value of coins', Journal of Economic Psychology, 4, 335–47.

Bruce, V., Howarth, C., Clark-Carter, D., Dodds, A. and Heyes, A. (1983b) 'All change for the pound: human performance tests with different versions of the proposed UK one pound coin', Ergonomics, 26, 215–27.

Bruner, J. and Goodman, C. (1947) 'Value and need as organizing factors in perception', Journal of Abnormal and Social Psychology, 42, 33–44.

Bruyn, S. (1987) The Field of Social Investment, Cambridge: Cambridge University Press.

Buchholz, R. (1976) 'Measurement of beliefs', Human Relations, 29, 1177–88.

Buchholz, R. (1977) 'The belief structure of managers relative to work concepts measured by a factor analytic model', Personnel Psychology, 30, 567–587.

Buchholz, R. (1978) 'An empirical study of contemporary beliefs about work in American society', Journal of Applied Psychology, 63, 219–27.

Burgess, M. (1962) 'Poverty and dependency: some selected characteristics', Journal of Social Psychology, 47, 231–40.

Burgess, M. (1965) 'Poverty and dependency: some selected characteristics', Journal of Social Psychology, 47, 231–40.

Burgoyne, C. (1990) 'Money in marriage: how patterns of allocation both reflect and conceal power', Sociological Review, 38, 634–65.

Burgoyne, C. and Lewis, A. (1994) 'Distributive justice in marriage equality or equity?', Journal of Community and Applied Social Psychology, 4, 101–14.

Burgoyne, C. B. and Routh, D. A. (1991) 'Constraints on the use of money as a gift at Christmas: the role of status and intimacy', Journal of Economic Psychology, 12, 47–69.

Burgoyne, C., Roth, D., Marshall, G., Swift, A. and Roberts, S. (1994) 'Contested boundaries and the justice of the market' (submitted for publication).

Burns, R. (1981) The Self Concept: Theory, measurement, development and behaviour, London: Longman.

Burris, V. (1983) 'Stages in the development of economic concepts', Human Relations, 9, 791–812.

Calderwood. G. B. and Webley, P. (1992) 'Who responds to changes in taxation? The relationship between taxation and the incentive to work', Journal of Economic Psychology, 13, 735–48.

Caldwell, B. (ed.) (1984) Appraisal and Criticism in Economics, Boston: Allen and Unwin.

Cantril, H. (1965) The Patterns of Human Concerns, New Brunswick NJ: Rutgers University Press.

Carlson, J. and Parkin, M. (1975) 'Inflation expectations', Economica, 42, 123–38.

Carlson, L. and Grossbart, S. (1988) 'Parental style and consumer socialization of children', *Journal of Consumer Research*, 15, 77–94.

Carroll, J. S. (1992) 'How taxpayers think about their taxes: frames and values', in J. Slemrod (ed.), *Why People Pay Taxes: Tax compliance and enforcement*, Ann Arbor: University of Michigan Press.

Carstairs, V. and Morris, R. (1989) 'Deprivation: explaining differences in morality between Scotland and England and Wales', *British Medical Journal*, 299, 886–9.

Carter, C. (1971) *Wealth: An essay on the purpose of economics*, Harmondsworth: Pelican.

Catalano, R. and Dooley, C. (1977) 'Economic predictors of depressed mood and stressful life events', *Journal of Health and Social Behaviour*, 18, 292–307.

Catalano, R. and Dooley, C. (1979) 'The economy as stressor: a sectoral analysis', *Review of Social Economy*, 37, 175–88.

*Charity Trends*, 11th edn, 1987/8.

Chizmar, J. and Halinski, R. (1983) 'Performance in the Basic Economic Test (BET) and "Trade-offs"', *Journal of Economic Education*, 14, 18–29.

Claxton, J., Ritchie, J. and McDougall, G. (1983) 'Evaluating acceptability and effectiveness of consumer energy conservation programs', *Journal of Economic Psychology*, 4, 71–83.

Clower, R. W. and Johnson, M. B. (1968) 'Income, wealth and the theory of consumption', in N. Wolfe (ed.). *Value, Capital and Growth*, Edinburgh: Edinburgh University Press.

Coates, K. and Silburn, R. (1970) *Poverty: The forgotton Englishmen*, Harmondsworth: Penguin.

Cochrane, R. (1983) *The Social Creation of Mental Illness*, London: Longman.

Cochrane, R. and Robertson, A. (1973) 'The life events inventory: a measure of the relative severity of psychosocial stressors', *Journal of Psychosomatic Research*, 17, 215–18.

Codere, H. (1968) 'Money-exchange systems and a theory of money', *Man*, 3, 557–77

Coffield, F. (1984) 'Learning to live with unemployment: what future for education in a world without jobs?', unpublished paper.

Cohen, M., Rea, S. and Lerman, R. (1970) 'Micro-model of labor supply', Bureau of Labor Statistics Staff Paper No. 4, Washington D.C.: US Government Printing Office.

Collins, H. and Pinch, T. (1982) *Frames of Meaning: The social construction of extraordinary science*, London: Routledge.

Connolly, K. (1985) 'Can there be a psychology for the third world?' *Bulletin of British Psychological Society*, 38, 249–357.

Cook, J., Hepworth, S., Wall, T. and Warr, P. (1981) *The Experience of Work*, London: Academic Press.

Cook, T. D. and Curtin, T. R. (1987) 'The mainstream and the underclass: why are the differences so salient and the similarities so unobstrusive', in J. C. Masters and W. P. Smith (eds), *Social Comparison, Social Justice and Relative Deprivation: Theoretical, empirical and policy perspectives*, Hillsdale NJ: Lawrence Erlbaum.

Cook, V. (1971) 'A comparison of work values of disadvantaged black males with the work values of advantaged black males in an urban setting', PhD thesis, Washington, Catholic University.

Cooper, C. and Davidson, M. (1982) *High Pressure: Working lives of women managers*, London: Fontana.

Cordes, J. J., Galper, H. and Kirby, S. N. (1990) 'Causes of over-withholding: forced saving transaction costs?', working paper, George Washington University, Economics Department.

Cornish, D. B. (1978) *Gambling: A review of the literature*, London: Home Office Research Study, no. 42.

Coser, L. (1964) *The Functions of Conflict*, New York: Free Press.

Coughlin, R. (1982) *Ideology, Public Opinion and Welfare Policy*, Institute of International Studies, University of California, Berkeley.

Coward, B., Feagin, J. and William, J. (1974) 'The culture of poverty debate: some additional data', *Social Problems*, 21, 621–34.

Cowell, F. A. (1990) *Cheating the Government*, Cambridge, MA: MIT Press.

Cowell, F. A. (1992) 'Tax evasion and inequity', *Journal of Economic Psychology*, 13, 521–43.

Cram, F. and Ng, S. (1989) 'Children's endorsement of ownership attributes', *Journal of Economic Psychology*, 10, 63–75.

Crow, J. (1970) 'Do genetic factors contribute to poverty?', in V. Allen (ed.), *Psychological Factors in Poverty*, Chicago: Markham.

Cullis, J. and Lewis, A. (1985) 'Some hypotheses and evidence on tax knowledge and preferences', *Journal of Economic Psychology*, 6, 271–87.

Cullis, J., Jones, P. and Morrissey, O. (1993a) 'Evaluating the Poll Tax as a tax reform', *Local Government Studies*, 19, 77–91.

Cullis, J., Jones, P. and Morrissey, O. (1993b) 'The charge of the tax brigade: a case study of government failure and tax reforms', *European Journal of Political Economy*, 9, 407–25.

Cullis, J., Lewis, A. and Winnett, A. (1992) 'Paying to be good? UK ethical investments'. *Kyklos*, 45 (1), 3–24.

Cummings, S. and Taebel, V. (1978) 'The economic socialisation of children: a neo-Marxist analysis', *Social Problems*, 26, 198–210.

Dahlbäck, O. (1990) 'Personality and risk-taking', *Personality and Individual Differences*, 11, 1235–42.

Dahlbäck, O. (1991) 'Saving and risk taking', *Journal of Economic Psychology*, 12, 479–500.

Dalton, G. (1971) *Economic Anthropology and Development*, London: Basic Books.

Dancy, J. (1978) 'Education about unemployment: a reflective element', *Oxford Review of Education*, 4, 289–94.

Danziger, K. (1958) 'Children's earliest conception of economic relationships', *Journal of Social Psychology*, 47, 231–40.

Davidson, C. and Gaitz, C. (1974) 'Are the poor different? A comparison of work behaviour and attitudes among the urban poor and non-poor', *Social Problems*, 22, 229–45.

Davidson, D. and Kilgore, J. (1971) 'A model for evaluating the effectiveness of economic education in primary grades', *Journal of Economic Education*, 3, 17–25.

Davies, C. (1992) 'The Protestant ethic and the comic spirit of capitalism', *British Journal of Sociology*, 43, 421–42.

Davis, E., Grube, J. and Morgan, M. (1984) 'Attitudes towards poverty and related social issues in Ireland', unpublished report, Trinity College, Dublin.

Davis, J. (1991) *The Greening of Business*, Oxford: Blackwell.

Davis, K. and Taylor, R. (1979) *Kids and Cash: Solving a parent's dilemma*, La Jolla, CA: Oak Tree.

Dawson, J. (1975) 'Socio-economic differences in size-judgements of discs and coins by Chinese Primary VI children in Hong Kong', *Perceptual and Motor Skills*, 41, 107–10.

Dayton, C. (1981) 'The young person's job search: insights from a study', *Journal of Counselling Psychology*, 28, 321–33.

de Groot, H. and Pommer, E. (1987) 'Budget-games and the private and social demand for mixed public goods', *Public Choice*, 52, 257–72.

de Groot, H. and Pommer, E. (1989) 'The stability of stated preferences for public goods: evidence from recent budget-games', *Public Choice*, 60, 123–32.

de Kam, F. (1992) 'Tax reform: dreaming about tough realities', *Journal of Economic Psychology*, 13, 679–86.

Deacon, A. (1978) 'The scrounging controversy: public attitudes towards the unemployed in contemporary Britain', *Social and Economic Administration*, 12, 120–35.

Dholakia, R., Dholakia, N. and Firat, A. (1983) 'From social psychology to political economy: a model of energy use behaviour', *Journal of Economic Psychology*, 3, 231–47.

Dickerson, M. G. (1984) *Compulsive Gambling*, London: Longman.

Dickinson, J. (1990) 'Adolescent representation of socio-economic status', *British Journal of Development Psychology*, 8, 351–71.

Dickson, J. and Buchholz, R. (1977) 'Managerial beliefs about work in Scotland and the USA', *Journal of Management Studies*, 14, 80–101.

Dickson, J. and Buchholz, R. (1979) 'Differences in beliefs, about work between managers and blue-collar workers', *Journal of Management Studies*, 16, 235–51.

Diener, E., Horowitz, J. and Emmons, R. (1985) 'Happiness of the very wealthy', *Social Indicators Research*, 16, 263–74.

Dildine, L., (1987) 'Effects on Industry' in Pechman, J. A. (ed.), *Tax Reform and the U.S. Economy*, Washington, DC: Brookings.

Dillman, D., Rosa, E. and Dillman, J. (1983) 'Lifestyle and home energy consumption in the United States', *Journal of Economic Psychology*, 3, 299–315.

Dittmar, H. (1992) *The Social Psychology of Material Possessions: To have is to be*, Hemel Hempstead: Harvester Wheatsheaf.

Dohrenwend, B. and Dohrenwend, B. (1969) *Social Status and Psychological Disorder: A causal inquiry*, New York: Wiley.

Dominic, A. and Kinder, K. (1984) *Ethical Investing*, Reading, MA: Addison-Wesley.

Donaldson, C. and Gerard, K. (1993) *Economics of Health Care Financing*, London: Macmillan.

Donaldson, R. (1992) *Key Issues in Business Ethics*, London and New York: Academic Press.

Donaldson, T. (1992) *The Ethics of International Business*, Oxford: Oxford University Press.

Donovan, A. and Oddy, M. (1982) 'Psychosocial aspects of unemployment: an investigation into the emotional and social adjustment of school leavers', *Journal of Adolescence*, 5, 15–30.

Dooley, D and Catalano, R. (1979) 'Economic life, and disorder changes: time-series analyses', *American Journal of Community Psychology*, 7, 381–96.

Dooley, D. and Catalano, R. (1980) 'Economic change as a cause of behavioural disorder', *Psychological Bulletin*, 87, 450–68.

Douglas, M. (1982) *In the Active Voice*. London: Routledge and Kegan Paul.

Douglas, M. and Isherwood, B. (1980) *The World of Goods: Towards an anthropology of consumption*, Harmondsworth: Penguin.

Duesenberry, J. (1949) *Income, Saving and the Theory of Consumer Behaviour*, Cambridge, MA: Harvard University Press.

Dumais, J., Kinney, M. and Ricci, S. (1991) 'IRS efforts to help businesses: small business program initiatives', in J. Slemrod (ed.) *Closing the Tax Gap: Alternatives to Enforcement*, Washington DC: IRS document 7302.

Earl, P. (1983) *The Economic Imagination*, New York: Sharpe.

Easterlin, R. (1973) 'Does money buy happiness?', *The Public Interest*, 30, 3–10.

Easterlin, R. A. (1974) 'Does economic growth improve the human lot?', in P. A. David and M. W. Reder (eds), *Nations and Household in Economic Growth*, New York: Academic Press.

EBRD (1993) 'Changes in real output in former communist states 1990–1992', European Bank Reconstruction and Development Economic Review. *Current Economic Issues*, July.

Edgell, S. and Duke, V. (1982) 'Reactions to the public expenditure cuts: occupational class and party realignment', *Sociology*, 16, 431–9.

Edgell, S. and Duke, V. (1991) *A Message of Thatcherism*, London: Harper-Collins.

EIRIS. *The Ethical Investment Research Service*, London.

Eisenberg, P. and Lazarsfeld, P. (1938) 'The psychological effects of unemployment', *Psychological Bulletin*, 35, 79–96.

Eisenberger, R. and Shank, D. (1985) 'Personal work ethic and effort training affect cheating', *Journal of Personality and Social Psychology*, 49, 520–8.

Ekins, P. (1992) *Wealth Beyond Measure*, London: Gaia.

Elffers, H. (1991) *Income Tax Evasion: Theory and measurement*, Dordrecht: Kluwer.

Elffers, H., Robben, H. S. J. and Hessing, D. J. (1991) Under-reporting income: who is the best judge – tax payer or tax inspector?', *Journal of the Royal Statistical Society* (series A, 154, part 1), 125–7.

Elffers, H., Robben, H. S. J. and Hessing, D. J. (1992) 'On measuring tax evasion', *Journal of Economic Psychology*, 13, 545–67.

Elffers, H., Weigel, R.H. and Hessing, D. J. (1987) 'The consequences of different strategies for measuring tax evasion behavior', *Journal of Economic Psychology*, 8, 311–37.

Eling, A. (1992) 'Employers evaluation of Dutch tax reform', *Journal of Economic Psychology*, 13, 4, 609–24.

Elster, J. (1991) 'Justice and the allocation of scarce resources', paper presented at the joint SASE and IAREP conference, Stockholm School of Economics.

Emler, N. and Dickinson, J. (1985) 'Children's representation of economic inequalities: the effects of social class', *British Journal of Developmental Psychology*, 3, 191–98.

Emmison, M. (1983) 'The economy: its emergence in media discourse', in H. Davis and P. Walton (eds), *Language, Image, Media*, Oxford: Blackwell.

Epstein, Y. and Babad, E. (1982) 'Economic stress: notes on the psychology of inflation', *Journal of Applied Social Psychology*, 12, 85–99.

Etzioni, A. (1988) *The Moral Dimension*, New York: The Free Press.

Etzioni, A. (1991a) 'A socio-economic perspective on friction', paper presented at the joint IAREP/SASE conference, Stockholm School of Economics, Sweden.

Etzioni, A. (1991b) 'Eastern Europe: the wealth of lessons', Monograph, the Socio-Economic Project, 714H Gelman Library, The George Washington University.

Evans, R. (1993) 'Soothsaying or science: falsification, uncertainty and social change in macro-economic modelling', MSc thesis, University of Bath.

Eysenck, M. and Eysenck, M. (1982) 'Effects of incentive on cued recall', *Quarterly Journal of Experimental Psychology*, 34, 489–98.

Faber, R. J. and O'Guinn, T. C. (1988a) Compulsive consumption and credit abuse', *Journal of Consumer Policy*, 11, 109–21.

Faber, R. J. and O'Guinn, T. C. (1988b) 'Dysfunctional consumer socialization: a search for the roots of compulsive buying', IAREP Brussels.

Fallowfield, L. (1990) *The Quality of Life: The missing measurement in health care*. London: Souvenir Press.

Faver, C. (1982) 'Achievement orientation, attainment values, and women's employment', *Journal of Vocational Behaviour*, 20, 67–80.

Feagin, J. (1972) 'Poverty: we still believe that God helps them who help themselves', *Psychology Today*, 6, 101–29.

Feagin, J. (1975) *Subordinating the Poor*, Englewood Cliffs, NJ: Prentice Hall.

Feather, N. (1974) 'Explanations of poverty in Australian and American samples: the person, society and fate', *Australian Journal of Psychology*, 26, 199–216.

Feather, N. (1982) 'Unemployment and its psychological correlations: a study of depressive symptoms, self-esteem, Protestant ethic values, attributional style, and apathy', *Australian Journal of Psychology*, 34, 309–23.

Feather, N. (1983) 'Causal attributions and beliefs about work and unemployment among adolescents in state and independent secondary schools', *Australian Journal of Psychology*, 35, 211–32.

Feather, N. (1991) 'Variables relating to the allocation of pocket money to children: Parental reasons and values', *British Journal of Social Psychology*, 30, 221–333.

Feather, N. (1992) 'Expectancy-value theory and unemployment effects', *Journal of Occupational Psychology*, 65, 315–30.

Feather, N. and Barber, J. (1983) 'Depressive reactions and unemployment', *Journal of Abnormal Psychology*, 92, 185–95.

Feather, N. and Bond, M. (1983) 'Time structure and purposeful activity among employed and unemployed university graduates', *Journal of Occupational Psychology*, 56, 241–54.

Feather, N. and Davenport, P. (1981) 'Unemployment and depressive effect: a motivational and attributional analysis', *Journal of Occupational Psychology*, 56, 241–54.

Feather, N. and O'Brien, G. (1986) 'A longitudinal study of the effects of employment and unemployment on school-leavers', *Journal of Occupational Psychology*, 59, 121–44.

Fenichel, O. (1947) 'The drive to amass wealth', in H. Fenichel and O. Rapoport (eds), *The Collected Papers of Otta Finichel*, New York: Norton.

Ferenczi, S. (1926) *Further Contributions to the Theory and Techniques of Psychoanalysis*, London: Knopf.

Festinger, L. (1954) 'Inequality in social exchange', in L. Berkowitz (ed.), *Advances in Experimental Social Psychology*, vol. 2, New York: Academic Press.

Fields, D. and Stanley, W. (1970) 'Incentives, disincentives and the income tax: futher empirical evidence', *Public Finance*, 25, 3, 381–415.

Filley, A. and Aldag, R. (1978) 'Characteristics and measurement of an organisational typology', *Academy of Management Journal*, 21, 578–91.

Fineman, S. (1979) 'A psychological model of stress and its application to managerial unemployment', *Human Relations*, 32, 323–45.

Fishbein, M. and Ajzen, I. (1975) *Belief, Attitude, Intention and Behavior*, Reading, MA: Addison-Wesley.

Fisher, I. (1911) *The Purchasing Power of Money*, New York: Macmillan.

Fisher, I. (1930) *The Theory of Interest*, New York: Macmillan.

Fleming, D. and Lavercombe, S. (1982) 'Talking about unemployment with school-leavers', *British Journal of Guidance and Counselling*, 10, 22–33.

Forgas, J., Morris, S. and Furnham, A. (1982) 'Lay explanations of wealth: attributions for economic success', *Journal of Applied Social Psychology*, 12, 381–97.

Forman, N. (1987) *Mind over Money*, Toronto: Doubleday.

Fournier, S. and Richins, M. L. (1991) 'Some theoretical and popular notions concerning materialism', *Journal of Social Behaviour and Personality*, 6, 403–14.

Fowler, B., Littlewood, B. and Madigan, R. (1977) 'Immigrant school-leavers and the search for work', *Sociology*, 11, 65–85.

Fox, K. (1978) 'What children bring to school: the beginnings of economic education', *Social Education*, 10, 478–81.

Foxall, G. (1994) 'Environment-impacting consumer behaviour: a framework of social marketing and demarketing', *Perspectives on Marketing Management*, 4, 27–53.

Frank, R. (1985) *Choosing the Right Pond: Human behaviour and the quest for status*, Oxford: Oxford University Press.

Frank, R. (1988) *Passions within Reason*, New York: Norton.

Frank, R., Gilovich, T. and Regan, D. (1993) 'Does studying economics inhibit co-operation?', *Journal of Economic Perspectives*, 7, (2), 159–71.

Franklin, J. A. and Andrews, G. (1989) 'Stress and the onset of agorophobia' *Australian Psychologist*, 24, 203–19.

Fraser, C. (1980) 'The social psychology of unemployment', in M. Jeeves (ed.), *Psychology Survey*, no. 3, London: Allen and Unwin.

Free, A. and Cantril, H. (1968) *The Political Beliefs of Americans*, New York: Simon and Schuster.

Freud, S. (1908) *Character and Anal Eroticism*, London: Hogarth.

Freud, S. (1928/1961) 'Dostoevsky and parricide', in J. Strachey (ed.), *The Standard Edition of the Complete Psychological Works of Freud*, vol. 21, London: Hogarth Press.

Friedland, N., Maital, S. and Rutenberg, A. (1978) 'A simulation study of income tax evasion', *Journal of Public Economics*, 10, 107–16.

Friedlander, F. (1966) 'Importance of work versus non-work among socially and occupationally stratified groups', *Journal of Applied Psychology*, 50, 437–41.

Friedlander, F. and Greenberg, S. (1971) 'Effect of job attitudes, training and organisation climate on performance of the hard-core unemployed', *Journal of Applied Psychology*, 55, 287–95.

Friedman, M. (1957) *A Theory of the Consumption Function*, Princetown NJ: Princetown University Press.

Friedman, M. (1962) *Capitalism and Freedom*, Chicago: University of Chicago Press.

Fromm, E. (1980) *To Have or to Be*, New York: Harper and Row, 1976/Bungay: Abacus.

Fruensgaard, K., Benjaminsen, S., Joensen, S. and Helstrup, K. (1983) 'Follow-up of a group of unemployed patients consecutively admitted to an emergency psychiatric department', *Social Psychiatry*, 18, 129–35.

Fruth, H. G., Baur, M. and Smith, J. E. (1976) 'Children's conception of social institutions: a Piagetian framework', *Human Development*, 19, 351–74.

Fryer, D. (1986) 'Employment deprivation and personal agency during unemployment', *Social Behaviour*, 1, 3–23.

Fuchs, V. R. (1982) 'Time preference and health: an explaratory study', in V. R. Fuchs (ed.), *Economic Aspects of Health*, Chicago: University of Chicago Press.

Furby, L. (1980a) 'The origins and development of early possessive behaviour', *Political Psychology*, 2, 30–42.

Furby, L. (1980b) 'Collective possession and ownership: a study of its judged feasibility and desirability', *Social Behaviour and Personality*, 8, 165–84.

Furby, L. (1991) 'Understanding the psychology of possessions and ownership: a personal memoir and an appraisal of our progress', *Journal of Social Behaviour and Personality*, 6, 457–63.

Furnham, A. (1981) *The Psychology of Social Situations*, Oxford and New York: Pergamon.

Furnham, A. (1982a) 'The Protestant work ethic and attitudes towards unemployment', *Journal of Occupational Psychology*, 55, 277–86.

Furnham, A. (1982b) 'Why are the poor always with us? Explanations for poverty in Britain', *British Journal of Social Psychology*, 20, 311–82.

Furnham, A. (1982c) 'Explanations for unemployment in Britain', *European Journal of Social Psychology*, 12, 335–52.

Furnham, A. (1982d) 'The perception of poverty among adolescents', *Journal of Adolescence*, 5, 135–47.

Furnham, A. (1983a) 'Mental health and unemployment status: a preliminary study', *British Journal of Counselling and Guidance*, 11, 197–201.

Furnham, A. (1983b) 'Attitudes to the unemployed receiving social security', *Human Relations*, 36, 135–50.

Furnham, A. (1983c) 'Inflation and the estimated sizes of notes', *Journal of Economic Psychology*, 4, 349–52.

Furnham, A. (1983d) 'The A-type behaviour pattern, mental health and health locus of control beliefs', *Social Science and Medicine*, 17, 1569–72.

Furnham, A. (1983e) 'Attributions for affluence', *Personality and Individual Differences*, 4, 31–40.

Furnham, A. (1983f) 'The Protestant work ethic, human values and attitudes towards taxation', *Journal of Economic Psychology*, 8, 112–29.

Furnham, A. (1984a) 'Many sides of the coin: the psychology of money usage', *Personality and Individual Differences*, 5, 95–103.

Furnham, A. (1984b) 'Work values and belief in Britain', *Journal of Occupational Behaviour*, 5, 281–91.

Furnham, A. (1985a) 'Attitudes to, and habits of, gambling in Britain', *Personality and Individual differences*, 6, 493–502.

Furnham, A. (1985b) 'Why do people save? Attitudes to, and habits of saving money in Britain', *Journal of Applied Social Psychology*, 15, 354–73.

Furnham, A. (1985c) 'The determinants of attitudes towards social security recipients', *British Journal of Social Psychology*, 24, 19–27.

Furnham, A. (1987) 'The determinants and structure of adolescents' beliefs about the economy', *Journal of Adolescence*, 10, 353–71.

Furnham, A. (1988) *Lay Theories*, Oxford and New York: Pergamon.

Furnham, A. (1990a) 'A content, correlational, and factor analytic study of seven questionnaire measures of the Protestant work ethic', *Human Relations*, 43, 383–99.

Furnham, A. (1990b) *The Protestant Work Ethic: The psychology of work – relations beliefs and behaviours*, London: Routledge.

Furnham, A. and Bland, K. (1983) 'The Protestant work ethic and conservatism', *Personality and Individual Differences*, 4, 205–6.

Furnham, A. and Bochner, S. (1985) *Culture Shock: Psychological reactions to unfamiliar environments*, London: Methuen.

Furnham, A. and Bond, M. (1986) 'Hong Kong Chinese explanations for wealth', *Journal of Economic Psychology*, 4, 447–60.

Furnham, A. and Cleare, A. (1988) 'School children's conceptions of economics: prices, wages, investments and strikes', *Journal of Economic Psychology*, 9, 467–79.

Furnham, A. and Gunter, B. (1984) 'Just world beliefs and attitudes towards the poor', *Journal of Social Psychology*, 23, 265–69.

Furnham, A. and Hesketh, B. (1989) 'Explanations for unemployment in Great Britain and New Zealand', *Journal of Social Psychology*, 129, 169–81.

Furnham, A. and Jones, S. (1987) 'Children's views regarding possessions and their theft', *Journal of Moral Education*, 16, 18–30.

Furnham, A. and Lewis, A. (1986) *The Economic Mind: the social psychology of economic behaviour*, Hemel Hempstead: Harvester Wheatsheaf.

Furnham, A. and Quilley, R. (1989) 'The Protestant work ethic and the prisoner's dilemma game', *British Journal of Social Psychology*, 28, 79–87.

Furnham, A. and Rose, M. (1987) 'Alternative ethics: the relationship between the wealth, work and leisure ethic', *Human Relations*, 40, 561–71.

Furnham, A. and Thomas, P. (1984a) 'Pocket-money: a study of economic education', *British Journal of Developmental Psychology*, 2, 205–12.

Furnham, A. and Thomas, P. (1984b) 'Adults' perception of the economic socialization of children', *Journal of Adolescence*, 7, 217–31.

Furnham, A. and Weissman, D. (1985) 'Judging the value of British coins: a developmental and cross-cultural study', unpublished paper.

Furth, H. (1980) *The World of Grown-ups*, New York: Elsevier.

Furth, H. G., Baur, M. and Smith, J. E. (1976) 'Children's conception of social institutions: a Piagetian framework', *Human Development*, 19, 351–74.

Fyons, L., Salilli, F., Maehr, M. and Desai, K. (1983) 'A cross-cultural exploration into the meaning of achievement', *Journal of Personality and Social Psychology*, 44, 1000–13.

Galbraith, J. (1958) *The Affluent Society*, London: Hamish Hamilton.

Galbraith, J. (1977) *The Age of Uncertainty*, London: André Deutsch.

Gallup, G. and Newport, F. (1990) 'Americans strongly in tune with the purpose of Earth day 1990', *Gallup Poll*, 54, 1–5.

Gans, H. (1972) 'The positive functions of poverty', *American Journal of Sociology*, 78, 275–89.

Ganster, D. (1980) 'Individual differences and task design: a laboratory experiment', *Organizational Behaviour and Human Performance*, 26, 131–48.

Ganster, D. (1981) 'Protestant ethic and performance: a re-examination', *Psychological Reports*, 48, 335–8.

Geller, E., Winett, R. and Everett, E. (1982) *Preserving the Environment: New strategies for behaviour change*, Elmsford, New York: Pergamon.

Gersick, C. (1991) 'Revolutionary change theories: a multi-level exploration of the punctuated equilibrium paradigm', *Academy of Management Review*, 16, 10–36.

Gigliotti, L. (1992) *Journal of Environmental Education*, 24 (1), 15–26.

Gilliard, C. J. (1989) 'The achieving society revisited', *Journal of Economic Psychology*, 10, 21–34.

Gillies, P. Elwood, J. and Hawlin, P. (1985) 'Anxieties in adolescents about unemployment and war', *British Medical Journal*, 291, 383–4.

Glen, D. (1990) 'From communalism to individualism', *The Public Perspective*, The Roper Centre, University of Connecticut, May/June 3–4.

Goetz, C. (1977) 'Fiscal illusion in state and local finance', in T. Borchering (ed.), *Budgets and Bureaucrats: The sources of government growth*, Durham: Duke University Press.

Golding, P. and Middleton, S. (1982) *Images of Welfare: Press and public attitudes to poverty*, Oxford: Martin Robertson.

Goldberg, H. and Lewis, R. (1978) *Money Madness: The Psychology of Saving, Spending, Loving and Hating Money*, London: Springwood.

Goldstein, B. and Eichborn, R. (1961) 'The changing Protestant ethic: rural patterns in health, work and leisure', *American Sociological Review*, 26, 557–65.

Goodwin, L. (1973) 'Middle-class misperceptions of the high life, aspirations and strong work ethics held by the welfare poor', *American Journal of Orthopsychiatry*, 43, 554–64.

Gordon, D. (1972) *Theories of Poverty and Underemployment*, Lexington: Lexington Books.

Gore, S. (1978) 'The effect of social support in moderating the health consequences of unemployment', *Journal of Health and Social Behaviour*, 19, 157–65.

Graham, H. (1987) 'Being poor: perceptions and coping strategies of lone mothers', in J. Brannen and G. Wilson (eds), *Give and Take in Families: Studies in resource distribution*, London: Allen and Unwin.

Grasmick, H. and Scott, H. (1982) 'Tax evasion and mechanisms of social control: a comparison of grand and petty theft', *Journal of Economic Psychology*, 2, 213–30.

Green, D. (1986) *Challenge to the National Health Service (NHS)*, London: Institute for Economic Affairs.

Greenberg, J. (1977) 'The Protestant work ethic and reactions to negative performance evaluations on a laboratory task', *Journal of Applied Psychology*, 62, 682–90.

Greenberg, J. (1978) 'Equity, equality and the Protestant ethic: Allocating rewards following fair and unfair competition', *Journal of Experimental Social Psychology*, 14, 217–26.

Greenberg, J. (1979) 'Protestant ethic endorsement and the fairness of equity inputs', *Journal of Research in Personality*, 13, 81–90.

Greenberger, E., Stenberg, L. and Vaux, A. (1981) 'Adolescents who work: health and behavioural consequences of job stress', *Developmental Psychology*, 17, 691–703.

Grierson, P. (1978) 'The origins of money', *Research in Economic Anthropology*, 1, 1–35.

Griffiths, M. D. (1990) 'Addiction to fruit machines: a preliminary study among young males', *Journal of Gambling Behaviour*, 6, 113–25.

Griffiths, M. D. (1991) 'Psychobiology of the near-miss in fruit machine gambling', *Journal of Psychology*, 125, 347–57.

Groenland, E. A. G. (1992) 'Developing a dynamic research strategy for the economic psychological study of taxation', *Journal of Economic Psychology*, 13, 589–96.

Grunert, K. and Olander, F. (1989) *Understanding Economic Behaviour*, Dordrecht: Kluwer.

Grygier, T. (1961) *The Dynamic Personality Inventory: Manual*, Windsor: NFER.

Guimond, S., Begin, G. and Palmer, D. (1989) 'Education and causal attributions: The development of "Person-Blame" and "System-Blame" ideology', *Social Psychology Quarterly*, 52, 126–14.

Guion, R. and Landy, F. (1972) 'The meaning of work and the motivation to work', *Organizational Behaviour and Human Performance*, 8, 308–39.

Gunnarsson, J. and Wahlund, R. (1993) Household financial strategies: do they exist?', paper given at the eighteenth IAREP conference, Moscow.

Gurin, G. and Gurin, G. (1970) 'Expectancy theory in the study of poverty', *Journal of Social Issues*, 26, 83–104.

Gurney, R. (1980a) 'Does unemployment affect the self-esteem of school-leavers?', *Australian Journal of Psychology*, 32, 175–82.

Gurney, R. (1980b) 'The effects of unemployment on the psychosocial development of school-leavers', *Journal of Occupational Psychology*, 53, 205–13.

Gurney, R. (1981) 'Leaving school, facing unemployment and making attributions about the causes of unemployment', *Journal of Vocational Behaviour*, 18, 79–91.

Güth, W. and Tietz, R. (1990) 'Ultimatum bargaining behaviour: a survey and comparison of experimental results', *Journal of Economic Psychology*, 11, 417–49.

Güth, W., Wärneryd, K.-E. and Lea, S. E. G. (1992) 'Editorial: economic psychology and experimental economies', *Journal of Economic Psychology*, 13 (2).

Hackman, J. and Oldham, G. (1980) *Work Redesign*, Reading, MA: Addison-Wesley.

Haire, M. and Morrison, F. (1957) 'School children's perception of labour and management', *Journal of Social Psychology*, 46, 179–97.

Hammarström, A. (1986) *Youth Unemployment and Health*. Stockholm: SIP.

Hammond, P. and Williams, R. (1976) 'The Protestant ethic thesis: a social psychological assessment', *Social Forces*, 54, 579–89.

Hanley, A. and Wilhelm, M. (1992) 'Compulsive buying: a exploration into self-esteem and money attitudes', *Journal of Economic Psychology*, 13, 5–18.

Hansen, H. (1985) 'The economics of early childhood education in Minnesota', *Journal of Economic Education*, 16, 219–24.

Hardin, G. (1968) 'The tragedy of commons', *Science*, 162, 1243–48.

Hargreaves, D. (1981) 'Unemployment, leisure and education', *Oxford Review of Education*, 7, 197–210.

Harper, D. (1991) 'The role of psychology in the analysis of poverty: some suggestions', *Psychology and Developing Societies*, 3, 193–201.

Harrison, R. (1976) 'The demoralizing experience of prolonged unemployment', *Department of Employment Gazette*, 4, 339–48.

Hartley, J. (1980) 'The personality of unemployed managers: myths and measurement', *Personal Review*, 9, 12–18.

Harvey, J., Ickes, W. and Kidd, R. (eds) (1975) *New Directions in Attribution Research*, Hillsdale, NJ: Erlbaum.

Hasseldine, D. J. and Bebbington, K. J. (1991) 'Blending economic deterrence and fiscal psychology models in the design of responses to tax evasion: the New Zealand experience', *Journal of Economic Psychology*, 12, 299–324.

Haste, H. and Torney-Purta, J. (eds) (1992) *The Development of Political Understanding: A new perspective* (New Directions for Child Development, 56), San Francisco: Jossey-Bass.

Hayes, J. and Nutman, P. (1981) *Understanding the Unemployed*, London: Tavistock.

Heath, A. (1992) 'The attitudes of the underclass', in Smith, D. J. (ed.), *Understanding the Underclass*, London: Policy Studies Institute.

Hebb, D. (1955) 'Drives and the CNS', *Psychological Review*, 62, 243–54.

Heider, F. (1958) *The Psychology of Interpersonal Relationships*. New York: Wiley.

Heikkinnen, M. A., Aro, H. and Lonnqvist, J. (1992) 'The partner's views on precipitant stressor in suicide', *Acto Psychiatrica Scandinavica*, 85, 380–4.

Heberlein, T. and Warriner, G. (1983) 'The influence of price and attitude on shifting residential electricity consumption from on- to off-peak periods', *Journal of Economic Psychology*, 4, 107–30.

Henry, S. (1978) *The Hidden Economy*, Oxford: Martin Robertson.

Hepworth, S. (1980) 'Moderating factors of the psychological impact of unemployment', *Journal of Occupational Psychology*, 53, 139–45.

Herskovitz, M. (1952) *Economic Anthropology*, New York: Norton.

Herzberg, F. (1966) *Work and the Nature of Man*, Cleveland, OH: World Publishing.

Herzberg, F., Mausner, B. and Snyderman, B. (1959) *The Motivation to Work*, New York: Wiley.

Hess, R. (1970) 'The transmission of cognitive strategies in poor families', in V. Allen (ed.), *Psychological Factors in Poverty*, Chicago: Markham.

Hessing, D. and Elffers, H. (1985) 'Economic Man or Social Man', in H. Brandstätter and E. Kirchler (eds), *Economic Psychology*, Linz: Trauner.

Hessing, D. and Elffers, H. (1986) 'Attitude toward death, fear of being declared dead too soon, and donation of organs after death', *Omega*, 17 (2), 115–26.

Hessing, D. J., Elffers, H., Robben, H. S. J. and Webley, P. (1992) 'Does deterrence deter? Measuring the effect of deterrence of tax compliance in field studies and experimental studies', in J. Slemrod (ed.), *Why People Pay Taxes: Tax compliance and enforcement*, Ann Arbor: University of Michigan Press.

Hessing, D. J., Kinsey, K. A., Elffers, H. and Weigel, R. H. (1988). 'Tax evasion research: measurement strategies and theoretical models', in W.F. van Raaij, G.M. van Veldhoven and K.-E. Wärneryd (eds), *Handbook of Economic Psychology*, Dordrecht: Kluwer.

Hewitt, D. (1986) 'Fiscal illusions from grants and the level of state and federal expenditure', *National Tax Journal*, 39, 471–83.

Hey, J. (1992) 'Experiments in economics and psychology', in S. E. G. Lea, P. Webley and B. Young (eds), *New Directions in Economic Psychology*, Vermont: Elgar.

Hill, A. (1976) 'Methodological problems in the use of factor analysis: a critical review of the experimental evidence for the anal character', *British Journal of Medical Psychology*, 49, 145–59.

Hill, C. (1977) 'The determinants of labor supply for the working urban poor', in G. Cain and H. Watts *Income Maintenance and Labor Supply*, Chicago: Rand-McNally.

Hill, J. (1978) 'The psychological impact of unemployment', *New Society*, 12 January.

Himmelstrand, U. (1992) *Interfaces in Economic and Social Analysis*, London and New York: Routledge.

Hitchcock, J., Munroe, R. and Munroe, R. (1976) 'Coins and countries: the value-sized hypothesis', *Journal of Social Psychology*, 100, 307–8.

Hite, P. (1991) 'Reasons for preparer usage by small business owners: how compliant are they?', in *Closing the Tax Gap: Alternatives to enforcement*, Washington, DC: IRS, document 7302.

Ho, R. (1986) *Adherence to Protestant Work Ethic Values and Helping Judgements towards the Unemployed*, unpublished paper.

Hodgkinson, V. and Weitzmann, M. (1990) *Giving and Volunteering in the United States: Findings from a national survey*, Washington, DC: Independent Sector.

Hodgson, J. and Brenner, M. (1968) 'Successful experience: training hard-core unemployed', *Harvard Business Review*, 46, 148–56.

Hollis, M. and Nell, E. (1975) *Rational Economic Man*, Cambridge: Cambridge University Press.

Holmes, T. and Rahe, R. (1967) 'The social readjustment rating scale', *Journal of Psychosomatic Research*, 11, 213–18.

Hopson, B. and Adams, J. (1976) 'Towards an understanding of transition', in J. Adams, J. Hayes and B. Hopson (eds), *Transition*, London: Martin Robertson.

Hornik, J. (1989) 'Economic time preference and individual smoking behaviour'.

Horton, R. and Weidenaar, D. (1975) 'Wherefore economic education?', *Journal of Economic Education*, 7, 40–4.

Huber, J. and Form, W. (1973) *Income and Ideology*, New York: Free Press.

Hudson, J. (1982) *Inflation: a theoretical survey and synthesis*, Boston, MA: Allen and Unwin.

Hulin, C. and Blood. M. (1968) 'Job enlargement, individual differences and worker responses', *Psychological Bulletin*, 69, 41–55.

Hurlock, E. (1972) *Child Development*, New York: McGraw-Hill.

Hussein, G. (1985a) 'Is money an acceptable gift in Cyprus?', *Perceptual and Motor Skills*, 61, 70–4

Hussein, G. (1985b) 'An examination of the psychological aspects of money', unpublished MPhil. thesis, University of Exeter.

Ingels, S. and O'Brien, M. (1985) 'The effects of economic instruction in early adolescence', *Theory and Research in Social Education*, 4, 279–94.

Inglehart, R. and Rabier, J.-R. (1986) 'Aspirations adapt to situations – but why are the Belgians so much happier than the French?', in F. M. Andrews (ed.), *Research on the Quality of Life*, Ann Arbor, MI: Institute for Social Research.

Irving, K. and Siegal, M. (1983) 'Mitigating circimstances of children's perceptions of criminal justice', *British Journal of Developmental Psychology*, 1, 179–88.

Isachsen, A. J., Samuelson, S. O. and Strøm, S. (1985) 'The behaviour of taxpayers', in W. Gärtner and A. Wenig (eds), *The Economics of the Shadow Economy*, Berlin: Springer.

Iverson, L., Sabroe, S. and Dansgaard, M. (1989) 'Hospital admissions before and after shipyard closure', *British Medical Journal*, 299, 1073–76.

Jackson, P., Stafford, E., Banks, M. and Warr, P. (1983) 'Unemployment and psychological distress in young people', *Journal of Applied Psychology*, 68, 525–35.

Jacobs, D. F. (1986) 'A general theory of addictions: a new theoretical model', *Journal of Gambling Behaviour*, 2, 15–31.

Jahoda, G. (1979) 'A cross-cultural perspective on experimental social psychology', *Personality and Social Psychology Bulletin*, 5 (2), 142–8.

Jahoda, G. (1981) 'The development of thinking about economic institution: the bank', *Cahiers de Psychologie Cognitive*, 1, 55–78.

Jahoda, G. and Woerdenbagch, A. (1982) 'The development of ideas about an economic institution: a cross-national replication', *British Journal of Social Psychology*, 21, 337–8.

Jahoda, M. (1979) 'The impact of unemployment in the 1930s and the 1970s', *Bulletin of the British Psychological Society*, 32, 309–14.

Jahoda, M. (1981) 'Work, employment and unemployment: values, theories and approaches in social research', *American Psychology*, 36, 184–91.

Jahoda, M. (1982) Employment and Unemployment: A social-psychological analysis, Cambridge: Cambridge University Press.

Jahoda, M., Lazarfeld, P. and Zeisel, H. (1933) *Marienthal: The sociography of an unemployed community*, London: Tavistock.

Jahoda, T. G. (1983) 'European "lag" in the development of an economic concept: a study in Zimbabwe', *British Journal of Developmental Psychology*, 1, 110–20.

James, S. and Nobes, C. (1992) *The Economics of Taxation*, 4th edn, Hemel Hempstead: Prentice Hall.

Jenkins, R., MacDonald, A., Murray, J. and Strathdee, G. (1982) 'Minor psychiatric, morbidity and the threat of redundancy in a professional group', *Psychological Medicine*, 12, 799–807.

Jensen, A. and Reynolds, C. (1982) 'Race, social class and ability patterns on the WISC-R', *Personality and Individual Differences*, 3, 423–35.

Joe, V. (1974) 'Personality correlates of conservatism', *Journal of Social Psychology*, 93, 309–10.

Joe, V., Jones, R. and Miller, R. (1981) 'Value pattern of a conservative', *Personality and Individual Differences*, 2, 25–30.

Jones-Lee, M. W. (1976) *The Value of Life: an economic analysis*, Oxford: Martin Robertson.

Kahneman, D., Knetsch, D. and Thaler, R. (1986) 'Fairness as a constraint on profit seeking', *American Economic Review*, 76, 728–41.

Kahnemann, P. and Tversky, A. (1979) 'Prospect theory, an analysis of decision-making under risk', *Econometrica*, 47, 263–92.

Kanto, A. J., Rosenqvist, G. and Suvas, A. (1992) 'On utility estimation of racetrack betters', *Journal of Economic Psychology*, 13, 491–8.

Kaplan, G. and Camacho, T. (1983) 'Perceived health and mortality: a nine year follow-up of the human laboratory cohort', *American Journal of Epidemiology*, 117, 292–304.

Kasl, S. and Cobb, S. (1970) 'Blood pressure changes in men undergoing job loss', *Psychosomatic Medicine*, 32, 19–38.

Kasser, T. and Ryan, R. (1993) 'A dark side of the American Dream: Correlations of financial success as a central life aspiration', *Journal of Personality and Social Psychology*, 65, 410–22.

Katona, G. (1975) *Psychological Economics*, Amsterdam and New York: Elsevier.

Katona, G. (1977) *Psychological Analysis of Economic, Behaviour*. Westport: Greenwood Press.

Katsenelinboigen, A. (1977) 'Coloured markets in the Soviet Union', *Soviet Studies*, XXIX, 1, 62–85.

Katz, J. (1970) 'A new approach to the study of school motivation in minority group children', in V. Allen (ed.), *Psychological Factors in Poverty*, Chicago: Markham.

Kaufmann, P., Ortmeyer, G. and Smith, N. (1991) 'Fairness in consumer pricing', *Journal of Consumer Policy*, 14, 117–40.

Kazemier, B. and van Eck, R. (1992) 'Survey investigations of the hidden economy: some methodological results', *Journal of Economic Psychology*, 13, 569–87.

Kelman, H. C. (1965) 'Manipulation of human behavior: an ethical dilemma for the social scientist', *Journal of Social Issues*, 21, 31–46.

Kelvin, P. (1980) 'Social psychology 2001: the social psychology bases and implications of structural unemployment', in R. Gilmour and S. Duck (eds), *The Development of Social Psychology*, London: Academic Press.

Kelvin, P. and Jarrett, J. (1985) *Unemployement: Its social psychological effects*, Cambridge: Cambridge University Press.

Kemp, S. and Willetts, K. (1994) 'The value of services supplied by the New Zealand government', *Journal of Economic Psychology*, 15 (in press).

Kershaw, D. (1972) 'A negative income-tax experiment', *Scientific American*, 227 (Oct.), 4, 19–25.

Keynes, J. M. (1936) *The General Theory of Employment, Interest and Money*. London: Macmillan.

Kidron, A. (1978) 'Work values and organisational commitment', *Academy of Management Journal*, 21, 239–47.

Kinsey, A., Pomeroy, W. and Martin, C. (1948) *Sexual Behaviour in the Human Male*, Philadelphia: Saunders.

Kinsey, K. A. (1984) *Theories and Models of Tax Cheating* (Taxpayer Compliance Project Working Paper 84–2), Chicago, IL: American Bar Foundation.

Kinsey, K. A. (1988) *Measurement Bias or Honest Disagreement? Problems of validating measures of tax evasion* (ABF Working Paper, no. 8811), Chicago: American Bar Foundation.

Kinsey, K. A. (1992) Deterrence and alienation effects of IRS enforcement: an analysis of survey data', in J. Slomrod (ed.), *Why people pay taxes*, Ann Arbor: University of Michigan Press.

Kinsey, K. A. (1993) 'Evaluating equity: the impact of tax policy on public perceptions of tax fairness', *Researching Law*, 4, 2–3.

Kirchler, E. (1988) 'Diary reports on daily economic decisions of happy versus unhappy couples', *Journal of Economic Psychology*, 9, 327–57.

Kirkpatrick, D. (1990) 'Environmentalism: the new crusade', Fortune, 12 February.

Klamer, A. (1983) *Conversations with Economists*, Totowa: Allaneld and Rowman.

Klamer, A. (1988) *The Consequences of Economic Rhetoric*, Cambridge: Cambridge University Press.

Klamer, A., McCloskey, D. and Solow, R. (1988) *The Consequences of Economic Rhetoric*, New York: Cambridge University Press.

Klein, R. (1977) 'The conflict between professionals, consumers and bureaucrats', *Journal of the Irish Colleges of Physicians and Surgeons*, 6 (3), 88–91.

Klein-Hesselink, D. and Spruit, I. (1992) 'The contribution of unemployment to socio-economic health differences', *International Journal of Epidemiology*, 21, 329–37.

Kline, P. (1967) 'An investigation into the Freudian concept of the anal character', unpublished PhD thesis, University of Manchester.

Kline, P. (1971) *Ai3Q Test*, Windsor: NFER.

Kline, P. (1972) *Fact and Fantasy in Freudian Theory*, London: Methuen.

Komarovsky, M. (1940) *The Unemployed Man and His Family*, New York: Dryden.

Kourilsky, M. (1977) 'The kinder-economy: a case of kindergarten pupils' acquisition of economic concepts', *The Elementary School Journal*, 77, 182–91.

Kourilsky, M. and Campbell, M. (1984) 'Sex differences in a simulated classroom economy: children's beliefs about entrepreneurship', *Sex Roles*, 10, 53–66.

Krafchik, M. (1983) 'Unemployment and vagrancy in the 1930s: deterrence, rehabilitation and the depression', *Journal of Social Policy*, 12, 195–214.

Kuhn, T. (1970) *The Structure of Scientific Revolutions*, Chicago: University of Chicago Press.

Kuran, T. (1992) 'The unthinkable and the unthought', paper presented at the SASE conference, University of California, Irvine, March.

Kurz, M., Spiegelman, R. G. and West, R. W. (1973) 'The experimental horizon and the role of time preference for the Seattle–Denver income maintenance experiments', Stanford: Stanford Research Institute, Memorandum no 21.

Kuznets, S. (1966) *Modern economic growth*, New Haven, CT: Yale University Press.

La France, M. and Cicchetti, C. (1979) 'Perceived responsibility and blame for economic success and failure: Social class and employment status comparison', *Journal of Applied Social Psychology*, 9, 466–75.

Lambert, W., Soloman, R. and Watson, P. (1949) 'Reinforcement and extinction as factors in size estimation', *Journal of Experimental Psychology*, 39, 637–41.

Lancaster, K. J. (1966) 'A new approach to consumer theory', *Journal of Political Economy*, 74, 132–57

Lane, R. (1983) *Money and the varities of happiness*, paper at ISPP meeting, Oxford.

Lane, R. (1991) *The Market Experience*, Cambridge: Cambridge University Press.

Langford, M. (1992) 'Who should get the kidney machine?', *Journal of Medical Ethics*, 18, 12–17.

Langner, T., Herson, J. Greene, E., Janeson, J. and Goff, T. (1970) 'Children of the city: affluence, poverty and mental health', in V. Allen (ed.), *Psychological Factors in Poverty*, Chicago: Markham.

Lavercombe, S. and Fleming, D. (1981) 'Attitudes and duration of unemployment among sixteen-year-old school-leavers', *British Journal of Guidance and Counselling*, 9, 36–45.

Lavik, R. and Lunde, T. (1991) 'Expensive attitudes: a structural model of environmental consciousness and the willingness to pay for "green products"', paper given at, IAREP/SASE conference, Stockholm School of Economics, June.

Lea, S. (1981) 'Inflation, decimalization and the estimated sizes of coins', *Journal of Economic Psychology*, 1, 79–81.

Lea, S. and Webley, P. (1981) 'Théorie psychologique de la monnaie', paper given at the Economic Psychology Conference, Paris.

Lea, S. E. G., Tarpy, R. M. and Webley, P. (1987) *The Individual in the Economy*, Cambridge: Cambridge University Press.

Lea, S. E. G., Walker, C. M. and Rooijmans, J. G. (1992) 'The concept of debt: an experimental investigation', paper presented at the IAREP colloquium, Frankfurt.

Lea, S. E. G., Walker, C. M. and Webley, P. (1992) 'An interview study of the origins of problem debt', paper presented at the conference of the Society for the Advancement of Socio-Economics, Irvine, March.

Lea, S. E. G., Webley, P. and Levine, R. M. (1993) 'The economic psychology of consumer debt', *Journal of Economic Psychology*, 14, 85–119.

Lea, S., Webley, P. and Young, B. (1992) *New Directions in Economic Psychology*, Vermont: Elgar.

Leahy, R. (1981) 'The development of the conception of economic inequality: descriptions and comparisons of rich and poor people', *Child Development*, 52, 523–32.

Lee, B., Jones, S. and Lewis, D. (1990) 'Public beliefs about the causes of homelessness', *Social Forces*, 69, 253–65.

Leeflang, R. Klein-Hesselink, D. and Spruit, I. (1992) 'Health effects of unemployment II: Men and women', *Social Science and Medicine*, 34, 351–63.

Leibenstein, H. (1976) 'Micro-micro theory, agent–agent trade and x-efficiency', in K. Dopfer (ed.), *Economics in the Future*, London: Macmillan.

Leiser, D. (1983) 'Children's conceptions and economics: the constitution of a cognitive domain', *Journal of Economic Psychology*, 4, 297–317.

Leiser, D., Sevón, G. and Lévy, D. (1990) 'Children's economic socialization: summarizing the cross-cultural comparison of ten countries', *Journal of Economic Psychology*, 11, 591–614.

Lerner, M. (1980) *The Belief in a Just World*, New York: Plenum.

Levinger, G. and Moles, O. (1979) *Divorce and Separation: Context, causes and consequences*, New York: Basic Books.

Lewis, A. (1978) 'Perceptions of tax rates', *British Tax Review*, 6, 358–66.

Lewis, A. (1981) 'Attributions and politics', *Personality and Individual Differences*, 2, 1–4.

Lewis, A. (1982) *The Psychology of Taxation*, Oxford: Martin Robertson.

Lewis, A. and Cullis, J. (1988) 'Preferences, economics and the economic psychology of public sector preference formation', *Journal of Behavioural Economics*, 17, 19–32.

Lewis, A. and Cullis, J. (1990) 'Ethical investments: preferences and morality', *Journal of Behavioural Economics*, 19, 395–411.

Lewis, A. and Furnham, A. (1986) 'Reducing unemployment: lay beliefs about how to reduce current unemployment', *Journal of Economic Psychology*, 6, 75–85.

Lewis, A. and Jackson, D. (1985) 'Voting preferences and attitudes to public expenditure: some new data', *Political Studies*, 33, 457–66.

Lewis, A. and Snell, M. (1986) 'Increasing kidney transplantation in Britain', *Social Science and Medicine*, 10, 1075–80.

Lewis, A. and Warneryd, K.-E. (1994) *Ethics and Economic Affairs*, London and New York: Routledge.

Lewis, A. and Webley, P. (1994) 'Social and ethical investing: beliefs, preferences and the willingness to sacrifice financial return', in A. Lewis and K.-E. Warneryd (eds), *Ethics and Economic Affairs*, London and New York: Routledge.

Lewis, A., Sandford, C. and Pleming, C. (1979) 'A survey of attitudes towards wealth, the wealthy, and the proposed annual wealth tax', report, Bath University.

Lewis, A., Snell, M. and Furnham, A. (1987) 'Lay explanations for the causes of unemployment in Britain: economic, individualistic, societal and fatalistic?', *Political Psychology*, 8, 427–39.

Lewis, O. (1951) *Life in a Mexican Village*, Urbana, IL: University of Illinois.

Lewis, O. (1965) *The Children of Sanchez*, Harmondsworth: Penguin.

Lewis, O. (1968) *La Vida*, London: Panther.

Lied, T. and Pritchard, R. (1976) 'Relationship between personality variables and components of the expectancy–valence model', *Journal of Applied Psychology*, 61, 463–7.

Liem, R. and Atkinson, T. (1982) *The work and unemployment project*, unpublished paper.

Liem, R. and Rayman, P. (1982) 'Health and social costs of unemployment', *American Psychologist*, 37, 116–23.

Lindqvist, A. (1981) 'A note on determinants of household saving behaviour', *Journal of Economic Psychology*, 1, 39–57.

Litwak, E., Hooyman, N. and Warren, D. (1973) Ideological complexity and middle American rationality', *Public Opinion Quarterly*, 37, 317–32.

Livingstone, S. M. and Lunt, P. K. (1992) 'Predicting personal debt and debt repayment: psychological, social and economic determinants', *Journal of Economic Psychology*, 13, 111–34.

Long, S. B. and Schwartz, R. (1987) 'The impact of IRS Audits on Taxpayer Compliance: A Field Experiment in Specific Deterrence', paper presented at the annual meeting of the Law and Society Association, Washington, D.C.

Long, S. B. and Swingen, J. (1988) 'The role of legal complexity in shaping taxpayer compliance', in P. J. Van Koppen, D. J. Hessing and G. Van den Heuvel (eds), *Lawyers on Psychology and Psychologists on Law*, Amsterdam: Swets and Zeitlinger.

Lowenstein, G. (1988) 'Frames of mind in intertemporal choice', *Management Science*, 34, 200–14.

Lowry, R. (1991) *Good Money: a Guide to profitable social investing in the '90s*, New York: Norton.

Luft, J. (1957) 'Monetary value and the perceptions of persons', *Journal of Social Psychology*, 46, 245–51.

Lunt, P. K. and Livingstone, S. M. (1991) 'Psychological, social and economic determinants of saving: comparing recurrent and total savings', *Journal of Economic Psychology*, 12, 621–41.

Lunt, P. K. and Livingstone, S. M. (1992) *Mass Consumption and Personal Identity*, Buckingham: Open University Press.

Luther, R. and Matatko, J. (1991) 'The investment of performance of "ethical" unit trusts', paper presented at the British Accounting Association, April.

Lynn, M. and Grassman, A. (1990) 'Restaurant tipping: an examination of three "rational" explanations', *Journal of Economic Psychology*, 11, 169–81.

Lynn, R. (1991) *The Secret of the Miracle Economy: Different national attitudes to competitiveness and money*, London, SAU.

Ma, L. C. and Smith, K. (1992) 'Social correlations of Confucian ethics in Taiwan', *Journal of Social Psychology*, 132, 655–9.

MacDonald, A. (1971a) 'Correlates of the ethics of personal conscience and the ethics of social responsibility', *Journal of Consulting and Clinical Psychology*, 37, 443.

MacDonald, A. (1971b) 'Relation of birth order to morality types and attitudes towards the poor', *Psychological Reports*, 29, 732.

MacDonald, A. (1972) 'More on the Protestant ethic', *Journal of Consulting and Clinical Psychology*, 39, 116–22.

MacFadyen, A. and MacFadyen, H. (1986) *Economic Psychology: Intersections in theory and application*, Amsterdam: North Holland.

Mair, B. and Raffe, D. (1983) 'The transition from school to work in 1980/81: a dynamic account', *British Educational Research Journal*, 9, 57–70.

Maital, S. (1982) *Minds, Markets and Money*, New York: Basic Books.

Maital, S. and Maital, S. (1993) (eds) *Economics and Psychology*, Vermont: Elgar.

Makeham, P. (1980) 'Youth unemployment: an examination of evidence on youth unemployment using national statistics', London, Department of Employment, Reach paper, no. 10.

Markova, J., Lockyer, R. and Forbes, C. (1980) 'Self-perception of employed and unemployed haemophiliacs', *Psychological Medicine*, 10, 559–65.

Marr, W. and Raj, B. (1983) *How Economists Explain*, Lanham: University Press of America.

Marsden, D. and Duff, E. (1975) *Workless*, Harmondsworth: Penguin.

Marshall, H. and Magruder, L. (1960) 'Relations between parent money education practices and children's knowledge and use of money', *Child Development*, 31, 253–84.

Maslow, A. (1970) *Motivation and Personality*, New York: Harper, 1954/Harper and Row.

Matza, D. and Miller, H. (1976) 'Poverty and proletariat', in R. Merton and R. Nisbet (eds), *Contemporary Social Problems*, New York: Harcourt, Brace and Jovanovich.

McBarnet, D. (1992) 'The construction of compliance and the challenge for control: the limits of noncompliance research', in J. Slemrod (ed.), *Why People Pay Taxes: Tax compliance and enforcement*, Ann Arbor: University of Michigan Press.

McClelland, D. (1961) *The Achieving Society*, Princeton, NJ: Van Nostrand.

McCloskey, D. (1987) *The Rhetoric of Economics*, Minneapolis: University of Minnesota Press.

McCloskey, D. (1990) *If You're So Smart: The narrative of economic expertise*. Chicago: University of Chicago Press.

McCracken, G. (1990) *Culture and Consumption*, Indianopolis: Indiana University Press.

McCrohan, K. F. (1982) 'The use of survey research to estimate trends in non-compliance with federal income taxes', *Journal of Economic Psychology*, 2, 231–40.

McCurdy, H. (1956) 'Coin perception studies and the concept of schemata', *Psychological Review*, 63, 160–8.

McGraw, K. M. and Scholz, J. T. (1991) 'Appeals to civic virtues versus attention to self-interest: effects on tax compliance', *Law and Society Review*, 25, 471–98.

McGuire, W. (1980) 'The development of theory in social psychology', in R. Gilmour and S. Duck (eds), *The Development of Social Psychology*, London: Academic Press.

McIntyre, R. (1992) 'Neo-classical hegemony in eastern Europe: made to rain', paper presented at the SASE conference. University of California, Irvine, March.

Mckenzie, R. (1971) 'An exploratory study of the economic understanding of elementary school teachers', *Journal of Economic Education*, 3, 26–31.

McKenzie, R. and Tullock, G. (1978) *The New World of Economics*, Homewood, IL: Irwin.

McNeal, J. (1987) *Children as Consumers: Insights and implications*, Lexington: Lexington Books.

Menezes, M. (1991) 'Ethical implications of product policy decisions', paper presented at the joint SASE and IAREP conference, Stockholm School of Economics.

Merrens, M. and Garret, J. (1975) 'The Protestant ethic, scale as a predictor of repetitive work performance', *Journal of Applied Psychology*, 60, 125–7.

Merton, R. (1957) 'The role-set: problems in sociological theory', *British Journal of Sociology*, 8, 106–20.

Merton, R. (1938) 'Social structure and anomie', *American Sociological Review*, 3, 672–82.

Merton, R. (1968) *Social Theory and Social Change*, New York: Free Press.

Merton, R. and Nisbett, R. (1976) *Contemporary Social Problems*, New York: Harcourt, Brace, Jovanovich.

Messick, D., Wilke, H., Brewer, M., Kramer, R., Zembe, P. and Lui, L. (1983) 'Individual adaptations and structural change as solutions to social dilemmas', *Journal of Personality and Social Psychology*, 44, 294–309.

Micromegas (1993) 'Money', Micromegas synthesis paper, Paris, Micromegas.

Milanovic, D. (1989) *Liberalization and Entrepreneurship: Dynamics of reform in socialism and capitalism*. New York: M. E. Sharpe.

Milham, S., Bullock, R. and Hosie, K. (1978) 'Juvenile unemployment: a concept due for re-cycling', *Journal of Adolescence*, 1, 11–24.

Miller, L. and Horn, T. (1955) 'Children's concepts regarding debt', *The Elementary School Journal*, 56, 406–12.

Mintel International Group (1991) *Special Report: The green consumer*, London.

Mirels, H. and Garrett, J. (1971) 'The Protestant work ethic as a personality variable', *Journal of Consulting and Clinical Psychology*, 36, 40–4.

Mischel, W. (1981) *Introduction to Personality*, New York: Holt, Rinehart and Winston.

Modigliani, F. and Brumberg, R. (1954) 'Utility analysis and the consumption function: an interpretation of the data', in K. K. Kurihara (ed.), *Post-Keynesian Economics*. New Brunswick, NJ: Rutgers University Press.

Moran, E. (1970) 'Varieties of pathological gambling', *British Journal of Psychiatry*, 116, 593–7.

Moscovici, C. (1981) 'On social representation', in J. Forgas (ed.), *Social Cognition*, London: Academic Press.

Mosler, H.-J. (1993) 'Self-dissemination of environmental – responsible behaviour: the influence of trust in a commons dilemma game', *Journal of Environmental Psychology*, 13, 111–23.

Nakhaie, M. (1993) 'Knowledge of profit and interest among children in Canada', *Journal of Economic Psychology*, 14, 147–60.

Nelson-Horchler, J. (1988) 'Safety: a tough sell', *Industry Week*, 236 (1), 24.

Newson, J. and Newson, E. (1976) *Seven Year Olds in the Home Environment*, London: Allen and Unwin.

Ng, S. (1983) 'Children's ideas about the bank and shop profit: developmental stages and the influence of cogniture contrasts and conflict', *Journal of Economic Psychology*, 4, 209–21.

Nobel, T. (1981) *Structure and Change in Modern Britain*, London: Batsford.

O'Brien, G. (1986) *Psychology of Work and Unemployment*, Chichester: Wiley.

O'Brien, G. and Feather, N. (1990) 'The relative effects of unemployment and quality of employment on the affect, work values and personal control of adolescents', *Journal of Occupational Psychology*, 63, 151–65.

O'Brien, M. and Ingels, S. (1985) *The Development of the Economic Values Inventory*, Chicago: University of Chicago Press.

O'Brien, M. and Ingels, S. (1987) 'The economic values inventory', *Research in Economic Education*, 18, 7–18.

O'Brien, G and Kabaroff, B. (1979) 'Comparison of unemployment and employed workers on values, locus of control and health variables', *Australian Psychologist*, 14, 143–54.

Olsen, M. (1983) 'Public acceptance of consumer energy conservation strategies', *Journal of Economic Psychology*, 4, 183–96.

Olson, G. and Schober, B. (1993) 'The satisfied poor', *Social Indicators Research*, 28, 173–93.

Orford, J. (1976) *The Social Psychology of Mental Disorder*, Harmondsworth: Penguin.

Osgood, M. (1977) 'Rural and urban attitudes towards the poor', *Social Work*, 22, 41–7.

Osmond, M. and Grigg, C. (1978) 'Correlates of poverty: the interaction of individual and family characteristics', *Social Forces*, 56, 1099–120.

Overlaet, B. and Lagrou, L. (1981) 'Attitude towards a redistribution of income', *Journal of Economic Psychology*, 1, 197–215.

Pandey, T., Kakkar, S. and Bohra, K. (1982) 'The functional perception of poverty in India', *Journal of Social Psychology*, 117, 149–50.

Pareek, U. (1970) 'Poverty and motivation: figure and ground', in V. Allen (ed.), *Psychological Factors in Poverty*, Chicago: Markham.

Parker, I. (1989) *The Crisis in Modern Social psychology – and How to End it*, London: Routledge.

Parkes, C. (1975) *Bereavement: Studies of grief in adult life*, Harmondsworth: Penguin.

Patterson, J. and Locksley, G. (1981) 'How fifth formers see the unions', *Labour Research*, 11, 23–5.

Payne, M. and Furnham, A. (1985) 'Explaining the causes of poverty in the West Indies: a cross-cultural comparison', *Journal of Economic Psychology*, 6, 215–29.

Payne, M. and Furnham, A. (1990) 'Causal attributions of unemployment in Barbados', *Journal of Social Psychology*, 130, 169–81.

Pearce, J. (1991) 'From socialism to capitalism: the effects of Hungarian human resources practices', *Academy of Mangement Executive*, 5 (4), 75–88.

Pearce, J. (1992) 'Adaptive interaction patterns in post-socialist Hungary: institutional trust', paper presented at the fourth annual International Conference of The Society for the Advancement of Socio-Economics, University of California, Irvine.

Pearce, J. and Branyiczki, I. (1993) 'Revolutionizing bureaucracies: managing change in Hungarian state-owned enterprises', *Journal of Organizational Change Management*, 6 (2), 53–64.

Penner, L. and Rokeach, M. (1969) 'The effects of employment condition on value systems', *Papers in Psychology*, 3, 47–51.

PIRC (1990) UK pension fund investment and South Africa', Briefing paper, No. 4, Pension Investment Research Consultants, London.

Platt, S. (1984) 'Unemployment and suicidal behaviour: a review of the literature', *Social Science and Medicine*, 19, 93–115.

Platt, S. and Kreitman, N. (1990) 'Long-term trends in parasuicide and unemployment in Edinburgh, 1968–1987', *Social Psychiatry and Psychiatric Epidemiology*, 25, 56–61.

Polanyi, G. and Wood, J. (1974) *How much inequality?*', London: Institute of Economic Affairs.

Pollio, H. and Gray, T. (1973) 'Change-making strategies in children and adults', *Journal of Psychology*, 84, 173–9.

Prince, M. (1993a) 'Self-concept, money beliefs and values', *Journal of Economic Psychology*, 14, 161–73.

Prince, M. (1993b) 'Women, men and money styles', *Journal of Economic Psychology*, 14, 175–82.

Pym, D. (1980) 'Towards a dual economy and emancipation from employment', *Futures*, 6, 223–37.

Rachlin, H. (1980) 'Economics and behavioural psychology', in J. Stadden (ed.), *Limits to Action*, New York: Academic Press.

Rachlin, H. (1989) *Judgement, Decision and Choice*. New York: Freeman.

Rae, J. and Drury, J. (1993) 'Reification and evidence in rhetoric on economic recession: some methods used in the UK Press, final quarter 1990', *Discourse and Society*, 4, 329–56.

Raelin, J. (1981) 'A comparative study of later work experience among full-time, part-time, and unemployment male youth', *Journal of Vocational Behaviour*, 19, 315–27.

Raffe, D. (1983) 'Employment instability among less-qualified young workers', *British Journal of Guidance and Counselling*, 11, 21–34.

Rahe, R., Floistad, I., Bergan, T., Ringdal, R., Gerhardt, R., Gunderson, E. and Arthur, R. (1974) 'A model of life changes and illness research', *Archives of General Psychiatry*, 31, 172–7.

Rainwater, L. (1970) 'Neutralizing the disinherited: some psychological aspects of understanding the poor', in V. Allen (ed.), *Psychological Factors in Poverty*, Chicago: Markham.

Ramsett, D. (1972) 'Toward improving economic education in the elementary grades', *Journal of Economic Education*, 4, 30–5.

Ray, J. (1970) 'Christianism ... the Protestant ethic among unbelievers', *Journal of Christian Education*, 13, 169–76.

Ray, J. (1982) 'The Protestant ethic in Australia', *Journal of Social Psychology*, 116, 127–38.

Reid, I. (1977) *Social Class Differences in Britain*, London: Open Books.

Resnik, A. and Stern, B. (1977) 'Children's television advertising and brand choice: a laboratory experiment', *Journal of Advertising*, 6, 11–17.

Richins, M. L. and Scott, D. (1992) 'A consumer values orientation for materialism and its measurement: scale development and validation', *Journal of Consumer Research*, 19, 303–16.

Rim, Y. (1977) 'Significance of work and personality', *Journal of Occupational Psychology*, 50, 135–8.

Rim, Y. (1982) 'Personality and attitudes connected with money', paper given at the Economic Psychology Conference, Edinburgh.

Rim, Y. (1984) 'Explanations for poverty: personality aspects', *Personality and Individual Differences*, 1, 123–4.

Ritzema, H. J. (1992) 'An extended and behavioral life-cycle model: the intermediary role of time preference', paper presented at the fourth International Conference of the Society for the Advancement of Socio-Economics, Irvine.

Ritzema, H. J. and Homan, M. E. (1991) *Schulden en bezittingen in Nederland: determinanten van schuldposities bij Nederlandse huishoudens*. [Debts and assets in the Netherlands: the determinants of debt positions in Dutch households]. 's-Gravenhage: SWOKA.

Robben, H. S. J., Webley, P., Weigel, R. H., Wärneryd, K-E, Kinsey, K. A., Hessing, D. J., Alvira Martin, F., Elffers, H., Wahlund, R. Van Langenhove, L., Long, S. B. and Scholz, J.T. (1991) 'Decision frame and opportunity as determinants of tax cheating: an international experimental study', *Journal of Economic Psychology*, 11, 341–64.

Roberts, K., Duggan, J. and Noble, M. (1982) 'Out-of-school youth in high unemployment areas', *British Journal of Guidance and Counselling*, 10, 1–11.

Robertson, A. and Cochrane, R. (1976) 'Attempted suicide and cultural change: an empirical investigation', *Human Relations*, 9, 863–83.

Robinson, R. and Bell, W. (1978) 'Equality, success and social justice in England and the United States', *American Sociological Review*, 43, 125–43.

Rodgers, B. (1991) 'Models of stress, vulnerability and affective disorder', *Journal of Affective Disorders*, 21, 1–13.

Roker, D. (1990) 'Socio-economic values in adolescence', in S. E. G. Lea, P. Webley and B. M. Young (eds), *Applied Economic Psychology in the 1990s*, Exeter: Washington Singer Press.

Rosansky, L. (1994) 'Moral and ethical dimensions of managing a multinational business', in A Lewis. and K.-E. Warneryd (eds), *Ethics and Economic Affairs*, London and New York: Routledge.

Rose, R. (1991) *Between State and Market* (Monograph no. 196), Centre for the Study of Public Policy, University of Strathclyde, Glasgow.

Rosen, B. (1959) 'Race, ethnicity and the achievement syndrome', *American Sociological Review*, 24, 47–60.

Rotter, J. (1967) 'A new scale of measurement of interpersonal trust', *Journal of Personality*, 35, 651–65.

Rowntree, B. and Lasker, B. (1911) *Unemployment: A social study*, Toronto: Macmillan.

Rowntree, B. S. (1901) *Poverty: A study of town life*, London: Macmillan.

Rubinstein, C. (1980) 'Your money and your life', *Psychology Today*, 12, 47–58.

Rubinstein, W. (1974) 'Men of property: some aspects of accommodation, inheritance and power among top British wealth holders', in P. Standworth and A. Giddens (eds), *Elites and Power in British Society*, Cambridge: Cambridge University Press.

Runciman, W. (1966) *Relative Deprivation and Social Justice*, London: Routledge.

Ryan, W. (1971) *Blaming the Victim*, New York: Partheon.

Sachs, W. (1983) 'Are energy – intensive life – images fading? The cultural meaning of the automobile in transition', *Journal of Economic Psychology*, 3, 347–65.

Sandford, C. T. (1978) *The Economics of Public Finance*, Oxford: Pergamon.

Schapiro, M. and Ahlberg, D. (1983) 'Income aspirations, unemployment and suicide: an analysis and forecast of US postwar suicides by age and sex', unpublished paper.

Scherhorn, G. (1990) 'The addictive trait in buying behaviour', *Journal of Consumer Policy*, 13, 33–51.

Scherhorn, G., Reisch, L.A. and Raab, G. (1990) 'Addictive buying in West Germany: an empirical study', *Journal of Consumer Policy*, 13, 355–87.

Scholz, J., McGraw, K and Steenbergen M. (1992) 'Will taxpayers ever like taxes?' Responses to the U.S. Tax Reform Act of 1986, *Journal of Economic Psychology*, 13, 4, 625–56.

Schug, M. and Birkey, C. (1985) 'The development of children's economic reasoning', paper presented at the annual meeting of the American Educational Research Association, Chicago.

Scitovsky, T. (1976) *The Joyless Economy*, Oxford: Oxford University Press.

Sen, A. (1977) 'Rational fools: a critique of the behavioural foundations of economic theory', *Philosophy and Public Affairs*, 6, 317–44.

Sevon, E. and Weckstrom, S. (1989) 'The development of reasoning about economic events: a study of Finnish children', *Journal of Economic Psychology*, 10, 495–514.

Shackle, G. (1949) *Expectation in Economics*, Cambridge: Cambridge University Press.

Shamir, B. (1983) 'A note on tipping and employee perceptions and attitudes', *Journal of Occupational Psychology*, 56, 255–60.

Shamir, B. (1985) 'Unemployment and "free-time": the role of Protestant work ethic and work involvement', *Leisure Studies*, 4, 333–45.

Shamir, B. (1986) 'Protestant work ethic, work involvement and the psychological impact of unemployment', *Journal of Occupational Behaviour*, 1, 25–38.

Shamir, B. (1987) 'The stability of the Protestant work ethic and work involvement', unpublished paper.

Shefrin, H. M. and Thaler, R. (1988) 'The behavioral life-cycle hypothesis', *Economic Inquiry*, 26, 609–43.

Shinn, M. and Weitzman, B. (1990) 'Research on homelessness: an introduction', *Journal of Social Issues*, 46, 1–11.

Shultz, T. and Coddington, M. (1981) 'Development of the concepts of energy conservation and entropy', *Journal of Experimental Child Psychology*, 31, 131–53.

Siegal, M. (1981) 'Children's perception of adult economic needs', *Child Development*, 52, 379–82.

Silverstein, D. (1987) 'Managing social responsibility in a changing legal environment', *American Business Law Journal*, 25, 523–66.

Simon, H. (1957) *Models of Man*, Wiley: New York.

Simon, H. (1976) 'From substantive to procedural rationality', in, S. Latsis (ed.), *Method and Appraisal in Economics*, Cambridge: Cambridge University Press.

Simon, W. and Gagnon, J. (1976) 'The anomie of affluence: a post-Mertonian conception', *American Journal of Sociology*, 82, 356–77.

Singh, S.and Vasudeva, P. (1977) 'A factorial study of the perceived reasons for poverty', *Asian Journal of Psychology and Education*, 2, 51–6.

Slemrod, J. (1985) 'An empirical test for tax evasion', *Review of Economics and Statistics*, 5, 232–8.

Smart, R. (1979) 'Drinking problems among employed, unemployed and shift workers', *Journal of Occupational Medicine*, 11, 731–6.

Smith, A. (1776/1937) *An Inquiry into the Nature and Causes of the Wealth of Nations*, New York: The Modern Library.

Smith, K. W. and Kinsey, K. A. (1987) 'Understanding taxpaying behaviour: a conceptual framework with implications for research', *Law and Society Review*, 21, 639–63.

Smith, S. and Razzell, P. (1975) *The Pools Winners*, London: Caliban.

Smith, V. (1991) *Papers in Experimental Economics*, Cambridge: Cambridge University Press.

Snelders, H. M. J. J., Hussein, G., Lea, S. E. G. and Webley, P. (1992) 'The polymorphous concept of money', *Journal of Economic Psychology*, 13, 71–92.

Solomon, M. R. (1983) 'The role of products as social stimuli: a symbolic interactionism perspective', *Journal of Consumer Research*, 10, 319–29.

Sonuga-Barke, E. and Webley, P. (1993) *Children's Saving: A study in the development of economic behaviour*. Hove: Lawrence Erlbaum.

Spencer, H. (1891) *Essays*, vol. III, London: Macmillan.

Spitze, G. and Waite, L. (1981) 'Wives' employment: the role of husbands' perceived attitudes', *Journal of Marriage and the Family*, 12, 117–24.

Stacey, B. (1982) 'Economic socialization in the pre-adult years', *British Journal of Social Psychology*, 21, 159–73.

Stacey, B. and Singer, M. (1985) 'The perception of poverty and wealth among teenagers', *Journal of Adolescence*, 8, 231–41.

Stafford, E. (1982) 'The impact of the Youth Opportunities Programme on young people's employment prospects and psychological well-being', *British Journal of Guidance and Counselling*, 10, 12–21.

Stigler, G. J. and Becker, G. S. (1977) 'De gustibus non est disputandum', *American Economic Review*, 67, 76–90.

Stirling, A. (1982) 'Preparing school leavers for unemployment', *Bulletin of the British Psychological Society*, 35, 421–2.

Stone, E. (1975) 'Job scope, job satisfaction, and the Protestant ethic', *Journal of Vocational Behaviour*, 7, 215–24.

Stone, E. (1976) 'The moderating effect of work-related values on the job scope–job satisfaction relationship', *Organisational Behaviour and Human Performance*, 15, 147–67.

Stone, P. (1994) 'Exit or voice? Lessons from companies in South Africa', in A. Lewis and K.-E. Warneryd (eds), *Ethics and Economic Affairs*, London and New York: Routledge.

Stouffer, S. *et al.* (1949) *The American Soldier*, vol. 1, Princeton NJ: Princeton University Press.

Strauss, A. (1952) 'The development and transformation of monetary meanings in the child', *American Sociological Review*, 17, 275–86.

Sullivan, T., Thompson, K., Wright, R, Gross, G. and Spady, D. (1980) *Social Problems: Divergent perspectives*, New York: Wiley.

Sutton, R. (1962) 'Behaviour in the attainment of economic concepts', *Journal of Psychology*, 53, 37–46.

Swift, A., Marshall, G. and Burgoyne, C. (1992) 'Which road to social justice?', *Sociology Review*, 2, 28–31.

Swinburn, P. (1981) 'The psychological impact of unemployment on managers and professional staff', *Journal of Occupational Psychology*, 54, 47–64.

Tajfel, H. (1981) *Human Groups and Social Categories*, Cambridge: Cambridge University Press.

Takahashi (in press) 'Understanding of the banking business in Japan: is economic prosperity accompanied by economic literacy?', *British Journal of Developmental Psychology*.

Tan, H. and Stacey, B. (1981) 'The understanding of socio-economic concepts in Malaysian Chinese school children', *Child Study Journal*, 11, 33–49.

Tang, T. (1992) 'The meaning of money revisited', *Journal of Organisation Behaviour*, 13, 197–202.

Tang, T. (1993a) 'A factor analytic study of the Protestant work ethic', *Journal of Social Psychology*, 133, 109–11.

Tang, T. (1993b) 'The meaning of money: extension and exploration of the money ethic scale in a sample of university students in Taiwan', *Journal of Organizational Behaviour*, 14, 93–9.

Tarde, G. (1902) *La Psychologie économique*. Paris: Alcan.

Taylor-Gooby, P. (1983) 'Moralism, self-interest and attitudes to welfare', *Policy and Politics*, 11 (2), 145–60.

Teahan, J. (1969) 'Future time perspective and job success: a group-oriented approach for faciliating the work adjustment of the hard core unemployed', Department of Labor, Washington, DC.

Thaler, R. H. (1990) 'Saving, fungibility and mental accounts', *Journal of Economic Perspectives*, 4, 193–205.

Thaler, R. H. and Shefrin, H. M. (1981) 'An economic theory of self-control', *Journal of Political Economy*, 89, 392–406.

Thaler, R. H. and Ziemba, W. T. (1987) 'Parimutuel betting markets: racetracks and lotteries; *Journal of Economic Perspectives*, 2, 161–74.

Thoits, P. and Hannan, M. (1979) 'Income and psychological distress: the impact of an income-maintenance experiment', *Journal of Health and Social Behaviour*, 20, 120–38.

Thurnwold, R. (1932) *Economics in Primitive Communities*, Oxford: Oxford University Press.

Thurow, L. (1969) 'The optimum lifetime distribution of consumption expenditures', *American Economic Review*, 59, 334–40.

Tiffany, D., Cowan, J. and Tiffany, P. (1970) *The Unemployed: A social psychological portrait*, Englewood Cliffs, NJ: Prentice-Hall.

Tokunaga, H. (1993) 'The use and abuse of consumer credit: application of psychological theory and research', *Journal of Economic Psychology*, 14, 285–316.

Townsend, P. (1979) *Poverty in the United Kingdom*, Harmondsworth: Penguin.

Trower, P., Bryant, B. and Argyle, M. (1978) *Social Skills and Mental Health*, London: Methuen.

Tushman, M. and Romanelli, E. (1985) 'Organizational evolution: a metamorphosis model of convergence and reorientation', *Research in Organizational Behaviour*, 7, 171–222.

Tversky, A. and Kahneman, D. (1981) 'The framing of decisions and the psychology of choice', *Science*, 211, 453–8.

Tyszka, T. and Sokolovska, J. (1992) 'Perceptions and judgments of the economic system', *Journal of Economic Psychology*, 13 (3), 421–48.

Uusitalo, L. and Djerf, K. (1983) 'Determinants of gasoline consumption', *Journal of Economic Psychology*, 4, 149–65.

van Raaij, W. F. (1993) 'Postmodern consumption', *Journal of Economic Psychology*, 14, 541–63.

van Raaij, W. F., van Veldhoven, G. M. and Wärneryd, K-E. (1988) *Handbook of Economic Psychology*, Dordrecht: Kluwer.

van Veldhoven, G. M. and Groenland, E. A. G. (1993) 'Exploring saving behaviour: a framework and a research agenda', *Journal of Economic Psychology*, 14, 507–22.

Vanderberg, S. (1970) 'Genetic factors in poverty: a psychologist's point of view', in V. Allen (ed.), *Psychological Factors in Poverty*. Chicago: Markham.

Veblen, T. (1953) *The Theory of the Leisure Class*, New York: Mentor; London: Macmillan.

Veblen, T. (1979) *The theory of the leisure class*, Harmondsworth: Penguin (originally published 1899).

Vecchio, R. (1981) 'Workers' beliefs in internal versus external determinants of success', *Journal of Social Psychology*, 114, 199–207.

Vedlitz, A. (1988) 'A question of values: conservatives and the culture of poverty' *Social Justice Research*, 2, 235–48.

Veenhoven, R. (1989) 'National wealth and individual happiness', in K. G. Gruenert and F. Olander (eds), *Understanding Economic Behaviour*, Dordrecht: Kluwer.

Verges, P. (1987) 'A social and cognitive approach to economic representations. In W. Doise and S. Moscovici (eds), *Current Issues in European Psychology*, vol. 1, Cambridge: Cambridge University Press.

Vogel, J. (1974) 'Taxation and public opinion in Sweden: an interpretation of recent survey data', *National Tax Journal*, 27, 499–513.

von Mises, L. (1978) *The Ultimate Foundation of Economic Science*, Kansas: Sheed, Andrew and McKeel.

Voskamp, U. and Wittke, V. (1991) 'Industrial restructuring in the former German Democratic Republic', *Politics and Society*, 19 (3), 341–71.

Vroom, V. (1964) *Work and Motivation*, New York: Wiley.

Wagner, R. (1976) 'Revenue structure, fiscal illusion and budgetary choice', *Public Choice*, 25, 45–61.

Wagstaff, G. (1983) 'Attitudes to poverty, the Protestant ethic and political affiliation: a preliminary investigation', *Social Behaviour and Personality*, 11, 45–7.

Wahlund, R. (1989) 'Perception and judgement of marginal tax rates after a tax reduction', in K. G. Grunert and F. Ölander (eds), *Understanding Economic Behaviour*, Dordrecht: Kluwer.

Wahlund, R. (1992) 'Tax changes and economic behaviour: the case of tax evasion', *Journal of Economic Psychology*, 13, 657–77.

Wahlund, R. and Wärneryd K.-E. (1988) 'Aggregate saving and the behaviour of saving groups in Sweden accompanying a tax reform', in S. Maital (ed.), *Applied Behavioural Economics*, vol. 1, Hemel Hempstead: Harvester Wheatsheaf.

Waite, P. (1988) 'Economic awareness: context, issues and concepts', *Theory and Practice*, 4, 16–29.

Walls (1983) *Pocket-money Monitor*, Walton on Thames: Bird's Eye Walls.

Walls (1989) *Pocket Money Monitor*, Walton on Thames: Bird's Eye Walls.

Walstad, W. (1979) 'Effectiveness of a USMES in service economic education programme for elementary school teachers' *Journal of Economic Education*, 11, 1–20.

Walstad, W. and Watts, M. (1985) Teaching economics in the schools: a review of survey findings', *Journal of Economic Psychology*, 16, 135–46.

Wanous, J. (1974) 'Individual differences and reactions to job characteristics', *Journal of Applied Psychology*, 59, 616–22.

Wärneryd, K.-E. (1983) 'The saving behaviour of households', paper presented at the conference, Saving in a Time of Economic Stagnation, Scheveningen.

Wärneryd, K.-E. (1989) 'Improving psychological theory through studies of economic behaviour: the case of saving', *Applied Psychology*, 38, 213–36.

Warr, P. (1981) 'Psychological aspects of employment and unemployment', *Psychological Medicine*, 11, 125–36.

Warr, P. (1983) 'Work, jobs and unemployment', *Bulletin of the British Psychological Society*, 36, 305–11.

Warr, P. (1984) 'Reported behaviour changes after job loss', *British Journal of Social Psychology*, 23, 271–5.

Warr, P. (1987) *Work, Unemployment and Mental Health*, Oxford: Clarendon Press.

Warr, P and Jackson, P. (1984) 'Men without jobs: some correlations of age and length of unemployment', *Journal of Occupational Psychology*, 57, 77–85.

Warr, P. and Parry, G. (1982) 'Paid employment and women's psychological well-being', *Psychological Bulletin*, 91, 498–516.

Warr, P. and Payne, R. (1983) 'Social class and reported changes in behaviour after job loss', *Journal of Applied Social Psychology*, 13, 206–22.

Warr, P., Jackson, P. and Banks, M. (1982) 'Duration of unemployment and psychological well-being in young men and women', *Current Psychological Research*, 2, 207–14.

Waters, L., Bathis, N. and Waters, C. (1975) 'Protestant ethic attitudes among college students', *Educational and Psychological Measurement*, 35, 447–50.

Watts, A. (1978) 'The implications of school-leavers unemployment for careers education in schools', *Journal of Curriculum Studies*, 3, 233–50.

Wayne, F. (1989) 'An instrument to measure adherence to the Protestant Ethic and contemporary work values', *Journal of Business Ethics*, 8, 793–804.

Weber, M. (1905) *The Protestant Ethic and the Spirit of Capitalism*, New York: Scribners.

Webley, P. (1983) 'Growing up in the modern economy', paper presented at the sixth International Conference on Political Psychology.

Webley, P. and Lea, S. E. G. (1993a) 'The partial unacceptability of money as repayment for neighbourly help', *Human Relations*, 46, 65–76.

Webley, P. and Lea, S. E. G. (1993b) 'Towards a more realistic psychology of economic socialization', *Journal of Economic Psychology*, 14, 461–72.

Webley, P. and Wilson, R. (1989) 'Social relationships and the unacceptability of money as a gift', *Journal of Social Psychology*, 129, 85–91.

Webley, P., Lea, S. E. G. and Hussein, G. (1983) 'A characteristics approach to money and the changeover from 1 pound note to 1 pound coin', paper presented at the eighth International Symposium on Economic Psychology, Bologna.

Webley, P., Lea, S. and Portalska, R. (1983) 'The unacceptability of money as a gift', *Journal of Economic Psychology*, 4, 233–8.

Webley, P., Lea, S. E. G. and Walker, C. M. (1993) 'Debt, borrowing and saving', in S. V. Malakhov (ed.), *Economic Psychology and Behavioral Economics*, Moscow: Academy of National Economy.

Webley, P., Levine, M. and Lewis, A. (1991) 'A study in economic psychology: children's saving in a play economy', *Human Relations*, 44, 127–46.

Webley, P., Robben, H. S. J., Elffers, H. and Hessing, D. J. (1991) *Tax Evasion: An experimental approach*, Cambridge: Cambridge University Press.

Weigel, R. H., Hessing, D. J. and Elffers, H. (1987) 'Tax evasion research: a critical appraisal and a theoretical model', *Journal of Economic Psychology*, 8, 215–35.

Wernimont, P. and Fitzpatrick, S. (1972) 'The Meaning of Money', *Journal of Applied Psychology*, 56, 218–61.

Westin, S. (1990) *Unemployment and Health*, Trondheim: TAPIR.

Whitehead, D. (1986) 'Student's attitudes to economic issues', *Economics*, Spring, 24–32.

Whiteley, P. (1981) 'Public opinion and the demand for social welfare in Britain', *Journal of Social Policy*, 10, 453–76.

Wicker, A. (1969) 'Attitudes versus actions: the relationship of verbal and overt behavioural responses to attitude objects', *Journal of Social Issues*, 25, 41–78.

Wight, J. (1992) 'The communitarian movement: lessons for eastern Europe', paper presented at the conference of National Building, American University of Bulgaria, Blagoevgrad, August.

Williams, A. (1985) 'Economics of coronary artery by-pass grafting', *British Medical Journal*, 291 (1249), 326–9.

Williamson, J. (1974) 'Beliefs about the motivation of the poor and attitudes towards poverty policy', *Social Problems*, 18, 634–48.

Wilson, G. (1973) *The Psychology of Conservatism*, London: Academic Press.

Wilson, G. (1991) 'Exposure to panhandling and beliefs about poverty causation', *Social Science Research*, 76, 14–16.

Winefield, A. and Tiggemann, M. (1989) 'Job loss versus failure to find work as psychological stressors in the young unemployed', *Journal of Occupational Psychology*, 62, 79–85.

Winefield, A. and Tiggemann, M. (1990) 'Employment status and psychological well-being: a longitudinal study', *Journal of Applied Psychology*, 75, 455–9.

Winefield, A., Tiggemann, M. and Winefield, H. (1991) 'The psychological impact of unemployment and unsatisfactory employment in young men and women: longitudinal and cross-sectional data', *British Journal of Psychology*, 82, 473–86.

Winefield, A., Tiggemann, M. and Winefield, H. (1992) 'Unemployment distress, reasons for job loss and causal attributions for unemployment among young people', *Journal of Occupational and Organizational Psychology*, 65, 213–18.

Winefield, A., Winefield, H., Tiggemann, M. and Goldney, R. (1991) 'A longitudinal study of the psychological effects of unemployment and unsatisfactory employment on young adults', *Journal of Applied Psychology*, 76, 424–31.

Winocur, S. and Siegal, M. (1982) 'Adolescent's judgements of economic arrangements', *International Journal of Behavioural Development*, 5, 357–65.

Winston, G. C. (1980) 'Addiction and backsliding: a theory of compulsive consumption', *Journal of Economic Behavior and Organization*, 1, 295–324.

Wiseman, T. (1974) *The Money Motive*, London: Hodder and Stoughton.

Witroyl, S. and Wentworth, N. (1983) 'A paired comparison scale of children's preference for monetary and material rewards used in investigations of incentive effects', *Journal of Genetic Psychology*, 142, 17–23.

Witte, A. D. and Woodbury, D.F. (1985) 'The effect of tax laws and tax administration on tax compliance: the case of US individual income tax', *National Tax Journal*, 38, 1–13.

Wollack, S., Goodale, J., Whiting, J. and Smith, P. (1971) 'Development of the survey of work values', *Journal of Applied Psychology*, 55, 331–8.

Wong, M. (1989) 'Children's acquisition of economic knowledge: Understanding banking in Hong Kong and the USA', in J. Valsiner (ed.), *Child Development in Cultural Context*, Norwood, NJ: Ablex.

Wosinski, M. and Pietras, M. (1990) 'Economic socialization in Polish children in different macro-economic conditions', *Journal of Economic Psychology*, 11, 515–28.

Yamauchi, K. and Templer, D. (1982) 'The development of a money attitude scale', *Journal of Personality Assessment*, 46, 522–8.

Younger, J., Arrowood, A. and Hemsley, G. (1977) 'And the lucky shall inherit the earth: perceiving the causes of financial success and failure', *European Journal of Social Psychology*, 7, 509–15.

Zabukovec, V. and Polic, M. (1990) 'Yugoslavian children in a situation of rapid economic changes', *Journal of Economic Psychology*, 11, 529–43.

Zaslavskaya, T. (1992) 'Public opinion in the last months of the Soviet Union', *The Republic Perspective*, 3, (2), 32–4.

Zelizer, V. A. (1985) *Pricing the Priceless Child: The changing social value of children*, New York: Basic Books.

Zimmerman, M. and Hartley, W. (1982) 'High blood pressure among employed women: a multi-factor discriminant analysis ', *Journal of Health and Social Behaviour*, 23, 205–20.

Zinser, O., Perry, J. and Edgar, R. (1975) 'Affluence of the request value of donations and sharing behaviour in preschool children', *Journal of Psychology*, 89, 301–5.

Zolatos, X. (1981) *Economic Growth and Declining Social Welfare*, New York: New York University Press.

Zullow, 1991 'Pessimistic rumination in popular songs and new magazines predict economic recession via decreasing consumer optimism and spending', *Journal of Economic Psychology*, 12, 501–26.

# Index